PAN Y MANTEQUILLA

Practical Conversational Spanish

Third Edition

Nicholas F. Sallese
St. John's University

Laura B. Fernández
Former Associate, New York State
Education Department

 HEINLE & HEINLE PUBLISHERS, INC.
Boston, Massachusetts 02210 U.S.A.

Cover Photo: Foto du Monde/The Picture Cube
Cover Design: Carol H. Rose
Illustrations: Rocco Alberico, Ray Bauer, Margarita Rosa Ortiz, José Delgado-Guitart, David White
Production Editor: Elinor Y. Chamas

DEDICATORIA

El refrán dice . . . *A buen hambre, no hay pan duro.* Aunque parezca difícil el estudio de una lengua extranjera, el estudiante con la volantad de aprender sigue la senda del aprendizaje hasta llegar al triunfo.

Este libro está dedicado a nuestros estudiantes de ayer y del mañana y a todos aquellos que quieran añadir una nueva dimensión a su preparación cultural.

Ofrecemos un ramillete verbal al Gobernador del Estado de Nueva York Mario M. Cuomo y a su linda señora Matilda, pareja de tres culturas y amantes de la lengua de Cervantes.

CONTENIDO

Parte 1: Lengua y práctica

UNIT

Parte 2: Gramática esencial

UNIT 1   **220**

Definite article — Indefinite article — Uses of the definite article —
Conjugation of the verb **llegar**

UNIT 2   **223**

Gender of nouns — Conjugation of the verbs **aprender** and **tener**

UNIT 3   **227**

Plural of nouns — Conjugation of the verbs **escribir** and **hacer**

UNIT 4   **230**

Gender of adjectives — Plural of adjectives — Conjugation of the verb
dar

UNIT 5   **233**

Position of adjectives — Apocopation of adjectives — Conjugation of the
verb **ir**

UNIT 6   **236**

Augmentatives — Diminutives — Pejoratives — Adverbs — Conjugation
of the verb **saber**

UNIT 7   **240**

Comparison of adjectives — **Tanto ... como** — Conjugation of the verb
conocer

PREFACE

PAN Y MANTEQUILLA, Third Edition, represents a thorough revision of a highly successful textbook for elementary and intermediate conversation courses in Spanish. Especially notable in this edition is the emphasis on practical, functional vocabulary to motivate students to begin talking right from the start.

PAN Y MANTEQUILLA takes students out of the classroom and into the midst of everyday life in the Hispanic World. The thematic concept of travel takes them on a delightful journey over 30 chapters from the travel agency in Unit 1, through modes of travel, finding lodging, dining, shopping, and an array of sports and amusements.

Another major improvement in this edition is the incorporation of career information in every chapter. The demand for Spanish-speaking professionals in business, industry, and commerce is increasing dramatically. *Oficios y profesiones*, a new section, has been tailored to address this specific vocational need.

The 30 units of PAN Y MANTEQUILLA are geared to the time frame of a normal course offering and enriched with the useful language patterns and motivating conversational stimuli that satisfy the prerequisites of "vida cotidiana." Each of the units in this third edition employs the building block formula introduced in the two previous editions. A noun with a high frequency count of usage in the theme of the unit is joined to a high frequency count verb to create a verb phrase. Twenty such phrases introduced at the beginning of each unit provide students with pertinent and practical bases for communicating in a given situation. Once mastered, these verb phrases are used in conversational patterns common to the native speaker of Spanish. A dialog, comprehension exercises, and conversational stimuli round out the students' opportunities to practice the original verb phrases. It is important to note that units may be shuffled about and even omitted in order to satisfy specific objectives—each unit may precede, follow, or be combined with any other unit.

The three preliminary units present the sounds and mechanics of the Spanish language and a list of everyday expressions. An abundance of direct cognates included in this section gives confidence to the student struggling for fluency in Spanish. One or two weeks of class time should be spent on these early units before Unit One is begun.

The essentials of grammar, so necessary for retention, effectiveness of instruction, and appreciation of the foreign tongue, have also been incorporated into this program of language instruction. This third edition is divided into two parts. First is *Lengua y práctica*, containing Units 1-30. In the second part, *Gramática esencial*, each of the 35 units presents clearly explained points of grammar, irregular verb conjugations, information on word formation in Spanish, and appropriate accompanying exercises. This format allows students to see the language in action before structure is introduced. As in the previous editions, PAN Y MANTEQUILLA is a practical course that spotlights career Spanish without foresaking an optional and extremely flexible presentation of grammar.

The essential elements of Part One, *Lengua y práctica* include:

Expresiones apropiadas: Twenty basic nouns normally associated with the theme of the lesson are joined with twenty basic verbs to create useful verb phrases.

Variaciones del vocabulario: Variations on several of the introductory verb phrases illustrate the multiple possibilities of Spanish expression.

Vocabulario en acción: The twenty introductory linguistic patterns are used in everyday idiomatic Spanish.

Cuestionario: This exercise elicits specific responses designed to review the basic vocabulary of the unit and to reinforce comprehension.

Modelos de conversación: Five conversational patterns utilizing the basic vocabulary of the lesson are presented for practice.

Diálogo: Anecdotal dialogs appropriate to the theme of the unit highlight the lesson. Marginal notes are included for unfamiliar vocabulary.

Comprensión: Questions related to the dialog, as well as more open-ended questions encourage student participation.

Vamos a hablar: Picture stimuli and thought-provoking discussion questions bring into sharp focus the elements of the lesson and its everyday application.

Dichos y refranes: Proverbs or sayings are presented in cartoon form.

Oficios y profesiones: Appropriate jobs and professions are described in each of the units as a point of departure for career-oriented conversation.

Repasito: A brief review of the nomenclature of the lesson is presented in test form.

Muchísimas gracias . . . to Carmen Rolleri, who made the keys of the typewriter sing in preparing the manuscript . . . to all our colleagues who have brought the Spanish language to so many eager students through the medium of *PAN Y MANTEQUILLA* and especially to Professor Ruth Bennett of Queens College, Professor Maria Dominicis of St. John's University, Professor Jesus Nuevo of York College (CUNY) . . . y un abrazo cordial para Dr. Xavier Fernández, "el caballero jubilado."

PAN Y MANTEQUILLA

PRELIMINARY UNIT 1

Los sonidos de la lengua española

Sounds of the Spanish Language

LAS VOCALES ESPAÑOLAS (SPANISH VOWELS)

VOWEL	ENGLISH SOUND	SPANISH SOUND
a	father, *ah*!	samba, cha-cha-cha, Panamá
e	they, m*a*de	mate, legal, Eva
e	let, m*e*t	escape, etcétera, Pepe
i	machine, *ea*t	idea, Cantinflas, Ibiza
o	oh, no	chocolate, polo, Oviedo
o	for, c*o*st	conga, motor, Orestes
u	r*u*le, m*oo*n	rumba, ultimatum, Cuba
y	bee	y, ¡huy!

EL ALFABETO ESPAÑOL (SPANISH ALPHABET)

There are thirty letters in the Spanish alphabet. The letters **k** and **w** appear mainly in foreign words. **Ch**, **ll**, and **rr** are treated as single consonants. In dictionaries, **ch**, **ll**, and **ñ** follow **c**, **l**, and **n** respectively.

corporal	**Lima**	**niño**
Cholula	**llama**	**niña**

Rr is listed in dictionaries as in English.

horrible
Hortensia

a (a) **adobe, África, Alabama, Álamo, albino, álbum, alcohol, animal, arena, Argentina, armadillo, aroma, Atlas, axis**

b (be) **B** is pronounced like the *b* in the English word *boy*, but with slightly less explosion of the lips.

Babel, Babieca, balance, bamba, banana, bar, barón, base, basílica, Benito, bolero, Bolivia, brutal

c (ce) **C** has two sounds in Spanish:
1. Before **e** and **i**, **c** is pronounced like the English *s* of *silly* in Spanish America, and like the English *th* of *think* in Spain.

Cecilia, celestial, censor, central, cereal, ceremonial, El Cid, Cielito Lindo, circular, civil

2. Before **a**, **o**, and **u** and consonants, **c** is pronounced like the *c* in *copper*. (EXCEPTION: **cz   czar, czarina**)

cable, California, capital, cartel, clamor, club, coaxial, color, confusión, cornucopia, cáncer, crisis, cucaracha, curable

ch (che)   Ch is pronounced like the *ch* in the English word *cherry*.

chalet, Chapala, Chapultepec, Chichicastenango, Chihuahua, Chimbote, China, chinchilla, chirimoya

d (de)   D is pronounced like the hard, dentalized *d* in the English word *dog* when it is the first letter of a word. In all other instances, it assumes a less dentalized and softer pronunciation approximating the English *th* sound in *thin*.

Damián, debate, decimal, decisión, diabetes, diagnosis, digestión, dimensión, diploma, director, doctor, dogma, Dolores

cadáver, Canadá, cardinal, pedal, pseudo, radio

e (e)   **enchilada, enigma, epidermis, Eritrea, exclusión**

f (efe)   F is pronounced the same as in English.

fandango, fatal, federal, festival, feudal, Fiat, fiesta, fiscal, floral, Florida, fraternal, fundamental, funeral, furor

g (ge)   G has two sounds in Spanish:
1. Before **e** and **i**, **g** is soft and is pronounced like the Spanish **j** sound (see **j** below).

general, génesis, genial, genital, Gibraltar, Giralda

2. Before **a**, **o**, and **u** and consonants, **g** is hard and is pronounced like the English *g* in *go*.

gala, Galileo, gastritis, gaucho, gazpacho, glacial, Gloria, golf, góndola, gradual, granular, grave, Guadalupe, guardián

h (hache)   H is silent in Spanish.

Alhambra, Haití, hepatitis, hernia, héroe, hexagonal, Honduras, Honolulú, honor, honorable, horizontal, horrible, hospital, hotel, humor

i (i)   **impenetrable, impostor, inaugural, incisión, inclusión, indecisión, India, individual**

j (jota)   J is a guttural sound formed deep in the throat. It approximates a rasping English *h* sound, but there is no English equivalent.

Don Juan, La Jolla, jade, jai-alai, Jalisco, Jamaica, Jerez, Jesús, jota, Juanita, judicial, Júpiter

k (ka)   K is not a Spanish letter and appears only in words of foreign origin. It is pronounced like the English *k*.

Kansas, Kenya, kilociclo, kilogramo, kilómetro, kimono (quimono), kindergarten, kiosko, kipu (quipu), koala, Kremlín, kriptón

l (ele)   L is pronounced like the English *l* in *lip*, with the tip of the tongue in the front part of the mouth.

labor, latín, Las Vegas, laurel, lava, legal, legión, León, liberal, limbo, lintel, local, loco, Luz

ll (elle)   Ll is pronounced like the *lli* in the English word *million* in Spain. In Spanish America, it is pronounced like the *y* in *yes*.

caballero, Callao, collar, llama, llano, Mallorca, Pancho Villa, Sevilla, Villalobos

m (eme)   M is pronounced like the English *m*.

machete, maestro, mango, Marco Polo, marimba, Martín, material, matrimonial, máximum, Maya, melodrama, memorial, mestizo, mineral

n (ene)   N is pronounced like the English *n*.

Napoleón, nasal, natural, neutral, Niágara, Nicaragua, noble, nocturnal, nominal, normal, notable, numeral

ñ (eñe)   Ñ is pronounced like the *ny* in the English word *canyon*.

Cataluña, doña, mañana, ñame, piñata, señor, señorita, vicuña

o (o)   **oasis, occidental, octagonal, Olga, ópera, opinión, oral, Oscar**

p (pe)   P is pronounced like the English *p* in *patio*, but is less explosive and less breathy. P before s is not pronounced (**psicología, pseudónimo**).

pampa, Pancho, papaya, particular, pastor, penal, personal, piano, Pilar, plan, plural, popular, Puerto Rico

q (cu)   Q is pronounced like the English *k* in *king*. It occurs only in the combination **qu**.

Don Quijote, Quebec, Querétaro, Quesada, quetzal, Quetzalcoatl, Quevedo, Quijana, quinta, Quintana, Quito, quorum

r (ere)   R is a trilled sound made by flipping the tongue once on the roof of the mouth. When **r** is the first letter of a word, the tongue is flipped more than once.

radial, radical, rancho, rector, regular, religión, Rembrandt, resistible, revisión, Río Grande, ritual, robot, rodeo, romance, rumor, rural

rr (erre)   Rr is a trilled sound made by flipping the tongue two or more times on the roof of the mouth.

arroz con pollo, Barranquilla, burro, corrosión, errata, error, horror, irreducible, irregular, irreparable, irritable, terror, Zorro

s (ese)   S is generally pronounced like the English *s* in *sent*.

               sable, sacramental, sacristán, Sahara, saliva, salmón, salón, San Salvador, sector, siesta, Simón

t (te)   T is pronounced almost like the English *t* in *tea*, but with the tongue closer to the teeth and with less breath than in English.

               taco, talismán, Tampa, tapir, tarántula, tango, tenor, Titicaca, Tobías, toga, Toledo, total, tractor, tuberculosis

u (u)   **ulterior, umbilical, unilateral, unión, unisexual, unisón, universal, Uruguay, utopía.**

v (ve)   V is similar to the sound of the English *b*. Avoid the hard *v* sound.

               Valdivia, vapor, variable, vector, Venezuela, versión, Víctor, Victoria, vicuña, Vietnam, vigor, Virginia, vodka

w (doble v,   W is not a Spanish letter and occurs only in foreign words. It is pronounced
doble u)   like the English *w*.

               Wagner, Walt Whitman, Wamba, Wanda, Wáshington, watusi, Wéstminster, Whig, whisky, Winston, Wisconsin

x (equis)   X is pronounced like the English *x* in examination, varying between the English *eks* and *egz* sounds. The x in **México** and **mexicano** is an exception and is pronounced like the Spanish **j**. X before a consonant is pronounced like the hissed *s* in the English word *sissy*.

               excursión, experimental, extra, México, Taxco, Xochimilco

y (i griega)   Y is pronounced like the English *y* in *yes*

               Yerma, yoga, yogurt, Yolanda, Yucatán, Yuma

z (zeta)   Z in Spanish America is pronounced like the English *s* in *silver*. In parts of Spain, it is pronounced like the *th* in *thermometer*.

               zamacueca, Zanzíbar, Zaragoza, zarzuela, zigzag, Zorrilla, Zulú

LAS COMBINACIONES DE VOCALES (VOWEL COMBINATIONS)

1. **A**, **e**, and **o** are strong vowels.
2. **I**, **u** and **y** are weak vowels.
3. The combination of a strong and a weak vowel forms one syllable (diphthong) with the stress on the strong vowel.

Los diptongos con a (Diphthongs with a)

ai   **paisaje** (*countryside*), **baile** (*dance*), **fraile** (*monk*)
au   **autor** (*author*), **astronauta** (*astronaut*), **inaugurar** (*to inaugurate*)
ay   **Uruguay, Paraguay**

Los diptongos con e (Diphthongs with e)

ei   **reina** (*queen*), **aceite** (*oil*), **seis** (*six*)
eu   **Eustaquio** (*Eustace*), **feudal** (*feudal*), **Europa** (*Europe*)
ey   **ley** (*law*), **rey** (*king*), **Camagüey**

Los diptongos con i (Diphthongs with i)

ia   **biblia** (*bible*), **tiara** (*tiara*), **diablo** (*devil*)
ie   **septiembre** (*September*), **griego** (*Greek*), **diez** (*ten*)
io   **palacio** (*palace*), **patio** (*patio*), **estudio** (*study*)

Los diptongos con o (Diphthongs with o)

oi   **heroico** (*heroic*), **Moisés** (*Moses*), **oiga** (*listen*)
oy   **hoy** (*today*), **soy** (*I am*), **estoy** (*I am*)

Los diptongos con u (Diphthongs with u)

ua   **Nicaragua, agua** (*water*), **suave** (*soft*)
ue   **jueves** (*Thursday*), **puente** (*bridge*), **pueblo** (*town*)
uo   **cuota** (*quota*), **duodécimo** (*twelfth*), **antiguo** (*old*)

4. Two adjacent strong vowels form separate syllables and not a diphthong.

    lo/or (*poetic form*), **cano/a** (*canoe*), **ide/a** (*idea*), **corre/o** (*mail*)

5. Two weak vowels form a diphthong. The stress within the syllable falls on the second vowel of the combination.

    ciu/dad (*city*), **rui/do** (*noise*), **muy** (*very*)

6. In the combination of a strong vowel (**a, e, o**) between two weak vowels (**i, u, y**) (triphthong), the stressed vowel usually has a written accent.

    a/ve/ri/guáis (*you ascertain*), **en/viáis** (you send), **Pa/ra/guay**

7. The written accent over a weak vowel in a diphthong splits the diphthong into two syllables. The weak vowel is then treated as a strong vowel.

    ba/úl (*trunk*), **o/í/do** (*ear*), **se/rí/a** (*it would be*)

EL SILABEO (SYLLABICATION)

1. A single consonant (including **ch**, **ll**, and **rr**) between vowels forms a syllable with the vowel that follows it.

Pa/na/má	*Panama*	**po/llo**	*chicken*
pa/lo/ma	*dove*	**pe/rro**	*dog*
mu/cha/cho	*boy*		

2. Combinations of two consonants between vowels are generally divided. The first consonant forms a syllable with the preceding vowel, and the second consonant unites with the following vowel.

lec/cio/nes	*lessons*	**pal/ma**	*palm*

3. Consonants followed by **l** or **r** (except **rl**, **sl**, **tl**) are not separated. Both consonants form one syllable with the following vowel.

te/a/tro	*theatre*	BUT:	
co/pla	*couplet*	**per/la**	*pearl*
no/ble	*noble*	**is/la**	*island*
re/gla	*rule*	**at/le/ta**	*athlete*

4. Combinations of three consonants are usually divided after the first consonant of the combination.

no/viem/bre	*November*	**miem/bro**	*member*
Lon/dres	*London*	**siem/pre**	*always*
sem/brar	*to seed*		

5. The letters of a prefix are inseparable, forming a single syllable.

sub/ra/yar	*to underline*	**ex/pre/sar**	*to express*
des/con/ten/to	*discontent*	**trans/por/te**	*transport*

6. When **s** precedes another consonant, it forms a syllable with the preceding vowel.

es/toy	*I am*	**obs/tan/te**	*standing*
cons/truc/ción	*construction*	**cons/pi/rar**	*to conspire*
as/tró/lo/go	*astrologer*		

LA ACENTUACIÓN (ACCENTUATION)

1. Words ending in a vowel, **n**, or **s** are stressed on the next to the last syllable.

in/te/re/san/te	*interesting*	**die/ta**	*diet*
con/tra/ban/do	*contraband*	**co/men**	*they eat*
im/pe/ne/tra/ble	*impenetrable*	**ha/blas**	*you speak*

2. Words ending in any consonant except **n** or **s** are stressed on the last syllable.

cu/rio/si/**dad**	*curiosity*	hos/pi/**tal**	*hospital*
e/lec/to/**ral**	*electoral*	glan/du/**lar**	*glandular*
ins/pec/**tor**	*inspector*		

3. The written accent is used when a syllable is stressed in a manner different from the general rules.

e/vo/lu/**ción**	*evolution*	ki/**ló**/me/tro	*kilometer*
hi/**pó**/cri/ta	*hypocritical*	ins/tan/**tá**/ne/o	*instantaneous*
ca/**fé**	*coffee, café*		

4. The written accent is also employed to distinguish words similar in spelling and pronunciation but different in meaning.

sí	*yes*	**té**	*tea*
si	*if*	**te**	*you* (pronoun)
sólo	*only* (adverb)	**¿qué?**	*what?*
solo	*alone*	**que**	*that*
más	*more*	**¿cómo?**	*how?*
mas	*but*	**como**	*I eat; like*

LA PUNTUACIÓN ESPAÑOLA (SPANISH PUNCTUATION)

.	**el punto**
,	**la coma**
;	**el punto y coma**
:	**los dos puntos**
...	**los puntos suspensivos**
··	**la diéresis, la crema**
—	**la raya** (*dash*)
-	**el guión** (*hyphen*)
`	**el acento grave**
´	**el acento (agudo)**
^	**el acento circunflejo, el signo de intercalación**
« »	**las comillas**
'	**el apóstrofe**
/	**la raya** (*slash*)
( )	**el paréntesis**
[ ]	**los corchetes**
¡ !	**los signos (puntos) de admiración, los signos (puntos) admirativos**
¿ ?	**los signos (puntos) de interrogación, los signos (puntos) interrogantes**
*	**el asterisco**
#	**el signo de número**

$ el signo del dólar
%   el signo de porcentaje
ç   la cedilla
~   la tilde
↑   la flecha
∧   el punto de omisión

1. The dash is commonly used in Spanish to indicate dialog or a direct quotation. It is the equivalent of English quotation marks.

    — ¿Cómo estás?   *"How are you?"*
    — Muy bien, gracias.   *"Very well, thank you."*

2. An inverted question mark begins an interrogative sentence in Spanish. The question mark used in English is placed at the end of the Spanish question.

    — ¿Cómo se llama Vd.?   *"What is your name?"*
    — ¿Cuál es la fecha de hoy?   *"What is today's date?"*

3. An inverted exclamation point begins an exclamatory sentence in Spanish. The exclamation point used in English is placed at the end of the Spanish exclamation.

    — ¡Atención!   *"Attention!"*
    — ¡Socorro!   *"Help!"*

4. Capital letters are used in Spanish in the same situations as in English with the exceptions of the days of the week, the months of the year, languages, nationalities and titles.

Los días de la semana (Days of the week)

lunes	Monday	sábado	Saturday
martes	Tuesday	domingo	Sunday
miércoles	Wednesday	hoy	today
jueves	Thursday	ayer	yesterday
viernes	Friday	mañana	tomorrow

The days of the week in Spanish are masculine and use the article **el** (singular) or **los** (plural). The article is often expressed as *on* in English.

Escuchamos el radio los domingos.   *We listen to the radio on Sundays.*

Ejercicio (Exercise)

Complete las oraciones siguientes (Complete the following sentences):

1. Hoy es_____.   4. No tengo clases los_____ y los_____.
2. Ayer fue _____.   5. _____ es el día de visita.
3. Y mañana será _____.   6. El primer día de la semana es _____.

Los meses del año (Months of the year)

enero	*January*	**julio**	*July*
febrero	*February*	**agosto**	*August*
marzo	*March*	**septiembre**	*September*
abril	*April*	**octubre**	*October*
mayo	*May*	**noviembre**	*November*
junio	*June*	**diciembre**	*December*

The months of the year are masculine in Spanish.

Ejercicio (Exercise)

Complete las oraciones siguientes (Complete the following sentences):

1. El mes presente es _____.
2. Celebramos la Navidad (*Christmas*) en el mes de _____.
3. _____ es el mes del Día de la Independencia norteamericana.
4. El Día de San Valentín ocurre en el mes de _____, y la fiesta de San Patricio en el mes de _____.
5. La primavera termina en el mes de _____, y el invierno termina en el mes de _____.

Las estaciones del año (Seasons of the year)

The seasons of the year are not capitalized in Spanish or English.

el invierno	*winter*	**el verano**	*summer*
la primavera	*spring*	**el otoño**	*fall (autumn)*

Ejercicio (Exercise)

Escoja la estación apropiada (Pick out the appropriate season):

1. la nieve (*snow*)
2. la playa (*beach*)
3. las hojas doradas (*golden leaves*)
4. las semillas (*seeds*)
5. el esquiar (*skiing*)
6. el Día de Dar las Gracias (*Thanksgiving*)
7. el Día de los Santos Inocentes (*April Fools' Day*)
8. el calor (*heat*)
9. el césped (*lawn*)
10. la Nochebuena (*Christmas Eve*)

País o continente o región *(Country or continent or region)*	*Habitante o nacionalidad* *(Inhabitant or nationality)*
África	africano (–a)
Albania	albanés
Alemania (*Germany*)	alemán
América	americano
Arabia	árabe
Asia	asiático
Australia	australiano
Austria	austríaco
Bélgica (*Belgium*)	belga
Brasil	brasileño
Canadá	canadiense
Corea	coreano
Checoeslovaquia	checoeslovaco
China	chino
Dinamarca (*Denmark*)	danés
Egipto	egipcio
Escandinavia (*Scandinavia*)	escandinavo
Escocia (*Scotland*)	escocés
España	español
Europa	europeo
(Islas) Filipinas	filipino
Finlandia	finlandés
Francia	francés
Gran Bretaña	británico
Grecia (*Greece*)	griego
Hawaii	hawaiano
Holanda	holandés
Hungría	húngaro
India	indio
Inglaterra (*England*)	inglés
Irán	iranio, persa
Irlanda (*Ireland*)	irlandés
Israel	israelí
Italia	italiano
Japón	japonés
Norteamérica	norteamericano
Noruega (*Norway*)	noruego
Oriente	oriental
Palestina	palestino
Polonia (*Poland*)	polaco
Portugal	portugués

Puerto Rico	puertorriqueño
Rumania	rumano
Rusia	ruso
Siria	sirio
Sudamérica, Suramérica	sudamericano, suramericano
Suecia (*Sweden*)	sueco
Suiza (*Switzerland*)	suizo
Tibet	tibetano
Turquía (*Turkey*)	turco
Unión Soviética	soviético
Yugoeslavia	yugoeslavo
Vietnam	vietnamés

Ejercicio (Exercise)

Repita la expresión empleando la forma adjetival (Repeat the expression employing the adjective (adjectival) form):

MODELO: unas pirámides **de Egipto**
            unas pirámides **egipcias**

1. un poema de Irlanda
2. una familia de Francia
3. un florista de España
4. unos productos de América
5. un cantador de Portugal
6. unos turistas de Inglaterra
7. una santa de Italia
8. un embajador del Canadá
9. la civilización de Palestina
10. unas bicicletas del Japón
11. una estatua de la China
12. unos misioneros de África
13. un edificio de Grecia
14. una cerveza de Alemania
15. unos tulipanes de Holanda
16. unos relojes de Suiza

Títulos (Titles)

doña María	don Juan	señor Sánchez	señora Martín	señorita Pardo

Abbreviations of titles are capitalized.

Da. María	D. Juan	Sr. Sánchez	Sra. Martín	Srta. Pardo

Ejercicios de pronunciación y comprensión (Exercises of pronunciation and comprehension)

A.   *Pronuncie Vd. las siguientes palabras españolas (Pronounce the following Spanish words):*

1. adiós
2. alpaca
3. amigo
4. bronco
5. café
6. caramba
7. corral
8. cucaracha

9.	coyote	15.	hombre	21.	parasol	27.	sombrero
10.	chile con carne	16.	mantilla	22.	patio	28.	tapioca
11.	chocolate	17.	maracas	23.	plaza	29.	toreador
12.	Don Quijote	18.	mosquito	24.	peso	30.	vista
13.	gusto	19.	negro	25.	poncho		
14.	hacienda	20.	olé	26.	pronto		

B. *Pronuncie Vd. en español los nombres de los siguientes lugares en los EE.UU.* (*Pronounce in Spanish the names of the following locations in the U.S.*):

1.	Amarillo	9.	Laredo	17.	Palo Alto	25.	San Pedro
2.	Arizona	10.	Las Vegas	18.	Pasadena	26.	Santa Ana
3.	California	11.	Los Ángeles	19.	Sacramento	27.	Santa Bárbara
4.	Catalina	12.	Modesto	20.	San Antonio	28.	Santa Fe
5.	Colorado	13.	Montana	21.	San Bernardino	29.	Texas (Tejas)
6.	El Paso	14.	Monterrey	22.	San Diego	30.	Yuma
7.	Florida	15.	Nevada	23.	San Francisco		
8.	La Jolla	16.	Nogales	24.	San José		

C. *Pronuncie Vd. los siguientes nombres españoles* (*Pronounce the following Spanish surnames*):

1.	Castillo	8.	González	15.	Ponce	22.	Torres
2.	Castro	9.	Gutiérrez	16.	Romero	23.	Valdés
3.	Colón	10.	Hernández	17.	Ruiz	24.	Vega
4.	Cruz	11.	Miranda	18.	Sánchez	25.	Velázquez
5.	Flores	12.	Moreno	19.	Santiago	26.	Zorrilla
6.	Gallego	13.	Ortíz	20.	Segovia		
7.	Gómez	14.	Pérez	21.	Soto		

D. *Pronuncie Vd. las siguientes frases y dé el significado en inglés* (*Pronounce the following phrases and give their English meaning*):

VOCABULARIO NUEVO (NEW VOCABULARY)

el *the* (masculine singular) **un** *a* (masculine singular)
la *the* (feminine singular) **una** *a* (feminine singular)

1.	el toro bravo	10.	un curso universitario
2.	una dama española	11.	un presidente amable
3.	una señora italiana	12.	la fotografía cómica
4.	un profesor inteligente	13.	un rancho mexicano (mejicano)
5.	el chico loco	14.	la guitarra flamenca
6.	una idea calculada	15.	un animal estúpido
7.	un general victorioso	16.	un actor notable
8.	el edificio grande	17.	la música moderna
9.	el océano pacífico	18.	una novela erótica

19. el cantor famoso
20. la tragedia nacional
21. una tempestad tropical
22. un patio circular
23. una clase interesante
24. un diplomático norteamericano

25. un marinero peruano
26. un automóvil antiguo
27. un aeroplano holandés
28. el programa oficial
29. un problema internacional
30. una tesis doctoral

E. *Pronuncie Vd. y traduzca al inglés* (*Pronounce and translate into English*):

me gusta — *I like*
de el — **del** (**de los**) — *of the*
de la — **de la** (**de las**) — *of the*

1. Me gusta el vino de la región de la Rioja.
2. Me gusta el café de Colombia.
3. Me gusta el metal zinc.
4. Me gusta el caviar de Rusia.
5. Me gusta la televisión de Nueva York.
6. Me gusta la historia de Ali Babá.
7. Me gusta la historia del Canal de Panamá.
8. No me gusta la historia del ángel Lucifer.
9. No me gusta el tutor italiano.
10. No me gusta la alfalfa de la Argentina. Sólo me gusta la alfalfa de América.
11. Me gustan los vinos de la región de Rioja.
12. No me gustan los hoteles de la China.
13. Me gustan los restaurantes de Roma.
14. No me gustan los autos del Japón.
15. Me gustan los sofás de Macy's.
16. No me gustan los mangos de la Florida.
17. Me gustan los sombreros de México.
18. No me gustan los taxis de París.
19. Me gustan las siestas.
20. No me gustan los coyotes de Arizona y Montana.

NOTE: The verb **gustar** appears only in the third person singular and the third person plural. Translation is made easier by changing the sentence from *I like it* to *It is pleasing to me*.

PRELIMINARY UNIT 2

Los pronombres personales y los verbos

Subject Pronouns and the Verb Story

LOS PRONOMBRES PERSONALES (SUBJECT PRONOUNS)

SINGULAR		PLURAL	
yo	*I*	nosotros (-as)	*we*
tú	*you* (familiar)	vosotros (-as)	*you* (familiar)
él	*he*	ellos	*they* (masculine)
ella	*she*	ellas	*they* (feminine)
usted (Vd.)	*you* (formal)	ustedes (Vds.)	*you* (formal)

The familiar **tú** is used when addressing persons of intimate acquaintance, children, animals, and God. The formal **usted** is used when addressing strangers or persons with whom one has a formal relationship, **Nosotras** and **vosotras** refer only to female persons. Spanish pronouns, with the exception of their abbreviated forms, are not capitalized.

LOS VERBOS (VERBS)

Spanish verbs have five properties.

1. person: first, second, and third person
2. number: singular or plural
3. time: present, past, or future tense
4. mood: indicative, subjunctive, and commands
5. voice: active or passive

Spanish verbs are classified according to their ending.

-ar   first conjugation   **-ir**   third conjugation
-er   second conjugation

The form of the verb ending in **-ar**, **-er**, or **-ir** is called the *infinitive*. It is composed of the stem plus the infinitive ending.

cant +	**ar**	**cantar**	*to sing*	**escrib +**	**ir**	**escribir**	*to write*
beb +	**er**	**beber**	*to drink*				

LOS VERBOS DE LA PRIMERA CONJUGACIÓN (FIRST CONJUGATION VERBS)

SINGULAR		PLURAL	
yo cant**o**	I sing	nosotros (-as) cant**amos**	we sing
tú cant**as**	you sing	vosotros (-as) cant**áis**	you sing

SINGULAR		PLURAL	
él canta	he sings	ellos cantan	they sing
ella canta	she sings	ellas cantan	they sing
Vd. canta	you sing	Vds. cantan	you sing

Los verbos regulares de la primera conjugación (Regular first conjugation verbs)

bailar	to dance	**limpiar**	to clean
conversar	to converse	**mirar**	to look at
estudiar	to study	**nadar**	to swim
firmar	to sign	**olvidar**	to forget
hablar	to speak	**trabajar**	to work

Ejercicios (Exercises)

VOCABULARIO NUEVO (NEW VOCABULARY)

a	to
al	to the
y	and
no	no (placed before verb)
en	in
con	with
pero	but

A. Exprese en inglés (Express in English):

1. María nada en el océano.
2. Yo converso con Carmen.
3. Ellos firman el documento.
4. Nosotros hablamos español.
5. Tú miras la televisión.
6. Vd. trabaja en Nueva York.
7. Carlos y Francisco limpian el interior del hotel.
8. Yo estudio el piano.
9. Los turistas bailan la rumba.
10. Vosotros olvidáis las guitarras.

B. Complete Vd. el pensamiento (Complete the thought):

1. Yo converso en español, pero Vd. no _____ .
2. El profesor habla portugués, pero yo no _____ :
3. Clara nada en el océano, pero nosotros no _____ .
4. Ellos trabajan en México, pero tú no _____ .
5. Nosotros bailamos, pero Dolores y Héctor no _____ .

LOS VERBOS DE LA SEGUNDA CONJUGACIÓN (SECOND CONJUGATION VERBS)

SINGULAR		PLURAL	
yo bebo	I drink	nosotros (-as) beb**emos**	we drink
tú beb**es**	you drink	vosotros (-as) beb**éis**	you drink
él beb**e**	he drinks	ellos beb**en**	they drink
ella beb**e**	she drinks	ellas beb**en**	they drink
Vd. beb**e**	you drink	Vds. beb**en**	you drink

Verbos regulares de la segunda conjugación (Regular second conjugation verbs)

aprender	*to learn*	**leer**	*to read*
comer	*to eat*	**meter**	*to put*
comprender	*to comprehend*	**responder**	*to answer*
correr	*to run*	**suspender**	*to suspend*
creer	*to believe*	**temer**	*to fear*

Ejercicios (Exercises)

A. *Exprese Vd. en inglés (Express in English)*:

1. Yo aprendo el español.
2. Ellos comen el chocolate.
3. Vd. comprende el problema.
4. Nosotros corremos al auto.
5. Él responde al profesor.
6. Doris teme el léon.
7. El profesor suspende la clase.
8. Las señoritas leen el texto.
9. Homero y Lucía meten la crema en el café.
10. ¿Crees la anécdota?

B. *Asocie Vd. cada sujeto en grupo 1 con el verbo apropiado en grupo 2 (Match each subject in group 1 with the appropriate verb in group 2)*:

Group 1

1. Yo
2. Tú
3. Él
4. Nosotros
5. Vds.

Group 2

1. comes una banana.
2. respondemos en clase.
3. comprendo la anécdota.
4. aprenden la biología.
5. lee la novela.

VERBOS DE LA TERCERA CONJUGACIÓN (THIRD CONJUGATION VERBS)

SINGULAR		PLURAL	
yo escrib**o**	I write	nosotros (-as) escrib**imos**	we write
tú escrib**es**	you write	vosotros (-as) escrib**ís**	you write
él escrib**e**	he writes	ellos escrib**en**	they write
ella escrib**e**	she writes	ellas escrib**en**	they write
Vd. escrib**e**	you write	Vds. escrib**en**	you write

Verbos regulares de la tercera conjugación (Regular third conjugation verbs)

abrir	*to open*	**partir**	*to leave*
consumir	*to consume*	**permitir**	*to permit*
insistir	*to insist*	**recibir**	*to receive*
interrumpir	*to interrupt*	**resistir**	*to resist*
omitir	*to omit*	**vivir**	*to live*

Ejercicios (Exercises)

A. *Exprese Vd. en inglés* (Express in English):

1. Ricardo recibe el telegrama.
2. El señor interrumpe la conversación.
3. Yo omito el acento.
4. Alicia abre el libro de texto.
5. Anita consume los bombones.
6. Nosotros vivimos en el Perú.
7. El profesor no permite conversaciones en clase.
8. ¿Insiste en hablar español?

B. *Exprese Vd. en español* (Express in Spanish):

1. I write the novel.
2. He resists.
3. David omits the verb.
4. We interrupt the class.
5. They live in México.

C. *Sustituya Vd. la forma apropiada del verbo* (Substitute the appropriate form of the verb):

1. Nosotros amamos la libertad. (él, Juan, Vds.)
    We love liberty.
2. Tú indicas el lugar. (el profesor, nosotros, Paco y Carmen)
    You indicate the place.
3. Él organiza un club. (ella, vosotros, los estudiantes)
    He is organizing a club.
4. Ella posee la tierra. (Don José, los García, tú)
    She possesses the land.

5. Vd. come el pan. (los animales, ellas, el turista)
   You eat the bread.
6. Nosotros bebemos café. (Mamá, vosotras, yo)
   We drink coffee.
7. Vosotros descubrís la verdad. (María y yo, papá y mamá, ellos)
   You discover the truth.
8. Ellos escriben una carta. (el sargento y el general, el prisionero, tú)
   They write a letter.
9. Ellas omiten el número. (el presidente, Vds., ellas)
   They omit the number.
10. Vds. insisten en las vacaciones. (el señor, los pilotos, Consuelo y Concepción)
    You insist on vacations.

SER AND ESTAR

There are two verbs in the Spanish language that are equivalent to the English verb *to be*. **Ser** is used in situations that are inherent and permanent. **Estar** is employed when the thought of the sentence implies temporary condition or location. (See Grammar Section)

Present tense of ser

yo **soy**	I am	nosotros (-as) **somos**	we are
tú **eres**	you are	vosotros (-as) **sois**	you are
él **es**	he is	ellos **son**	they are
ella **es**	she is	ellas **son**	they are
Vd. **es**	you are	Vds. **son**	you are

Present tense of estar

yo **estoy**	I am	nosotros (-as) **estamos**	we are
tú **estás**	you are	vosotros (-as) **estáis**	you are
él **está**	he is	ellos **están**	they are
ella **está**	she is	ellas **están**	they are
Vd. **está**	you are	Vds. **están**	you are

Ejercicios

A. *Concentre Vd. la atención en el significado de los cognados y lea las oraciones en voz alta (Concentrate on the meaning of the cognates and then read the sentences aloud):*

1. Pizarro es el conquistador del Perú.
2. San Fernando es una región de California.
3. El jaguar es un animal de las Américas.
4. El bar del motel es popular.
5. Don Juan es el héroe del drama.
6. Ricardo Burton es un actor del cine.
7. El chile con carne de la cafetería es horrible.

8. El plan del doctor y del barón no es original.
9. El caballero en el auto no es de la fiesta.
10. La lava es un mineral, y el mango es una fruta.

B. *Pronuncie Vd. y concentre la atención en el significado (Pronounce and concentrate on the meaning):*

1. ¿Es la península de la Florida?
2. ¿Es el álbum de María?
3. ¿Es el televisor de David?
4. Es el club de golf.
5. Es el aroma de la azalea.
6. ¿Es el corral del burro?
7. Es un dragón de la China.
8. Es una idea terrible.
9. Es un error grave.
10. ¿Es el cable del radio?

C. *Lea Vd. las oraciones en voz alta y concentre la atención en el significado (Read the sentences aloud and concentrate on the meaning):*

1. El auto está en el garaje.
2. El criminal está en el calabozo.
3. La pampa está en la parte central de la Argentina.
4. Elena está en el Canadá con la mamá de Víctor.
5. El canal está en Panamá.
6. Susana y Teresa están en la catedral.
7. Estamos en octubre.
8. Estoy en el patio con el papá de Carolina.
9. Ricardo Montalbán está al piano en el bar del Club Oasis Tropical.
10. Los generales están en el hotel.

D. *Pronuncie Vd. y concentre la atención en el significado (Pronounce and concentrate on the meaning):*

1. ¿Está normal la señorita?
2. ¿Está Bárbara en la plaza?
3. ¿Está loco el dictador?
4. ¿Está el presidente en la capital?
5. ¿Está melancólico el doctor?
6. ¿Está Rusia en Europa?
7. ¿Están contentas las personas en la villa?
8. ¿Están los turistas en Puerto Rico?
9. ¿Está Nicolás en el aeroplano?
10. ¿Está el hombre en el auto?

NOTE: **Ser** answers the questions *who?* and *what?*
        Estar answers the questions *where?* and *how?*

PRELIMINARY UNIT 3

Gente y situaciones   *People and situations*

Las expresiones de cortesía (Expressions of courtesy)

Muchas gracias.	*Thank you very much.*	**No hay de qué.**	*Think nothing of it.*
Se lo agradezco.	*I appreciate it.*	**Con su permiso.**	*With your permission.*
Estoy muy agradecido.	*I am very grateful.*	**Dispénseme.**	*Excuse me.*
¿En qué puedo servirlo (-la)?	*What can I do for you?*	**Con mucho gusto.**	*With pleasure.*
		Tenga la bondad de (ir).	*Please (go).*
¿Puedo ayudarlo (-la)?	*May I help you? Can I help you?*	**Por favor (continúe).**	*Please (continue).*
Es Vd. muy amable.	*You are very kind.*	**Hágame el favor de (salir).**	*Please (leave).*
De nada.	*Think nothing of it. (You are welcome.)*		

Ejercicio (Exercise)

Complete Vd. las frases siguientes (Complete the following sentences):

1. Un señor **dice** a una señorita ———————————————————— . (says)
2. La profesora dice ———————————————————— .
3. El hombre en la **tienda** dice ———————————————— . (store)
4. Mamá dice ———————————————————— .
5. Cuando recibe un **regalo** María dice ————————————— . (present)

Las presentaciones (Introductions)

Permítame presentarme.	*Permit me to introduce myself.*
Quiero presentar . . .	*I want to present . . .*
Me llamo (Juan Valdés).	*My name is (Juan Valdés).*
Permítame presentarle al señor (a la señora) López.	*Allow me to introduce Mr. (Mrs.) López to you.*
A sus órdenes.	*At your service.*
Tanto gusto.	*Glad to know you.*
Tengo mucho gusto en conocerlo (-la).	*I'm glad to make your acquaintance.*
El gusto es mío.	*The pleasure is mine.*

Ejercicio (Exercise)

Exprese en español (Express in Spanish):

1. I want to introduce myself, Philip Rey, at your service.
2. John introduces Mary to Mr. López.
3. My name is Joseph.
4. It's a pleasure to meet you, Mr. García.
5. The pleasure is all mine.

Los saludos y las despedidas (Greetings and farewells)

Hola, María	*Hello, Mary.*
Buenos días, señora.	*Good morning,*
Buenas tardes,	*madam.*
señor.	*Good afternoon, sir.*
Buenas noches,	*Good evening*
Juana.	*(night), Jane.*
¿Qué tal?	*How are things?*
¿Cómo le va?	*How goes it?*
¡Que le vaya bien!	*May all go well.*
¿Qué hay de nuevo?	*What's new?*
¡Qué gusto de verlo!	*It's a pleasure to see you!*

¿Cómo está Vd.?	*How are you?*
Hasta luego.	*See you later.*
Hasta la vista.	*Till we meet again.*
Hasta mañana.	*Until tomorrow.*
¡Que se divierta!	*Have a good time!*
Recuerdos a todos.	*Remember me to everybody.*
Saludos a todos.	*My regards to everyone.*
Feliz viaje.	*Pleasant trip.*
Felices fiestas.	*Happy holidays.*
Adiós.	*Good-bye.*

Ejercicio (Exercise)

Traduzca Vd. al español. (Translate into Spanish):

1. Good afternoon, madam.
2. Good morning, sir. How are you?
3. It's a pleasure to see you John. How is everything?
4. See you later, Jane.
5. What's new, Angel?

Las preguntas (Questions)

¿Cuánto cuesta . . . ?	*How much does . . . cost?*
¿Cuánto cobra por . . . ?	*What are you charging for . . . ?*
¿Adónde se va para comprar . . . ?	*Where do you go to buy . . . ?*
¿Dónde está . . . ?	*Where is . . . ?*
¿Dónde se encuentra . . . ?	*Where is . . . located?*
¿De dónde es Vd.?	*Where are you from?*
¿Con quiénes van a . . . ?	*With whom are they going to . . . ?*
¿Qué sabe Vd. de . . . ?	*What do you know about . . . ?*
¿Sabe Vd. que . . . ?	*Do you know that . . . ?*
¿Adónde va este tranvía?	*Where does this trolley go . . . ?*
¿Cúal prefiere Vd.?	*Which do you prefer?*
¿A qué hora . . . ?	*At what time . . . ?*
¿En qué mes . . . ?	*In what month . . . ?*
¿Qué es un . . . ?	*What is a . . . ?*
¿Cómo se llega a . . . ?	*How does one get to . . . ?*
¿Cómo es la comida en . . . ?	*How is the food in . . . ?*
¿Qué le dice el señor a . . . ?	*What does the man say to . . . ?*
¿Cómo se deletrea . . . ?	*How do you spell . . . ?*
¿Es posible + inf.?	*Is it possible to . . . ?*

Las instrucciones para la clase (Instructions for class)

Silencio, por favor.	*Silence, please.*
Levántese Vd. (Levántense Vds.)	*Stand up.*
Siéntese Vd. (Siéntense Vds.)	*Sit down.*
Abra Vd. el libro. (Abran Vds.)	*Open the book.*
Cierre Vd. el libro. (Cierren Vds.)	*Close your book.*
Escuche Vd. (Escuchen Vds.)	*Listen.*
Preste Vd. atención. (Presten Vds.)	*Pay attention.*
Corrija Vd. su trabajo. (Corrijan Vds.)	*Correct your work.*
Siga Vd. (Sigan Vds.)	*Continue.*
Repita Vd. (Repitan Vds.)	*Repeat.*
En voz más alta.	*Louder.*
Escríbalo en la pizarra.	*Write it on the blackboard.*
Dígalo en español.	*Say it in Spanish.*
Más despacio, por favor.	*Slower, please.*
Responda Vd. a la pregunta. (Respondan Vds.)	*Answer the question.*
Conteste Vd. la pregunta. (Contesten Vds.)	
Mire Vd. el libro. (Miren Vds.)	*Look at the book.*

PARTE 1
Lengua y práctica

UNIT 1

La agencia de viajes　　　　The Travel Agency

Expresiones apropiadas (Appropriate Phrases)

1.	estar de vacaciones	to be on vacation
2.	consultar el (la) agente de viajes	to consult the travel agent
3.	revalidar el pasaporte	to validate (renew) the passport
4.	gozar de los folletos de viajes	to enjoy the travel brochures
5.	preparar un itinerario	to prepare an itinerary
6.	comprar un billete de ida y vuelta	to buy a round-trip ticket
7.	pagar con tarjeta de crédito	to pay with a credit card
8.	confirmar la reservación	to confirm the reservation
9.	viajar en primera (segunda) clase	to travel first (second) class
10.	llegar a la destinación	to arrive at the destination
11.	guiar al (a la) turista	to guide the tourist
12.	llevar una maleta	to carry a suitcase
13.	pasar por la aduana	to go through customs
14.	revisar el equipaje	to check the baggage
15.	ayudar a los turistas	to help the tourists
16.	alquilar un coche	to rent a car
17.	buscar alojamiento	to look for lodging
18.	hablar con el (la) guía	to speak with the guide
19.	visitar los lugares de interés	to visit the places of interest
20.	disfrutar del viaje	to enjoy the trip

Variaciones del vocabulario (Vocabulary Variations)

el boleto	ticket
el destino	destination
la excursión, el recorrido	trip
el hospedaje	lodging
la reserva	reservation
la valija	suitcase (valise)

Vocabulario en acción (Vocabulary in Action)

Traduzca (Translate):

1. He is on vacation in Mexico.
2. Juanita consults a travel agent.
3. We renew our passports.
4. They enjoy the travel brochures.
5. The travel agent prepares the itinerary.
6. She buys a round-trip ticket.
7. We pay with a credit card.
8. The boy confirms his reservation.
9. Do you (Uds.) travel first class in Spain?
10. They arrive at the destination.

11. She guides tourists in Peru.
12. You *(Ud.)* carry your suitcases.
13. Everybody *(todo el mundo)* goes through customs.
14. The customs inspector *(el aduanero)* checks the baggage.
15. Do you *(tú)* help the tourists?
16. I'm renting a car in Puerto Rico.
17. We look for lodging in the Dominican Republic.
18. Pepe speaks with the guide.
19. They are visiting places of interest in Venezuela.
20. Everybody enjoys the trip.

Expresiones útiles (Useful Expressions)

LOS PAÍSES HISPANOAMERICANOS (COUNTRIES OF SPANISH AMERICA)

PAÍS (Country)	CAPITAL (Capital City)	GENTILICIO (Nationality)
Argentina	Buenos Aires	argentino (-a)
Bolivia	La Paz	boliviano (-a)
Colombia	Bogotá	colombiano (-a)
Costa Rica	San José	costarricense
Cuba	La Habana	cubano (-a)
Chile	Santiago	chileno (-a)
Ecuador	Quito	ecuatoriano (-a)
El Salvador	San Salvador	salvadoreño (-a)
Guatemala	Ciudad de Guatemala	gautemalteco (-a)
Honduras	Tegucigalpa	hondureño (-a)
México	Ciudad de México	mexicano (-a)
Nicaragua	Managua	nicaragüense (-a)
Panamá	Ciudad de Panamá	panameño (-a)
Paraguay	Asunción	paraguayo (-a)
Perú	Lima	peruano (-a)
Puerto Rico	San Juan	puertorriqueño (-a)
República Dominicana	Santo Domingo	dominicano (-a)
Uruguay	Montevideo	uruguayo (-a)
Venezuela	Caracas	venezolano (-a)

Ejercicio (Exercise)

Identifique la capital con el país (Match the capital with the country):

1. Argentina
2. Bolivia
3. Ecuador
4. Perú
5. Honduras

6. Puerto Rico
7. Colombia
8. Chile
9. Nicaragua
10. Venezuela

a. Tegucigalpa
b. Buenos Aires
c. Quito
d. Bogotá
e. La Paz

f. Caracas
g. Santiago
h. Managua
i. San Juan
j. Lima

AMÉRICA DEL NORTE

El Océan
Atlántico

Chicago

Nuevo México

Arizona

Nueva York

Los Ángeles

Texas

Miami

ANTILLAS MAYORES

CUBA
La Habana

LA REPÚBLICA
DOMINICANA
Santo Domingo

AMÉRICA CENTRAL

PUERTO RICO
San Juan

9 3

11 20

1

2
4

5

8

10

6
7

1. MÉXICO — México D. F.
2. GUATEMALA — Guatemala
3. HONDURAS — Tegucigalpa
4. EL SALVADOR — San Salvador
5. NICARAGUA — Managua
6. COSTA RICA — San José
7. PANAMÁ — Panamá
8. ZONA DEL CANAL
9. BELICE — Belmopan

12

13

14

AMÉRICA DEL SUR

El Océano Pacífico

15

19

16

18

10. VENEZUELA — Caracas
11. COLOMBIA — Bogotá
12. ECUADOR — Quito
13. ISLAS GALÁPAGOS (Archipiélago de Colón)
14. PERÚ — Lima
15. BOLIVIA — (La Paz & Sucre)
16. CHILE — Santiago
17. ARGENTINA — Buenos Aires
18. URUGUAY — Montevideo
19. PARAGUAY — Asunción
20. ANTILLAS HOLANDESAS — Aruba, Curaçao

17

ASIA

EUROPA

Madrid

ESPAÑA

ISLAS
CANARIAS   GIBRALTAR

El Sahara Español

ÁFRICA

Fernando Póo
(Guinea Ecuatorial)

El Océano Índio

AUSTRALIA

El mundo hispánico

MONEDA (CURRENCY)

PAÍS (Country)	MONEDA (Currency)
Alemania	marco
Argentina	peso
Bolivia	peso
Brasil	cruzeiro
Colombia	peso
Costa Rica	colón
Cuba	peso
Chile	escudo
Ecuador	sucre
El Salvador	colón
España	peseta
Francia	franco
Guatemala	quetzal
Honduras	lempira
Inglaterra	libra esterlina
Italia	lira
Japón	yen
México	peso
Nicaragua	córdoba
Panamá	balboa
Paraguay	guaraní
Perú	sol
Puerto Rico	dólar
República Dominicana	peso
Uruguay	peso
Venezuela	bolívar

Ejercicio

Identifique la moneda con el país (Match the currency with the country):

1. Francia
2. Inglaterra
3. Italia
4. España
5. Alemania
6. México
7. Venezuela

a. libra esterlina
b. lira
c. peso
d. peseta
e. marco
f. bolívar
g. franco

Cuestionario (Questionnaire)

Complete las siguientes frases (Complete the following sentences):

1. Los turistas van a la agencia de viajes para comprar _____ .

2. Es necesario planear un _____ antes de viajar.
3. El verano es la época de _____ para muchos maestros y estudiantes.
4. Se puede ahorrar dinero cuando el viajero compra un billete de _____ .
5. Se pueden apreciar escenas de España en _____ .
6. Cuando el viajero no tiene dinero suficiente, puede pagar con una _____

7. Los viajeros ricos en general viajan _____ .
8. Al llegar a un país extranjero, el viajero tiene que pasar por _____ .
9. _____ es el señor que muestra a los turistas los puntos de interés en una ciudad.
10. _____ es el permiso para entrar en un país extranjero.

Modelos de conversación (Conversational Patterns)

Repita y substituya las expresiones dadas (Repeat and substitute with the given expressions):

1. **Ya tenemos el billete de ida y vuelta.**
   _____ **el itinerario.**
   _____ **el pasaporte.**

   We already have our round-trip ticket.
   _____ our itinerary.
   _____ our passport.

2. **Este verano pensamos ir a España.**
   _____ **a México.**
   _____ **de vacaciones.**

   This summer we intend to go to Spain.
   _____ to Mexico.
   _____ on vacation.

3. **Vamos a consultar a la agente de viajes.**
   _____ **el itinerario.**
   _____ **el folleto de viaje.**

   Let's consult the travel agent.

   _____ the itinerary.
   _____ the travel brochure.

4. **Espéreme en correos.**
   _____ **en la aduana.**
   _____ **en el coche.**

   Wait for me at the post office.
   _____ in customs.
   _____ in the car.

5. **¿Dónde está la tarjeta de crédito?**
   _____ **el equipaje?**
   _____ **la maleta?**

   Where is the credit card?
   _____ the baggage?
   _____ the suitcase?

Diálogo (Dialogue)

Esposa:	¡**Qué** emoción! Nuestro hijo regresa de Europa.	*(What!)*
Esposo:	Sí, bastante **trabajé** para mandarlo a Italia.	*(I worked)*
Esposa:	Aquí está mi hijito. ¡Es tan inteligente! **Seguro que** conoce todos los monumentos de Italia.	*(certainly)*
Esposo:	Seguro que no los conoce.	
Esposa:	¡Paquito, un **abrazo** para tu mamá! Cuéntame algo de los monumentos de Italia.	*(embrace)*
Paquito:	Es un país precioso. Pero sus monumentos principales están en ruinas. Están en **estado** de inmediata **reparación**.	*(state/repair)*

Comprensión (Comprehension)

1. ¿De dónde regresa Paquito?
2. ¿Quién ha pagado su viaje?
3. ¿Qué le dice su madre al recibirlo?
4. ¿Qué piensa Paquito de los monumentos principales?
5. ¿Adónde viajará Ud. este año en sus vacaciones?
6. ¿Por qué viajan muchos turistas a España todos los años?
7. ¿Adónde van los turistas para preparar un itinerario de viaje a Europa?
8. ¿Qué ventajas hay en un viaje a Suramérica para los estudiantes de español?
9. ¿Por qué es ventajoso comprar un billete de ida y vuelta?

Vamos a hablar (Let's Talk)

A. ¡Usted acaba de ganar el premio gordo ($50,000.00) de la lotería del estado! Por supuesto Ud. va a hacer un viaje con sus seres queridos—quizás a La Costa del Sol, quizás a Acapulco o a cualquier otro lugar. Mencione todas las preparaciones que se necesitan para efectuar un viaje al exterior. De acuerdo con sus planes haga un itinerario de su viaje.

(You have just won the grand prize ($50,000.00) of the state lottery! Of course, you will take a trip with your loved ones—perhaps to the Costa del Sol, Acapulco, or some other place. Discuss all the preparations that are needed for a trip abroad. In accordance with your plans, make an itinerary for your trip.)

B. Complete Ud. el siguiente diálogo entre un agente de viajes y una cliente que quiere hacer un viaje a Puerto Rico. (Complete the following dialogue between a travel agent and a client who wants to take a trip to Puerto Rico.)

Agente: Buenas tardes, señorita. ¿En qué puedo servirle?
Cliente: _____
Agente: Sí, tenemos muchos vuelos para Puerto Rico.
Cliente: _____
Agente: El vuelo va a costar $200 por un billete de ida y vuelta y hay un avión que sale a las once de la noche cada día de la semana.
Cliente: _____
Agente: Voy a enviar el billete del vuelo a su casa. Mil gracias. Hasta luego, señorita.
Cliente: _____

C. Comente Ud. sobre los pensamientos del individuo que en época helada del invierno se enfrenta con un cartel de anuncio de viaje a un lugar atractivo y asoleado. (Comment on the thoughts of an individual who in a cold period of winter comes face to face with a travel poster of an attractive and sunny place.)

D. Prepare un itinerario para una excursión escolar a un país hispanoamericano. (Prepare an itinerary for a student excursion to a Spanish American country.)

Dichos y refranes (Sayings and Proverbs)

—Dicen que hay huelga de aviones para Puerto Rico.

—Hombre prevenido, nunca fue vencido.

Oficios y profesiones (Jobs and Professions)

el (la) agente de viajes	*travel agent*
el vendedor (la vendedora) de billetes	*ticket seller*
el dependiente (la dependienta) de reservaciones	*reservations clerk*
el dependiente (la dependienta) de información	*information clerk*
el (la) agente de seguros de viajes	*travel-insurance agent*
el aduanero (la aduanera)	*customs inspector*
el oficial de la inmigración	*immigration officer*
el guardia (la guardiana) de la frontera	*border guard*
el cónsul	*consul*
el maletero (la maletera)	*porter*
el (la) taxista	*taxi driver*
el chófer (de limosina)	*chauffeur (limousine)*
el (la) agente de coches de alquiler	*car-rental agent*
el hostelero, el posadero (la posadera), el mesonero (la mesonera), el fondista	*innkeeper*
el dueño (la dueña) de casa para viajeros o turistas (casa de huéspedes)	*tourist-home owner (boarding house)*

Ejercicio

Complete las siguientes definiciones (Complete the following definitions):

1. El hombre que se encarga de las maletas es _____.
2. La mujer que prepara el itinerario de viaje es _____.
3. El representante del gobierno en el extranjero es _____.
4. El chófer de un taxi es _____.
5. El individuo que revisa el equipaje es _____.
6. La mujer que alquila coches es _____.
7. El individuo que vende billetes es _____.

Repasito (Review)

Prueba—Escoja la traducción apropiada (Test—Choose the appropriate translation):

1.	las vacaciones	a.	reservation
2.	el itinerario	b.	passport
3.	la aduana	c.	vacation
4.	la tarjeta de crédito	d.	travel agent
5.	el viaje	e.	suitcase
6.	la maleta	f.	itinerary
7.	el agente de viajes	g.	customs
8.	el billete	h.	trip
9.	el pasaporte	i.	credit card
10.	la reservación	j.	ticket

Unit 2

Viajar en avión   *Air Travel*

Expresiones apropiadas

1.	llegar a tiempo al aeropuerto	*to arrive on time at the airport*
2.	buscar la línea aérea	*to look for the airline*
3.	confirmar el vuelo	*to confirm the flight*
4.	comprar los seguros de vuelo	*to buy flight insurance*
5.	abordar el avión	*to board the plane*
6.	confiar en el piloto (el copiloto)	*to trust the pilot (copilot)*
7.	reservar un asiento de ventana	*to reserve a window seat*
8.	abrochar el cinturón de seguridad	*to fasten the seat belt*
9.	gozar del panorama	*to enjoy the view*
10.	volar a máxima altitud	*to fly at the maximum altitude*
11.	marearse	*to get airsick*
12.	temer la turbulencia	*to fear turbulence*
13.	ir al lavatorio	*to go to the washroom*
14.	llamar a la azafata	*to call the flight attendant (stewardess)*
15.	tomar un calmante	*to take a tranquilizer*
16.	hablar con un pasajero (una pasajera)	*to speak with a passenger*
17.	comer una comida en vuelo	*to have a meal in flight*
18.	anunciar el aterrizaje (el despegue)	*to announce the landing (takeoff)*
19.	aterrizar en la pista de aterrizaje	*to land on the runway*
20.	salir por la puerta de pasajeros	*to leave through the passenger gate*

Variaciones del vocabulario

el aeródromo	*airport*
el aeromozo (la aeromoza)	*flight attendant*
el aeroplano	*airplane*
la altura	*altitude*
el capitán (la capitana)	*pilot (captain)*
el cuarto de caballeros (damas)	*men's (ladies') room*
el excusado, el retrete, el lavamanos, el inodoro, el baño	*bathroom*
le llegada	*landing, arrival*
la píldora tranquilizadora, el tranquilizador	*tranquilizer*
la salida	*takeoff*

Vocabulario en acción

Traduzca:

1. I always arrive on time at the airport.
2. The tourists look for the airline.

3. Do you (tú) confirm your flight?
4. He buys flight insurance.
5. The tourists board the airplane at seven o'clock.
6. Do you (Ud.) trust the pilot?
7. She always reserves a window seat.
8. The passengers fasten their seat belts.
9. We enjoy the view.
10. The airplane flies at the maximum altitude.
11. They get airsick.
12. We fear turbulence.
13. The passengers go to the washroom.
14. The woman calls the flight attendant.
15. José takes a tranquilizer.
16. The flight attendant talks with the passengers.
17. We have a meal in flight.
18. The pilot announces the arrival in La Paz.
19. The plane lands on the runway at six o'clock.
20. We leave through the passenger gate.

Cuestionario

Complete las siguientes frases:

1. Para volar se utiliza un _____ .
2. El hombre que maneja un avión se llama el _____ .
3. _____ asiste a los pasajeros.
4. Sirven unas _____ muy ricas en los aviones.
5. Se puede ver _____ abajo por la ventana.
6. El avión se mueve mucho con la _____ .
7. El avión aterriza en _____ .
8. Iberia y T.W.A. son dos _____ que vuelan a España.
9. El pasajero nervioso toma _____ .

Modelos de conversación

Repita y substituya las expresiones dadas:

1. **Confían en el piloto.**   They trust the pilot.
   _____ **el copiloto.**   _____ the copilot.
   _____ **la azafata.**   _____ the flight attendant.
2. **La azafata ayuda a los pasajeros.**   The flight attendant helps the passengers.
   _____ **al piloto.**   _____ pilot.
   _____ **a los turistas.**   _____ tourists.
3. **Los pasajeros abordan el avión.**   The passengers board the plane.
   _____ **reservan un asiento.**   _____ reserve a seat.
   _____ **confirman el vuelo.**   _____ confirm their flight.

4. **El piloto anuncia el despegue.**   The pilot announces the takeoff.
    _____ habla con los pasajeros.   _____ speaks to the passengers.
    _____ aterriza el avión.   _____lands the plane.
5. **¿Dónde está el aeromozo?**   Where is the flight attendant?
    ¿_____ calmante?   _____ tranquilizer?
    ¿_____ lavatorio?   _____ washroom?

Diálogo

Capitán:	Señoras y señores. Les habla el capitán del avión. Parece que nos hemos encontrado con una **tempestad**. Les agradezco que se abrochen los cinturones. Gracias.	*(storm)*
Abuela:	¡María santísima! ¿Dónde está mi **botellita** de calmantes?	*(little bottle)*
Niña:	¡Qué interesante! Me siento como en una **montaña rusa**.	*(roller coaster)*
Juan:	**Bésame**, Catalina. **Quizás sea** la última vez. Dáme un beso antes de morir.	*(kiss me/it may be)*
Catalina:	Tengo mucho miedo. Me voy a marear. **Abrázame**, Juan. No quiero morir.	*(hug me)*
Capitán:	Le tempestad ha terminado. Ya pueden **soltar** sus cinturones.	*(unfasten)*
Abuela:	Gracias a Dios.	
Juan:	Bésame, Catalina. Mira que nos hemos salvado.	
Catalina:	No me hables, Juan. Tú eres un oportunista.	
Niña:	¡Qué lástima! **Se acabó** la aventura.	*(ended)*
Azafata:	**No hay mal que por bien no venga.**	*(Every dark cloud has a silver lining.)*

Comprensión

1. ¿Qué recomendación hizo el capitán a los pasajeros?
2. ¿Qué causó la turbulencia en el avión?
3. ¿Cuál de los pasajeros no tiene miedo?
4. ¿Cuándo busca Catalina el amor de Juan?
5. ¿Le gustan a usted los refranes *(proverbs)*?
6. ¿Sabe Ud. otro refrán?
7. Cuando Ud. viaja en avión, ¿tiene Ud. miedo?

Vamos a hablar

A. Preguntas
1. Nombre usted cinco clases de empleados que trabajan para una línea aérea.
2. ¿En qué consiste el trabajo de un piloto? ¿De una azafata?
3. ¿Cómo se siente la mayoría de los pasajeros que viajan en avión?

4. ¿Recuerda Ud. su primer vuelo en avión? ¿Cuáles fueron sus pensamientos la noche anterior del viaje? ¿Qué emociones experimentó Ud. al abordar el avión? Describa el despegue . . . el vuelo . . . el aterrizaje.

5. ¿Ha volado de nuevo? ¿Adónde? ¿Cómo fue el viaje?

B. Complete Ud. el siguiente diálogo entre una aeromoza en la sección de reservación de vuelos y un cliente que quiere viajar a la República Dominicana.

Aeromoza: ¿Puedo servirle?

Cliente: _____

Aeromoza: Hay un vuelo a las once de la noche que tiene dos asientos vacíos.

Cliente: _____

Aeromoza: Sí, hace escala primero en el aeropuerto internacional de Miami antes de cruzar el mar para llegar a la destinación.

Cliente: _____

Aeromoza: No es posible. Hay jaulas (*cages*) especiales de vuelo en las que pueden viajar los perros.

Cliente: _____

Aeromoza: Sí, y también Diners Club. El billete de ida vale $300 dólares. Mil gracias por incluir nuestra línea en sus planes de viaje.

_____

Dichos y refranes

—Aunque tengo miedo de volar, vamos a México este verano.

—Ver es creer.

Oficios y profesiones

el dependiente (la dependienta) de reservaciones	*reservation clerk*
el taquillero (la taquillera)	*ticket seller*
el (la) agente de seguros de vuelo	*flight-insurance agent*
el mecánico (la mécanica) de aviones	*airplane mechanic*
el maletero (la maletera)	*luggage porter*
los empleados de la carga	*cargo handlers*
los vigilantes (las vigilantas) de los detectores electrónicos	*electronic-detector guards*
el piloto	*pilot*
el copiloto	*copilot*
el navegante	*navigator*
los empleados de la torre del aeropuerto	*tower personnel*
los controladores de vuelo	*flight controllers*

Ejercicio

Complete las siguientes definiciones:

1. El _____ es el que conduce el avión.
2. El que lleva las maletas para un viajero es el _____.
3. La persona que vende billetes en el aeropuerto se llama el _____.
4. Antes de entrar en un avión, los pasajeros pasan por la puerta donde están los

   _____.

5. El que hace las reparaciones de un avión es el _____.
6. Antes de aterrizar, el piloto espera las señales de los _____.
7. Si Ud. quiere cambiar su vuelo, Ud. tiene que hablar con el (la) _____.

Repasito

Prueba-Escoja la traducción apropiada:

1.	el vuelo	a.	flight attendant
2.	el avión	b.	seat belt
3.	la línea aérea	c.	arrival
4.	el piloto	d.	flight
5.	el aeropuerto	e.	airplane
6.	la azafata	f.	airline
7.	la llegada	g.	pilot
8.	los seguros de vuelo	h.	airport
9.	el cinturón de seguridad	i.	runway
10.	la pista de aterrizaje	j.	flight insurance

UNIT 3

Viajar en tren   *Train Travel*

Expresiones apropiadas

1.	llegar a la estación del tren	*to arrive at the train station*
2.	pararse en el andén	*to stand on the platform*
3.	leer el horario	*to read the timetable*
4.	poner las maletas en la red de equipajes	*to put the suitcases on the luggage rack*
5.	sentarse en el coche-club	*to sit in the club car*
6.	preferir el coche de fumar	*to prefer the smoking car*
7.	dar el boleto al conductor (a la conductora)	*to give the ticket to the conductor*
8.	comer en el coche-comedor	*to eat in the dining car*
9.	llamar al maletero (a la maletera)	*to call the porter*
10.	dormir en el coche-cama	*to sleep in the sleeping car*
11.	pasar por un túnel	*to go through a tunnel*
12.	jugar a las cartas en el coche-club	*to play cards in the club car*
13.	reparar la locomotora	*to repair the locomotive*
14.	oír el sonido de los rieles	*to hear the sound of the rails*
15.	mirar los vagones de carga	*to look at the freight cars*
16.	ver el vagón rojo de cola	*to see the red caboose*
17.	gozar del viaje en el ferrocarril	*to enjoy the railroad trip*
18.	beber en el coche-mirador	*to drink in the observation car*
19.	dar al maletero (a la maletera) los talones del equipaje	*to give the porter the baggage stubs*
20.	tomar el metro	*to take the subway*

Variaciones del vocabulario

los carriles, los raíles	*rails*
el coche-bar	*club car*
el coche de carga	*freight car*
el coche Pullman	*Pullman car*
el ferrocarril subterráneo	*subway*
el furgón de cola, el vagón del conductor	*caboose*
el mozo (la moza) de la estación, el mozo de servicio	*porter*
el revisor (la revisora), el cobrador (la cobradora) de billetes*	*conductor*
el vagón de fumar	*smoking car*
el vagón mirador	*observation car*

Vocabulario en acción
Traduzca:

1.   The passengers arrive at the train station.
2.   We stand on the platform.
3.   She reads the timetable.
4.   The porter puts the suitcases on the luggage rack.
5.   The tourists sit in the club car.
6.   My friend prefers the smoking car.
7.   Do you *(tú)* give your ticket to the conductor?
8.   The students eat in the dining car.
9.   Aunt Alice calls the porter.
10. My brother and I sleep in the same *(mismo)* sleeper car.
11. The train goes through a tunnel.
12. My friends and I play cards in the club car.
13. They repair the locomotive before the trip.
14. I hear the sound of the tracks.
15. I'm looking at the freight cars.
16. Do you *(Ud.)* see the red caboose?
17. The tourists enjoy their railroad trip.
18. The men are having a drink in the observation car.
19. We give the baggage stubs to the porter.
20. I take the subway at 7:15.

Cuestionario
Complete las siguientes frases:

1.   El vagón en que sirven comidas se llama _____.
2.   Se puede jugar a las cartas en _____.
3.   Las camas para turistas se encuentran en _____.
4.   Los trenes se mueven rápidamente sobre _____.
5.   Los pasajeros esperan la llegada del tren sobre _____.
6.   _____ chequea los billetes de los pasajeros.
7.   La maquina que tira los vagones es _____.
8.   Se puede fumar en _____.

Modelos de conversación
Repita y substituya las expresiones dadas:

1.   **Los pasajeros esperan en el andén.**   The passengers wait on the platform.
     _____ en la estación.   _____ in the station.
     _____ el metro.   _____ for the subway.
2.   **Mi esposo está en el coche-club.**   My husband is in the club car.
     _____ coche-comedor.   _____ dining car.
     _____ coche-cama.   _____ sleeping car.

3. ¿Dónde está el horario?   Where is the timetable?
    ¿_____ maletero?   _____ porter?
    ¿_____ conductor?   _____ conductor?
4. El equipaje está en la red de   The luggage is on the luggage rack.
    equipaje.
    _____ el coche-cama.   _____ in the sleeping car.
    _____ la estación del   _____ in the train station.
    tren.
5. El conductor está en la locomotora.   The conductor is in the locomotive.
    _____ el vagón de   _____ caboose.
    cola.
    _____ el vagón de   _____ freight car.
    carga.

Diálogo

Oscar:	Siempre la misma existencia **aburrida** y **pesada**. No cambia la rutina diaria.	*(boring/monotonous)*
Félix:	Sí. Tienes razón. Tomamos el tren de Nueva York cada lunes por la mañana. Salimos de Washington cada viernes por la tarde.	
Oscar:	Me **fastidia** este viaje. Siempre el mismo paisaje, el mismo conductor, las mismas comidas, y las mismas caras todos los días.	*(bores)*
Félix:	Conozco exactamente el lugar en donde estamos en nuestro viaje, por los ruidos particulares del tren al correr sobre los rieles. ¡BOOM! ¡PAF! ¡CHAS!	
Oscar:	**¿Qué pasó?**	*(What happened?)*
Félix:	¡No sé!	
Conductor:	¡Pasajeros! Es un choque de dos trenes. **Salgan** inmediatamente del tren por las ventanas, y **cuidado** con los **vidrios rotos**.	*(Leave)* *(be careful/broken windows)*
Oscar:	¡Gracias a Dios, estamos **sanos y salvos**! Bendita sea la vida pesada y aburrida. Nunca voy a condenarla.	*(safe and sound)*
Félix:	¡Amén!	

Comprensión

1. ¿Dónde viven Oscar y Félix?
2. ¿Por qué están aburridos los compañeros de viaje?
3. ¿Cómo sabe Félix dónde está en cada momento de su viaje?
4. ¿Quién explicó a los pasajeros lo que sucedió?
5. ¿Cómo se salvaron los pasajeros?
6. ¿Qué es lo que Oscar y Félix nunca van a condenar?

7.   ¿Cuáles son las ventajas de viajar en tren?
8.   ¿Le gusta a Ud. viajar en tren? ¿Por qué?
9.   Algunas naciones en Europa y un país en Asia tienen trenes muy cómodos y corren sobre los rieles con gran velocidad. ¿Cuáles son?
10. Nombre Ud. algunas líneas ferroviarias en los Estados Unidos.

Vamos a hablar

A.   Observe bien el dibujo y responda a las preguntas.

1.   ¿Cómo se llama el tipo de tren que corre en el subterráneo de una ciudad?
2.   ¿En qué estación para este tren subterráneo?
3.   ¿Qué piensa el hombre que espera el tren?
4.   ¿Qué piensa el conductor?
5.   Describa el grafito.
6.   ¿Por qué las tarifas de tren son más caras cada año?
7.   ¿Qué crímenes son comunes en los metros (trenes subterráneos) de la ciudad?

B.   ¿Cómo es la vida de las personas que viajan de un lugar a otro? ¿Es ventajoso viajar en tren? ¿Por qué algunos hombres y mujeres de negocios no viajan en tren? ¿Viaja Ud. en tren?

C.   ¿En qué ocasión quieren los padres comprar un tren eléctrico de juguete? Relate la conversación entre un padre y el dependiente de una tienda de juguetes que vende trenes modelos. ¿Es Ud. uno de los afortunados que en su niñez le obsequiaron un tren eléctrico? ¿Qué clase de tren fue?

Dichos y refranes

—¡Después de tantos años, viajo a mi tierra!

—Más vale tarde que nunca.

Oficios y profesiones

el guardia (la guardiana) (del cruce de ferrocarriles)	*watchman (woman)*
el operador (la operadora) de los semáforos ferroviarios	*signal man (woman)*
el (la) maquinista (ingeniero) del tren	*train engineer*
el mozo (la moza) del coche-cama	*sleeping car attendant*
el vendedor (la vendedora) de boletos	*ticket seller*
el despachador (la despachadora)	*dispatcher*
el anunciador (la anunciadora) del tren	*train announcer*
el reparador (la reparadora) de los rieles	*track repairman*
el mozo (la moza) del coche-comedor	*dining car waiter (waitress)*
el maletero (la maletera)	*redcap*
el empleado (la empleada) de la estación de trenes	*station attendant*
el oficial (la oficiala) de la oficina de objetos perdidos y encontrados	*official of the lost and found office*

Ejercicio

Complete las siguientes definiciones:

1. El hombre que lleva las maletas al tren es _____.
2. La persona que da direcciones en el altoparlante de una estación de trenes es _____.
3. Otra palabra para maquinista del tren es _____.
4. La persona que trabaja en el coche Pullman es _____,
5. La mujer que vende billetes es _____.
6. El individuo que repara los rieles es _____.

Repasito

Prueba—Escoja la traducción apropiada:

1. el conductor
2. el coche-comedor
3. la estación del tren
4. el metro
5. el ferrocarril
6. el maletero
7. el vagón
8. el coche-club
9. el andén
10. el coche de fumar

a. train station
b. railroad
c. club car
d. smoking car
e. platform
f. conductor
g. subway
h. railroad car
i. dining car
j. porter

UNIT 4

Viajar en autobus   *Bus Travel*

Expresiones apropiadas

1. esperar en la parada del autobús   *to wait at the bus stop*
2. estacionar el autobús   *to park the bus*
3. saludar con la mano al conductor (la conductora) del autobús   *to wave at the bus driver*
4. embarcarse en el (subir al) autobús   *to board (get on) the bus*
5. preguntar por el precio del pasaje   *to ask the price of the fare*
6. pagar la mitad de la tarifa para los niños   *to pay half-fare for children*
7. dar el cambio exacto   *to give the exact change*
8. pedir al conductor (a la conductora) un billete de transbordo   *to ask the bus driver for a transfer*
9. caminar por el pasillo   *to walk down the aisle*
10. coger un asiento del frente   *to take a front seat*
11. sentarse en un asiento de atrás   *to sit in a rear seat*
12. reclinarse en su asiento   *to recline in your seat*
13. leer los carteles de anuncios   *to read the advertising posters*
14. mirar por la ventanilla del autobús   *to look out the bus window*
15. viajar en un autobús de dos pisos   *to ride a double-decker bus*
16. tirar del cordón   *to pull the cord*
17. salir (bajar) del autobús por la puerta de salida   *to leave (get off) the bus through the exit door*
18. ir al terminal del autobús   *to go to the bus terminal*
19. subir al tranvía   *to get on the trolley car*
20. averiguar sobre un autobús escolar   *to inquire about a school bus*

Variaciones del vocabulario

los anuncios	*advertising posters*
el chófer de autobús, el guagüero (la guaguera)	*bus driver*
la guagua, el bus, el camión	*bus*
el medio pasaje	*half-fare*
la transferencia	*transfer*
el trole	*trolley*

Vocabulario en acción

Traduzca:

1. The people wait at the bus stop.
2. The driver parks the bus.
3. The children wave at the bus driver.
4. You *(Ud.)* board the bus at the bus stop.
5. He asks the price of the fare.
6. She pays half-price for her children.
7. You *(tú)* give the exact change.
8. María asks the bus driver for a transfer.
9. The gentleman walks down the aisle.
10. We take a front seat.
11. The children sit in seats in the rear.
12. I like to recline in my seat.
13. Do you *(Uds.)* read the advertising posters?
14. My friend looks out the bus window.
15. In England we like to ride a double-decker bus.
16. I pull the cord.
17. The passengers leave the bus through the exit door.
18. The bus goes to the bus terminal.
19. The workers get on a trolley car.
20. The students ask about the school bus.

Expresiones útiles

LAS SEÑALES DE TRÁNSITO (TRAFFIC SIGNS)

alto (pare)	*stop*
parada	*bus stop*
despacio	*slow*
precaución	*caution*
ceda el paso	*yield*
curva	*curve*
peligro	*danger*
desvío (desviación)	*detour*
carretera dividida	*divided highway*
no pase	*do not pass*
conserve su derecha	*keep to the right*
trabajadores	*men working*
confluencia	*merging traffic*
puente angosto	*narrow bridge*
no se estacione	*no parking*
no vire a la izquierda (derecha)	*no left (right) turn*
no vire en U	*no U turn*

calle de dirección única	*one-way street*
peatones	*pedestrians*
a la derecha con luz roja	*right turn on red light*
F.C. (ferrocarril)	*railroad*
zona escolar	*school zone*
velocidad máxima . . . k.p.h.	*speed limit . . . kilometers per hour*
círculo (glorieta) de tráfico	*traffic circle*

Ejercicio

Dé el equivalente en español:

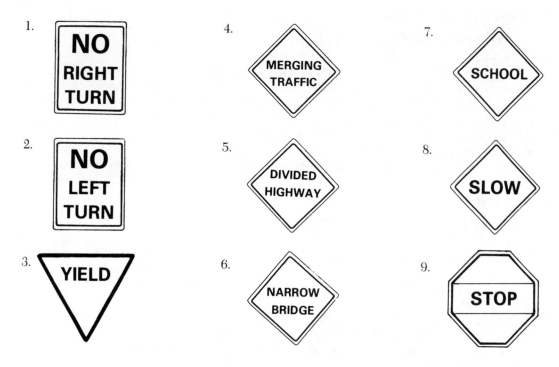

1. NO RIGHT TURN
2. NO LEFT TURN
3. YIELD
4. MERGING TRAFFIC
5. DIVIDED HIGHWAY
6. NARROW BRIDGE
7. SCHOOL
8. SLOW
9. STOP

LOS ANUNCIOS (PUBLIC SIGNS)

cuidado con el perro	*beware of dog*
prohibido hacer camping	*camping prohibited*
caja, cajero(a)	*cashier*
cerrado	*closed*
entrada	*entrance*
salida	*exit*
se alquila	*for rent*
se vende	*for sale*
información	*information*
se prohibe la entrada	*keep out*

Ejercicio

¿Qué anuncio ve Ud. en . . . ?

1. ¿el teatro?
2. ¿el supermercado?
3. ¿un apartamiento?
4. ¿una casa?
5. ¿el aeropuerto?
6. ¿un autobús?

Cuestionario

Complete las siguientes frases:

1. Los alumnos viajan en _____.
2. _____ maneja el autobús.
3. Al subir al autobús, hay que pagar _____ .
4. En Londres usan _____ .
5. Estoy cansado. Espero que haya un _____ libre en este autobús.
6. Los pasajeros leen _____ que aparecen en el techo del vehículo.
7. Yo siempre pido _____ para subir al segundo autobús.
8. A los niños les gusta mirar por _____ .
9. Al llegar a su destinación es necesario tirar del _____ para que pare el autobús.

Modelos de conversación

Repita y substituya las expresiones dadas:

1. **Los pasajeros suben al autobús.**
   _____ bajan del autobús.
   _____ tiran del cordón.

   The passengers board the bus.
   _____ get off the bus.
   _____ pull the cord.

2. **Me siento en el pasillo.**
   _____ un asiento del frente.
   _____ un asiento de atrás.

   I sit in the aisle.
   _____a front seat.
   _____a rear seat.

3. **Prefiero sentarme en un asiento al lado del pasillo.**
   _____cerca de la ventana.
   _____cerca de la puerta de salida.

   I prefer to sit in an aisle seat.
   _____ near the window.
   _____ near the exit door.

4. **Me gustan los tranvías.**
   _____ autobuses de dos pisos.
   _____ carteles de anuncios.

   I like trolleys.
   _____double-decker buses.
   _____advertising posters.

5. **El conductor del autobús pide el pasaje.**

The driver of the bus asks for the fare.

———————————————

cambio exacto.

——————————————— **billete de transbordo.**

———————————————exact

fare.

———————————————transfer.

Diálogo

Soldado: ¿Cuánto es el pasaje?

Chófer: Cincuenta centavos. Póngalos en la **cajita,** por favor *(fare box)* . . . Hay solamente seis asientos libres en el centro del autobús.

Soldado: Gracias. Es Ud. muy amable. ¿Dónde? . . . Ah, ya veo uno. El asiento junto a la señorita.

Señorita: Perdóneme, señor. ¿Tiene un **fósforo?** *(match)*

Soldado: Sí, señorita, pero se prohíbe **fumar** en el autobús. *(to smoke)*

Señorita: No es para ahora. Voy a fumar el cigarillo en unos minutos al bajar en la parada próxima.

Soldado: A sus órdenes, señorita, y si me permite, yo mismo voy a **encenderle** el cigarillo. *(to light)*

Comprensión

1. ¿Cuánto paga el pasajero y dónde deposita el dinero?
2. ¿Dónde se sienta?
3. ¿Quién habla primero y qué dice?
4. ¿Qué está prohibido en el autobús?
5. ¿Qué sugiere el soldado?
6. ¿Es difícil hablar con un desconocido en un autobús? Generalmente, ¿de qué se trata en la conversación?
7. ¿Por qué no es buena idea fumar?
8. ¿Qué tenemos que poner sobre la mesa cuando los invitados fuman en casa?
9. En su ciudad, ¿cuánto vale el pasaje del metro, autobús, taxi y tranvía?

Vamos a hablar

A. Describa Ud. tres individuos que todas las mañanas esperan el autobús para ir al trabajo.

B. Adivine en qué época era una cosa muy común viajar en tranvía en los Estados Unidos. ¿Cuál es la ventaja de viajar en tranvía? El tranvía es el símbolo de una de las ciudades estadounidenses. Describa esa ciudad.

C. ¿Recuerda Ud. sus días en el autobús escolar? Relate las conversaciones o charlas entre los estudiantes de la escuela superior (secundaria) al regresar a sus casas respectivas después de un día de clase.

Dichos y refranes

—Eres el payaso del barrio.

—En cada circo hay un payaso.

Oficios y profesiones

el **conductor** (la **conductora**)	*bus driver*
el **despachador** (la **despachadora**)	*dispatcher*
el **empleado** (la **empleada**) **de carga**	*cargo loader*
el (la) **guía**	*tour guide*
el **mecánico** (la **mecánica**)	*mechanic*
el **maletero** (la **maletera**)	*baggage handler*
el **taquillero** (la **taquillera**)	*ticket seller*

Ejercicio

Desempeñe Ud. el papel de guía y presente Ud. las atracciones de su ciudad.

Repasito

Prueba — Escoja la traducción apropiada:

1.	el pasaje	a.	aisle
2.	el asiento	b.	bus terminal
3.	el conductor del autobús	c.	transfer
4.	el pasillo	d.	seat
5.	la puerta de salida	e.	exact change
6.	el billete de transferencia	f.	fare
7.	la parada del autobús	g.	window
8.	el terminal del autobús	h.	bus driver
9.	el cambio exacto	i.	bus stop
10.	la ventanilla	j.	exit door

UNIT 5

Viajar por vapor   *Steamship Travel*

Expresiones apropiadas

1.	navegar (embarcarse) en un barco	*to sail (embark) on a ship*
2.	salir del muelle	*to leave the pier*
3.	contemplar el mar	*to contemplate the sea*
4.	caminar por la cubierta	*to walk on deck*
5.	inclinarse sobre la baranda	*to lean over the rail*
6.	llamar al camarero (a la camarera)	*to call the steward (maid)*
7.	tomar una píldora para el mareo	*to take a pill for seasickness*
8.	mirar las gaviotas	*to watch the sea gulls*
9.	regresar al camarote	*to return to the stateroom*
10.	mirar por una portilla	*to look out a porthole*
11.	usar un salvavidas	*to use a life preserver*
12.	ponerse un chaleco salvavidas	*to put on a life jacket*
13.	sentarse en un bote salvavidas	*to sit in a lifeboat*
14.	jugar al tejo	*to play shuffleboard*
15.	reposar en una silla de la cubierta	*to relax in a deck chair*
16.	comer con el capitán (la capitana)	*to dine with the captain*
17.	ver la costa del mar	*to see the seacoast*
18.	observar la marea	*to observe the tide*
19.	entrar al puerto	*to enter the harbor*
20.	dar gracias a la tripulación	*to thank the crew*

Variaciones del vocabulario

el barco de vela	*sailing vessel*
el barco transoceánico	*transoceanic ship, ocean liner*
el (la) comandante	*captain*
la costa marítima	*seacoast*
el océano	*ocean*
la porta	*porthole*
el vapor	*ship*

Vocabulario en acción

Traduzca:

1. The newlyweds (*los recién casados*) embark on a ship.
2. The ship leaves the pier.
3. We contemplate the sea.
4. The passengers walk on deck.
5. The man leans over the rail.
6. His friend calls the steward.
7. I take a pill for seasickness.

8. The crew watches the sea gulls.
9. The sick man returns to his stateroom.
10. Do you *(tú)* look out the porthole in your stateroom?
11. The passengers use life preservers.
12. They wear life jackets.
13. We all sit in a lifeboat.
14. We like to play shuffleboard.
15. The tourists relax in deck chairs.
16. All of us dine with the captain.
17. I can see the seacoast.
18. Do you *(Ud.)* observe the tide?
19. The ship enters the harbor.
20. The passengers thank the crew.

Cuestionario

Complete las siguientes frases:

1. En un naufragio *(shipwreck)* los pasajeros llevan _____ y se sientan en
   _____.
2. Muchas personas toman _____ cuando el mar está turbulento.
3. En una de las últimas noches de la excursión todo el mundo come con el
   _____.
4. La ventana del vapor se llama _____.
5. Muchos pasajeros juegan _____ en la cubierta.
6. Muchos pasajeros descansan y leen libros en _____.
7. _____ vuelan sobre _____.
8. Desde la baranda se ve _____ en el horizonte.

Modelos de conversación

Repita y substituya las expresiones dadas:

1. **Los pasajeros están en la cubierta.**   The passengers are on the deck.
   _____ en el camarote.   _____ in the stateroom.
   _____ a la baranda.   _____ at the rail.
2. **El barco navega hacia la costa.**   The ship sails towards the coast.
   _____ el muelle.   _____ pier.
   _____ el puerto.   _____ harbor.
3. **Ese viajero pesimista busca píldoras**   That pessimistic traveler looks for
   para el mareo.   seasickness pills.
   _____ el chaleco salvavidas.   _____ the life jacket.
   _____ el bote salvavidas.   _____ the lifeboat.
4. **Reposo en la silla de cubierta.**   I relax in the deck chair.
   _____ jugando al tejo.   _____ playing shuffleboard.
   _____ mirando las gaviotas.   _____ looking at the sea gulls.

5. **El comandante colombiano es muy**   That Colombian captain is very nice.
    simpático.
    El capitán italiano _____ .   The Italian captain _____ .
    El camarero francés _____ .   The French steward _____ .

Diálogo

Capitán: ¡Atención: ¡Atención! Les habla el Capitán Sorol-
            la. ¡**Pónganse** los salvavidas! Repito—¡Pónganse los   *(put on)*
            chalecos salvavidas!

Marcelo: ¡Qué barbaridad! Todavía no he terminado de
            afeitarme. ¿Cómo puedo salir a la cubierta con   *(shaving myself)*
            tanto **jabón** en la cara?   *(soap)*

Mercedes: Mejor estás **medio** afeitado que **ahogado.**   *(half/drowned)*

Marcelo: Basta con tus **consejos,** mujer. Ya veo que estás   *(advice)*
            nerviosa. **¿Tienes miedo?**   *(Are you afraid?)*

Mercedes: Estoy nerviosísima. ¿Vamos a **hundirnos?**   *(sink)*

Capitán: **Bien hecho,** señores pasajeros. El ejercicio de   *(well done)*
            salvamento está terminado. Regresen Uds. a los
            camarotes. Gracias por su cooperación.

Marcedo: **Por fin** me puedo afeitar la otra **mitad** de la cara.   *(finally/half)*

Comprensión

1. ¿Qué instrucciones da el capitán a los pasajeros?
2. ¿Qué problema tiene Marcelo?
3. ¿Está nerviosa Mercedes?
4. ¿Qué hace Marcelo al regresar al camarote?
5. ¿Cuáles son las ventajas de viajar en un barco transoceánico?
6. ¿Cuáles son las desventajas de viajar por vapor?
7. Si Ud. tuviera la oportunidad de viajar por vapor, ¿por dónde quisiera navegar?
8. ¿Por qué es desventajoso navegar en un barco transoceánico si uno está a dieta?

Vamos a hablar

A. Uno de los deportes más emocionantes es el de las regatas. ¿Qué espectáculo? Son
        bien conocidas las regatas a remos entre Harvard y Yale o las regatas internacionales
        de barcos de vela. ¿Qué tipo de regata prefiere Ud.? ¿Ha participado en alguna
        regeta o solamente la ha presenciado? Exprese sus ideas sobre esta materia.

B. Describa el viaje de Cristóbal Colón al Nuevo Mundo en las carabelas La Niña, La
        Pinta y la Santa María.

C. Observe bien el dibujo y responda a las preguntas.

1. ¿Adónde va el hombre en el barco?
2. ¿Qué hacen las personas en el muelle?
3. Identifique el pájaro.
4. Describa el vapor.

Dichos y refranes

—¿Puedo besarte, mi amor?

—Quien no se aventura,
no cruza la mar.

Oficios y profesiones

la tripulación	*crew*
el jefe (la jefa) de la tripulación	*crew chief*
el marinero (la marinera)	*seaman (woman)*
el capitán (la capitana)	*captain*
el ayudante (la ayudanta) de primera	*first mate*
el enfermero (la enfermera) del barco	*ship's nurse*
el médico (la médica) del barco	*ship's doctor*
el contador (la contadora) del barco	*purser*
el director (la directora) de actividades sociales	*social director*
el mozo de cámara	*cabin boy*
la camarera	*chambermaid*
el mozo (la moza) de cubierta	*deck boy (girl)*
el despensero (la despensera) de vinos	*wine steward (stewardess)*
el operador (la operadora) del remolcador	*tugboat operator*
el (la) policía del puerto	*harbor police*
el navegante (la navegadora)	*navigator*
el operador (la operadora) del radio	*radio operator*

Ejercicio

Describe el trabajo . . . :

1. del navegante
2. del mozo de cubierta
3. de la directora de actividades sociales
4. del contador del barco
5. de la operadora del radio

Repasito

Prueba—Escoja la traducción apropiada:

1. el océano
2. el barco
3. el puerto
4. el camarero
5. la gaviota

a. steward
b. dock
c. lifeboat
d. sea gull
e. ocean

6. el muelle
7. el camarote
8. el bote salvavidas
9. la portilla
10. el capitán

f. porthole
g. stateroom (cabin)
h. port
i. captain
j. ship

UNIT 6

Viajar en automóvil   Automobile Travel

Expresiones apropiadas

1.	pararse en la parada de taxis	*to stop at the taxi stand*
2.	llamar un taxi	*to hail a taxi*
3.	dar direcciones al (a la) taxista	*to give directions to the taxi driver*
4.	pagar el costo de la carrera	*to pay the taxi fare*
5.	dar propina al (a la) taxista	*to tip the taxi driver*
6.	alquilar un coche	*to rent a car*
7.	mostrar la licencia de chófer	*to show one's driver's license*
8.	pedir la matrícula del coche	*to ask for the car registration*
9.	pagar por el seguro del automóvil	*to pay for automobile insurance*
10.	inflar las llantas	*to inflate the tires*
11.	chequear el aceite y el agua	*to check the oil and water*
12.	engrasar el coche	*to lubricate the car*
13.	llenar el tanque de gasolina en la gasolinera	*to fill the gas tank at the gas station*
14.	leer el mapa de carreteras	*to read the road map*
15.	arrancar el coche	*to start the car*
16.	conducir (manejar) el coche	*to drive the car*
17.	cambiar una llanta desinflada	*to change a flat tire*
18.	mirar la placa de matrícula	*to look at the license plate*
19.	hacer cola (los autos) en una gasolinera	*to form a line (of cars) at a gas station*
20.	poner el coche en el garaje	*to put the car in the garage*

Variaciones del vocabulario

el carro, el auto	*automobile*
el garaje	*gas station*
la goma pinchada	*flat tire*
el número de matrícula, la chapa de circulación	*license plate*

Vocabulario en acción

Traduzca:

1. The men stop at the taxi stand.
2. They hail a taxi.
3. Anthony gives directions to the taxi driver.
4. Uncle Oscar pays the taxi fare.
5. He gives the driver a tip.
6. The woman rents a car.
7. She shows her driver's license.
8. Do they ask for the car registration?

9. How much do we pay for automobile insurance?
10. She inflates the tires of her car.
11. Please check *(Chequee Ud.)* the oil and water.
12. Do you *(tú)* need to lubricate the car?
13. We fill up the tank at the gas station.
14. My sister reads the road map during the trip.
15. The chauffeur starts the car.
16. Dad drives the car.
17. A.A.A. *(La Asociación automovilística de América)* changes the flat tire.
18. That man is looking at our license plate.
19. There are many cars in line today.
20. He puts his car in the garage every night.

Expresiones útiles

TIPOS DE VEHÍCULOS DE LA CARRETERA (TYPES OF ROAD VEHICLES)

la ambulancia	*ambulance*
el autobús	*bus*
el autobús escolar	*school bus*
el auto-casa	*house trailer*
el auto de policía	*police car*
la bicicleta	*bicycle*
el camión	*truck*
el camión basurero	*garbage truck*
el camión de mudanzas	*moving van*
el camión de remolque	*trailer truck*
la camioneta	*station wagon*
el camión-grúa	*tow truck*
el camper	*camper*
el coche de remolque	*trailer*
el convertible (el descapotable)	*convertible*
el coupé	*coupe*
el jeep	*jeep*
la limosina	*limousine*
la minicicleta	*minibike*
la motocicleta	*motorcycle*
la motoneta	*moped*
el ómnibus de excursión	*sightseeing bus*
el quitanieve	*snowplow*
el sedán	*sedan*
el vagón volquete	*dump truck*
el van	*van*
los vehículos de construcción	*construction vehicles*

Ejercicio

Nombre Ud. el vehículo que . . . :

1. remueve la nieve.
2. recoge la basura de las casas.
3. se emplea en la construcción de un edificio.
4. usan los novios en la boda.
5. lleva a los estudiantes.
6. transporta a los enfermos.
7. usa la policía.
8. transporta a los turistas.

Cuestionario

Complete las siguientes frases:

1. Es necesario poner _____ en el tanque del coche.
2. El policía quiere ver _____ del chófer.
3. Falta gasolina, vamos a parar en la primera _____ .
4. _____ del taxi es muy caro.
5. Durante el invierno, papá pone nuestro coche en _____ .
6. En las vacaciones, yo siempre _____ de Hertz.
7. El estado requiere que pongamos _____ en el coche.
8. Cada 2000 millas de manejar el coche es buena idea _____ .
9. Es más cómodo viajar en _____ por las calles de las ciudades extranjeras.

Modelos de conversación

Repita y substituya las expresiones dadas:

1. **El coche necesita agua.**
   _____gasolina.
   _____aceite.

   The car needs water.
   _____gasoline.
   _____oil.

2. **Mamá y papá pagan el seguro del automóvil.**
   _____la matrícula .

   _____la placa de matrícula.

   Mother and Dad pay for the car insurance.
   _____car registration.
   _____license plates.

3. **¿Sabe alquilar un coche?**
   ¿_____arrancar _____?
   ¿_____manejar _____?

   Do you know how to rent a car?
   _____start _____?
   _____drive _____?

4. **Ponga la matrícula en el coche.**
   _____el mapa de carreteras en el coche.
   _____la chapa de circulación en el coche.

   Put the registration in the car.
   _____road map in the car.
   _____license plate on the car.

5.   **El taxi está al lado del garaje.**   The taxi is on the side of the garage.
     _____**de la gasolinera.**   _____gas station.
     _____**de la parada de**   _____taxi stand.
     taxis.

Diálogo

Caballero:	Mis llantas necesitan aire. **Y haga** el favor de **chequear** el radiador.	*(gentleman/do)* *(to check)*
Jovenzuelo:	Inmediatamente **lo chequeo todo**, señor.	*(young boy/I'll check everything)*
Caballero:	El **parabrisas** está **sucio.** Por favor **límpielo.**	*(windshield/dirty/clean it)*
Jovenzuelo:	Sí, señor. ¿Qué **cantidad** de gasolina desea Ud.?	*(quantity)*
Caballero:	¿Gasolina? Yo no deseo gasolina. **Vengo aquí solamente por** sus servicios. Gracias por su **ayuda.**	*(I come here)* *(only for help)*
Jovenzuelo:	**¡Qué trabajo!**	*(What a job!)*

Comprensión

1.   ¿Qué necesitan las llantas del coche?
2.   ¿Qué otros servicios necesita el cliente de la gasolinera?
3.   ¿Qué pregunta el jovenzuelo?
4.   ¿Cuál es la respuesta del caballero?
5.   ¿Por qué es difícil trabajar en una gasolinera?
6.   ¿Qué pasó con el precio de la gasolina este año?
7.   ¿Por qué son populares los autos compactos?
8.   ¿Cuántos kilómetros debe recorrer un auto por cada litro de gasolina para que se considere económico?

Vamos a hablar

A.   Dicen que algunos hombres cuidan sus autos mejor que su propia salud. ¿Está Ud. de acuerdo? Hable Ud. sobre esta cosa muy común.

B.   ¿Prefiere Ud. un auto grande o uno de clase económica? ¿Qué marca de auto maneja Ud.?

C. Describa esta escena de la Carretera Panamericana que atraviesa los Andes del Perú.

D. ¿Cuáles son sus ideas sobre la dependencia de nuestro país del petróleo árabe?

Dichos y refranes

—¿Por qué será que el mecánico de la gasolinera repara el coche de nuestros vecinos en medio día, y nosotros tenemos que esperar una semana?

—La peor rueda del carro es la que más rechina.

Oficios y profesiones

el ingeniero (la ingeniera)	*engineer*
el (la) maquinista	*machinist*
el mecánico (la mecánica)	*mechanic*
el chófer	*chauffeur*
el chófer de prueba	*test driver*
el camionero (la camionera)	*trucker*
el operario (la operaria) del remolcador	*tow-truck operator*
el instructor (la instructora) de manejar (conducir)	*driving instructor*
el reparador (la reparadora) de guardafangos	*body and fender worker*
el vendedor (la vendedora) de automóviles	*car salesperson*
el chatarrero (la chatarrera)	*junk dealer*
el (la) agente de seguros para automóviles	*car-insurance agent*
el ayudante (la ayudanta) de la gasolinera	*gasoline station attendant*
el dueño (la dueña) del almacén de piezas para automóviles	*automobile-parts store owner*
el engrasador (la engrasadora)	*"grease monkey"*
el ayudante (la ayudanta) de garaje (de estacionamiento)	*garage (parking) attendant*

Ejercicio

Complete las siguientes definiciones:

1. _____ limpia el parabrisas en la gasolinera.
2. La persona que enseña a manejar el coche es _____.
3. Después de un choque el operario del remolcador lleva el coche dañado al _____.
4. _____ vende seguros.
5. La persona que pone lubricante en el motor es _____.
6. El radio de mi coche está dañado, voy a llevarlo al _____.
7. Al llegar al hotel, el _____ estaciona su coche.
8. Quiero comprar un coche. Voy a hablar con _____.

Repasito

Prueba—Escoja la traducción apropiada:

1.	el chófer	a.	garage
2.	la taxista	b.	driver's license
3.	la chapa de circulación	c.	tank
4.	el garaje	d.	registration
5.	la gasolinera	e.	road map
6.	la licencia	f.	driver
7.	la llanta pinchada	g.	gas station
8.	la matrícula	h.	license plate
9.	el tanque	i.	flat tire
10.	el mapa de carreteras	j.	taxi driver

UNIT 7

La aduana   *Customs*

Expresiones apropiadas

1.	solicitar un pasaporte	*to apply for a passport*
2.	mostrar su partida de nacimiento	*to show your birth certificate*
3.	someter (presentar) un certificado de sanidad	*to submit a health certificate*
4.	recibir una visa	*to receive a visa*
5.	pasar por el detector electrónico	*to walk through the electronic detector*
6.	pesar el equipaje	*to weigh the baggage*
7.	pagar por el exceso de equipaje	*to pay for excess baggage*
8.	firmar la declaración	*to sign the declaration*
9.	ir al lugar de la inspección del equipaje	*to go to the baggage inspection area*
10.	dar los talones del equipaje al aduanero (a la aduanera)	*to give the baggage tags to the customs inspector*
11.	abrir las maletas	*to open the suitcases*
12.	obedecer la ley	*to obey the law*
13.	confiscar el contrabando	*to confiscate the contraband*
14.	recibir una multa	*to get a fine*
15.	traer mercancías libres de impuestos	*to bring in duty-free merchandise*
16.	cobrar el impuesto	*to collect the tax*
17.	necesitar una licencia de exportación	*to need an export license*
18.	pegar en las maletas un sello de la inspección de la aduan	*to paste a customs inspection sticker on the suitcases*
19.	preguntar por el tipo de cambio	*to ask about the exchange rate*
20.	entrar en el país como inmigrante	*to enter the country as an immigrant*

Variaciones del vocabulario

la contribución	*tax*
la etiqueta	*tag, ticket*
el exceso de peso, el peso de añadidura, el sobrecargo	*excess baggage*

Vocabulario

Traduzca:

1. Puerto Ricans do not need a passport to enter the United States.
2. Do you have your birth certificate?
3. You *(Ud.)* submit your health certificate.
4. He receives his visa.
5. The passengers walk through the electronic detector.

6. Do they weigh the baggage?
7. They pay 20 pesos for the excess baggage.
8. The tourists sign their declarations.
9. The tourists go to the baggage inspection area.
10. We give the baggage tags to the customs inspector.
11. We open our suitcases.
12. It is necessary to obey the law.
13. He confiscates the contraband.
14. The man pays his fine.
15. Travelers bring in a lot of duty-free merchandise.
16. The customs inspectors collect the tax.
17. They need an export license.
18. The customs inspector pastes inspection stamps on our suitcases.
19. The guide inquires about the exchange rate.
20. Each year many people enter the country as immigrants.

Cuestionario

Complete las siguientes frases:

1. El hombre que rompe *(breaks)* _____ va a la cárcel.
2. Cada año muchos _____ llegan a nuestro país.
3. El aduanero hace _____ .
4. Los turistas tienen el derecho de traer cien dólares en _____ .
5. La aduanera pone _____ en la maleta del viajero.
6. El certificado de _____ y la partida de _____ son dos requisitos para entrar en este país.
7. Las maletas pesan doscientas libras, señor. Tiene Ud. que pagar _____ .
8. Ponga Ud. la lista de sus compras en _____ y fírmela.
9. La casa exportadora requiere una _____ para exportar pieles de llama.

Modelos de conversación

Repita y substituya las expresiones dadas:

1. **Para exportar mercancías se necesita una licencia.**

   _____un impuesto.

   _____un sello de inspección de la aduana.

2. **La aduanera mira al inmigrante.**

   _____el pasaporte.

   _____la visa.

In order to export merchandise one needs a license.

   _____a tax.

   _____a customs inspection sticker.

The customs inspector looks at the immigrant.

   _____passport.

   _____visa.

3. **¡Muestre su certificado de sanidad, por favor!**

¡———— partida de nacimiento, ————!

¡———— talón de equipaje, ———!

Please show me your certificate of health.

————————————birth certificate.

————————————baggage tag.

4. **El hombre del contrabando pasa por el detector electrónico.**

————————————**abre la maleta.**

————————————**paga una multa.**

The man with the contraband goes through the electronic detector.

————————————————————opens the suitcase.

————————————————————pays a fine.

5. **El turista se aprovecha de las mercancías libres de impuesto.**

————————**lee la ley de aduana.**

————————**firma la declaración.**

The tourist takes advantage of the duty-free merchandise.

————————reads the customs law.

————————signs the declaration.

Diálogo

Aduanero:	¡Señores! Por favor, abran las maletas.
Carmen:	¿Qué pasa, Margarita? ¿Estás enferma?
Margarita:	Todavía no . . . pero si **encuentran** el perfume que compré en París voy a necesitar las **sales aromáticas.** *(they find)* *(smelling salts)*
Carmen:	¿Dónde **lo escondiste?** *(did you hide it)*
Margarita:	Entre la ropa interior y las **medias panti.** ¡Qué miedo tengo! ¡Dios me libre! ¿Me van a poner en la cárcel? Tal vez me pongan una multa. *(pantyhose)*
Aduanero:	Cierren las maletas, señoritas. Todo está en orden. Con **caras** tan inocentes como las suyas no hay necesidad de inspeccionar sus maletas. Es tonto pensar que mujeres tan simpáticas como Uds. lleven contrabando. *(faces)*
Margarita:	¡Qué suerte encontrar a un aduanero que tiene confianza en la gente!

Comprensión

1. ¿Qué anuncia el aduanero?
2. ¿Dónde escondió Margarita el perfume?
3. ¿Por qué no inspeccionó el aduanero las maletas de las dos señoritas?
4. ¿Dónde esconden los criminales las drogas y las mercancías prohibidas?
5. ¿Quiénes son los que no tienen que pasar por la inspección de la aduana?
6. ¿Qué frontera de los Estados Unidos es difícil de proteger?
7. ¿Por qué es difícil el oficio de aduanero?

Vamos a hablar

A. Por la aduana pasan muchas cosas raras—objetos que traen los turistas al regresar a los Estados Unidos o emigrantes que llegan al país por primera vez. Haga Ud. el papel de aduanero(a) y mencione esta noche a su esposa(o), a la hora de cenar, algunas cosas curiosas que sucedieron durante el día en el aeropuerto.

B. A veces los viajeros tienen que esperar horas enteras en la aduana hasta que el aduanero inspeccione el equipaje. ¿Conoce Ud. los reglamentos de la aduana y las estipulaciones que le permiten llevar mercancía y efectos personales? ¿Qué riesgos corren los turistas que meten contrabando en sus equipajes? ¿Cuál es el problema que existe hoy?

Dichos y refranes

—Tu mamá me dijo que tu papá y tú roncáis como dos leones.

—De tal palo, tal astilla.

Oficios y profesiones

el presidente (la presidenta)	*president*
el vicepresidente (la vicepresidenta)	*vice-president*
el oficial (la oficiala) del gabinete	*cabinet officer*
el jefe (la jefa) del estado	*chief executive*
el senador (la senadora)	*senator*
el (la) congresista	*congressman (woman)*
el (la) representante	*representative*
el gobernador (la gobernadora)	*governor*

el (la) asambleísta	*assemblyman (woman)*
el secretario (la secretaria)	*secretary*
el tesorero (la tesorera)	*treasurer*
el alcalde (la alcaldesa)	*mayor*
el concejal (la concejala)	*councilman (woman)*
el embajador (la embajadora)	*ambassador*
el comisionado (la comisionada)	*commissioner*
el (la) cónsul	*consul*
el primer ministro (la primera ministra)	*premier*
el ministro (la ministra)	*minister*
el rey	*king*
la reina	*queen*
el príncipe	*prince*
la princesa	*princess*
el dictador (la dictadora)	*dictator*

Ejercicio

Complete las siguientes definiciones:

1. La representante de un gobierno en el extranjero es _____.
2. La mujer que se encarga de los asuntos financieros es _____.
3. Un miembro del concejo municipal es _____.
4. El jefe de una ciudad es _____.
5. El jefe del estado es _____.
6. El jefe de los Estados Unidos es _____.

Repasito

Prueba—Escoja la traducción apropiada:

1.	la licencia	a.	custom's stamp
2.	la inspección de equipaje	b.	declaration
3.	el sello de aduana	c.	duty-free merchandise
4.	el aduanero	d.	license
5.	la declaración	e.	tag
6.	la multa	f.	contraband
7.	el talón	g.	fine
8.	la partida de nacimiento	h.	birth certificate
9.	el contrabando	i.	baggage inspection
10.	las mercancías libres de impuestos	j.	customs inspector

UNIT 8

El hotel y el motel   Hotel and Motel

Expresiones apropiadas

1.	hacer reservación de un cuarto por teléfono	to make a room reservation by telephone
2.	estacionar el coche en el estacionamiento del hotel	to park the car in the hotel parking area
3.	registrarse en la oficina de reservaciones	to register at the reservation desk
4.	pedir una cama doble (sencilla)	to ask for a double (single) bed
5.	esperar en el vestíbulo	to wait in the lobby
6.	seguir al botones al ascensor	to follow the bellhop to the elevator
7.	abrir la puerta con una llave	to open the door with a key
8.	usar el jabón y la toalla	to use the soap and the towel
9.	llamar (por teléfono) para el servicio de cuartos	to call (by phone) for room service
10.	disfrutar de la vista del mar	to enjoy the ocean view
11.	sentarse en el balcón	to sit on the balcony
12.	prender la calefacción (el aire acondicionado)	to turn on the heater (air conditioner)
13.	visitar el café	to visit the coffee shop (café)
14.	tomar una bebida en el salón de coctel	to have a drink in the cocktail lounge
15.	comer en la terraza	to dine on the terrace
16.	poner un letrero "No moleste" en la puerta	to leave a "Do Not Disturb" sign on the door
17.	cerrar la puerta del motel con llave y cadena	to lock the motel door with a key and a chain
18.	desayunar en cama	to have breakfast in bed
19.	dar propina a la camarera	to tip the maid
20.	pagar la cuenta del hotel	to pay the hotel bill

Variaciones del vocabulario

el calefactor	heater
la cama de matrimonio (matrimonial)	double bed
la criada	chambermaid
la habitación	room
las reservaciones, la caja, la carpeta	reservation desk
el salón de entrada, el foyer	lobby

Vocabulario en acción

Traduzca:

1. I always make a room reservation by telephone.
2. He parks the car in the hotel parking area.

3.   The man and his wife register at the reservation desk.
4.   Do you *(Ud.)* want a single bed or a double bed?
5.   We wait for our friends in the lobby.
6.   The guests follow the bellhop to their rooms.
7.   The bellhop opens the door with a key.
8.   She uses the soap and the towel.
9.   My husband loves to call for room service.
10. We enjoy the ocean view.
11. We sit on the balcony of the hotel room.
12. Where do you turn on the heater?
13. I visit the coffee shop to have coffee.
14. The friends have a drink in the cocktail lounge.
15. Tonight we're dining on the terrace.
16. The guests leave a "Do Not Disturb" sign on the door.
17. My husband always locks the door with a key and a chain.
18. What a pleasure *(¡Qué placer!)* to have breakfast in bed.
19. Do you *(Uds.)* tip the maid?
20. I pay the hotel bill with a credit card.

Expresiones útiles

EL CUARTO DE BAÑO (THE BATHROOM)

la alfombra de baño	*bathmat*
los azulejos	*tiles*
la bañadera	*bathtub*
el botiquín (para medicina)	*medicine cabinet*
el cepillo para el cabello	*hairbrush*
el cepillo para los dientes	*toothbrush*
la cortina de la ducha	*shower curtain*
los cosméticos	*cosmetics*
la crema de afeitar	*shaving cream*
la cubeta del inodoro	*toilet bowl*
el desodorante	*deodorant*
la ducha	*shower*
el espejo	*mirror*
la esponja	*sponge*
la hojita de afeitar	*razor blade*
la loción para después de afeitarse	*after-shave lotion*
la navaja de afeitar, la máquina de afeitar	*razor*
el paño para lavarse	*washcloth*
el papel higiénico	*toilet paper*
la pasta dentrífica	*toothpaste*

el peine	comb
la toalla de baño	bath towel
el toallero	towel rack

Ejercicio

Dé un sustantivo que se relacione con las cosas siguientes:

1. el pelo
2. el baño
3. la cara
4. los dientes
5. la ducha
6. la medicina

EL HOGAR (THE HOME)

la alcoba, el dormitorio	bedroom
el armario	clothes closet
el balcón	balcony
la cerca	fence
la cocina	kitchen
el comedor	dining room
la contraventana	shutter
el cuarto de baño	bathroom
el cuarto de estudio, el gabinete	study, den
la despensa	pantry
el desván	attic
la entrada para coches	driveway
la escalera	staircase
el jardín	garden
el pasillo	hall
la puerta	door
la sala, el salón	living room
la sala de recreo	recreation room
el sótano	basement
la ventana	window
el vestíbulo	vestibule, lobby

Ejercicio

Describa su casa o apartamiento.

Cuestionario

Complete las siguientes frases:

1. El _____ nos ayuda con las maletas.
2. El botones nos da _____ del cuarto.
3. Tomamos _____ para subir al segundo piso.
4. Mi esposo da la _____ al botones.
5. El cuarto es grande y tiene _____.
6. Por la noche, cuando tenemos hambre, llamamos al _____.
7. Para beber un coctel, necesitamos ir al _____.

Modelos de conversación

Repita y substituya las expresiones dadas:

1. **La camarera llega pronto.**
   El botones _____ .
   El ascensor _____ .
2. **Te encuentro en la terraza.**
   _____ **el salón de coctel.**
   _____ **el vestíbulo.**
3. **¿Tiene el motel vista del mar?**
   ¿_____**cuartos con aire acondicionado?**
   ¿_____**un café?**
4. **Pídale las llaves al botones.**
   _____ **el número del cuarto** _____ .
   _____ **el servicio de cuartos** _____ .
5. **La camarera se ocupa de su jabón.**

   La oficina _____ **cuenta.**
   El botones _____ **calefacción.**

The maid will arrive shortly.
The bellboy _____ .
The elevator _____ .
I'll meet you on the terrace.
_____ cocktail lounge.
_____ lobby.
Does the motel have an ocean view?
_____ air-conditioned rooms?
_____ a coffee shop?
Ask the bellboy for the keys.
_____ the room number.
_____ room service.
The chambermaid takes care of your soap.
The desk _____ bill.
The bellhop _____ heater.

Diálogo

Joven:	¿Cuánto cuesta ir de aquí al Hotel San Carlos?
Taxista:	Un dólar.
Joven:	¿Y cuánto **me cobra** por el equipaje?
Taxista:	Eso va **gratis**.

(will it cost me)
(free)

Joven: Pues entonces hágame el favor y lléveme el equipaje.
             Yo voy **a pie**.   *(on foot)*
Taxista: ¡Estos jóvenes de hoy día!

Comprensión

1.   ¿A dónde quiere ir el joven?
2.   ¿Qué pregunta el joven al entrar en el taxi?
3.   ¿Cuánto quiere cobrarle el taxista?
4.   ¿Por qué decide no tomar el taxi?
5.   ¿Cree Ud. que los taxistas son amables?
6.   ¿Por qué es interesante el oficio de taxista?
7.   ¿Es peligroso ser taxista? ¿Por qué?
8.   Según la costumbre, ¿cuánto se debe dar como propina al chófer de un taxi?

Vamos a hablar

A.   Preguntas

   1. ¿Qué clase de servicios presta el botones?
   2. ¿Cuánto da Ud. de propina al botones?
   3. ¿Por qué es difícil el trabajo de los botones?
   4. ¿Hay chicas que desempeñan este oficio? Si no, ¿por qué?

B.   Adivine Ud. qué dice el individuo cuando llega al hotel del pueblo y no encuentra alojamiento.

C.   ¿Cuál es su hotel predilecto? Explique las razones por su selección. ¿Qué servicios de entretenimiento ofrecen los grandes hoteles?

D.   Empleando los siguientes ideas comerciales, prepare un anuncio para la radio.

   1. ¡Qué lugar para espectáculos!
   2. Apropiado para sus conferencias.
   3. Todo es nuevo y de suprema elegancia.
   4. Cene y vea una revista de Broadway.
   5. Una joya de la ciudad.
   6. El hotel favorito de los viajeros.
   7. Teatros y comercios a pocos pasos del hotel.

Dichos y refranes

—Antes de casarme, tu hermana era cortés y nunca echaba blasfemias.

—Quien con perros se acuesta, con pulgas se levanta.

Oficios y profesiones

el administrador (la administradora) del hotel	*hotel administrator*
el (la) detective del hotel	*hotel detective*
el dependiente (la dependienta) del hotel	*hotel clerk*
el (la) telefonista	*telephone operator*
el cajero (la cajera)	*cashier*
el portero (la portera), el maletero (la maletera)	*porter*
el (la) botones	*bellhop*
el ascensorista	*elevator operator*
el sastre	*tailor*
la costurera	*seamstress*
el tintorero (la tintorera)	*dry cleaner*
la lavandera	*laundry woman*
el cocinero (la cocinera), el chef	*cook (chef)*
el (la) lavaplatos	*dishwasher*
el mozo (la moza), el camarero (la camarera)	*waiter (waitress)*
el criado, el camarero	*valet*
la criada, la camarera	*chambermaid*

Ejercicio

Complete las siguientes definiciones:

1. Cuando Ud. quiere telefonear a su familia, llame al (a la) _____.
2. Cuando se daña el vestido, se lleva al (a la) _____.
3. Cuando sus joyas son robadas, llame al (a la) _____.
4. Cuando los platos están sucios, llame al (la) _____.
5. Cuando necesita más jabón, llame al (a la) _____.

Repasito

Prueba—Escoja la traducción apropiada:

1. el servicio de cuartos
2. el botones
3. la propina
4. la carpeta
5. el café
6. el cuarto
7. el vestíbulo
8. el ascensor
9. el salón de coctel
10. la cama de matrimonio

a. tip
b. reservation desk
c. room
d. cocktail lounge
e. elevator
f. double bed
g. room service
h. lobby
i. coffee shop
j. bellhop

UNIT 9

La barbería   *The Barbershop*

Expresiones apropiadas

1.	sentarse en la silla del barbero	*to sit in the barber's chair*
2.	cortarse el pelo	*to get a haircut*
3.	pedir que le den un champú	*to ask for a shampoo*
4.	lavar el pelo	*to wash one's hair*
5.	dar masaje al cuero cabelludo	*to massage the scalp*
6.	dejar crecer las patillas	*to grow long sideburns*
7.	usar el esquilador	*to use the clippers*
8.	usar las tijeras	*to use scissors*
9.	aplicar una toalla caliente	*to apply a hot towel*
10.	poner la crema de afeitar	*to apply shaving cream*
11.	afeitar la barba con una navaja	*to shave the beard with a razor*
12.	recortar el bigote	*to trim one's moustache*
13.	empapar la cara con la loción de afeitar	*to soak the face with after-shave lotion*
14.	peinar el pelo	*to comb one's hair*
15.	hacer la raya con un peine y un cepillo	*to part one's hair with a comb and a brush*
16.	ponerse un tupé	*to put on a toupee*
17.	mirarse en el espejo	*to look in the mirror*
18.	hacerse la manicura	*to manicure the nails*
19.	embetunar los zapatos	*to polish the shoes*
20.	dar propina al barbero (a la barbera)	*to tip the barber*

Variaciones del vocabulario

el cabello	*hair*
hacerse las manos	*to manicure the nails*
lavar la cabeza	*to shampoo one's hair*
el pelado	*haircut*
el peluquero (la peluquera)	*barber, hairdresser*

Vocabulario en acción

Traduzca:

1. The little boy sits in the barber's chair.
2. I'm going to get a haircut tomorrow.
3. You *(tú)* always ask for a shampoo.
4. The barber washes the little boy's hair.
5. The barber massages the scalp of his client.
6. Today, young men want to grow long sideburns.
7. We don't use clippers.
8. The barber uses scissors.

9. In this barbershop they apply a hot towel.
10. The man applies shaving cream.
11. He shaves the beard with a razor.
12. Papa trims his moustache.
13. The barber always soaks my face with after-shave lotion.
14. Do you *(Ud.)* comb your hair before class?
15. The girls part their hair with a comb and a brush.
16. The bald *(calvo)* man puts on a toupee.
17. The children look in the mirror.
18. I like to manicure my nails.
19. The barber's son shines the customer's shoes.
20. I always tip the barber.

Cuestionario

Complete las siguientes frases:

1. El hombre que arregla el pelo se llama _____.
2. Para arreglar el pelo se va a _____
3. Después de lavar el pelo, el barbero _____.
4. El barbero le afeita la _____.
5. El señor quiere que le recorten _____.
6. El señor pide que le empapen _____.
7. Soy calvo, necesito un _____.
8. Después de afeitarlo, le dan un _____.
9. Para cortar el pelo, se necesitan _____.

Modelos de conversación

Repita y substituya las expresiones dadas:

1. **Por favor recorte el bigote.**   Please trim the moustache.
    _____ **las patillas.**   _____ the sideburns.
    _____ **la barba.**   _____ the beard.
2. **Siempre uso un peine.**   I always use a comb.
    _____ **el esquilador.**   _____ the clippers.
    _____ **la navaja.**   _____ the razor.
3. **Déme una navaja, por favor.**   Give me a razor, please.
    _____ **un espejo,** _____ .   _____ mirror _____ .
    _____ **una toalla caliente,** _____ .   _____ hot towel _____ .
4. **Este es un buen peine.**   This is a good comb.
    _____ **cepillo.**   _____ brush.
    _____ **tupé.**   _____ toupee.
5. **Lleva el pelo largo.**   He has long hair.
    _____ **las patillas largas.**   _____ long sideburns.
    _____ **la barba.**   _____ a beard.

Diálogo

Barbero:	Me imagino que Ud. quiere un corte de pelo.
Joven:	¿Un corte de pelo? **No, por cierto.** *(indeed not)*
Barbero:	**Entonces** ¿quiere Ud. una afeitada? *(then)*
Joven:	**Tampoco.** La barba **tarda un año en crecer.** *(not that either/takes a year to grow)*
Barbero:	¿Entonces qué hace Ud. en una barbería?
Joven:	Quiero un champú y **brillantina** para el cabello. *(hair tonic)* Hoy es el día de mi **boda.** Y mi novia es una chica *(wedding)* ideal.
Barbero:	**¡Pobre muchacha!** *(poor girl)*

Comprensión

1. ¿Quiere el joven un corte de pelo?
2. ¿Cuánto tiempo tarda en crecer la barba?
3. ¿Por qué va el joven a la barbería?
4. ¿Qué día es?
5. Exprese Ud. su opinión sobre el pelo largo de los muchachos.
6. ¿Cómo cortan el pelo en la marina?
7. ¿Cree Ud. que los hombres son más vanidosos con su pelo que las mujeres?
8. ¿Cuánto cuesta hoy un buen pelado en una barbería que se especializa en estilo de peinados?
9. Mencione Ud. todos los servicios que ofrece una barbería de lujo.

Vamos a hablar

A. Describa la escena en una barbería militar cuando un recluta nuevo entra para su primer corte de pelo.

B. En una oración completa identifique por el vocabulario siguiente una persona bien conocida.

1. el rubio (la rubia) — *blonde*
2. el pelirrojo (la pelirroja) — *redhead*
3. el moreno (la morena) — *brunette*
4. el pelo negro — *black hair*
5. el calvo — *bald man*
6. el pelo encanecido — *gray hair*
7. los rizos — *curls*
8. la barba — *beard*
9. la barba de chivo — *goatee*
10. el bigote — *moustache*

C. Los hombres y las mujeres tienen el complejo de envejecerse y acuden a los métodos modernos, como la cirugía plástica, para quitarse las arrugas y otros defectos faciales. Lo más común para rejuvenecerse es el tinte del cabello para esconder las canas, y para la calvicie se usa tupés o pelucas. ¿Cuáles son sus opiniones sobre este fenómeno social?

Dichos y refranes

—Hace un cuarto de siglo que trabajo como barbero y todavía no soy rico.

—¿Echaste la plata en un saco roto?

Oficios y profesiones

el **barbero** (la **barbera**)	*barber*
el **peluquero** (la **peluquera**), el **peinador** (la **peinadora**)	*hairdresser*
el **teñidor** (la **teñidora**) de pelo	*hair dryer*
el (la) **masajista**	*masseur, masseuse*
el **dermatólogo** (la **dermatóloga**)	*dermatologist*
el (la) **manicurista**	*manicurist*
el **maquillador** (la **maquilladora**)	*makeup artist*
el **confeccionador** (la **confeccionadora**) de tupés o de pelucas	*toupee or wig maker*
el **pedicuro** (la **pedicura**)	*pedicurist*
el (la) **recepcionista**	*receptionist*

Ejercicio

Complete las siguientes definiciones:

1. La persona que corta las uñas de las manos es _____.
2. El hombre que tiñe el pelo es _____.
3. El individuo que corta el pelo es _____.
4. El especialista en maquillaje es el _____.
5. La persona que corta las uñas de los pies es _____.
6. La mujer que fabrica tupés es _____.

Repasito

Prueba—Escoja la traducción apropiada:

1.	la navaja	a.	scissors
2.	el pelo	b.	comb
3.	la raya	c.	hot towel
4.	la silla del barbero	d.	mirror
5.	las patillas	e.	razor
6.	las tijeras	f.	beard
7.	la barba	g.	sideburns
8.	la toalla caliente	h.	hair
9.	el espejo	i.	barber's chair
10.	el peine	j.	part

UNIT 10

El salón de belleza   *The Beauty Parlor*

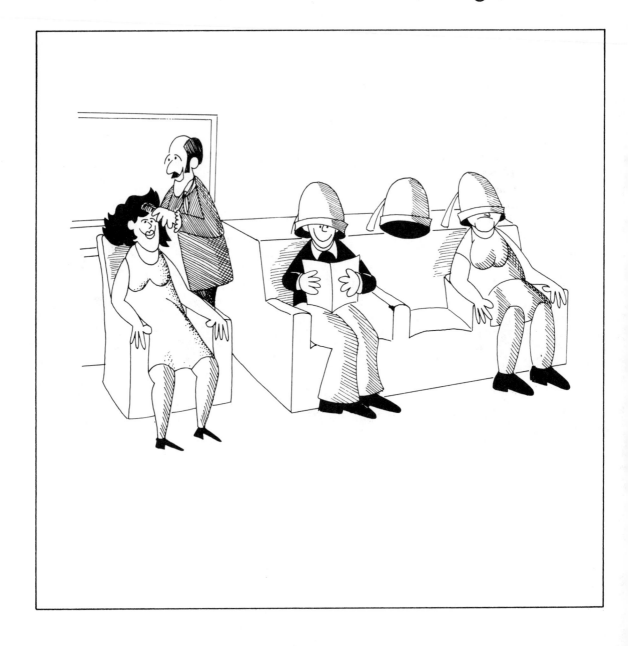

Expresiones apropiadas

1.	teñir el pelo	*to dye one's hair*
2.	lavar al cabello	*to wash one's hair*
3.	enjuagar el pelo	*to rinse one's hair*
4.	usar acondicionador	*to use hair conditioner*
5.	secar el pelo con una secadora	*to dry one's hair with a hair dryer*
6.	desenredar la cabellera	*to untangle long hair*
7.	poner laca en el pelo	*to spray the hair*
8.	rizar el pelo	*to curl the hair*
9.	peinar a la moda	*to style hair*
10.	pintar (limar) las uñas	*to polish (file) the nails*
11.	limpiar el cutis	*to clean one's skin*
12.	suavizar la piel	*to smooth the skin*
13.	maquillar los ojos	*to make up the eyes*
14.	quitar la pintura de las pestañas	*to take off mascara*
15.	poner colorete	*to put on rouge*
16.	aplicar lápiz labial	*to apply lipstick*
17.	empolvar la cara	*to powder the face*
18.	seleccionar un perfume	*to choose a perfume*
19.	sacar las cejas	*to tweeze the eyebrows*
20.	poner crema suavizadora	*to apply cold cream*

Variaciones del vocabulario

la barra de labios	*lipstick*
colorear el pelo	*to dye one's hair*
encrespar el pelo	*to curl the hair*
enjabonar el pelo	*to shampoo one's hair*
el peinado	*hairstyle*
el polvo facial	*face powder*

Vocabulario en acción

Traduzca:

1. He dyes his hair, doesn't he?
2. The young girl washes her hair twice a week.
3. Then she rinses her hair.
4. They always use hair conditioner.
5. We dry our hair with our new hair dryer.
6. The girl needs to untangle her long hair.
7. He sprays his hair every day.
8. You (*Ud.*) curl your hair, don't you?
9. The hairdresser styles his hair.
10. Do you (*tú*) polish your nails?

11. I clean the skin every morning.
12. The lady smooths her skin with cold cream.
13. Juana uses mascara to make up her eyes.
14. She takes off the mascara before going to bed.
15. That woman is putting on rouge.
16. She puts on lipstick after eating.
17. I powder my face.
18. You *(Uds.)* always choose a French perfume.
19. She tweezes her eyebrows every week.
20. Before going to bed, I apply cold cream.

Expresiones útiles

LOS COLORES (COLORS)

rojo	*red*
naranjado	*orange*
amarillo	*yellow*
verde	*green*
azul	*blue*
púrpura, morado	*purple*
marrón	*brown*
negro	*black*
blanco	*white*
gris	*gray*
color de oro, dorado	*gold*
plateado	*silver*
rosado	*pink*
beige	*beige*
aguamarina	*aquamarine*
azul turquesa	*turquoise blue*
violeta	*violet*
multicolor	*multicolored*

Ejercicio

Dé el color apropiado de los objetos siguientes:

1. una naranja
2. un tomate
3. una rosa
4. una planta
5. la nieve
6. el cielo
7. una banana

Cuestionario

Responda Ud. en oraciones completas:

1. ¿Necesito una cita *(appointment)*?
2. ¿Hacen permanentes en este salón de belleza?
3. ¿Puede hacer algo con este pelo lacio *(straight)*?
4. ¿De qué color debo teñirme el pelo?
5. Quiero un lavado. ¿Es posible?
6. ¿Cuánto tiempo tengo que estar debajo de la secadora?
7. ¿Tiene Ud. un espejo de mano?

Modelos de conversación

Repita y substituya las expresiones dadas:

1. **Menos pintura de las pestañas, por favor.**
   _____ colorete, _____.
   _____ perfume, _____.

   Less mascara, please.
   _____ rouge, _____ .
   _____ perfume, _____ .

2. **Me gusta ese lápiz labial.**
   _____ **ese peinado.**
   _____ **esa crema suavizadora.**

   I like that lipstick.
   _____ hairstyle.
   _____ cold cream.

3. **No use acondicionador.**
   _____ **secadora.**
   _____ **laca.**

   Don't use conditioner.
   _____ a hair dryer.
   _____ hairspray.

4. **¿Es caro este polvo facial?**
   ¿_____ **este lápiz labial?**
   ¿_____ **esta secadora?**

   Is this face powder expensive?
   _____ lipstick _____?
   _____ dryer _____?

5. **Por favor, déme la crema.**
   _____ **la laca.**
   _____ **el perfume.**

   Please give me the cream.
   _____ hairspray.
   _____ perfume.

Diálogo

Franco:	Hola, Margarita. ¿Cómo estás? ¿Qué quieres hoy?	
Margarita:	Un champú por favor.	
Franco:	**De veras** tienes una cabellera preciosa.	*(really)*
Margarita:	**Eso mismo creo yo.**	*(I agree)*
Franco:	**¿La cuidas** mucho?	*(do you take good care of it)*
Margarita:	¡Ah, sí! La **guardo todas las noches** en la **gaveta** de las **pelucas.**	*(I keep/every night/ drawer/wigs)*

Comprensión

1.   ¿Para qué va Margarita al salón de belleza?
2.   ¿Cómo responde Margarita a las **alabanzas** *(compliments)* del peluquero?
3.   ¿Qué pregunta Franco?
4.   ¿Dónde guarda Margarita su cabellera?
5.   ¿Cuál es su opinión sobre las pelucas para las mujeres? ¿Para los hombres?

Vamos a hablar

A.   Relate los estilos de peinados de las mujeres que Ud. recuerde desde la época de su niñez.

B.   Describa Ud. las actividades de una modelo de moda preparándose para una sesión con los fotógrafos. Mencione Ud. los diferentes expertos de belleza que ayudan a prepararla y los productos que usan.

Dichos y refranes

—Querido . . . ayer me diste cien pesos para hacer las compras, pero con los precios tan altos no me sobró ni un centavo para ir mañana al salón de belleza.

—Los dineros del sacristán, cantándose se vienen y cantándose se van.

Oficios y profesiones

el diseñador (la diseñadora) de peinados	*hair designer*
el peinador (la peinadora)	*hairdresser*
el cortador (la cortadora) de pelo	*hair cutter*

el (la) colorista de pelo	*hair dyer*
el maquillador (la maquilladora)	*makeup artist*
el (la) manicurista	*manicurist*
el pedicuro (la pedicura)	*pedicurist*
el (la) masajista	*masseur (masseuse)*
el dermatólogo (la dermatóloga)	*dermatologist*
el cirujano estético	*plastic surgeon*
(la cirujana estética)	
el (la) fabricante de productos de	*manufacturer of beauty products*
belleza	
el (la) perfumista	*perfume dealer*
el vendedor (la vendedora) de pelucas	*wig merchant*

Ejercicio

Asocie el oficio con el objeto o acción:

1. el perfume
2. el peinado
3. las tijeras
4. la cirugía
5. una peluca
6. la piel
7. el masaje

Repasito

Prueba—Escoja la traducción apropiada:

1. la laca   a. face
2. la secadora   b. dryer
3. la cara   c. skin
4. el colorete   d. nail
5. el ojo   e. rouge
6. la pintura de las pestañas   f. hairspray
7. la cabellera   g. conditioner
8. acondicionador   h. long hair
9. la uña   i. mascara
10. el cutis   j. eye

*U*NIT 11

**La sastrería,
la tintorería,
y la lavandería**

*The Tailor Shop,
Dry Cleaner
and Laundry*

Expresiones apropiadas

1.	recoger la ropa sucia	to gather the dirty clothes
2.	separar la ropa de lava y pon	to separate the wash-and-wear clothing
3.	lavar la ropa en la máquina de lavar	to wash the clothes in the washing machine
4.	añadir el blanqueador	to add bleach
5.	blanquear las sábanas	to bleach the sheets
6.	sacar la ropa de la secadora	to remove the clothes from the dryer
7.	almidonar los cuellos de las camisas	to starch the collars of the shirts
8.	planchar la ropa limpia en la tabla de planchar	to iron the clean clothes on the ironing board
9.	llevar la ropa sucia a la tintorería	to take the soiled clothes to the dry cleaner
10.	quitar la mancha de la blusa	to remove the stain from the blouse
11.	limpiar en seco los trajes	to dry clean the suits
12.	remendar los pantalones	to mend the slacks
13.	poner la ropa en una percha	to put the clothes on a hanger
14.	enseñar la chaqueta al sastre	to show the jacket to the tailor
15.	coser un botón	to sew on a button
16.	acortar el vestido	to shorten the dress
17.	planchar los blue jeans en la planchadora	to press the blue jeans on the (tailor's) press
18.	comprar un perchero	to buy a clothes rack
19.	colgar la ropa con perchas	to hang the clothes with hangers
20.	coser el dobladillo con una máquina de coser	to sew the hem with a sewing machine

Variaciones del vocabulario

el blanqueo	bleach
el colgadero	clothes rack
inarrugable	wash-and-wear
la lavadora	washing machine
la mesa de planchar	ironing board
los vaqueros	blue jeans

Vocabulario

Traduzca:

1. Pepe gathers his dirty clothes.
2. He separates the wash-and-wear clothes.
3. He washes them in the washing machine.
4. He adds bleach to the water.
5. Mother bleaches the sheets

6. I remove the clothes from the dryer.
7. Do you *(Ud.)* starch the collars of your shirts?
8. Do you *(tú)* iron the clean clothes on the ironing board?
9. Dad takes his dirty clothes to the dry cleaner.
10. They remove the stains from his suit.
11. They dry clean his suits.
12. Grandma mends the slacks.
13. Thomas puts the clothes on a hanger.
14. Grandpa shows his jacket to the tailor.
15. I'm sewing a button on this suit now.
16. Mama shortens her dress.
17. Do you want to press your blue jeans on the tailor's press?
18. We're going to buy a new clothes rack.
19. We hang our clothes on hangers.
20. I'm sewing a hem with a sewing machine.

Cuestionario

Complete las siguientes frases:

1. Debo añadir _____ para limpiar esta ropa blanca.
2. No es necesario planchar las camisas y pantalones de _____.
3. El lugar donde cosen trajes se llama _____.
4. ¡Hijo, pon *(put)* tu ropa limpia en _____!
5. _____ es esencial para lavar la ropa sucia.
6. Después de secar la ropa, la saca de _____.
7. Acabo de comprar un vestido nuevo. ¿Dónde puedo arreglarlo? ¿Hay un _____ allí que cosa bien?

Modelos de conversación

Repita y substituya las expresiones dadas:

1. **La mujer va a lavar la ropa sucia.**

    _____con blanqueo.
    _____en la máquina de
    lavar.
2. **Déme jabón para las camisas.**
    _____blanqueador _____ .
    _____almidón _____ .

The woman is going to wash the dirty clothes.

    _____ with bleach.
    _____ in the
    washing machine.
    Give me soap for the shirts.
    _____ bleach _____ .
    _____ starch _____ .

3. **En la lavandería tienen una planchadora.**   At the laundry they have a press.

_____ una tabla de planchar.   _____ an ironing board.

_____ percheros.   _____ clothes racks.

4. **Estos pantalones necesitan una percha.**   These slacks need a clothes hanger.

_____ plancharse.   _____ to be ironed.

_____ un botón.   _____ a button.

5. **Papá limpia sus pantalones.**   Papa cleans his slacks.

_____ su chaqueta.   _____ jacket.

_____ sus camisas.   _____ shirts.

Diálogo

Tomás:	¿Hacen Uds. alteraciones?	
Tintorero:	De todo tipo. ¿En qué puedo servirlo?	
Tomás:	Quiero arreglar este traje, porque **me veo muy grueso** en él. ¿Se puede hacer?	*(I look very fat)*
Tintorero:	Sí, pero necesitamos **al menos** un mes.	*(at least)*
Tomás:	¿Por qué un mes?	
Tintorero:	Para darle tiempo **a que baje de peso.**	*(to lose weight)*

Comprensión

1. ¿Dónde tiene lugar el diálogo?
2. ¿Qué quiere Tomás?
3. ¿Cuánto tiempo necesita el sastre para arreglar su traje?
4. ¿Por qué tanto tiempo?
5. ¿Cuánto tiempo tarda su tintorero en plancharle un traje?

Vamos a hablar

A. Preguntas

1. ¿Cuánto se paga por un vestido hecho a mano por un sastre?
2. ¿Quiénes son mejores en el arte de coser—las mujeres o los hombres?
3. ¿Qué ropa favorita quiere Ud. guardar a pesar de ser vieja?
4. Mencione Ud. toda su ropa exterior y la tela de que está hecha.

B.   Describa la escena.

Dichos y refranes

—Mi amor, yo sé que este mes andamos escasos de dinero, y por eso, voy a llevar un traje viejo a la boda.

—No hay mal que por bien no venga.

Oficios y profesiones

la criada	*maid*
el sirviente (la sirvienta)	*servant*
el mayordomo	*butler*
el criado	*valet*
la criada para la limpieza	*cleaning woman*
la lavandera	*laundry woman*
el cocinero (la cocinera)	*cook*
la tutora	*governess*
el maestro práctico (la maestra práctica)	*tutor*
el secretario (la secretaria personal)	*personal secretary*
el (la) guardaespaldas	*bodyguard*
el enfermero práctico (la enfermera práctica)	*practical nurse*
el niñero (la niñera)	*baby-sitter*

Ejercicio

Complete las siguientes definiciones:

1. La chica que cuida a los bebés es_____.
2. La persona que cocina es_____.
3. La mujer que limpia casas es_____.
4. El individuo que enseña a los niños es_____.
5. La mujer que lava la ropa se llama_____.

Repasito

Prueba—Escoja la traducción apropiada:

1.	la tabla de planchar	a.	hem
2.	el sastre	b.	rack
3.	la mancha	c.	hanger
4.	el dobladillo	d.	clean clothes
5.	la máquina de lavar	e.	button
6.	el botón	f.	ironing board
7.	la ropa limpia	g.	dirty clothes
8.	el perchero	h.	washing machine
9.	la ropa sucia	i.	tailor
10.	la percha	j.	stain

*U*NIT 12

Servicios médicos   *Medical Services*

Expresiones apropiadas

1.	sentirse mal	to feel sick
2.	tener dolor	to suffer pain
3.	esperar en el consultorio del médico (de la médica) (del cirujano/de la cirujana)	to wait in the doctor's (surgeon's) office
4.	ir a la clínica	to go to the clinic
5.	entrar en la sala de emergencia	to enter the emergency room
6.	hablar con el (la) internista	to speak with the intern
7.	hacerse un examen físico	to get a physical examination
8.	dar una inyección	to give an injection
9.	sacarse los rayos X (las radiografías)	to have X-rays taken
10.	necesitar puntos (una receta)	to require stitches (a prescription)
11.	recibir una transfusión	to receive a transfusion
12.	andar con muletas	to walk on crutches
13.	estar en la sala de operaciónes	to be in the operating room
14.	llamar al enfermero (a la enfermera)	to call the nurse
15.	pedir una silleta	to ask for a bedpan
16.	sentarse en una silla de ruedas	to sit in a wheelchair
17.	visitar a un (una) paciente en el hospital	to visit a patient in the hospital
18.	estar embarazada	to be pregnant
19.	dar a luz	to give birth
20.	hacer (arreglar) una cita con el (la) dentista	to make an appointment with the dentist

Variaciones del vocabulario

la casa de socorro	clinic
la consulta	doctor's office
el chequeo	physical examination
el pato, la chata, la bacinilla	bedpan
el quirófano, el cuarto de operaciónes	operating room
la sala de socorro, el cuarto de emergencia	emergency room
el venoclisis	transfusion

Vocabulario en acción

Traduzca:

1. I feel sick.
2. He suffers a lot of pain.

3. We wait in the surgeon's office.
4. The sick man goes to the clinic.
5. The sick woman enters the emergency room.
6. They speak with the interns in the hospital.
7. My boss gets a physical examination each year.
8. The doctor gives the little boy an injection.
9. It is necessary to have an X-ray of your chest.
10. You (*Ud.*) need about ten stitches.
11. That patient is receiving a blood transfusion.
12. I have to walk on crutches for six weeks.
13. The doctor is in the operating room at least three hours every day.
14. Are you (*tú*) calling the nurse?
15. He asks for a bedpan.
16. The patient is sitting in a wheelchair.
17. We visit a patient in the hospital.
18. Pilar is pregnant again.
19. Grace gives birth to twins (*gemelos*).
20. I'm making an appointment with my dentist for next Tuesday.

Expresiones útiles

LAS PARTES EXTERNAS DEL CUERPO HUMANO (EXTERNAL PARTS OF THE BODY)

la boca	*mouth*	**la mano**	*hand*
el brazo	*arm*	**la mejilla**	*cheek*
la cabeza	*head*	**la muñeca**	*wrist*
la cadera	*hip*	**el muslo**	*thigh*
la cara	*face*	**la nariz**	*nose*
la cintura	*waist*	**el ojo**	*eye*
el codo	*elbow*	**la oreja**	*ear*
el cuello	*neck*	**el pecho**	*chest, breast*
el dedo	*finger*	**el pie**	*foot*
el dedo del pie	*toe*	**la piel**	*skin*
la espalda	*back*	**la pierna**	*leg*
la frente	*forehead*	**el pulgar**	*thumb*
el hombro	*shoulder*	**la rodilla**	*knee*
los labios	*lips*	**el tobillo**	*ankle*

LAS PARTES INTERNAS DEL CUERPO HUMANO (INTERNAL PARTS OF THE BODY)

el apéndice	*appendix*	**el bazo**	*spleen*
la arteria	*artery*	**el cerebro**	*brain*

la columna vertebral	spinal cord	los intestinos	intestines
el corazón	heart	la lengua	tongue
los dientes	teeth	el músculo	muscle
la espina dorsal	spine	el nervio	nerve
el esqueleto	skeleton	el pulmón	lung
el estómago	stomach	el riñón	kidney
la garganta	throat	la sangre	blood
el hígado	liver	el seno del cráneo	sinus
el hueso	bone	la vena	vein
		la vesícula biliar	gallbladder

LOS CINCO SENTIDOS (THE FIVE SENSES)

oír (el oído)	to hear (sound)
oler (el olfato)	to smell (odor, scent)
gustar (el gusto)	to taste (taste)
tocar (el tacto)	to touch (touch)
ver (la vista)	to see (sight)

Ejercicio

Complete las oraciones:

1. Para besar utilizamos _____ .
2. Para caminar utilizamos _____ .
3. Para escribir utilizamos _____ .
4. Para hablar utilizamos _____ .
5. Para oír utilizamos _____ .
6. Para oler utilizamos _____ .
7. Para pensar utilizamos _____ .
8. Para respirar utilizamos _____ .
9. Para sentir utilizamos _____ .
10. Para ver utilizamos _____ .

LAS ENFERMEDADES (AILMENTS)

la alergia	allergy
la anemia	anemia
la apendicitis	appendicitis
el ataque de corazón	heart attack
el dolor de cabeza	headache
el dolor de estómago	stomachache
el dolor de muelas	toothache
la escarlata	scarlet fever
la fiebre	fever

la fiebre del heno	hay fever
la herida	sore
la hinchazón	swelling
la hipertensión arterial	high blood pressure
la infección	infection
la influenza	influenza
la laringitis	laryngitis
el mareo	seasickness
la nerviosidad	nervousness
la papera	mumps
la pulmonía	pneumonia
el resfriado	cold
el sarampión	measles
la tirantez	strain
la tonsilitis	tonsillits
la torcedura	sprain
la úlcera	ulcer
el vértigo	dizziness
las viruelas locas	chicken pox

Ejercicio

Asocie una enfermedad con las partes del cuerpo que siguen:

1. la cabeza
2. el corazón
3. los dientes
4. la garganta
5. la piel
6. los pulmones
7. la sangre
8. la nariz
9. el estómago

Cuestionario

Responda Ud. en oraciones completas:

1. Me siento mal. ¿Hay un médico aquí?
2. Por favor, ¿pueden llamar una ambulancia?
3. ¿Dónde está la sala de emergencia?
4. ¿Cómo ocurrió el accidente?
5. ¿Tiene ella una fiebre alta?
6. ¿Es una enfermedad contagiosa?
7. ¿Tiene Ud. alergia contra la penicilina?
8. ¿Dónde tiene Ud. dolor todavía?

Modelos de conversación

Repita y substituya las expresiones dadas.

1. **El internista examina al paciente.**   The intern examines the patient.
   El cirujano _____ .   The surgeon _____ .
   La dentista _____ .   The dentist _____ .
2. **El paciente necesita radiografías.**   The patient requires X-rays.
   _____ **un chequeo físico.**   _____ an examination.
   _____ **puntos.**   _____ stitches.
3. **Llévela a la sala de emergencia.**   Take her to the emergency room.
   _____ **a la sala de operaciónes.**   _____ operating room.
   _____ **al consultorio de la médica.**   _____ doctor's office.
4. **El médico da una transfusión de**   The doctor gives a blood transfusion.
   sangre.
   _____ **receta.**   _____ prescription.
   _____ **inyección.**   _____ an injection.

5. **La enfermera la quita la silleta al**   The nurse removes the bedpan from the
   paciente.   patient.
   _____ **las muletas** __ .   _____ crutches _____ .
   _____ **la silla de**   _____ wheelchair _____ .
   ruedas _____ .

Diálogo

Paciente:	Doctor, **no me opere de nuevo la pierna. Ya van** cinco operaciones.	*(don't operate again on my leg/you have already completed)*
Médico:	Dos días buscando la **bala** y no la podemos encontrar en la **herida**. No **me explico** esto.	*(bullet)* *(wound/understand)*
Paciente:	¿Qué buscan Uds.?	
Médico:	Buscamos la bala.	
Paciente:	Haberlo dichos antes. La tengo en el **bolsillo** .	*(pocket)*
Médico:	**¡Ahora sí que lo mato!**	*(now I'll certainly kill you)*

Comprensión

1. ¿Cuántas operaciones sufre el paciente?
2. ¿Cuántos días pasa el médico en busca de la bala?
3. ¿Qué es lo que no puede explicarse el médico?
4. ¿Dónde tiene la bala el paciente?
5. Describa Ud. sus días en el hospital.

Vamos a hablar

A. Diga algo sobre los numerosos pleitos (*court cases*) contra los médicos.

B. Haga Ud. un comentario sobre los investigadores científicos que tratan de curar las enfermedades de la población.

Dichos y refranes

—No estés tan triste, mi amor. Olvídate del choque del Cadillac.

—Cinco dedos en una mano, a veces hacen provecho, y a veces, hacen daño.

Oficios y profesiones

el médico (la médica)	*doctor*
el enfermero (la enfermera)	*nurse*
el ayudante (la ayudanta) de enfermera	*nurse's aide*
el administrador (la administradora) del hospital	*hospital administrator*
el técnico (la técnica) del laboratorio	*lab technician*
el asistente (la asistenta) en un hospital	*orderly*
el conductor (la conductora) de la ambulancia	*ambulance driver*
el técnico (la técnica) de radiografía	*X-ray technician*
el anestesiólogo (la anestesióloga)	*anesthesiologist*
el cirujano (la cirujana)	*surgeon*

el médico (la médica) general	*general practitioner*
el interno (la interna) de hospital	*intern*
el (la) especialista	*specialist*
el (la) terapeuta	*therapist*
el ortopédico (la ortopédica)	*orthopedist*
el (la) osteópata	*osteopath*
el oftalmólogo (la oftalmóloga)	*opthalmologist*
el neurólogo (la neuróloga)	*neurologist*
el ginecólogo (la ginecóloga)	*gynecologist*
el cardiólogo (la cardióloga)	*cardiologist*
el cirujano (la cirujana) estético(a)	*plastic surgeon*
el (la) psiquiatra	*psychiatrist*
el patólogo (la patóloga)	*pathologist*
el radiólogo (la radióloga)	*radiologist*
el dietético (la dietética)	*dietician*
el médico (la médica) forense	*coroner*
el (la) podiatra	*podiatrist*
el quiropráctico (la quiropráctica)	*chiropractor*
el parmédico (la paramédica)	*paramedic*

Ejercicio

¿Cuántos oficios médicos puede Ud. mencionar sin mirar esta lección?

Repasito

Prueba—Escoja la traducción apropiada:

1. la sala de emergencia
2. el médico
3. los puntos
4. el dolor
5. el hospital
6. el dentista
7. el consultorio
8. la inyección
9. la radiografía
10. el paciente

a. hospital
b. patient
c. X-ray
d. stitches
e. dentist
f. injection
g. doctor's office
h. pain
i. emergency room
j. doctor

UNIT 13

La farmacia

The Pharmacy

Expresiones apropiadas

1.	frotar con el alcohol	to rub on alcohol
2.	tomar el antiácido	to take antacid
3.	sacar el antiséptico del gabinete de medicina	to get the antiseptic from the medicine cabinet
4.	tomar la aspirina	to take aspirin
5.	aplicar una bolsa de hielo	to apply an ice bag
6.	necesitar un tranquilizador	to need a tranquilizer
7.	ponar una curita en el arañazo	to put a bandage on the scratch
8.	confiar en el farmacéutico (la farmacéutica)	to trust the pharmacist
9.	poner la gasa en la herida	to put gauze on the wound
10.	poner las gotas en los ojos	to put eyedrops into the eyes
11.	comprar la medicina	to buy the medicine
12.	tragar las píldoras	to swallow the pills
13.	pedir una pastilla para el dolor	to ask for a painkiller
14.	recetar pastillas para dormir	to prescribe sleeping pills
15.	poner las píldoras en una botella	to put the pills in a bottle
16.	llenar una recenta	to fill a prescription
17.	leer la temperatura en el termometro	to read the temperature on the fever thermometer
18.	poner la venda en la herida	to put a bandage on the sore
19.	tomar vitaminas cada día	to take vitamins every day
20.	poner tintura de yodo	to put on iodine

Variaciones del vocabulario

la botica	drugstore
el boticario (la boticaria)	druggist
el cendal	gauze
la prescripción	prescription
el rasguño	scratch
el tranquilizante, el calmante	tranquilizer

Vocabulario en acción

Traduzca:

1. Dad rubs alcohol on the scratch.
2. After I eat a pizza I have to take an antacid.
3. Is the antiseptic in the medicine cabinet?
4. He takes two aspirins every four hours.
5. It is a good idea to apply an ice bag.
6. Very nervous people sometimes need a tranquilizer.
7. The nurse puts a bandage on the scratch.

8. I trust my pharmacist.
9. The doctor puts gauze on the wound.
10. The doctor puts eyedrops into my eyes.
11. Do you *(Uds.)* buy medicine at this pharmacy?
12. I can't swallow this big pill.
13. She is asking for a painkiller.
14. Many surgeons prescribe sleeping pills for their patients.
15. The druggist puts the pills in the bottle.
16. Do you *(Ud.)* fill prescriptions?
17. Can you *(tú)* read the temperature on this thermometer?
18. The nurse puts a bandage on the sore.
19. My son and I take vitamins every day.
20. We do not put iodine on the infection.

Cuestionario

Complete las siguientes frases:

1. El dueño de la farmacia se llama _____ .
2. Aplique _____ en la herida.
3. Estás muy nerviosa. ¿Por qué no te tomas un _____?
4. Tengo insomnio. ¿Que _____ me puedo recomendar?
5. _____ indica 39°C—Tienes fiebre.
6. Es muy saludable tomar _____ cada día.
7. Tome dos _____, beba mucha agua y acuéstese temprano.
8. El médico recetó _____ para los ojos.
9. Tiene dolores muy fuertes. ¿Por qué no le dan _____?
10. Yo recomiendo _____ para dolores del estómago y para la indigestión.

Modelos de conversación

Repita y substituya las expresiones dadas:

1. **¿Puede venderme un paquete de gasa?**

    ¿ _____ **vendas?**

    ¿ _____ **curitas?**

    Can you sell me a package of gauze?

    _____ bandages?

    _____ bandages?

2. **Déme una botella de alcohol.**

    _____ **pastillas para el dolor.**

    _____ **pastillas para dormir.**

    Give me a bottle of alcohol.

    _____ painkillers.

    _____ sleeping pills.

3. **Mi doctor me receta gotas para los ojos.**   My doctor prescribes eyedrops.

    _____un tranquilizador.   _____ a tranquilizer.

    _____vitamina C.   _____ Vitamin C.

4. **Tengo dolor de cabeza. Necesito aspirina.**   I have a headache. I need aspirin.

    _____dolor de estómago. _____ un antiácido.   _____stomachache. _____ an antacid.

    _____una herida. _____ un antiséptico.   _____ cut. _____ an antiseptic.

5. **Tome una pastilla cada cuatro horas.**   Take one tablet every four hours.

    _____píldora _____ .   _____pill _____ .

    _____píldora de vitaminas _____ .   _____vitamin pill _____ .

Diálogo

Farmacéutica:	¿Qué le **sucede**, señor?	*(is happening)*
Paciente:	¡Oh! Me siento muy enfermo. Tengo un dolor muy **fuerte** en el estómago.	*(strong)*
Farmacéutica:	Le voy a dar algo para remediar su mal.	
Paciente:	Ud. es muy amable.	
Farmacéutica:	**No se preocupe.** Si esta medicina no da **resultado, vuelva** mañana, y le doy algo **mejor**.	*(don't worry)* *(results/come back/ better)*
Paciente:	¿Y no puede dar ahora ese algo mejor?	

Comprensión

1. ¿Dónde tiene lugar este diálogo?
2. ¿Qué le sucede al paciente?
3. ¿Qué le dice la farmacéutica?
4. ¿Cuál es la reacción del paciente?
5. ¿Le gustaría a Ud. ser farmacéutico?
6. Nobre Ud. una nueva medicina que apareció en los últimos años.
7. ¿De qué plantas vienen las drogas y medicinas nuevas?
8. Además de las medicinas, ¿qué otros productos se venden en las farmacias norteamericanas?

Vamos a hablar

A.   En un viaje de vacaciones al campo, es buena idea llevar una caja de primer auxilio, con todos los requisitos medicinales. ¿Qué debe llevar consigo en esta caja para proteger la salud de su familia?

B.   El **pesar demasiado** es uno de los mayores **enemigos** que tienen los hombres y las mujeres de todas las **edades**. Pos eso, abundan en el mercado los productos destinados a **adelgazar**, y las compañías que los fabrican **se enriquecen** con los millones que se gastan. Muchas personas hacen toda clase de ejercicios para perder peso. Todos hemos visto a los que corren más o menos **velozmente**. ¿Cómo anda Ud. de peso? ¿Necesita ganar o perder peso? ¿Conoce a alguien que **haya perdido** peso? ¿Cómo **lo consiguió?** Haga comentarios sobre el particular.

C.   ¿Cuáles son las medicinas que se deben tener en un gabinete de medicina en el hogar? ¿Qué precauciones debe tomar los padres para proteger la vida de los adolescentes y niños? ¿Qué dibujo o símbolo ponen los farmacéuticos en una botella de medicina que puede ser fatal?

Dichos y refranes

—¿Por qué estás tan alegre esta noche?

—Barriga llena, corazón contento.

Oficios y profesiones

el farmacéutico (la farmacéutica)	*pharmacist*
el boticario (la boticaria)	*druggist*
el técnico (la técnica) en medicina	*medical technician*
el médico (la médica) investigador	*medical research doctor*
el vendedor (la vendedora) de drogas	*drug salesperson*
el farmacólogo (la farmacióloga)	*pharmacologist*
el cajero (la cajera)	*cashier*
el dependiente (la dependienta)	*clerk*
el aprendiz (la aprendiza)	*pharmacy student*
el químico (la química)	*chemist*

Ejercicio

Describa las personas relacionadas con el personal de farmacia.

Repasito

Prueba—Escoja la traducción apropriada:

1.	la receta	a.	pharmacist
2.	la aspirina	b.	antiseptic
3.	la pastilla para dormir	c.	tranquilizer
4.	la curita	d.	painkiller
5.	la vitamina	e.	bandage
6.	el farmacéutico	f.	gauze
7.	la gasa	g.	vitamin
8.	la pastilla para el dolor	h.	aspirin
9.	el antiséptico	i.	sleeping pill
10.	el calmante	j.	prescription

UNIT 14

La librería y la tienda de tabaco y efectos de escritorio

The Bookstore and the Tobacco and Stationery Shop

Expresiones apropiadas

1.	fumar un cigarillo	to smoke a cigarette
2.	comprar una caja de cigarros	to buy a box of cigars
3.	encender su cigarrillo con un encendedor	to light one's cigarette with a cigarette lighter
4.	usar un filtro	to use a filter
5.	apagar el fósforo	to blow out the match
6.	llenar la pipa de tabaco	to fill the pipe with tobacco
7.	ordenar el papel de escritorio	to order stationery
8.	comprar una regla y sujetapapeles	to buy a ruler and paper clips
9.	escoger la tarjeta	to select a greeting card
10.	necesitar una goma de borrar y goma de pegar	to need an eraser and glue
11.	poner una cinta nueva en la máquina de escribir	to put a new ribbon in the typewriter
12.	imprimir las tarjetas de negocio	to print business cards
13.	afilar los lápices	to sharpen the pencils
14.	presillar los papeles	to staple the papers
15.	pegar recortes en un libro	to paste scraps in a book
16.	borrar el error en el papel de escribir a máquina	to erase the mistake on the typing paper
17.	sellar los sobres	to seal the envelopes
18.	escribir con un bolígrafo	to write with a ball-point pen
19.	gozar de libros cómicos	to enjoy comic books
20.	leer una novela	to read a novel

Variaciones del vocabulario

el borrador	eraser
la cachimba	pipe
la cola	glue
el cigarro	cigarette
la presilla	staple
el tabaco, el puro	cigar
la tarjeta comercial	business card
la tarjeta de felicitación	greeting card
el yesquero, el mechero	cigarette lighter

Vocabulario en acción

Traduzca:

1. Do you (*tú*) still smoke cigarettes?
2. He's buying a box of expensive cigars.

3. Her boyfriend lights her cigarette with a cigarette lighter.
4. I prefer to use a filter on my cigarettes.
5. Do not blow out (*no apague*) the match.
6. Grandpa fills his pipe with tobacco.
7. Let's order stationery.
8. Are you (*Ud.*) buying a ruler and paper clips?
9. My sister and I are selecting greeting cards.
10. We need an eraser and some glue.
11. She puts a new typewriter ribbon in the typewriter.
12. Do you (*Ud.*) print business cards?
13. The students sharpen their pencils.
14. He staples the papers on his desk.
15. Aurora is always putting scraps in a book.
16. A good secretary always erases mistakes on the typing paper.
17. They seal the envelopes.
18. I like to write with a ball-point pen.
19. The children enjoy comic books.
20. I like to read novels.

Cuestionario

Complete las siguientes frases:

1. Yo siempre fumo cigarillos con _____ .
2. Los cubanos producen los mejores _____ del mundo.
3. Aquí tienes un cigarillo, ahora necesitas un _____ para encenderlo.
4. Abuelito está limpiando su _____ antes de fumar.
5. Por favor, afile estos _____ .
6. Hice un error en el papel. Dame la _____ .
7. Ahora que fue Ud. nombrado vicepresidente del banco, tiene que comprar nuevos
   _____ .
8. ¿Dónde está _____ ? Quiero sacar el sello para mi colección.
9. Este diagrama necesita una línea recta. Emplee una _____ .

Modelos de conversación

Repita y substituya las expresiones dadas:

1. **Yo fumo puros.**   I smoke cigars.
   _____**cigarrillos.**   _____cigarettes.
   _____**una pipa.**   _____a pipe.
2. **Cómpreme un encendedor.**   Buy me a lighter.
   _____**un filtro.**   _____a filter.
   _____**tabaco.**   _____tobacco.

3. **El pone el lápiz en el bolsillo.**   He puts the pencil in his pocket.
   _____ el bolígrafo _____ .   _____pen _____ .
   _____ el sobre _____ .   _____envelope _____ .
4. **Me falta una goma de borrar.**   I'm missing an eraser.
   _____regla.   _____a ruler.
   _____presilla.   _____a staple.
5. **¿Le gusta a Ud. esta novela?**   Do you like this novel?
   ¿_____este papel de   _____this stationery?
   escritorio?
   ¿_____este sujetapapeles?   _____this paper clip?

Diálogo

Jovencita:	¿Tiene un **ejemplar** de *Thornbirds*?	*(copy)*
Vendedor:	No, pero tenemos otras novelas románticas.	
Jovencita:	No tengo interés en libros de amor.	
Vendedor:	¿Por qué entonces *Thornbirds*?	
Jovencita:	**La cubierta** del libro **hace juego** con las paredes de mi casa.	*(cover/matches)*
Vendedor:	¡Ay, qué gente!	

Comprensión

1. ¿Qué busca la jovencita?
2. ¿Lo encuentra?
3. ¿Qué le pregunta el vendedor de libros?
4. ¿Por qué no quiere comprar la jovencita otra novela romántica?
5. Nombre Ud. otra novela romántica.

Vamos a hablar

A. ¿Qué enfermedades se atribuyen al fumar? ¿Qué ley promulgó el cirujano general de los Estados Unidos?

B. ¿Cuándo molesta más el humo del cigarrillo a los que no fuman? ¿En qué negocios y lugares de trabajo se prohibe fumar? Mencione los lugares públicos en que antes se podía fumar y hoy no.

C. Hay muchas industrias satélites relacionadas con la industria del tabaco, por ejemplo, la fábrica de ceniceros (*ashtrays*). ¿Qué otras? Diga algo sobre este tema.

D. La venta de tarjetas es un negocio de muy buena ganancia en los Estados Unidos.

Hay tarjetas para cualquier ocasión a fin de expresar nuestros sentimientos íntimos. Los mensajes de las tarjetas expresan nuestros deseos mucho mejor de lo que pudiéramos hacer nosotros.

¿Envía Ud. muchas tarjetas? ¿A quiénes? ¿En qué ocasiones? Mencione las ocasiones tristes. Mencione las alegres. ¿Es Ud. partidario de las tarjetas de San Valentín? ¿Recuerda Ud. las palabras impresas en una tarjeta que Ud. mandó?

Dichos y refranes

—¿Por qué será que Luisa y Rafael siempre tienen las mejores butacas en el teatro y nosotros apenas podemos ver la función?

—Por dinero baila el perro.

Oficios y profesiones

el autor (la autora)	*author*
el editor (la editora)	*publisher*
el impresor (la impresora)	*printer*
el redactor (la redactora)	*editor*
el librero (la librera)	*book seller*
el papelero (la papelera)	*stationer, paper dealer (manufacturer)*
el agricultor (la agricultora) de tabaco	*tobacco farmer*
el tabacalero (la tabacalera)	*tobacconist*
el (la) fabricante de tabacos	*cigar maker, cigar dealer*

Ejercicio

Haga oraciones usando los nombres dados de oficios o profesiones.

Repasito

Prueba—Escoja la traducción apropiada:

1.	el papel de escritorio	a.	pen
2.	el cigarrillo	b.	match
3.	el lápiz	c.	envelope
4.	la tarjeta	d.	pipe
5.	el fósforo	e.	cigar
6.	la pipa	f.	stationery
7.	el cigarro	g.	eraser
8.	el sobre	h.	greeting card
9.	una goma	i.	pencil
10.	el bolígrafo	j.	cigarette

UNIT 15

El correo   *The Post Office*

Expresiones apropiadas

1.	ir al buzón	to go to the mailbox
2.	echar una carta al correo	to mail a letter
3.	saludar al cartero (a la cartera)	to greet the letter carrier
4.	olvidar el código postal	to forget the zip code
5.	enviar la carta por correo aéreo	to send the letter air mail
6.	mandar una carta certificada	to send a letter by certified mail
7.	pagar el correo de primera clase	to pay for first class mail
8.	hablar con el dependiente (la dependienta)	to speak to the mail clerk
9.	incluir la dirección del remitente	to include the return address
10	conocer al director (la directora) de correos	to know the postmaster
11.	recibir una carta de entrega especial	to receive a special delivery letter
12.	comprar un giro postal	to buy a postal money order
13.	guardar los matasellos	to save postmarks
14.	asegurar el paquete postal	to insure the parcel post package
15.	llevar el portacartas	to carry the mailbag
16.	lamer el sello	to lick the stamp
17.	corregir las señas	to correct the address
18.	poner la dirección en el sobre	to address the envelope
19.	pagar el sobrepeso	to pay the overweight
20.	firmar la tarjeta postal	to sign the postcard

Variaciones del vocabulario

el correo por avión	air mail
la postal	postcard
el recomendado, el correo registrado	certified or registered mail
la valija de correo	mailbag
la entrega inmediata	special delivery

Vocabulario en acción

Traduzca:

1. Raymond goes to the mailbox.
2. He mails a letter to Uncle Pepe.
3. We greet the letter carrier every morning.
4. I always forget the zip code on my letters.
5. It's faster to send the letter air mail.
6. Are you *(Ud.)* sending that letter by certified mail?
7. It's expensive to pay for first class mail.
8. I enjoy speaking to the mail clerk.

9.   We always include the return address.
10. Do you *(Uds.)* know the postmaster?
11. They receive a special delivery letter.
12. My mother often buys postal money orders.
13. Saving postmarks is an interesting hobby *(pasatiempo)* .
14. It is a good idea to insure parcel post packages.
15. Carrying mailbags is hard work.
16. I hate to lick postage stamps.
17. You *(tú)* must correct the mailing address.
18. They forget to address the envelope.
19. The company pays for the overweight.
20. We all sign the postcard.

Cuestionario

Complete las siguientes frases:

1.   El señor echa la carta en ———————— .
2.   Los sellos se venden en ———————— .
3.   Cuando vamos de vacaciones, siempre enviamos ———— a nuestros amigos íntimos.
4.   *Zip code* es ——— en español.
5.   ——— es el hombre que lleva las cartas.
6.   ——— es la mujer que vende sellos en el correo.
7.   La fecha de entrega se encuentra en ———————— .
8.   Los paquetes se envían por ———————— .
9.   Yo pongo la dirección en ———————— .
10. El dependiente pone todas las cartas en ———————— .

Modelos de conversación

Repita y substituya las expresiones dadas:

1.   **El cartero lleva las cartas.**   The letter carrier carries the letters.
     El director de correos ————— .   The postmaster ————————————— .
     El dependiente ————————— .   The mail clerk ————————————— .
2.   **Envíe la carta por correo aéreo.**   Send the letter air mail.
     —————————**certificada.**   —————————by certified mail.
     —————————**por entrega especial.**   —————————special delivery.
3.   **Hay un cargo adicional por correo**   There is an additional charge for
     registrado.   registered mail.
     —————————**correo certificado.**   —————————certified mail.
     —————————**sobrepeso.**   —————————overweight.
4.   **Muchas personas coleccionan sellos.**   Many people save stamps.
     —————————**matasellos.**   —————————postmarks.
     —————————**sobres.**   —————————envelopes.

5. **La tarjeta postal está en el correo.**   The postcard is in the post office.
_____**portacartas.**   _____mailbag.
_____**buzón.**   _____mailbox.

Diálogo

Manuel: ¡Soy rico! La semana pasada recibí una carta **bien**   *(well sealed)*
cerrada y certificada de mi **corredor de la bolsa** en   *(stockbroker)*
la cual anunció una **subida** en el precio de mis **accio-**   *(rise/stocks)*
nes. Pensaba comprar un chalet en las montañas.
Alicia: ¿Por qué no lo compraste?
Manuel: Porque **anteayer** llegó otra carta en que se anunció   *(day before yesterday)*
la bajada de precio de **dichas** acciones. Iba a vender   *(aforementioned)*
mi casa en la ciudad.
Alicia: ¿Por qué no la vendiste?
Manuel: Porque hoy recibí la tercera carta en que anunció el
corredor una nueva subida en el precio de las acciones.
Alicia: ¿Qué **harás?**   *(will you do)*
Manuel: Estas subidas y bajadas me atacan los nervios y me
vuelven loco. Voy a renunciar mi **apartado postal** en   *(post office box)*
el correo.

Comprensión

1. ¿Por qué es rico el accionista Manuel? ¿Por qué es pobre?
2. Cuando era rico, ¿qué iba a comprar?
3. Al ser pobre, ¿qué iba a vender?
4. Al oír el último precio de las acciones, ¿qué decide el accionista?
5. ¿Qué ventajas tiene un apartado postal? ¿Desventajas?

Vamos a hablar

A. Describa el trabajo de un cartero. ¿Qué peligros corre? ¿Qué placeres hay en su trabajo? ¿Conoce Ud. a su cartero? ¿Cómo se llama? Describa su personalidad.

B. Fíjese la próxima vez en la cara que ponen las personas cuando miran su correspondencia. ¿Cómo reaccionan con las cartas que contienen cuentas y con las que traen cheques?

C. ¿Cuál es el valor de coleccionar sellos? Según los aficionados la colección de "los sobres del primer día" es más interesante que un catálogo de sellos. Explique Ud. las razones.

Dichos y refranes

—¿Por qué no me tienes miedo?

—Perros que ladran, no muerden.

Oficios y profesiones

el administrador (la administradora) de correos	*postmaster (postmistress)*
el operador (la operadora) de computadora	*computer operator*
el vendedor (la vendedora) de sellos	*postal clerk*
el cartero (la cartera)	*letter carrier*
el repartidor (la repartidora) de paquetes postales	*parcel post delivery man (woman)*
el (la) filatelista	*philatelist*

Ejercicio
Describa la operadora de computadora.

Repasito

Prueba—Escoja la traducción apropiada:

1. la carta
2. el director de correos
3. el sello
4. la tarjeta
5. la entrega especial
6. el correo aéreo
7. el buzón
8. el correo de primera clase
9. el dependiente
10. el matasellos

a. stamp
b. postmark
c. air mail
d. letter
e. mailbox
f. first class mail
g. clerk
h. postcard
i. special delivery
j. postmaster

UNIT 16

El banco   *The Bank*

Expresiones apropiadas

1.	ir al banco de ahorros	*to go to the savings bank*
2.	pedirle al banquero (a la banquera) consejo financiero	*to ask the banker for financial advice*
3.	querer un libro de cheques	*to want a checkbook*
4.	pedir billetes nuevos	*to ask for new bills*
5.	poner el dinero en la cartera de bolsillo	*to put the money in a billfold*
6.	abrir la caja de seguridad	*to open the safe-deposit box*
7.	hablar con el cajero (la cajera)	*to speak with the teller*
8.	pagar el principal	*to pay the principal*
9.	abrir una cuenta corriente (de cheque)	*to open a checking account*
10.	escribir un cheque	*to write a check*
11.	depositar dinero en la cuenta de banco	*to deposit money in the bank account*
12.	necesitar cheques de viajeros	*to need traveler's checks*
13.	ahorrar dinero	*to save money*
14.	recibir por correo el estado de la cuenta	*to receive a bank statement in the mail*
15.	llenar el formulario de depósito	*to fill out the deposit slip*
16.	someter el formulario de retiro	*to submit a withdrawal slip*
17.	acumular el interés	*to collect the interest*
18.	leer la libreta de banco	*to read the bank book*
19.	verificar el saldo bancario	*to check the bank balance*
20.	solicitar un préstamo	*to apply for a loan*

Variaciones del vocabulario

la hoja de depósito	*deposit slip*
el saldo de la cuenta bancaria	*bank balance*

Vocabulario en acción

Traduzca:

1. I'm going to the savings bank.
2. He asks the banker for financial advice.
3. We want a new checkbook.
4. She always requests new bills.
5. José puts the money in a billfold.
6. They open a safe-deposit box.
7. Elena and I are speaking with the teller.
8. The buyer pays the principal.
9. My parents are opening a checking account.

10. The vice-president of the bank writes a check.
11. Do they deposit money in the bank account every week?
12. The tourists need traveler's checks.
13. Do you (Ud.) save money?
14. We receive a statement in the mail every month.
15. Are you (tú) filling out the deposit slip?
16. We submit the withdrawal slips.
17. They collect a lot of interest.
18. The teller reads the bank book.
19. The teller checks the bank balance.
20. My mother is applying for a loan.

Cuestionario

Complete las siguientes frases:

1. Los turistas en países extranjeros usan _____ .
2. Cuando se deposita dinero en el banco, es necesario escribir la suma en

   _____ .
3. Antes de sacar dinero del banco, hay que firmar _____ .
4. El dinero que se deja en el banco gana _____ .
5. Mis joyas están en _____ .
6. Si voy a comprar un auto nuevo este año, necesito _____ .
7. Cajero, ¿tengo que endosar este _____?
8. _____ calcula el interés en mi cuenta de ahorros.
9. ¿Quiere Ud. los _____ de $5, $10 o $20?

Modelos de conversación

Repita y substituya las expresiones dadas:

1. **Deposite el dinero en la cuenta corriente.**
   _____ el banco de ahorros.
   _____ la caja de seguridad.

   Deposit the money in the checking account.
   _____ savings bank.

   _____ safe-deposit box.

2. **Llene el formulario de depósito.**
   _____ formulario de retiro.
   _____ cheque.

   Fill out the deposit slip.
   _____ withdrawal slip.
   _____ check.

3. **Tengo que pagar con un cheque de viajeros.**
   _____ el interés.
   _____ con un billete.

   I have to pay with a traveler's check.
   _____ the interest.
   _____ with a bill.

4. **¿Recibe Ud. un estado de la cuenta?**   Are you receiving a bank statement?
    ¿——————**un préstamo?**   ————————————loan?
    ¿——————**una libreta de banco?**   ————————————bank book?

5. **¿Dónde está la banquera?**   Where is the banker?
    ¿——————**el cajero?**   ——————teller?
    ¿——————**la cartera de bolsillo?**   ——————billfold?

Diálogo

Estudiante universitario:	Tengo interés en obtener un préstamo.	
Banquera:	¿Qué cantidad tiene Ud. **en mente?**	*(in mind)*
Estudiante universitario:	**Alrededor** de mil dólares. Quiero comprar un **anillo de compromiso** para mi novia.	*(approximately)* *(engagement ring)*
Banquera:	¡Mil dólares! ¿Y qué garantía nos da Ud.?	
Estudiante universitario:	Pues, tengo una guitarra, un radio y muchos discos.	
Banquera:	¡Dios mío! ¡Una guitarra! Con ese tipo de **seguridad** no es posible darle el préstamo. Pero la **firma** de su padre en estos papeles es suficiente para darle el dinero.	*(collateral)* *(signature)*

Comprensión

1. ¿En qué tiene interés el estudiante universitario?
2. ¿Cuánto necesita el estudiante? ¿Por qué?
3. ¿Qué garantía da el estudiante?
4. ¿Qué necesita para recibir el dinero?
5. ¿Puede Ud. enumerar todos los servicios que ofrecen los bancos a sus clientes?

Vamos a hablar

A. Comente sobre lo difícil que es conseguir, el día de hoy, un préstamo de un banco. ¿Sabe Ud. qué interés pide el banco por un préstamo? ¿Por qué son una mala idea los préstamos?

B. ¿Por qué será buena idea usar cheques viajeros en su próximo viaje? Cuando pierde Ud. sus cheques viajeros, ¿qué tiene que hacer? ¿Sabe Ud. cuánto cobra el banco por cheques viajeros?

Dichos y refranes

—¡Caramba! me dijeron que las acciones iban a aumentar de precio, pero bajaron.

—No es oro todo lo que reluce.

Oficios y profesiones

el presidente (la presidenta) del banco	*bank president*
el vicepresidente (la vicepresidenta) del banco	*bank vice-president*
el cajero (la cajera)	*teller*
el cajero (la cajera) del auto banco	*drive-in window teller*
el (la) guardia del banco	*bank guard*
el director (la directora) del personal	*personnel director*
el jefe (la jefa) de la sucursal	*branch manager*
el chófer del carro blindado	*armored car driver*
el corredor (la corredora) de acciones (de la bolsa)	*stockbroker*
el (la) accionista	*stockholder*
el analizador (la analizadora) de acciones	*stock analyst*
el (la) gerente de hipotecas	*mortgage manager*
el notario (la notaria)	*notary public*

Ejercicio

Describa el trabajo de cinco de los oficios mencionados anteriormente.

Repasito

Prueba — Escoja la traducción apropiada:

1.	la caja de seguridad	a.	traveler's check
2.	el saldo bancario	b.	bank book
3.	el interés	c.	safe-deposit box
4.	el banco de ahorros	d.	money
5.	el cajero	e.	bill
6.	el cheque de viajeros	f.	bank balance
7.	el dinero	g.	checking account
8.	el billete	h.	savings bank
9.	la cuenta corriente	i.	teller
10.	la libreta de banco	j.	interest

UNIT 17

El colegio,
la universidad
y la biblioteca

The School,
University
and Library

Expresiones apropiadas

1.	leer los apuntes	*to read the notes*
2.	estar presente (ausente)	*to be present (absent)*
3.	cerrar el armario	*to close the locker*
4.	recibir las calificaciones	*to receive the report card*
5.	escribir en una libreta	*to write in a notebook*
6.	borrar la pizarra	*to erase the board*
7.	pagar la matrícula	*to pay the tuition*
8.	pertenecer al estudiantado	*to be a member of the student body*
9.	respetar la facultad	*to respect the faculty*
10.	abrir el libro de texto	*to open the textbook*
11.	responder al maestro (a la maestra)	*to answer the teacher*
12.	recibir buenas notas	*to receive good grades*
13.	fracasar este semestre	*to fail this semester*
14.	sentarse al pupitre	*to sit at the desk*
15.	poner un anuncio en el tablero	*to put a notice on the bulletin board*
16.	hacer su tarea de clase	*to do your homework*
17.	consultar con el bibliotecario (la bibliotecaria)	*to consult the librarian*
18.	repasar el catálogo de fichas	*to check the card catalogue*
19.	pedir prestado un libro de referencia	*to borrow a reference book*
20.	perder la tarjeta de la biblioteca	*to lose the library card*

Variaciones del vocabulario

las calificaciones	*grades*
el deber, el trabajo escolar, el trabajo en casa	*homework*
el escritorio	*desk*
el fichero	*card catalogue*
la gaveta	*locker*
el instructor (la instructora)	*teacher*
el libro de apuntes, el cuaderno	*notebook*
la obra de consulta, el libro de referencia	*reference book*
el pizarrón	*board*
el profesor (la profesora)	*teacher*
los profesores	*faculty*
salir bien (mal)	*to pass (to fail)*
la tarjeta, el boletín	*report card*

Vocabulario en acción

Traduzca:

1. The teacher reads the notes.
2. That student is absent today.
3. The girl closes her locker.
4. The students receive their report cards today.
5. The pupils write in their notebooks.
6. The teacher erases the blackboard.
7. The students pay their tuition in September.
8. He is a new member of the student body.
9. The students respect the faculty.
10. The female students open their textbooks.
11. They answer the teacher.
12. Diligent students receive good grades.
13. Few students fail the first semester.
14. The teacher sits at his desk.
15. Let's put a notice on the bulletin board.
16. It is necessary to do our homework for Spanish class.
17. The students consult the librarian.
18. The librarian checks the card catalogue.
19. The foreign student borrows a reference book.
20. The professor loses his library card.

Cuestionario

Complete las siguientes frases:

1. El alumno pertenece al _____ .
2. El profesor escribe las notas en _____ .
3. Tenemos que pagar _____ cada semestre.
4. Abran _____ en la página 32.
5. La maestra escribe la palabra en _____ .
6. No se puede sacar un libro de la biblioteca sin _____ .
7. El escritorio de los alumnos se llama _____ .
8. Mi uniforme de béisbol está en el _____ .
9. El estudiante escribe los apuntes en su _____ .
10. Los anuncios diarios aparecen en _____ .

Modelos de conversación

Repita y substituya las expresiones dadas:

1. **La universidad envía las notas a casa.**

The university sends the grades home.

_____ las
calificaciones _____ .

_____report card ___ .

_____ la cuenta de
matrícula _____ .

_____tuition bill ___ .

2. **El maestro se sienta detrás del escritorio.**

The teacher sits behind the desk.

El estudiante _____ **del pupitre.**

The student _____ the desk.

El bibliotecario _____ **de la mesa.**

The librarian _____ the table.

3. **El estudiante lee el libro de referencia.**

The student reads the reference book.

_____el libro de texto.

_____ textbook.

_____los apuntes.

_____ notes.

4. **La estudiante encuentra su tarea.**

The student finds her homework.

_____ tarjeta
de la biblioteca.

_____library card.

_____ libreta.

_____notebook.

5. **Los maestros quieren armarios nuevos.**

The teachers want new lockers.

_____ tableros
nuevos.

_____bulletin boards.

_____ pizarras
nuevas.

_____blackboards.

Diálogo

Profesor: ¿Cuál es el animal que acompaña a **los ciegos**? *(the blind)*
Pepito: El perro.
Profesor: Muy bien. ¿Cuál es el animal más **poderoso**? *(powerful)*
Antonio: El elefante.
Profesor: Tienes razón. ¿Cuál es el animal que nos da
alimento y abrigo? *(food and clothing)*
Panchito: Mi padre.

Comprensión

1. ¿Qué pregunta el profesor?
2. Según Pepito, ¿cuál es el animal que acompaña a los ciegos?
3. Según Antonio, ¿qué animal es el más poderoso?
4. ¿Cuál es el animal que da alimento y abrigo a Panchito?
5. ¿Cuál es el animal predilecto de Ud.?
6. ¿Sabe Ud. algo sobre el entrenamiento de perros que guían a los ciegos?

Vamos a hablar

A. Según su opinión . . .

1. ¿Qué es un muchacho bueno (una muchacha buena)?
2. ¿Qué es un muchacho malo (una muchacha mala)?

B. Haga una oración sobre la importancia de los computadores en la educación de los estudiantes de hoy día.

C. Según el concepto de algunos educadores ilustres, uno de los grandes valores de la universidad es su biblioteca. Explique la razón de esta idea.

D. Los atletas que se distinguen en el fútbol y béisbol tienen la ventaja de obtener contratos con un pago de cinco mil dólares por tres años a pesar de no haber terminado sus estudios. Opine Ud. sobre este acontecimiento social.

Dichos y refranes

—¿Has oído, Rogelio, que hay cursos para jubilados en sus setenta?

—Amor mío, para aprender nunca es tarde.

Oficios y profesiones

el maestro (la maestra)	*teacher*
el profesor (la profesora)	*teacher, professor*
el décano (la decana)	*dean*
el director (la directora)	*principal*
el bibliotecario (la bibliotecaria)	*librarian*
el (la) novelista	*novelist*
el poeta (la poetisa)	*poet*
el (la) ensayista	*essayist*
el dramaturgo (la dramaturga)	*playwright*
el (la) periodista	*journalist*
el conferenciante (la conferencianta)	*speaker*
el (la) intérprete	*interpreter*
el (la) artista	*artist*
el dibujante (la dibujadora)	*cartoonist*
el autor (la autora)	*author*
el escritor (la escritora)	*writer*
el traductor (la traductora)	*translator*

Ejercicio

Explique el trabajo de tres de estos profesionales.

Repasito

Prueba—Escoja la traducción apropiada:

1.	el estudiantado	a.	grades
2.	el bibliotecario	b.	report card
3.	la matrícula	c.	notebook
4.	el libro de referencia	d.	faculty
5.	las notas	e.	semester
6.	las calificaciones	f.	student body
7.	el tablero	g.	reference book
8.	la facultad	h.	tuition
9.	el semestre	i.	librarian
10.	el cuaderno	j.	bulletin board

UNIT 18

*La iglesia
y el templo*

*The Church
and Temple*

Expresiones apropiadas

1.	visitar la catedral	to visit the cathedral
2.	ir a la sinagoga	to go to the synagogue
3.	consultar el ministro (cura)	to consult the minister (priest)
4.	hablar con el rabino	to speak to the rabbi
5.	decorar el altar	to decorate the altar
6.	arrodillarse en el banco	to kneel on the pew
7.	rezar en la capilla	to pray in the chapel
8.	recibir la comunión (comulgar)	to receive communion
9.	cantar en el coro	to sing in the choir
10.	alabar a Dios	to praise God
11.	buscar el himno	to look for the hymn
12.	encender el incienso	to light the incense
13.	celebrar la misa	to celebrate the mass
14.	obedecer a la monja	to obey the nun
15.	leer la Biblia	to read the Bible
16.	confesar los pecados	to confess one's sins
17.	predicar desde el púlpito	to preach from the pulpit
18.	bendecir la congregación	to bless the congregacion
19.	escuchar el sermón	to listen to the sermon
20.	ponerse las vestimentas	to put on one's vestments

Variaciones del vocabulario

la homilía	sermon
los ornamentos, las vestiduras	vestments
el padre, el sacerdote	priest
el rabí	rabbi
la religiosa, la hermana, la madre	nun

Vocabulario en acción

Traduzca:

1. Are you (*Ud.*) visiting the new cathedral?
2. My friend goes to the synagogue every Saturday.
3. You (*Uds.*) consult your minister.
4. We're going to speak with the rabbi.
5. The nuns decorate the altar.
6. The family kneels on the pews.
7. I prefer to pray in the chapel.
8. All the members of my family receive communion every Sunday.
9. Does she sing in the choir?
10. We praise God.
11. The organist (*el organista*) is looking for the hymn.

12. The altar boy (*el monaguillo*) lights the incense.
13. The priest celebrates mass at seven o'clock.
14. Do you (*tú*) obey the nuns, Paul?
15. We like to read the Bible.
16. Do you (*Ud.*) confess all your sins?
17. The minister preaches from the pulpit.
18. The priest blesses the congregation.
19. We listen to the sermon.
20. The priest puts on his vestments.

Expresiones útiles

LOS PARENTESCOS (FAMILY RELATIONSHIPS)

la madre	*mother*
el padre	*father*
la hermana	*sister*
el hermano	*brother*
el medio hermano	*half brother*
la media hermana	*half sister*
el esposo (el marido)	*husband*
la esposa (la mujer)	*wife*
el hijo	*son*
la hija	*daughter*
la abuela	*grandmother*
el abuelo	*grandfather*
la bisabuela	*great-grandmother*
el bisabuelo	*great-grandfather*
la tía	*aunt*
el tío	*uncle*
el primo (la prima)	*cousin*
el sobrino	*nephew*
la sobrina	*niece*
la suegra	*mother-in-law*
el suegro	*father-in-law*
la cuñada	*sister-in-law*
el cuñado	*brother-in-law*
la nuera	*daughter-in-law*
el yerno	*son-in-law*
el padrastro	*stepfather*
la madrastra	*stepmother*
el prometido (la prometida)	*fiancé(e)*
la viuda	*widow*
el viudo	*widower*
el padrino	*godfather*
la madrina	*godmother*

Ejercicio

Complete las oraciones siguientes:

1. El hijo de mi tía es _____ .
2. La hija de mi madre es _____ .
3. La esposa de mi hijo es _____ .
4. La madre de mi padre es _____ .
5. La madre de mi esposo es _____ .
6. El hermano de mi madre es _____ .

Cuestionario

Complete las siguientes frases:

1. _____ celebra la misa.
2. Es costumbre leer _____ todos los días.
3. La mujer canta en _____ .
4. Los niños están sentados en _____ de la iglesia.
5. El ministro _____ desde el púlpito.
6. La gente va a la confesión para confesarse _____ .
7. _____ dirige los miembros de su sinagoga en una oración.

Modelos de conversación

Repita y substituya las expresiones dadas.

1. **El rabino está en el púlpito.**   The rabbi is at the pulpit.
   El sacerdote _____ .   The priest _____ .
   El ministro _____ .   The minister _____ .
2. **La congregación escucha el coro.**   The congregation listens to the choir.
   _____ **sermón.**   _____ sermon.
   _____ **el himno.**   _____ hymn.
3. **Muchos católicos van a confesarse.**   Many Catholics go to confession.
   _____ **misa.**   _____ mass.
   _____ **comulgar.**   _____ communion.
4. **El reza en el banco de la iglesia.**   He prays in the pew of the church.
   _____ **la capilla.**   _____ chapel.
   _____ **la sinagoga.**   _____ synagogue.
5. **La iglesia necesita vestimentas nuevas.**   The church needs new vestments.
   _____ **un altar nuevo.**   _____ a new altar.
   _____ **bancos nuevos.**   _____ new pews.

Diálogo

Turista:	¡Socorro! ¡Socorro!	*(help)*
Lugareño:	**¿Qué le pasa,** amigo?	*(villager/what's the matter?)*
Turista:	**Allí** hay un **espíritu.**	*(there/ghost)*
Lugareño:	¿Dónde?	
Turista:	En frente de la iglesia. Veo una figura de un **asno** en la **pared.**	*(donkey/wall)*
Lugareño:	**¡Qué hombre tan tímido!** Ve su **propia sombra** y tiene miedo.	*(what a timid man/own shadow)* *(you are afraid)*

Comprensión

1. ¿Qué grita el turista?
2. ¿Qué ve?
3. ¿Dónde está la figura del asno?
4. En realidad, ¿qué es el asno?
5. ¿Va Ud. al templo o a la iglesia? ¿Cuál?
6. ¿Cree Ud. que la religión es una consolación para el hombre?

Vamos a hablar

A. ¿Cuántos de los diez mandatos que Dios dió a Moisés en el Monte de Sinaí puede Ud. recitar?

B. ¿Qué opina Ud. sobre el celibato para los ministros de la iglesia?

C. Los psicólogos y los psiquiatras dicen que la confesión para los que creen es una purga que limpia y deja al hombre en santa paz y tranquilidad. Discuta este tema. ¿Por qué es difícil confesarse?

Dichos y refranes

—Cuando vamos a misa, ¿por qué te sientas siempre en el último banco de la iglesia?

—Dios dijo que los últimos serán los primeros.

Oficios y profesiones

el ministro	*minister*
el sacerdote, el cura, el padre	*priest*
el rabino, el rabí	*rabbi*
el párroco	*pastor*
el fraile	*monk*
el hermano (la hermana)	*brother (sister)*
la madre superiora	*mother superior*
la monja	*nun*
el cardenal	*cardinal*
el obispo	*bishop*
el arzobispo	*archbishop*
el monseñor	*monsignor*
el diácono (la diaconesa)	*deacon (deaconess)*
el misionero (la misionera)	*missionary*
el seminarista	*seminarian*
el vicario	*vicar*

Ejercicio

Haga oraciones usando todos los nombres dados.

Repasito

Prueba—Escoja la palabra apropiada:

1.	el púlpito	a.	God
2.	el banco	b.	choir
3.	la catedral	c.	altar
4.	la monja	d.	priest
5.	Dios	e.	communion
6.	el sacerdote	f.	chapel
7.	la comunión	g.	nun
8.	el coro	h.	pulpit
9.	la capilla	i.	cathedral
10.	el altar	j.	pew

*U*NIT 19

La estación de bomberos y la estación de policía

The Firehouse and the Police Station

Expresiones apropiadas

1.	dar la alarma de incendio	to set off the fire alarm
2.	manejar el camión de bomberos	to drive the fire engine
3.	abrir la boca de agua	to open the hydrant
4.	subir la escalera	to climb the ladder
5.	usar el extintor	to use the fire extinguisher
6.	coger la manguera	to grab the hose
7.	echar agua a las llamas	to throw water on the flames
8.	apagar el incendio	to put out the fire
9.	eliminar el humo	to eliminate the smoke
10.	saltar en la red	to jump into the net
11.	resucitar a los bomberos	to resuscitate the firefighters
12.	notificar a la policía	to notify the police
13.	seguir el coche de policía	to follow the police car
14.	llamar a un (una) detective	to call a detective
15.	cometer un crimen	to commit a crime
16.	identificar al (a la) criminal	to identify the criminal
17.	dar una citación	to give a summons
18.	tomar las huellas digitales	to take fingerprints
19.	quitarle las esposas	to take off the handcuffs
20.	disparar la pistola	to fire the pistol

Variaciones del vocabulario

el coche patrullero	police car
el (la) delincuente	criminal
el delito	crime
la huella dactilar	fingerprint
la mujer policía	policewoman

Vocabulario en acción

Traduzca:

1. The juvenile delinquents *(los delincuentes juveniles)* set off the fire alarm.
2. My father drives a fire engine.
3. The firemen open the fire hydrant.
4. The firefighters climb the ladder quickly.
5. Can you *(Ud.)* use a fire extinguisher?
6. They grab the hose and help the firemen.
7. It is not always a good idea to throw water on flames.
8. We put out the fire.
9. It is necessary to eliminate the smoke.
10. The victims *(las víctimas)* of the fire jump into the net.
11. The nurse resuscitates the fireman.

12. Do you *(Ud.)* notify the police when you see a crime?
13. The ambulance *(la ambulancia)* follows the police car.
14. The fireman calls the detective.
15. Many young people commit crimes.
16. Can you *(tú)* identify the criminal?
17. The policeman gives the man a summons.
18. The detective takes fingerprints in the criminal's home.
19. The policeman takes the handcuffs off the criminal.
20. The criminal fires a pistol.

Cuestionario

Complete las siguientes frases:

1. La víctima del incendio salta del tercer piso del edificio y cae en _____ .
2. Los bomberos apagan el incendio con _____ .
3. Cuando hay un incendio en la casa, es necesario dar _____ .
4. ¡Llame a la _____ ! Me robaron mis joyas de la habitación del hotel.
5. El policía pone _____ en las manos del criminal.
6. _____ robaron el dinero del banco.
7. Ponga _____ en la boca de agua.
8. No (se) muere la gente solamente a causa del incendio, sino a causa del
   _____ .
9. Para llegar al tercer piso del edificio, emplean _____ .
10. El policía dispara su _____ .

Modelos de conversación

Repita y substituya las expresiones dadas:

1. **Los camiones de bomberos van de prisa al incendio.**
   Los policías _____ .
   Los bomberos _____ .
2. **El extintor apaga el incendio.**
   El agua de la boca de agua _____ .
   El bombero _____ .
3. **Mucha gente (se) muere a causa del humo.**
   _____ incendio.
   _____ crimen.
4. **Traiga la manguera.**
   _____ **red.**
   _____ **escalera.**
5. **Llame a la estación de bomberos.**
   _____ **la estación de policía.**
   _____ **un policía o un detective.**

The fire engines rush to the fire.

The policemen _____ .
The firefighters _____ .
The fire extinguisher puts out the flame.
The water from the hydrant _____ .
The firefighter _____ .
Many people die because of smoke.

_____ fire.
_____ crime.
Bring the hose.
_____ net.
_____ ladder.
Call the firehouse.
_____ the police station.
_____ a policeman or a detective.

Diálogo

(Suena el teléfono.)

Teniente García: Este es el departamento de incendios. Soy   *(lieutenant)*
el teniente García de la estación de bomber-
os. ¿Hay un fuego?

Señora López: ¡No! Discúlpeme, señor. **Me equivoqué** en   *(I made a mistake)*
marcar el número de teléfono. No necesito
bomberos, sino la policía.

Teniente García: ¿Qué pasa, señora? ¿En qué puedo servirla?

Señora López: Mi esposo, Herminio López, salió de casa
hace dos días y no regresó.   *(two days ago)*

Teniente García: Si me da una descripción de él, **avisaré a** un   *(I shall advise)*
detective del **departamento de personas**   *(missing persons*
perdidas.   *bureau)*

Señora López: Es pequeño, **gordo, calvo,** tiene mal humor   *(fat/bald)*
y se viste como un **payaso.**   *(clown)*

Teniente García: Con esta excelente descripción estoy seguro
que la policía no va a tener ninguna
dificultad en encontrarlo.

Señora López: Ahora que lo pienso bien, **no se moleste** en   *(don't bother)*
llamar a la policía.

Comprensión

1. ¿Cómo se equivocó la señora López?
2. ¿A quién busca?
3. ¿Cuál es la descripción que da la señora de su esposo?
4. Al final, ¿qué le dice al bombero?
5. ¿Está Ud. casado? ¿Va Ud. a casarse?
6. Cuando Ud. ve un incendio, ¿qué debe hacer?
7. Cuando Ud. es testigo de un delito, ¿qué debe hacer?
8. ¿Por qué son héroes los bomberos y los policías?
9. ¿Está Ud. de acuerdo con la proposición de dar igual salario a los bomberos y a los policías?

Vamos a hablar

A. Diga algo sobre las mujeres en uniforme de policía.

B. ¿Ha recibido Ud. una citación de la policía? ¿Cuáles fueron sus pensamientos en ese momento? Describa Ud. un día en la corte de tráfico.

C. ¿Por qué hay tantos robos en las ciudades?

D. ¿Cree Ud. que los jueces son bastante severos en condenar a los culpables? ¿Es Ud. de los que creen que la policía de su estado debe dar muerte a los criminales incorregibles que matan a la gente?

Dichos y refranes

¿Te fijaste en el cutis de Dolores después de su operación facial?

—Aunque la mona se vista de seda, mona se queda.

Oficios y profesiones

el (la) **policía**	*policeman (woman)*
el (la) **policía auxiliar**	*auxiliary police*
el **jefe** (la **jefa**) **de policía**	*police chief*
el (la) **detective**	*detective*
el (la) **policía montado a caballo**	*mounted policeman (woman)*
el **guardia** (la **guardiana**) **de prisión**	*prison guard*
el **carcelero** (la **carcelera**)	*warden*
el **bombero** (la **bombera**)	*firefighter*
el **inspector** (la **inspectora**) **de incendios**	*fire inspector*
el **jefe** (la **jefa**) **de bomberos**	*fire chief*
el **abogado** (la **abogada**)	*lawyer*
el **fiscal** (la **fiscal**)	*prosecutor*
el **juez** (la **juez**)	*judge*

Ejercicio

Describa el trabajo de tres de las personas que desempeñan los oficios mencionados.

Repasito

Prueba—Escoja la traducción apropiada:

1.	el humo	a.	fire alarm
2.	el camión de bomberos	b.	net
3.	la boca de agua	c.	fireman
4.	la manguera	d.	ladder
5.	el crimen	e.	police car
6.	la red	f.	smoke
7.	la alarma de incendio	g.	crime
8.	la escalera	h.	fire engine
9.	el coche de policía	i.	hydrant
10.	el bombero	j.	hose

UNIT 20

La panadería   *The Bakery*

Expresiones apropiadas

1.	comer el pan blanco	to eat white bread
2.	tostar el pan de centeno	to toast the rye bread
3.	rebanar el pan de centeno moreno	to slice the pumpernickel bread
4.	servir el pan de pasas	to serve the raisin bread
5.	calentar el panecillo	to heat the roll
6.	amasar la masa	to knead the dough
7.	poner la masa en el horno	to put the dough in the oven
8.	probar los dulces	to try the pastries
9.	preparar las galletas	to prepare cookies
10.	querer flan	to want custard
11.	escarchar el pastel	to frost the cake
12.	adornar la torta de cumpleaños	to decorate the birthday cake
13.	preferir el pastel de queso (manzana, cereza)	to prefer the cheesecake (apple pie, cherry pie)
14.	glasear el pastel de frutas	to glaze the fruitcake
15.	sacar del horno la torta de chocolate	to take the chocolate cake out of the oven
16.	congelar el pastel de helado	to freeze the ice cream cake
17.	rellenar las empanadas de carne	to stuff the meat pies
18.	trabajar de panadero (panadera)	to work as a baker
19.	apreciar el trabajo del pastelero (de la pastelera)	to appreciate the work of the pastry chef
20.	hervir los churros en aceite	to boil the churros (doughnuts) in oil

Variaciones del vocabulario

el bizcocho de cumpleaños	birthday cake
el cake, el queque, la torta	cake
el pastelito, la galletica	cookie

Vocabulario en acción

Traduzca:

1. My young children eat white bread every day.
2. Do you *(Uds.)* toast your rye bread?
3. The baker slices the pumpernickel bread.
4. She often serves raisin bread.
5. Mom always warms the rolls for our Sunday dinner.
6. It is difficult to knead the dough.
7. I'm putting the dough in the oven.
8. Let's try the pastries.
9. Carlos is preparing cookies.

10. We want flan for dessert.
11. The baker frosts the cake.
12. The baker decorates the birthday cake.
13. Do you *(tú)* prefer cheesecake?
14. Grandma glazes her fruitcake every Christmas.
15. I just *(acabo de)* took the chocolate cake out of the oven.
16. Dad freezes the ice cream cake.
17. Are you *(Ud.)* stuffing the meat pies?
18. My father works as a baker.
19. Do you *(Ud.)* appreciate the work of the pastry chef?
20. You *(tú)* need to boil the doughnuts in oil.

Cuestionario

Complete las siguientes frases:

1. Para el desayuno yo como sólo _____ y café.
2. ¡Feliz cumpleaños! ¡Qué bonita _____ !
3. En la fiesta de Jorge Wáshington, mamá siempre sirve _____ .
4. _____ es el postre típico de España.
5. A los alemanes les gusta el pan de _____ .
6. En los restaurantes italianos siempre se encuentra el pastel de _____ .
7. _____ con helado es tradicional en los Estados Unidos.

Modelos de conversación

Repita y substituya las expresiones dadas.

1. **¿Quién prefiere el pastel de helado?**	Who prefers ice cream cake?
¿_____ **chocolate?**	_____ chocolate cake?
¿_____ **frutas?**	_____ fruit cake?
2. **Me llevo un pastel de queso.**	I'll take a cheesecake.
_____ **una empanada de carne.**	_____ a meat pie.
_____ **un pastel de manzana.**	_____ an apple pie.
3. **La panadera prepara el pan de centeno.**	The baker prepares the rye bread.
_____ **las galletas.**	_____ cookies.
_____ **las empanadas.**	_____ pies.
4. **¿Está hecho con pasas?**	Is it made with raisins?
¿_____ **queso?**	_____ cheese?
¿_____ **frutas?**	_____ fruit?
5. **¿Le gusta a Ud. el pan blanco?**	Do you like white bread?
¿_____ **de centeno?**	_____ rye bread?
¿_____ **de centeno moreno?**	_____ pumpernickel bread?

Diálogo

Dependiente:	¡Muy buenos días! ¿Qué tal, señor?
Cliente:	¿Es Ud. el dueño de esta panadería?
Dependiente:	No, es el señor Ramírez. Yo trabajo de dependiente. ¿Quiere algún pastel o unos panecillos **recién sacados** del horno?
Cliente:	En realidad no quiero **ni** panecillos **ni** pan, **tan sólo charlar** un **rato**. Soy **viudo** y estoy **solito** en **este mundo** .

(recently taken out)
(neither . . . nor)
(only to chat/while/ widower)
(alone/this world)

Comprensión

1. ¿Qué pregunta el cliente?
2. ¿Qué contesta el dependiente?
3. ¿Qué pregunta el dependiente al cliente?
4. ¿Por qué entra el cliente en la panadería?
5. ¿Desea Ud. panecillos, pan de centeno o pan de pasas para el desayuno?
6. ¿Cuál es su torta predilecta?
7. ¿Cuántas velitas le pusieron en su última torta de cumpleaños?

Vamos a hablar

A. Haga un comentario sobre el pastel de cerezas que se sirve el día que se celebra el cumpleaños de Jorge Washington. ¿Sabe Ud. la leyenda de la mentira de este presidente?

B. Describa las tortas o galletas que hacen

   (a) los italianos
   (b) los alemanes
   (c) los franceses
   (d) los españoles
   (e) los chinos
   ¿Cuál es su torta predilecta?

C. Describa la costumbre de la torta para festejar los cumpleaños en los Estados Unidos. Mencione algunos detalles de su última fiesta de cumpleaños.

D.   Mire el dibujo y responda a las preguntas.

1.   ¿Qué preparó el chico?
2.   ¿Por qué lo hizo?
3.   ¿Cómo salieron las galleticas?
4.   ¿Le pasó a Ud. esta calamidad doméstica?
5.   Si le hubiera pasado esta escena, ¿qué habría hecho Ud.?
6.   ¿Qué va a decir y hacer la madre al entrar en la cocina y encontrarse con esta escena?
7.   ¿En qué situación igual a la del dibujo se halló alguna vez un miembro de su familia?

Dichos y refranes

—Si no me hubiese casado contigo, tal vez hoy sería millonario.

—Antes que te cases, mira lo que haces.

Oficios y profesiones

el dueño (la dueña) de la tienda de dulces (confitería)	*candy store proprietor (confectionery)*
el confitero (la confitera)	*candy dealer*
el panadero (la panadera)	*bread maker*
el pastelero (la pastelera)	*pie, cake, and cookie baker*
el repostero (la respostera)	*fancy pastry cook, dessert chef*
el decorador (la decoradora) de pasteles	*cake decorator*
el vendedor (la vendedora) de alimentos congelados	*frozen foods dealer*

Ejercicio

Complete las siguientes definiciones:

1. La persona que vende alimentos congelados es _____ .
2. La mujer que decora pasteles es _____ .
3. La persona que hace los panes es _____ .
4. El individuo que hace los pasteles es _____ .
5. El vendedor de dulces es _____ .

Repasito

Prueba—Escoja la traducción apropiada:

1.	la torta de cumpleaños	a.	cheesecake
2.	la galleta	b.	bread
3.	el pastel	c.	dough
4.	la panadera	d.	custard
5.	el pastel de queso	e.	baker
6.	el panecillo	f.	cookie
7.	los dulces	g.	birthday cake
8.	la masa	h.	roll
9.	el flan	i.	cake
10.	el pan	j.	pastries

UNIT 21

La carnicería y la pescadería

The Butcher Shop and the Fish Market

Expresiones apropiadas

1.	cortar la carne	*to cut the meat*
2.	moler el bistec	*to grind the steak*
3.	colgar la pierna de cordero	*to hang the leg of lamb*
4.	desplumar el pollo	*to pluck the chicken*
5.	atar el rosbif	*to tie the roast beef*
6.	pesar las chuletas de puerco (cordero, ternera)	*to weigh the pork (lamb, veal) chops*
7.	rellenar el pavo	*to stuff the turkey*
8.	congelar (descongelar) el pato	*to freeze (defrost) the duck*
9.	separar el filete	*to separate the fillet*
10.	glacear el jamón	*to glaze the ham*
11.	contar las salchichas	*to count the frankfurters*
12.	freír el tocino	*to fry the bacon*
13.	poner migas de pan al filete de ternera	*to bread the veal cutlet*
14.	vender riñones	*to sell kidneys*
15.	cocer la longaniza	*to boil the sausage*
16.	sacar el hueso	*to take out the bone*
17.	recortar la grasa	*to trim the fat*
18.	preparar la lengua	*to prepare the tongue*
19.	cocinar las costillas	*to cook the spareribs*
20.	preferir la carne para guisar	*to prefer stew meat*

Variaciones del vocabulario

el biftec	*steak*
los chorizos, las salchichas	*sausages*
el perro caliente	*frankfurter, hotdog*
la tocineta	*bacon*

Vocabulario en acción

Traduzca:

1. The waiter cuts the meat.
2. Father grinds the steak.
3. They hang a leg of lamb in the butcher shop.
4. I don't like to pluck chickens.
5. Mama ties the roast beef.
6. You (Ud.) weigh the pork chops, don't you?
7. We're going to stuff the turkey.
8. She freezes the flounder.
9. The butcher separates the fillet.
10. Does your (Ud.) mother glaze the ham?

11. The butcher counts the frankfurters.
12. He fries bacon for breakfast.
13. Does she bread her veal cutlets?
14. The butcher sells kidneys every Monday.
15. Do you (*tú*) boil your sausages?
16. Does he take out the bone?
17. He trims all the fat from the meat.
18. I don't know how to prepare tongue.
19. We cook spareribs once a week in our home.
20. I prefer stew meat.

Expresiones útiles

LOS PESCADOS Y MARISCOS   (FISH AND SEAFOOD)

los camarones	*shrimp*
la langosta	*lobster*
el cangrejo	*crab*
el lenguado	*flounder*
el calamar	*squid*
el atún	*tuna*
el salmón	*salmon*
la ostra	*oyster*
la trucha	*trout*
el pez espada	*swordfish*
la macarela	*mackerel*
las veneras	*scallops*
las almejas	*clams*
los mejillones	*mussels*
las sardinas	*sardines*
el bacalao	*codfish*
la corvina	*white sea bass*
la anguila	*eel*
las anchoas	*anchovies*

Cuestionario

Complete las siguientes frases:

1. _____ a dos pesos la libra es una ganga.
2. Es necesario descongelar _____ antes de cocinarlo.
3. A los niños siempre les gustan_____ .
4. Mamá siempre sirve _____ a los gatos.
5. Rex, nuestro perro, siempre espera su _____ .
6. Hoy día _____ es carísimo.

7. A los italianos les gustan _____ .
8. Nunca servimos _____ en nuestra casa.
9. El Coronel de Kentucky vende _____ frito muy delicioso.

Modelos de conversación

Repita y substituya las expresiones dadas:

1. **¿Cuánto cuesta una libra de longaniza?**
    ¿_____ **cuestan dos libras de carne molida?**
    ¿_____ **cuestan doce salchichas?**

    How much is a pound of sausage?
    _____ are two pounds of chopped meat?
    _____ are twelve frankfurters?

2. **Quiero una pierna de cordero.**
    _____ **un pollo.**
    _____ **unas costillas.**

    I want a leg of lamb.
    _____ a chicken.
    _____ spareribs.

3. **¿Está tierno el filete de ternera?**
    ¿_____ **rosbif?**
    ¿_____ **biftec?**

    Is the veal cutlet tender?
    _____ roast beef _____?
    _____ steak _____?

4. **Tres libras de jamón, por favor.**
    _____ **carne para guisar, __ .**
    _____ **tocino, _____ .**

    Three pounds of ham, please.
    _____ stew meat, _____ .
    _____ bacon, _____ .

5. **¿Está barato el tocino hoy?**
    ¿_____ **pavo _____?**
    ¿_____ **puerco _____?**

    Is the bacon cheap today?
    _____ turkey _____?
    _____ pork _____?

Diálogo

Carnicero:	¡Buenos días! Hoy tenemos chuletas de puerco **frescas** y baratas. ¿Cuántas libras quiere?	*(fresh)*
Hombre:	La carne . . .	
Carnicero:	Sus **invitados** van a **saborear** la carne **más rica** del **mundo.**	*(guests/to taste/most delicious/world)*
Hombre:	Pero tengo . . .	
Carnicero:	Pero **nada,** aquí tiene Ud. la carne. Son dos dólares y cincuenta centavos.	*(nothing)*
Hombre:	Pero si es que **vengo a traer** su orden de carne para la semana. Está **afuera** en el **camión.**	*(I come to bring)* *(outside/truck)*
Carnicero:	¡Oh! Ud. es de la compañía **distribuidora.** ¡**Haberlo dicho antes,** hombre!	*(distributing)* *(you should have said so before)*

Comprensión

1. ¿Qué ganga *(bargain)* hay hoy en la carnicería?
2. Según el carnicero, ¡cómo está la carne?
3. ¿Cuánto cobra el carnicero por la carne?
4. ¿Por qué está el hombre en la carnicería?
5. ¿Qué clase de carne come Ud.?
6. ¿Compra Ud. la carne en una carnicería o en un supermercado? ¿Por qué?
7. ¿Cuál es la carne más barata? ¿Y la más cara?
8. ¿Cuáles son los peces que se pescan en las aguas, ríos o lagos cerca de su casa?

Vamos a hablar

A. ¿Hay un día especial en que se sirve pescado en su casa? ¿Es más barato el pescado que la carne? Dé ejemplos. ¿Cuánto vale una libra de bacalao? ¿De biftec? ¿Cuáles son los pescados que más le gustan? ¿Puede Ud. comparar el valor nutritivo del pescado con el de la carne? ¿Cuál es la ventaja de comprar pescado en una pescadería?

B. ¿Cómo le gusta preparado su biftec? ¿Qué parte del pollo prefiere Ud.? En el mercado de hoy compare Ud. el precio del pollo con el del biftec.

Dichos y refranes

—¡Cuánto me duele dar palmadas a nuestro hijo cuando no se porta bien!

—Juventud perezosa, vejez menesterosa.

Oficios y profesiones

el vaquero (la vaquera)	*cowboy (girl)*
el ranchero (la ranchera)	*rancher*

el ganadero (la ganadera)	cattle rancher
el pescador (la pescadora)	fisherman (woman)
el porquero (la porquera)	swine herder
el embaulador (la embauladora) de carne	meat packer
el pescador (la pescadora) de almejas	clam digger
el cortador (la cortadora) de carne	meat cutter

Ejercicio

Seleccione uno de estos oficios y explique el trabajo relacionado con el mismo.

Repasito

Prueba—Escoja la traducción apropiada:

1.	la longaniza	a.	lamb chop
2.	la chuleta de puerco	b.	roast beef
3.	el pavo	c.	sausage
4.	el filete	d.	ham
5.	el pato	e.	chopped meat
6.	el bistec	f.	fillet
7.	la carne molida	g.	pork chop
8.	la chuleta de cordero	h.	steak
9.	el rosbif	i.	turkey
10.	el jamón	j.	duck

UNIT 22

El supermercado   *The Supermarket*

Expresiones apropiadas

1.	buscar los alimentos congelados	*to look for frozen foods*
2.	gozar de los aperitivos	*to enjoy the appetizers*
3.	tomar las bebidas	*to have drinks*
4.	comer los bizcochos	*to eat the biscuits*
5.	llenar el carrito de compras	*to fill the cart with groceries*
6.	comprar el cereal	*to buy cereal*
7.	pagar los comestibles	*to pay for the food*
8.	servir el té y el café	*to serve tea and coffee*
9.	seleccionar las frutas y las verduras	*to select the fruits and vegetables*
10.	mirar los huevos	*to look at the eggs*
11.	beber el jugo de frutas	*to drink the fruit juice*
12.	examinar la fecha de la leche y de la crema	*to examine the date of the milk and cream*
13.	buscar la mayonesa y la salsa de tomate	*to look for the mayonnaise and the tomato sauce*
14.	vender la mantequilla y dar el pan gratis	*to sell the butter and give the bread free*
15.	rallar el queso	*to grate the cheese*
16.	acordarse de la sal y de la pimienta	*to remember the salt and pepper*
17.	dar cupones por las servilletas de papel y las toallas de papel	*to give coupons for paper napkins and paper towels*
18.	preguntar por el precio de venta del vinagre y del aceite	*to ask for the sale price of the vinegar and oil*
19.	olvidar el papel sanitario	*to forget the toilet paper*
20.	usar el detergente y el desinfectante	*to use detergent and disinfectant*

Variaciones del vocabulario

la manteca	*butter*
la nata	*cream*
el papel de inodoro	*toilet paper*
los refrescos	*cold beverages*
una rebanada de pan	*slice of bread*
las tapas	*appetizers*
el zumo	*juice*

Vocabulario en acción

Traduzca:

1. The customers look for the frozen foods.

2. Everybody enjoys appetizers.
3. Do you *(Uds.)* have drinks in the afternoon?
4. Do the children eat biscuits?
5. Every Saturday we go shopping *(ir de compras)* and fill the shopping cart.
6. Their father always buys cereal.
7. We pay for the food.
8. Do you *(tú)* serve tea after dinner?
9. I like to select fruits and vegetables.
10. We always look at the eggs.
11. Our family drinks a lot of fruit juice.
12. They examine the date of the milk and the cream.
13. I'm looking for the mayonnaise and the tomato sauce.
14. We sell the butter and give the bread free.
15. I need to grate the cheese.
16. I must remember the salt and pepper.
17. I have coupons for paper napkins and towels.
18. We ask for the sale price of the vinegar and oil.
19. You *(tú)* always forget the toilet paper!
20. Mother uses detergent and disinfectant.

Expresiones útiles

LAS VERDURAS (VEGETABLES)

el ajo	*garlic*
la alcachofa	*artichoke*
el apio	*celery*
el arroz	*rice*
la batata, el boniato	*sweet potato*
la berenjena	*eggplant*
el berro	*watercress*
los bretones	*brussels sprouts*
el brócoli	*broccoli*
la calabaza	*pumpkin, squash*
la cebolla	*onion*
la col, el repollo (morado)	*(red) cabbage*
la coliflor	*cauliflower*
los espárragos	*asparagus*
la espinaca	*spinach*
los frijoles, las habichuelas, las judía negras	*beans*
los garbanzos	*chick-peas*
los guisantes	*peas*
las habas	*lima beans*

la lechuga	*lettuce*
las lentejas	*lentils*
el maíz	*corn*
el nabo	*turnip*
las papas, las patatas	*potatoes*
el pepino	*cucumber*
el perejil	*parsley*
el pimiento picante, el ají, el chile, la guindilla	*hot pepper*
el quimgombó	*okra*
el rábano	*radish*
las remolachas	*beets*
el ruibarbo	*rhubarb*
las setas, los hongos, los champiñones	*mushrooms*
el tomate	*tomato*
el yame	*yam*
la zanahoria	*carrot*

LAS FRUTAS (FRUITS)

el aguacate	*avocado*
el albaricoque	*apricot*
el arándano agrio	*cranberry*
la cereza	*cherry*
la ciruela	*plum*
el dátil	*date*
la frambuesa	*raspberry*
las frambuesas azules	*blueberries*
la fresa	*strawberry*
la granada	*pomegranate*
la grosella	*currant*
el higo	*fig*
la lima, el limón verde	*lime*
el limón	*lemon*
la mandarina	*tangerine*
la manzana	*apple*
el melocotón, el durazno	*peach*
el melón	*cantaloupe, melon*
la naranja	*orange*
la nectarina	*nectarine*
el plátano, la banana	*banana*
la pera	*pear*
la piña	*pineapple*
la sandía, la patilla	*watermelon*
la toronja, el pomelo	*grapefruit*
las uvas	*grapes*

Ejercicio

¿Son frutas o legumbres?

1. los guisantes
2. los rábanos
3. las papas
4. las ciruelas
5. las fresas
6. las lentejas
7. las habas
8. los higos
9. las espinacas
10. las remolachas
11. las cerezas
12. las mandarinas

Cuestionario

Complete las siguientes frases:

1. Se utiliza _____ para lavar la ropa sucia.
2. ¡Cuidado con _____! Se rompen fácilmente.
3. A los niños les gustan _____ .
4. _____ es demasiado caro en esta época.
5. Falta _____ en el baño.
6. Me encanta una rebanada de pan con _____ .
7. Siempre compro _____ y _____ frescas.
8. _____ para el desayuno nos da las vitaminas esenciales.
9. Las compras se ponen en _____ .
10. En la lechería se compra _____ y _____ .

Modelos de conversación

Repita y substituya las expresiones dadas:

1. **Una botella de zumo de naranja, por favor.**
   _____ **leche,** _____ .
   _____ **crema,** _____ .

   A bottle of orange juice, please.
   _____ milk, _____ .
   _____ cream, _____ .

2. **No se olvide del detergente.**
   _____ **de las servilletas de papel.**
   _____ **de la mantequilla.**

   Don't forget the detergent.
   _____ paper napkins.
   _____ butter.

3. **Ponga el cereal en el carrito de compras.**
   _____ **pan** _____ .
   _____ **vinagre** _____ .

   Put the cereal in the shopping cart.
   _____ bread _____ .
   _____ vinegar _____ .

4.   ¿Cuál es el precio de estos bizcochos?   What is the price of these biscuits?
     ¿——————————— huevos?   ——————————— eggs?
     ¿——————————— aperitivos?   ——————————— appetizers?

5.   Para la fiesta necesitamos queso.   For the party we need cheese.
     ——————————— servilletas   ——————————— paper napkins.
     de papel.
     ——————————— bebidas.   ——————————— beverages.

Diálogo

Madre:	**A ver, hijito**, si compro cuatro litros de leche a sesenta centavos cada uno, ¿cuánto tengo que pagar?	*(let's see/little son)*
Hijo:	No sé, mamacita. Esa pregunta es muy difícil.	
Hija:	Es bien fácil: dos dólares, cuarenta.	
Padre:	¡Qué poco conoces a tu mamá!	
Madre:	¿Por qué dices eso?	
Padre:	Porque los niños no saben cómo tú **regateas** .	*(bargain)*

Comprensión

1.   ¿De qué trata el problema aritmético?
2.   ¿Por qué no puede el hijo resolver el problema?
3.   ¿Quién da la respuesta al problema?
4.   ¿Por qué va a costar la leche menos de dos dólares cuarenta centavos?
5.   Describa un regateo en su vida personal.

Vamos a hablar

A.   ¿Cuáles comestibles son exclusivamente preparados por hispanos y rara vez aparecen en la cocina norteamericana?

B.   Nuestros supermercados norteamericanos son la envidia del mundo. ¿Puede Ud. mencionar las secciones principales de un supermercado norteamericano?

C.   ¿Trabajó Ud. alguna vez en un supermercado—o quizás un amigo suyo (una amiga suya)? ¿Cuál fue su trabajo principal? ¿Le gustó?

Dichos y refranes

—Eres una esposa hermosísima y la cena de esta noche fue insuperable.

—Barriga llena, corazón contento.

Oficios y profesiones

el vendedor (la vendedora) de alimentos	*food salesman (woman)*
el verdulero (la verdulera)	*greengrocer*
el comerciante (la comercianta) de verduras	*vegetable merchant*
el vendedor (la vendedora) de frutas	*fruit merchant*
el huevero (la huevera)	*egg dealer*
el lechero (la lechera)	*dairyman (woman)*
el carnicero (la carnicera)	*butcher*
el salchichero (la salchichera)	*sausage maker*
el panadero (la panadera)	*bread maker*
el pastelero (la pastelera)	*pie and cake maker*
el cervecero (la cervecera)	*beer merchant*
el heladero (la heladera)	*ice cream merchant*
el cajero (la cajera)	*checker, cashier*
el director (la directora) del almacén	*warehouse manager*
el director (la directora) del supermercado	*supermarket manager*
el repartidor (la repartidora)	*delivery boy (girl)*
el inspector (la inspectora) de sanidad	*health inspector*

Ejercicio

Haga oraciones empleando los oficios mencionados. ¿Puede Ud. nombrar más oficios relacionados con el supermercado?

Repasito

Prueba—Escoja la traducción apropiada:

1.	la leche	a.	salt
2.	el jugo de frutas	b.	eggs
3.	los congelados	c.	beverages
4.	los huevos	d.	shopping cart
5.	el queso	e.	appetizers
6.	las servilletas de papel	f.	fruit juice
7.	los aperitivos	g.	frozen foods
8.	el carrito de compras	h.	paper napkins
9.	la sal	i.	milk
10.	las bebidas	j.	cheese

UNIT 23

La tienda de ropa de caballeros

The Men's Clothing Store

Expresiones apropiadas

1.	tener calor con el abrigo	*to be warm in one's overcoat*
2.	ponerse el traje	*to put on the suit*
3.	comprar vaqueros	*to buy blue jeans*
4.	acortarse los pantalones	*to shorten the slacks*
5.	botonarse la camisa	*to button the shirt*
6.	probarse una nueva chaqueta de sport	*to try on a new sport jacket*
7.	atar la corbata	*to tie the necktie*
8.	abrocharse el cinturón	*to fasten one's belt*
9.	quitarse los guantes	*to take off the gloves*
10.	desabotonarse la bata	*to unbutton one's robe*
11.	necesitar una camiseta	*to need an undershirt*
12.	cambiar los calzoncillos	*to exchange the shorts*
13.	saludar con el sombrero	*to tip one's hat*
14.	tejer un suéter	*to knit a sweater*
15.	alterar el chaleco	*to alter the vest*
16.	alquilar un traje de etiqueta	*to rent a tuxedo*
17.	llevar un uniforme	*to wear a uniform*
18.	lavar los calcetines	*to wash the socks*
19.	atarse los zapatos	*to lace one's shoes*
20.	envolver las zapatillas para un regalo	*to wrap the slippers as a gift*

Variaciones del vocabulario

los blue jeans	*blue jeans*
la correa	*belt*
las pantuflas	*slippers*
el sobretodo	*overcoat*
el vestido sastre	*suit*

Vocabulario en acción

Traduzca:

1. He's warm in that overcoat.
2. The man puts on his new suit.
3. The young boys are buying blue jeans.
4. He shortens his slacks.
5. The little boy can button his shirt.
6. He tries on a new sport jacket.
7. Can the little boy tie a necktie?
8. Edward fastens his belt.
9. Henry takes off his gloves.

10. The man unbuttons his robe.
11. Uncle Oscar needs new undershirts.
12. Let's exchange the shorts.
13. The soldier tips his hat.
14. Aunt Teresa is knitting a sweater for Christmas.
15. The tailor alters the vest.
16. We're renting tuxedos.
17. All of his employees wear uniforms.
18. Are you (*tú*) washing your socks?
19. The young lad laces his shoes for the first time.
20. The clerk wraps the slippers.

Cuestionario

Complete las siguientes frases:

1. Los pantalones azules, muy populares hoy, se llaman _____ .
2. Los enfermeros necesitan un _____ .
3. No me gusta llevar _____ .
4. Los trajes de moda incluyen un _____ .
5. Tengo frío a las manos. Necesito _____ .
6. En el invierno es necesario llevar _____ .
7. En Hawaii, los hombres llevan _____ chillones (*loud*).
8. Yo nunca llevo _____ .
9. Para los bailes formales, papá siempre se pone _____ .
10. Cuando regreso del trabajo, me saco el vestido y me pongo _____ .

Modelos de conversación

Repita y substituya las expresiones dadas:

1. **Necesito pantalones.**   I need slacks.
   _____ **una camisa.**   _____ a shirt.
   _____ **calcetines.**   _____ socks.
2. **¿Vende Ud. cinturones?**   Do you sell belts?
   ¿_____ **zapatillas?**   _____ slippers?
   ¿_____ **corbatas?**   _____ neckties?
3. **¿De qué tamaño son estos   What size are these shorts?
   calzoncillos?**

   ¿_____ **estas camisetas?**   _____ undershirts?
   ¿_____ **estas camisas?**   _____ shirts?
4. **Las corbatas son muy caras.**   The ties are very expensive.
   Las chaquetas _____ . The jackets _____ .
   Las batas _____ .   The robes _____ .

5.   ¿Cuánto vale este chaleco?   How much is this vest?
      ¿——————— traje de etiqueta?   ——————— tuxedo?
      ¿——————— abrigo?   ——————— overcoat?

Diálogo

Tendero:	**Bienvenido**, señor.	*(shopkeeper/welcome)*
Cliente:	Quiero comprar dos camisas.	
Tendero:	Tiene Ud. **suerte. Hoy llegaron** dos **docenas** de la **última moda.** Aquí están. ¿Cuál es **la medida** de su **cuello?**	*(lucky/today. . . arrived/dozen/latest style)* *(size/collar)*
Cliente:	Esas camisas rojas son para las mujeres. **Me disculpa,** pero **parece** que estoy en una tienda de modas femeninas.	*(you will forgive me)* *(it seems)*
Tendero:	Está Ud. **equivocado.** Mi tienda se especializa en ropa de caballeros que desean ser elegantes.	*(in error)*
Cliente:	Primero el pelo largo, ahora camisas de señora. **Seguramente** en el futuro **no se va** a poder distinguir entre los hombres y las mujeres.	*(surely/one is not going)*

Comprensión

1.   ¿Qué clase de camisas busca el cliente?
2.   ¿Por qué tiene suerte?
3.   Describa las camisas que vende el tendero.
4.   ¿Por qué se disculpa el cliente?
5.   ¿Ha tenido Ud. dificultad alguna vez de distinguir por las apariencias entre un hombre y una mujer?
6.   ¿Cómo se llaman los pantalones azules que llevan ambos sexos?
7.   ¿Qué prendas de vestir masculinas del último siglo no están de moda en nuestros días?
8.   Diga algo sobre las corbatas de hombres.

Vamos a hablar

A.   ¿Cree Ud. que la mayoría de los hombres quiere vestirse de moda? Dé las razones para su respuesta afirmativa o negativa.

B.   ¿Cuánto cuesta un par de zapatos de cuero para hombre? ¿Y de imitación de cuero? ¿Cuánto cuesta hoy una corbata de seda?

C.   Mire el dibujo y responda a las preguntas.

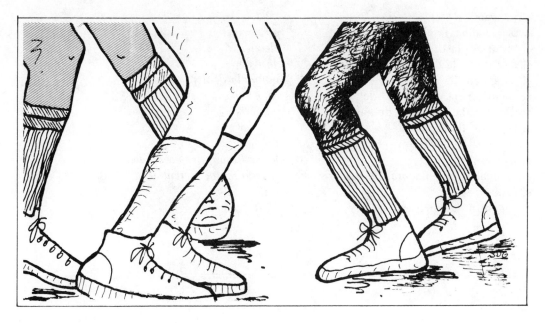

1. ¿A qué deporte juegan los jóvenes?
2. ¿Dónde están?
3. ¿Qué llevan en los pies?
4. Nombre Ud. tres deportes que requieren zapatos deportivos especiales.
5. Mencione Ud. las dos compañías más conocidas que venden zapatos deportivos.

Dichos y refranes

—Con mi esmoquin nuevo yo me veía muy distinguido ¿verdad?

—El hábito no hace el monje.

Oficios y profesiones

el (la) modelo	*model*
el planchador (la planchadora)	*presser*
el tintorero (la tintorera)	*cleaner*
el diseñador (la diseñadora)	*designer*
el paragüero (la paragüera)	*umbrella dealer*
el vendedor (la vendedora) de zapatos	*shoe salesman (woman)*
el director (la directora) de anuncios	*advertising manager*
el zapatero (la zapatera)	*cobbler*
el curtidor (la curtidora)	*tanner*
el mercero	*haberdasher, dry-goods dealer*
el alquilador (alguiladora) de tuxedos	*tuxedo rental merchant*
el sastre	*tailor*
el camisero (la camisera)	*shirt dealer*

Ejercicio

Escoja cinco palabras dadas y empleélas en oraciones interrogativas.

Repasito

Prueba—Escoja la traducción apropiada:

1.	los vaqueros		a.	socks
2.	el suéter		b.	pants, slacks
3.	la corbata		c.	shirt
4.	el cinturón		d.	suit
5.	los zapatos		e.	sport jacket
6.	los calcetines		f.	shoes
7.	la camisa		g.	belt
8.	la chaqueta sport		h.	sweater
9.	el traje		i.	blue jeans
10.	los pantalones		j.	necktie

*U*NIT 24

La tienda de ropa femenina

The Women's Clothing Store

Expresiones apropiadas

1.	probarse un vestido	*to try on a dress*
2.	ponerse los pantalones	*to put on the slacks*
3.	quitarse la falda	*to take off one's skirt*
4.	bordar la blusa	*to embroider one's blouse*
5.	dar una bufanda como regalo	*to give a scarf as a gift*
6.	coger su cartera (bolsa)	*to hold your wallet (purse)*
7.	chequear el largo de la enagua	*to check the length of your half slip*
8.	poner el chal alrededor del cuello	*to wrap the shawl around one's neck*
9.	coser una camisa de dormir	*to sew a nightgown*
10.	doblar el impermeable	*to fold the raincoat*
11.	tejer un suéter	*to knit a sweater*
12.	preferir panti-medias	*to prefer pantyhose*
13.	devolver el cinturón	*to return the belt*
14.	saludar con el pañuelo	*to wave your handkerchief*
15.	abrir el paraguas	*to open the umbrella*
16.	pedir medias de su talle	*to ask for stockings in your size*
17.	mirar los zapatos (las botas) en el espejo	*to look at the shoes (boots) in the mirror*
18.	secar el traje de baño	*to dry the bathing suit*
19.	hacer el dobladillo del traje de noche	*to hem the evening gown*
20.	colgar la chaqueta	*to hang up the jacket*

Variaciones del vocabulario

el bañador, el vestido de baño	*bathing suit*
la capa de agua, el chubasquero	*raincoat*
la chompa	*sweater*
el frac, el traje	*suit*
los pantalones flojos, los pantalones sueltos	*slacks*
el fustán	*slip*
la sombrilla	*umbrella*
el traje de dormir, la camisa de noche	*nightgown*
el vestido de noche	*evening gown*

Vocabulario en acción

Traduzca:

1. She wants to try on that dress.
2. Carlita puts on her new slacks.
3. She takes off her skirt.

4. My sister likes to embroider her blouses.
5. It's a good idea to give a scarf as a gift.
6. You *(Ud.)* must hold on to your wallet.
7. The woman often checks the length of her half slip.
8. My grandmother wears a shawl around her neck.
9. Are you *(tú)* sewing a nightgown?
10. She folds her raincoat carefully.
11. I'm knitting a sweater for my boyfriend.
12. She prefers pantyhose.
13. She returns the belt to the store.
14. The tourists on the ship wave their handkerchiefs.
15. It's raining. Let's open our umbrella.
16. It's important to ask for stockings in your size.
17. The customer looks at the boots in the mirror.
18. Do you *(tú)* dry your bathing suit?
19. We hem the evening gown.
20. She always hangs up her jacket.

Cuestionario

Complete las siguientes frases:

1. Para un baile formal la mujer lleva un _____ .
2. En la playa Margarita lleva _____ .
3. Para ir a la escuela me gusta llevar _____ y _____ .
4. Muchas mujeres llevan _____ en vez de faldas.
5. Me gusta dormir con _____ de seda.
6. En invierno es necesario llevar _____ .
7. Los pasajeros a bordo del vapor saludan con _____ .
8. Tengo frío; por eso llevo _____ .
9. Cuando llueve, usamos _____ y _____ .

Modelos de conversación

Repita y substituya las expresiones dadas:

1. **¿Tiene Ud. faldas de lana?**
   ¿_____ **un suéter de lana?**
   ¿_____ **vestidos de lana?**
2. **¿Pudiera mostrarme una enagua de nilón?**
   ¿_____ **medias de nilón?**
   ¿_____ **una blusa de nilón?**

Do you have wool skirts?
_____ a wool sweater?
_____ wool dresses?

Would you show me a nylon slip?

_____ nylon stockings?
_____ a nylon blouse?

3. **¿Son blusas de algodón?**   Are they cotton blouses?
    ¿_____ faldas _____?   _____ skirts?
    ¿_____ pantalones _____?   _____ slacks?
4. **Compro estas enaguas de seda.**   I'll buy these silk slips.
    _____estos trajes de noche de seda.   _____ evening gowns.
    _____estos vestidos de seda.   _____ dresses.
5. **¿Tiene un vestido de mi talla?**   Do you have a dress in my size?
    ¿_____ un vestido de noche _____ ?   _____ an evening gown _____ ?
    ¿_____ un traje de baño _____ ?   _____ a bathing suit _____ ?

Diálogo

Esposa:	¿Te gusta mi vestido nuevo?	
Esposo:	Sí, **me parece** muy elegante. **Te hace lucir** mucho más joven.	*(it looks to me/it makes you look)*
Esposa:	Gracias, **cariño**. Me lo voy a poner la próxima vez que **vayamos** al teatro .	*(dear)* *(we go)*
Esposo:	¡Qué coincidencia! Acabo de comprar dos **entradas** para el teatro.	*(tickets)*
Esposa:	¡Oh, qué fantástico! Voy a empezar a **vestirme** .	*(to get dressed)*
Esposo:	¡Buena idea! Las entradas son para mañana por la noche.	

Comprensión

1. ¿Qué acaba de comprar la esposa?
2. ¿Le gusta al marido el vestido?
3. ¿Cuándo piensa ella ponérselo?
4. ¿Por qué piensa el esposo que es buena idea vestirse con un día de anticipación?
5. ¿Le gusta a Ud. el teatro? ¿Por qué?

Dichos y refranes

—Te amo, y tú, ¿me amas?

—Shhh . . . . ¡Cállate, "Don Juan," las paredes tienen oídos!

Vamos a hablar

A. En Navidad se goza dando y recibiendo regalos, especialmente cuando uno los recibe. ¿Ha recibido Ud. alguna vez una prenda de vestir cuya moda o talla no le convenía? ¿Qué hizo?

B. La ropa que lleva la marca de un diseñador bien conocido es mucho más caro que la ropa "ordinaria." ¿Cuáles son las razones que tendría la gente en preferir gastar más para poseer productos de diseñador?

C. Imagínese que Ud. es una mujer ejecutiva (una mujer de negocios) haciendo la maleta para un viaje de negocios de dos días. Ud. sabe que tiene que asistir a dos reuniones importantes, a un cóctel y a un baile formal. Describa Ud. lo que empaquetaría en su maleta.

Oficios y profesiones

el (la) fabricante de vestidos   *dress manufacturer*
el peletero (la peletera)   *furrier*

el modisto (la modista)	dressmaker
la costurera	seamstress
el dependiente (la dependienta)	sales clerk
el sombrerero (la sombrerera)	hat maker
la modelo	model
el vendedora (la vendedora)	salesman (woman)
el cajero (la cajera)	cashier
el diseñador (la diseñadora) de ropa femenina	ladies' clothes designer

Ejercicio

Usando el vocabulario anterior, explique el trabajo de cada uno.

Repasito

Prueba—Escoja la traducción apropiada:

1. el vestido
2. la cartera
3. la falda
4. el paraguas
5. el traje de noche
6. la bufanda
7. el suéter
8. la blusa
9. las botas
10. la enagua

a. boots
b. blouse
c. dress
d. sweater
e. umbrella
f. skirt
g. wallet
h. scarf
i. evening gown
j. slip

UNIT 25

La joyería   *The Jewelry Shop*

Expresiones apropiadas

1.	gustarle a uno el color azul de la piedra	*to like the color blue of the stone*
2.	gustarle a uno el color violeta de la amatista	*to like the violet color of the amethyst*
3.	gustarle a uno el vario color del ópalo	*to like the many colors of the opal*
4.	gustarle a uno el color blanco de la perla	*to like the white color of the pearl*
5.	gustarle a uno el color verde del jade	*to like the green color of jade*
6.	no gustarle a uno el color rojo del rubí	*to dislike the red color of the ruby*
7.	no gustarle a uno el color amarillo del topacio	*to dislike the yellow color of the topaz*
8.	no gustarle a uno el brillo de la esmeralda	*to dislike the brilliance of the emerald*
9.	no gustarle a uno el fuego del zafiro	*to dislike the fire of the sapphire*
10.	no gustarle a uno las joyas de fantasía	*to dislike costume jewelry*
11.	premiar con un reloj de pulsera de oro	*to award a gold wristwatch*
12.	dar un anillo de compromiso	*to give an engagement ring*
13.	regalar un collar de plata	*to give a silver necklace as a gift*
14.	querer un brazalete (zarcillos) de oro	*to want a gold bracelet (earrings)*
15.	valorar el diamante	*to appraise the diamond*
16.	llevar un camafeo	*to wear a cameo*
17.	asegurar sus joyas	*to insure your jewels*
18.	escoger una montadura	*to select a setting*
19.	medir el anillo de boda	*to measure (for) a wedding ring*
20.	engarzar la joya en un anillo de platino	*to set the jewel in a platinum ring*

Variaciones del vocabulario

los aretes, los pendientes	*earrings*
la armadura	*setting*
el brillante	*diamond*
la pulsera	*bracelet*
la sortija de boda	*wedding ring*

Vocabulario en acción

Traduzca:

1. Jane likes the blue of the stone.
2. We like the violet of the amethyst.
3. They like the many colors of the opal.
4. My mother likes the white of the pearl.
5. The Chinese like the green of the jade.
6. Do you *(tú)* like the red of the ruby?
7. Everybody likes the color of the topaz.
8. Do you *(Uds.)* like the brilliance of the emerald?
9. I don't like the fire of the sapphire.
10. I dislike costume jewelry.
11. My professor was awarded a gold wristwatch.
12. Why don't you *(tú)* give her an engagement ring?
13. We give a silver necklace as a gift.
14. Many girls want gold bracelets.
15. Can you *(Ud.)* appraise the diamond?
16. Many women wear a cameo.
17. It is a good idea to insure your jewels.
18. It is very important to select a good setting.
19. Let's measure your finger for a wedding ring.
20. My girl friend wants a jewel set in platinum.

Cuestionario

Complete las siguientes frases:

1. Es costumbre dar _____ a la novia en su boda.
2. El _____ es azul y _____ es rojo.
3. Estas magníficas _____ son de Japón.
4. _____ es multicolor y tiene un fuego intenso.
5. En el traje tradicional español de la mujer, se ponen _____ en las orejas.
6. Muchos _____ se exportan de Africa.
7. _____ son menos caros que las joyas preciosas.
8. Muchas joyas chinas tienen piedras de _____ .
9. Elizabeth Taylor tiene un _____ solitario que vale dos millones de dólares.

Modelos de conversación

Repita y substituya las expresiones dadas:

1. **Odio las joyas de fantasía.**   I hate costume jewelry.
    ____ los zarcillos.   ____ earrings.
    ____ los anillos.   ____ rings.

2. **¿No sabe Ud. que un zafiro es azul?**   Don't you know a sapphire is blue?

    ¿——————— un rubí es rojo?   ——————— a ruby is red?

    ¿——————— el jade es verde?   ——————— jade is green?

3. **Ella está contenta con su anillo de**   She is happy with her engagement ring.
    compromiso.

    ——————— reloj de   ———————wristwatch.
    pulsera.

    ——————— camafeo.   ———————cameo.

4. **Quiero montar un topacio en este**   I want to set a topaz in this ring.
    anillo.

    ——————— una amatista ——— .   ——————— an amethyst ——————— .

    ——————— una perla ———— .   ——————— a pearl ——————— .

5. **¿Puedo cambiar el anillo de boda?**   May I exchange the wedding ring?

    ¿——————— el collar de perlas?   ——————— pearl necklace?

    ¿——————— el anillo de   ——————— platinum ring?
    platino?

Diálogo

Hombre: Acabo de darle una pulsera de oro a mi esposa **por ser**   *(because it is)*
            el día de nuestro aniversario.

Invitado: Ella **debe de ser** una mujer fantástica. **Estoy seguro**   *(guest/must be/*
            que la quieres muchísimo.   *I'm sure that)*

Hombre: ¡Ciertamente que sí! Y, de veras, me dio un regalo
            maravilloso.

Invitado: ¿Era un anillo? ¿Un reloj de pulsera?

Hombre: ¡No, no! Ella sabe bien que a mí no me gusta llevar
            joyas, así que más bien me regaló una pluma de oro.

Comprensión

1. ¿Qué acaba de darle a la esposa el hombre?
2. ¿Cuándo le da el señor la pulsera de oro a su esposa?
3. ¿Qué dice el invitado?
4. ¿Qué dijo el hombre de su esposa?
5. ¿Acertó el invitado correctamente qué regalo le dio a su esposo la mujer?
6. ¿Cómo demuestra el regalo de la esposa su consideración?

Vamos a hablar

A. ¿Cuántas piedras preciosas puede Ud. nombrar? Mencione el color de cada una de
    ellas.

B. Le gusta a Ud., en la ceremonia de bodas, la mutua entrega de anillos?

C. En nuestras ciudades hay vendedores ambulantes que ofrecen (según ellos) una
    ganga al público.

1. ¿Cree Ud. que estas clases de ventas son realmente gangas?
2. ¿Qué trata de vender este vendedor?
3. A veces hay amigos que se ofrecen a comprarle un brillante a un precio especial. ¿Es ésto buena idea? ¿Por qué piensa que a veces es favorable, y a veces no?
4. Nombre Ud. los artículos que tiene el vendedor en la mesita para la venta.
5. ¿Qué hace un policía cuando se enfrenta con los vendedores ambulantes?

Dichos y refranes

—Querido, cuando compres el brillante, ten cuidado de que no sea artificial.

—A mí no me dan gato por liebre.

Oficios y profesiones

el (la) orfebre	*goldsmith*
el calderero (la calderera)	*coppersmith*
el platero (la platera)	*silversmith*
el herrero (la herrera)	*blacksmith*
el vendedor (la vendedora) de joyas	*jewelry salesman (woman)*
el (la) diamantista	*diamond cutter, diamond merchant*
el pescador (la pescadora) de perlas	*pearl diver*
el diseñador (la diseñadora) de joyas	*jewelry designer*
el minero (la minera)	*miner*
el relojero (la relojera)	*watchmaker, watch repairman (woman)*

Ejercicio

Diga algo sobre el arte de los artesanos de México y del Perú.

Repasito

Prueba—Escoja la traducción apropiada:

1.	las joyas de fantasía	a.	emerald
2.	la montadura	b.	necklace
3.	el brazalete de plata	c.	gold wristwatch
4.	el camafeo	d.	sapphire
5.	el diamante	e.	earring
6.	el reloj pulsera de oro	f.	setting
7.	la esmeralda	g.	cameo
8.	el arete	h.	costume jewelry
9.	el zafiro	i.	silver bracelet
10.	el collar	j.	diamond

UNIT 26

La florería   *The Flower Shop*

Expresiones apropiadas

1.	hacer un ramo	to make a bouquet
2.	decorar con helechos	to decorate with ferns
3.	romper la maceta	to break the flowerpot
4.	plantar un cacto	to plant a cactus
5.	entregar la corona fúnebre	to deliver the funeral piece
6.	llevar el ramo de novia	to carry the bridal bouquet
7.	llevar una flor en el ojal	to wear a boutonniere
8.	poner las flores en un búcaro	to put the flowers in a vase
9.	hacer una corona de flores	to make a floral wreath
10.	echar el ramo de novia	to throw the bridal bouquet
11.	vender un jardín japonés	to sell a Japanese garden
12.	incluir una tarjeta de saludo	to include a greeting card
13.	hacerse florista	to become a florist
14.	enviar un corsage	to send a corsage
15.	entregar una caja de flores	to deliver a box of flowers
16.	oler las flores	to smell the flowers
17.	dar agua a las plantas	to water the plants
18.	trabajar en el invernadero	to work in the greenhouse
19.	sembrar las semillas	to plant the seeds
20.	cortar las flores·	to cut the flowers

Variaciones del vocabulario

el florero, el jarrón	vase
el hortelano	gardener (florist)
el invernáculo	greenhouse
el ramillete (de novia)	(bridal) bouquet
la simiente	seed
el tiesto	flowerpot

Vocabulario en acción

Traduzca:

1. I love to make bouquets.
2. We decorate the table with ferns.
3. Julio breaks the flowerpot.
4. The children plant a large cactus.
5. Can you *(tú)* deliver a funeral piece?
6. She's carrying a bridal bouquet of roses.
7. He wears a white boutonniere.
8. Can you *(Ud.)* put the flowers in a vase?
9. We're making a wreath of flowers.
10. She throws the bridal bouquet.

11. The florist sells many Japanese gardens.
12. Do you *(Ud.)* want to include a greeting card with the flowers?
13. Does she want to become a florist?
14. Are you sending your mother a corsage?
15. We deliver a box of flowers to the hospital.
16. I like to smell the flowers in a flower shop.
17. It is necessary to water these plants twice a week.
18. I want to work in a greenhouse.
19. They usually sow the seeds in March.
20. We cut the flowers.

Expresiones útiles

LAS FLORES (FLOWERS)

la amapola	*poppy*
la azalea	*azalea*
la begonia	*begonia*
el clavel	*carnation*
el clavelón	*marigold*
el crisantemo	*chrysanthemum*
el flox	*phlox*
la gardenia	*gardenia*
el geranio	*geranium*
el girasol	*sunflower*
el jacinto	*hyacinth*
el jazmín	*jasmine*
la lila	*lilac*
el lirio, la azucena	*lily*
la margarita	*daisy*
la nochebuena, la flor de Pascua	*poinsettia*
la orquídea	*orchid*
la petunia	*petunia*
la rosa	*rose*
la trompeta	*daffodil*
el tulipán	*tulip*
la violeta	*violet*
la zinia	*zinnia*

Ejercicio

Mencione una flor cuyo color corresponda con uno de los colores siguientes:

1. blanco
2. violeta

3. amarillo
4. rojo
5. rosado
6. azul
7. anaranjado
8. multicolor

Cuestionario

Complete las siguientes frases:

1. Para un funeral, se envía _____ .
2. _____ crecen en el desierto.
3. Las novias llevan _____ .
4. El novio lleva _____ .
5. Para que crezcan las flores, es necesario plantar _____ .
6. El hombre que arregla las flores se llama _____ .
7. Las plantas crecen bien en _____ .
8. Cada mes yo envío _____ de cristal con una sola rosa roja.
9. El florista pone la planta en _____ .

Modelos de conversación

Repita y substituya las expresiones dadas:

1. **¿Puede hacerme Ud. un ramo de flores?**   Can you make me a bouquet?

   ¿_____ corsage?   _____ corsage?
   ¿_____ ramo de novia?   _____ bridal bouquet?

2. **Por favor, mande esta caja de flores a mi casa.**   Please send this box of flowers to my home.

   _____ planta ____ .   _____ plant _____ .
   _____ maceta ____ .   _____ flowerpot _____ .

3. **Las flores crecen bien en la primavera.**   Flowers grow well in the spring.
   Las semillas _____ .   Seeds _____ .
   Los helechos _____ .   Ferns _____ .

4. **El florista nos da una corona.**   The florist gives us a wreath.
   _____ flor.   _____ flower.
   _____ flor on el ojal.   _____ boutonniere.

5.   **¿Cuánto vale este búcaro?**   How much is this vase?
     ¿——————— **jardín japonés?**   ——————— Japanese garden?
     ¿——————— **invernadero?**   ——————— greenhouse?

Diálogo

Jardinero: ¡Qué **placer** verla de nuevo, señora Cordero!   *(pleasure)*
                  ¿En qué puedo servirla?

Sra. Cordero: Estoy de muy mal **humor**. La planta recién   *(mood)*
                  comprada está **muerta**.   *(dead)*

Jardinero: ¿Cómo? ¿Está muerta? Es de las mejores
                  plantas que tenemos en nuestro invernadero.

Sra. Cordero: **Después de seguir** sus instrucciones **al pie de la**   *(after following/to the*
                  letra, me encuentro con la **pérdida** de la   *letter/I am faced with/*
                  planta. Cada noche **la pongo con cariño** bajo   *loss/I place it with*
                  una lámpara de rayos ultravioleta.   *care)*

Jardinero: ¡Lámpara de rayos ultravioleta! Con razón está
                  muerta.

Sra. Cordero: ¿Y para qué decirme entonces que **le hace falta**   *(it needs)*
                  mucho sol?

Comprensión

1.   ¿Por qué está de mal humor la señora Cordero?
2.   ¿De dónde viene la planta?
3.   ¿Dónde pone la señora Cordero la planta todas las noches?
4.   ¿Por qué está muerta la planta?
5.   ¿Para qué sirve un invernadero?

Vamos a hablar

A.   La Pascua Florida, que llega siempre en la primavera, es la fiesta de las flores,
         como lo dice su nombre.

     1.   ¿Qué hace su familia en la Pascua Florida?
     2.   Generalmente, ¿qué sirve la familia en la casa?
     3.   ¿Hay flores? ¿Quién y a quién las regala?
     4.   ¿Qué flores se compran en el verano? ¿En el invierno?

B. Diga algo sobre este anuncio de flores.

Florista Delgado

ARREGLOS FLORALES/RAMILLETES DE FLORES

Servidor de Vd. para toda ocasion

666-3566   (24 horas)

Dichos y refranes

—Deseo felicitar a mi madre.

—Diselo con flores.

Oficios y profesiones

el diseñador (la diseñadora) de flores   *floral designer*

el (la) florista	*florist*
el agricultor (la agricultora)	*farmer*
el jardinero (la jardinera), el horticultor (la horticultora)	*gardener*
el hacendado (la hacendada)	*farm owner*
el botánico (la botánica)	*botanist*

Ejercicio

Haga oraciones con los oficios mencionados.

Repasito

Prueba—Escoja la traducción apropiada:

1.	las semillas	a.	flower
2.	el jardín	b.	bouquet
3.	el invernadero	c.	florist
4.	el búcaro	d.	wreath
5.	la planta	e.	greenhouse
6.	la flor	f.	flowerpot
7.	una corona	g.	garden
8.	la maceta	h.	plant
9.	el florista	i.	vase
10.	el ramo	j.	seeds

UNIT 27

La tienda de muebles, de alfombras y de efectos eléctricos

The Furniture, Carpet and Appliance Store

Expresiones apropiadas

1.	forrar (tapizar) el sofá	*to cover (to upholster) the sofa*
2.	acostarse en el colchón	*to lie on the mattress*
3.	enchufar la lámpara	*to plug in the lamp*
4.	limpiar la alfombra	*to clean the rug*
5.	reparar la nevera	*to repair the refrigerator*
6.	buscar un televisor a colores	*to look for a color television set*
7.	regalar un lavaplatos	*to give a dishwasher as a present*
8.	garantizar una secadora de ropa	*to guarantee a clothes dryer*
9.	usar la aspiradora	*to use the vacuum cleaner*
10.	encerar la mesita de la sala	*to wax the cocktail table*
11.	hacer la cama	*to make the bed*
12.	regalar una secadora de pelo	*to give a hair dryer as a gift*
13.	apagar la afeitadora	*to shut off the razor*
14.	dañar la silla	*to damage the chair*
15.	pintar la mecedora	*to paint the rocking chair*
16.	abrir el gas (de la estufa)	*to turn on the gas (of the stove)*
17.	sentarse bajo una lámpara ultravioleta	*to sit under an ultraviolet lamp*
18.	mostrar una vajilla de porcelana	*to show a set of china*
19.	sentarse en un sillón	*to sit in an armchair*
20.	escribir en una máquina eléctrica	*to type on an electric typewriter*

Variaciones del vocabulario

el diván	*sofa*
la hornilla	*stove*
la loza	*china*
la refrigeradora	*refrigerator*
la silla de brazos	*armchair*

Vocabulario en acción

Traduzca:

1. My grandmother is upholstering her old sofa.
2. My husband and I lie on the mattress in the store.
3. She plugs in the lamp.
4. I clean my rugs every spring.
5. The mechanic is repairing our refrigerator.
6. Antonio is looking for a color television set.
7. We're giving our mother a new dishwasher as a gift.
8. They guarantee this clothes dryer.
9. My husband uses the vacuum cleaner every Saturday morning.
10. We wax the cocktail table.

11. Are you (*tú*) making the bed, Teresa?
12. My son uses the hair dryer every morning.
13. He shuts off the razor.
14. That man is damaging my chair.
15. I'm going to paint these rocking chairs.
16. Do you (*Ud.*) turn on the gas of the stove?
17. She is sitting under an ultraviolet lamp.
18. The shop is showing a set of china.
19. My husband sits in the armchair each night.
20. Do you (*Uds.*) know how to type with an electric typewriter?

Cuestionario

Complete las siguientes frases:

1. Todas las noches miramos _____ .
2. Hay demasiado polvo (*dust*) en este cuarto. ¿Dónde está _____?
3. Es casi indispensable _____ para el estudiante de la Universidad.
4. No me molestan los platos sucios. Tengo un _____ .
5. Voy a comprar _____ para mi hermana porque tiene el pelo muy largo.
6. Mi padre siempre se sienta en _____ .
7. Los jóvenes de hoy duermen en _____ de agua.
8. Muchas personas prefieren sentarse en una _____ mientras leen el periódico.
9. Descansa y pon los pies sobre _____ .
10. Las bebidas están en _____ .

Modelos de conversación

Repita y substituya las expresiones dadas:

1. **El vendedor nos enseña una mesa.** The salesman shows us a table.
   _____ silla. _____ chair.
   _____ cama. _____ bed.
2. **La mesa está vieja. Vamos a comprar una nueva.** The table is old. Let's buy a new one.
   La nevera _____ . The refrigerator _____ .
   La alfombra _____ . The carpet _____ .
3. **Estoy buscando un televisor a colores.** I'm looking for a color TV.
   _____ una lámpara ultravioleta. _____ an ultraviolet lamp.
   _____ una secadora de ropa. _____ a clothes dryer.
4. **Mi estufa no funciona.** My stove doesn't work.
   Mi lámpara _____ . My lamp _____ .
   Mi afeitadora _____ . My razor _____ .

5. **Cómpreme un lavaplatos.**   Buy me a dishwasher.
    _____**una secadora de ropa.**   _____ clothes dryer.
    _____**una aspiradora.**   _____ vacuum cleaner.

Diálogo

Dependiente:	**¿En qué puedo servirla,** señora? Tal vez puedo venderle un sofá estilo mediterráneo.	*(how can I help you?)*
Cliente:	No señor, necesito una nevera nueva.	
Dependiente:	Tenemos **algunos** modelos de **marca** Westinghouse, General Electric y Admiral.	*(some/brand)*
Cliente:	¿Son **caros o baratos?**	*(expensive or cheap)*
Dependiente:	Se venden a buenos precios.	
Cliente:	¿Puede Ud. **envíarmelo** hoy mismo? Aquí tiente mi tarjeta de crédito.	*(to send it to me)*
Dependiente:	Claro que sí. Pero dígame, ¿Por qué no puede usar ya su refrigerador viejo?	
Cliente:	Por falta de pago.	
Dependiente:	**¡Con razón tiene prisa!**	*(no wonder you're in a hurry!)*

Comprensión

1. ¿Qué compra la cliente?
2. ¿Por qué necesita una nevera?
3. ¿Qué modelos vende el dependiente en esta tienda?
4. ¿Son caras las neveras nuevas?
5. ¿Cómo va a pagar la cliente?
6. ¿Funciona bien la nevera en su casa?

Vamos a hablar

A. Actualmente se presentan muchos problemas sociales con la liberación de la mujer, especialmente cuando una madre se ausenta del hogar para ir a trabajar. Hay muchos casos en que los hombres ayudan en los quehaceres domésticos, mientras que sus esposas trabajan practicando sus carreras. (Esta idea es rechazada por los hombres españoles). ¿Ayuda su papá a su mamá en los quehaceres domésticos?

B. ¿Qué piensa Ud. del derecho que tiene un hombre de ir a la corte para reclamar dinero de su esposa rica que pide divorcio?

C.   Preguntas

1. ¿Cómo se planea una mudanza (*move*)?
2. Describa su última mudanza.
3. ¿Qué protección tienen los consumidores contra el daño de los muebles?
4. ¿Puede Ud. adivinar cuánto cuesta una mudanza desde San Franciso a Los Angeles y desde Nueva York a Miami?

Dichos y refranes

—¡Caramba! Con los precios tan altos, hay que comprar cuando el almacén tenga baratillo.

—Hay que bailar al son que le toquen.

Oficos y profesiones

el (la) comerciante de muebles	*furniture dealer*
el vendedor (la vendedora) de antigüedades	*antique dealer*
el (la) alfombrista	*carpet layer*
el (la) ebanista	*cabinet maker*
el (la) mueblista	*furniture maker*
el empapelador (la empapeladora)	*paper hanger*
el carpintero (la carpintera)	*carpenter*
el reparador (la reparadora) de aparatos	*appliance repairman (woman)*
el (la) negociante de aparatos	*appliance dealer*
el mecánico (la mecánica) de televisión	*television repairman (woman)*

Ejercicio

¿Puede Ud. nombrar cinco oficios más que sean de las categorías de muebles, alfombras y efectos eléctricos?

Repasito

Prueba—Escoja la traducción apropiada:

1.	la alfombra	a.	razor
2.	el lavaplatos	b.	mattress
3.	la loza	c.	china
4.	la secadora de pelo	d.	television set
5.	la estufa	e.	stove
6.	la mecedora	f.	refrigerator
7.	la afeitadora	g.	hair dryer
8.	la nevera	h.	rocking chair
9.	el televisor	i.	dishwasher
10.	el colchón	j.	rug

UNIT 28

La ferretería y la madadería

The Hardware Store and the Lumberyard

Expresiones apropiadas

1.	usar una sierra	*to use a saw*
2.	golpear los clavos con un martillo	*to hit the nails with a hammer*
3.	poner tornillos en la bisagra	*to put screws in the hinge*
4.	cortar la madera con un formón	*to cut the wood with a chisel*
5.	hacer un agujero con un taladro eléctrico	*to make a hole with an electric drill*
6.	pintar las paredes	*to paint the walls*
7.	limpiar las brochas con trementina	*to clean the paintbrushes with turpentine*
8.	poner el papel embreado en el tejado	*to put tarpaper on the roof*
9.	necesitar una llave	*to need a wrench*
10.	escoger el papel de empapelar	*to select the wallpaper*
11.	serrar los tablones	*to saw the planks*
12.	pegar la madera (laminada)	*to glue the wood (plywood)*
13.	verificar el nivel del suelo	*to check the level of the floor*
14.	subir por una escalera	*to climb a ladder*
15.	reemplazar las tejas	*to replace the roof tiles*
16.	afilar el hacha	*to sharpen the axe*
17.	cementar los ladrillos	*to cement the bricks*
18.	llevar la arena (el concreto) en una carretilla	*to carry the sand (the cement) in a wheelbarrow*
19.	medir con una regla	*to measure with a ruler*
20.	poner las herramientas en la caja de herramientas	*to put the tools in the toolbox*

Variaciones del vocabulario

el escoplo, el cincel	*chisel*
la inglesa	*wrench*
la madera contrachapada, el chapeado	*plywood*
el papel pintado, el empapelado	*wallpaper*
el pincel	*paintbrush*

Vocabulario en acción

Traduzca:

1. Ana is using a saw.
2. The boy hammers the nails with a hammer.
3. Do you (*Ud.*) put the screws in the hinge?
4. It is necessary to cut the wood with a chisel.
5. He makes a hole with an electric drill.

6. My wife paints the walls every year.
7. We always clean the paintbrushes with turpentine.
8. He puts tarpaper on the roof of his house.
9. I need a wrench.
10. Tomorrow we're going to select wallpaper for our dining room.
11. The neighbor's son saws the planks.
12. He glues the plywood.
13. Do you (*Uds.*) check the level of the floor?
14. He is afraid to climb the ladder.
15. Let's replace the tiles of the roof.
16. I always sharpen the axe before I use it.
17. We cement the bricks.
18. She carries the sand in a wheelbarrow.
19. It is a good idea to measure the wall with a ruler.
20. We put the tools in the toolbox.

Expresiones útiles

LOS ARBOLES (TREES)

el abedul	*birch*
el abeto rojo del norte	*spruce*
el álamo	*poplar*
el arce	*maple*
el bálsamo	*balsam*
el bambú	*bamboo*
la caoba	*mahogany*
el castaño	*chestnut*
el cedro	*cedar*
la cicuta	*hemlock*
el cornejo	*dogwood*
el chopo de Virginia	*cottonwood*
el ébano	*ebony*
el eucalipto	*eucalyptus*
el haya	*beech*
la magnolia	*magnolia*
la mimosa	*mimosa*
el nogal	*walnut*
el olivo	*olive*
el olmo	*elm*
la pacana	*pecan*
la palma	*palm*
el pinabete	*fir*
el pino	*pine*

el roble	*oak*
el sauce llorón	*weeping willow*
la secoya	*sequoia*
el serbal de los cazadores	*mountain ash*
el sicómoro	*sycamore*
el tilo	*linden*

Ejercicio

Escoja los árboles que se relacionen con los lugares geográficos siguientes:

1. Virginia
2. Vermont
3. el Japón
4. el Ecuador
5. Alemania
6. el Brasil
7. España
8. Italia
9. Oregón
10. Georgia
11. la Florida
12. Nueva York

Cuestionario

Complete las siguientes frases:

1. Muchas casas están construídas de _____ .
2. Tengo el martillo, pero no puedo encontrar _____ .
3. Los mecánicos siempre utilizan _____ en su trabajo.
4. Para cementar los ladrillos se emplea _____ .
5. Las maderas se cortan con _____ .
6. Los leñadores (*woodsmen*) cortan los árboles con _____ .
7. En el tejado de mi casa hay _____ .
8. Los pintores usan _____ para limpiar la pintura de las manos.
9. Se hacen los agujeros (*holes*) con _____ .

Modelos de conversación

Repita y substituya las expresiones dadas:

1. **Los ladrillos protegen la casa.**   Bricks protect the house.
   El papel embreado protege _____ .   Tarpaper protects _____ .
   Las tejas protegen _____ .   Roof tiles protect _____ .

2. **La caja de herramientas contiene llaves.**   The toolbox contains wrenches.

_____ **un martillo.**   _____ a hammer.

_____ **brochas.**   _____ paintbrushes.

3. **No puedo hallar los clavos.**   I can't find the nails.

_____ **tornillos.**   _____ screws.

_____ **formones.**   _____ chisels.

4. **Para Navidad, papacito va a recibir un taladro.**   Dad is going to receive a drill as a Christmas present.

_____ **hacha.**   _____ an axe _____ .

_____ **nivel.**   _____ a level _____ .

5. **¿Tiene Ud. en venta papel de empapelar?**   Do you have wallpaper for sale?

¿_____ **tablones?**   _____ planks _____?

¿_____ **madera laminada?**   _____ plywood _____?

Diálogo

Maderero:	¿Qué necesita, señor?	*(lumberman)*
Campesino:	Unas **tablas**, cinco libras de clavos y un litro de barniz para mi **infeliz** mujer.	*(farmer/boards)* *(poor)*
Maderero:	¿Es alta su mujer? ¿Es **gorda**? ¿Cuántas libras **pesa**?	*(fat)* *(does she weigh)*
Campesino:	Es alta y delgadita. ¿Por qué me pregunta tantas cosas personales?	
Maderero:	Necesito saber **la medida** de su mujer para darle tablas suficientemente grandes para construir su **ataúd**.	*(the size)* *(coffin)*
Campesino:	¡**No sea** Ud. loco! Gracias a Dios, mi mujer **aún** vive. ¡Las tablas son para **construir** un gabinete en la cocina!	*(don't be/still)* *(build)*

Comprensión

1. ¿Qué busca el campesino?
2. ¿Cuáles son las tres preguntas personales del maderero?
3. ¿Cómo reacciona el esposo?
4. ¿Por qué necesita tablas?
5. ¿Qué va a construir Ud. este año?

Vamos a hablar

A. Narre Ud. un episodio de su trabajo en casa, mencionando todas las herramientas que utilizó para realizar el proyecto.

B. Haga una oración con todos los materiales de construcción mencionados en el anuncio. (*Plywood* es un anglicismo.)

Buenvista Lumber

858-6239

MATERIALES DE CONSTRUCCION

- **Maderas**
- **Puertas**
- **Plywood**
- **Cabilla**

- **Pintura**
- **Herramientas**
- **Cemento**
- **Bloques**

- **Arena y piedra**

Abierto el sábado

Dichos y refranes

—Amorcito, tenemos que pintar la cocina antes de Navidad.

—Sí, querida. Mañana, manos a la obra. Ahora voy a soñar con los angelitos.

Oficios y profesiones

el (la) astronauta	*astronaut*
el operador (la operadora) de computadoras	*computer operator*
el navegante (la naveganta)	*navigator*
el ingeniero (la ingeniera) del espacio	*space engineer*
el piloto de pruebas	*test pilot*
el meteorólogo (la meteoróloga)	*meteorologist*
el ingeniero (la ingeniera) de seguridad	*safety engineer*
el físico (la física)	*physicist*
el ingeniero (la ingeniera) de comunicaciones	*communications engineer*
el hombre rana	*frogman*
la tripulación de tierra	*ground crew*
el personal médico	*medical personnel*
el mecánico (la mecánica) de aviación	*aviation mechanic*
el ingeniero (la ingeniera) de radar	*radar engineer*
el planeador (la planeadora) de vuelo	*flight planner*
el anunciador (la anunciadora) de control de la misión	*mission-control announcer*

Ejercicio

Describa los preparativos que se hacen en Cabo Cañaveral para una misión en el espacio.

Repasito

Prueba—Escoja la traducción apropiada:

1.	el taladro	a.	nail
2.	la llave	b.	chisel
3.	la brocha	c.	sand
4.	la sierra	d.	drill
5.	el concreto	e.	tarpaper
6.	el formón	f.	paintbrush
7.	el martillo	g.	saw
8.	el papel embreado	h.	wrench
9.	el clavo	i.	cement
10.	la arena	j.	hammer

UNIT 29

El restaurante   The Restaurant

Expresiones apropiadas

1.	ir a un restaurante	*to go to a restaurant*
2.	reservar una mesa	*to reserve a table*
3.	llamar al camarero (a la camarera)	*to call the waiter (waitress)*
4.	leer el menú	*to read the menu*
5.	ver la lista de los vinos	*to look at the wine list*
6.	seleccionar la especialidad	*to choose the dinner special*
7.	escoger el plato de mariscos	*to pick the seafood dish*
8.	pedir sopa y el plato principal	*to order soup and the entrée*
9.	comer pan y mantequilla	*to eat bread and butter*
10.	beber (tomar) un vaso de agua	*to drink a glass of water*
11.	disfrutar de las tapas y del postre	*to enjoy the appetizers and the dessert*
12.	tomar un coctel	*to have a cocktail*
13.	servir el vino a los invitados	*to serve the wine to the guests*
14.	preferir la cerveza fría	*to prefer cold beer*
15.	brindar por los recién casados	*to drink a toast for the newlyweds*
16.	saborear la bebida y la comida	*to savor the drink and the meal*
17.	tomar café (té)	*to have coffee (tea)*
18.	pasar (tener) un rato agradable	*to have a good time*
19.	pagar la cuenta	*to pay the check*
20.	dejar una propina	*to leave a tip*

Variaciones del vocabulario

el café solo	*black coffee*
el caldo, el consomé	*broth (soup)*
el entremés	*appetizer*

Vocabulario en acción

Traduzca:

1. My friend and I are going to a Spanish restaurant.
2. She reserves a table.
3. He calls the waiter.
4. They read the menu.
5. I look at the wine list.
6. My wife always chooses the dinner special.
7. Your sister picks the seafood dish.
8. Ricardo orders soup, doesn't he?
9. The children eat bread and butter.
10. María asks for a glass of water.
11. The young girl enjoys the dessert.
12. They have a cocktail before dinner.
13. The waiter serves the wine to the guests.
14. My father prefers a cold beer instead of wine.
15. Juan drinks a toast to the newlyweds.
16. I always savor my drink and my meal.
17. Do you (*Uds.*) have hot coffee?
18. We all have a good time at the restaurant.
19. My friend pays the check.
20. He leaves a tip for the waitress.

Cuestionario

Complete las siguientes frases:

1. Llame al restaurante para reservar una _____ .
2. Sirven muy buenas _____ en esta restaurante.
3. Deseo tomar un coctel. ¡Camarero, _____ por favor!
4. Se me cayó _____ al suelo. Camarero, ¿me puede traer otro?
5. Las comidas están descritas en _____ .
7. Con el postre me gustaría tomar _____ .
8. La señora paga _____ y deja _____ .

Modelos de conversación

Repita y substituya las expresiones dadas:

1. **Tomo té.**   I drink tea.
   _____ **café.**   _____ coffee.
   _____ **agua.**   _____ water.
2. **Voy a dejar las tapas.**   I'll skip the appetizers.
   _____ **la sopa.**   _____ soup.
   _____ **el postre.**   _____ dessert.
3. **Queremos un coctel.**   We want a cocktail.
   _____ **vino.**   _____ wine.
   _____ **cerveza.**   _____ beer.
4. **Tengo ganas de comer el plato de**   I feel like eating the seafood dish.
   mariscos.
   _____ **la**   _____ the special.
   especialidad.
   _____ **pan y**   _____ bread and butter.
   mantequilla.
5. **El precio del vino es atroz.**   The price of the wine is atrocious.
   _____ **de las tapas** _____ .   _____ appetizers _____ .
   _____ **de los mariscos** _____ .   _____ seafood _____ .

Diálogo

Señorita:	Por favor, **tráigame** una sopa **cualquiera.**	*(bring me/any)*
Camarero:	Aquí tiene su sopa de cebolla. Es la especialidad de la casa.	
Señorita:	Muchas gracias. ¡Qué bien **huele!**	*(it smells)*
Camarero:	¡Cuánto **me alegro!** Nuestro restaurante **se esmera** **por** servir bien a sus clientes.	*(I'm happy)* *(take pains to)*
Señorita:	¡Ah! ¡Qué horror! Hay un pelo en la sopa.	
Camarero:	Pues, la **culpa** no es nuestra. Yo soy **calvo** y el **cocinero** también.	*(blame/bald)* *(chef)*

Comprensión

1. ¿Qué pide la cliente?
2. ¿Qué le trae el camarero?
3. ¿De qué se queja la señorita?
4. ¿Qué responde el camarero?
5. ¿Cuál es su restaurante favorita?
6. Por lo general, ¿cuánto da Ud. de propina?

Vamos a hablar

A. Haga Ud. un diálogo para las dos escenas.

B. ¿Ha ido Ud. a un club nocturno? ¿Cuál? ¿Qué celebraba Ud. en esa ocasión? ¿Qué bebió? ¿Cuál fue su plato favorito? ¿Quiénes estaban sentados en la mesa? Describa el espectáculo (*show*). ¿Se acuerda cuánto fue la cuenta y quién la pagó? ¿Le gustaría volver al mismo club? ¿Por qué?

Dichos y refranes

 —¿Comiendo ahora? En la cena no vas a probar bocado.

 —El comer y el rascar, todo es empezar.

Oficios y profesiones

el anfitrión (la anfitriona)	*host (hostess)*
el tabernero (la tabernera)	*tavern keeper*
el socio (la socia) de un club	*club member*
el vendedor (la vendedora) de víveres	*food retailer*
el comerciante (la comercianta) de licores	*liquor dealer*
el director (la directora) de orquesta	*band director*
los músicos	*musicians*
el (la) cantante	*singer*
el cantinero (la cantinera)	*bartender*
el cocinero (la cocinera)	*chef*
el mayordomo (la mayordoma)	*steward*
el camarero, el mozo	*waiter*
la moza, la camarera	*waitress*
el lavador (la lavadora) de platos	*dishwasher*
el inspector (la inspectora) de sanidad	*health inspector*

Ejercicio

Defina el oficio de cada uno de los empleados de un cabaret o casino.

Repasito

Prueba—Escoja la traducción apropiada:

1.	el pan	a.	appetizer
2.	la mantequilla	b.	waiter
3.	la cuenta	c.	bread
4.	la lista de vinos	d.	butter
5.	la propina	e.	entrée
6.	la comida	f.	soup
7.	la sopa	g.	wine list
8.	el plato principal	h.	check
9.	el camarero	i.	tip
10.	la tapa	j.	meal

UNIT 30

Deportes y diversiones

Sports and Amusements

El béisbol (Baseball)

1.	el árbitro (la árbitra)	*umpire*
2.	el bate	*bat*
3.	el béisbol	*baseball*
4.	el cobertizo	*dugout*
5.	el estadio	*stadium*
6.	el jonrón	*homerun*
7.	el jugador (la jugadora)	*player*
8.	el lanzador (la lanzadora)	*pitcher*
9.	el receptor (la receptora)	*catcher*
10.	el strike	*strike*

Ejercicios

A. *Traduzca:*

1. The pitcher throws *(tira)* the baseball.
2. The baseball player bats *(batea)* the ball.
3. The umpira yells *(grita)* .
4. The catcher catches *(coge)* the ball.
5. The baseball player makes a homerun.

B. **Dibuje Ud.** un equipo de jugadores de béisbol en el **rombal** o, si puede, **corte** una foto del periódico, **mostrando** al equipo en acción. **Ponga** en español cómo **se dicen** las distintas posiciones de los jugadores.

(draw)
(diamond/cut)
(showing/put)
(are said)

El balompié, el fútbol (Football)

1.	el árbitro (la árbitra)	*referee*
2.	el atajo	*tackle*
3.	el caer del balón	*fumble*
4.	el casco	*helmet*
5.	el futbolista	*football player*
6.	el mozo del agua, al aguador	*water boy*
7.	el poste (de la meta)	*goalpost*
8.	la raya (de la meta)	*goal line*
9.	el tanto ganado	*touchdown*
10.	el uniforme	*uniform*

Ejercicios

A. *Traduzca:*

1. The football player puts on *(se pone)* his helmet.
2. The athlete reaches *(alcanza)* the goal line.

3. He makes a touchdown.
4. The referee calls it a fumble.
5. The water boy gives water to the football players.

B.   Haga Ud. el papel de anunciador(a) para la **emisora**   *(play the role/*
WABC. Se trata de un **partido** de fútbol entre su escuela   *radio station/game)*
y la escuela rival. Usando las expresiones que siguen,
hable Ud. del partido: anunciador(a) de deportes,
micrófono, la estación (o emisora). ¿Quién va **ganando**?   *(winning)*

El basquetbol (Basketball)

1. **el banco**   *bench*
2. **el jugador (la jugadora) de**   *basketball player*
    basquetbol
3. **el baloncesto**   *basketball*
4. **la cesta**   *basket*
5. **el empate**   *tie score*
6. **el entrenador (la entrenadora), el**   *coach*
    coach
7. **el gimnasio**   *gymnasium*
8. **el marcador**   *scoreboard*
9. **el punto**   *point*
10. **el sucio**   *foul*

Ejercicios

A. *Traduzca:*

1. He throws the ball into the basket.
2. It's a foul.
3. The basketball players are on the bench.
4. The coach is in the gymnasium.
5. It's a tie score.

B.   Muchas escuelas y universidades tienen equipos ex-
celentes de baloncesto. Los **torneos** de NCAA y de NIT   *(tournaments)*
atraen a mucha gente, vieja y joven. ¿Asiste Ud. a los   *(attract)*
partidos de baloncesto de su escuela? ¿Participa **de vez**
en cuando? ¿Cuántas personas se necesitan para un   *(from time to time)*
equipo? ¿Dónde vió el último partido? ¿Cuál fué el
mejor partido que ha visto Ud.? Discuta este tópico,
contestando las preguntas formuladas.

El tenis (Tennis)

1.	la cancha de tenis	court
2.	el cero, el nada	love
3.	el juego de dobles	doubles
4.	el juego de simples	singles
5.	la partida	set
6.	la pelota de tenis	tennis ball
7.	la raqueta	racquet
8.	la red	net
9.	el tenis	tennis shoes, tennis
10.	el (la) tenista	tennis player

Ejercicios

A. *Traduzca:*

1. We play doubles every week.
2. The tennis player serves the ball.
3. She returns the ball.
4. The ball hits (*da contra*) the net.
5. The score was 40-love.

B. ¿Sabe Ud. jugar al tenis? ¿Cuándo aprendió? ¿Quiénes son los mejores jugadores de hoy día? **Desarrolle** estas ideas. *(develop)*

El golf (Golf)

1.	el (la) golfista	golfer
2.	el muchacho (la muchacha) de golf	caddy
3.	la pelota de golf	golf ball
4.	los palos de golf	golf clubs
5.	el agujero (entrar en el agujero con un solo golpe)	hole (hole in one)
6.	el tee	tee
7.	la trampa de arena	sand trap
8.	el cubierto de césped	green
9.	el terreno	fairway
10.	el cochecillo (la carreta) de golf	golf cart

Ejercicios

A. *Traduzca:*

1. The caddy gives the golfer a golf club.

2. She puts the golf ball on the tee.
3. The golfer looks at the golf ball.
4. The ball goes into the sand trap.
5. The golfer hits (*dar un golpe*) the golf ball.

B. Si hay un deporte que **atrae** a gente de todas las   *(attracts)*
edades, lo es ciertamente el golf. Entre las **personas**
mayores parece ser el más popular. En algunas partes   *(adults)*
del país, donde el clima invita a ello, se construyen
hermosas casas residenciales **alrededor o al lado de** un   *(surrounding or at*
campo de golf, verde y **ondulado**. ¿Quiénes son los más   *the side / hilly)*
famosos jugadores de golf hoy día? ¿Ha servido Ud. al-
guna vez de caddy? Describa algo cómico que pasó en
un campo de golf. Dé su **parecer** sobre el mini-golf.   *(opinion)*

El juego de bolos (Bowling)

1.	**el anotador**	*scoresheet*
2.	**la bolera**	*bowling alley*
3.	**los bolos**	*pins*
4.	**el canal**	*gutter*
5.	**el golpe de fortuna, el «strike»**	*strike*
6.	**el jugador (la jugadora) de bolos**	*bowler*
7.	**el libre, el «spare»**	*spare*
8.	**la línea de sucia**	*foul line*
9.	**la máquina de poner los bolos**	*pinsetter*
10.	**la pelota de bolos**	*bowling ball*

Ejercicios

A. *Traduzca:*

1. The bowler makes a strike.
2. The bowler makes a spare.
3. She gets 300—a perfect score.
4. The ball goes into the gutter.
5. The ball misses the pins.

B. El juego de bolos es un deporte popular de la gente
trabajadora. Hay numerosas **ligas**, de hombres y muje-   *(working/leagues)*
res, y hay campeonatos, que se transmiten por televi-
sión. Algunos jugadores **lucen** camisas con el nombre de   *(display)*
la liga a que **pertenecen**. ¿Participa Ud. en este deporte?   *(they belong)*
¿Adónde va para jugar? ¿Ha hecho mucho progreso?
¿Ha ganado algún premio? Discuta este tema.

El patinaje sobre el hielo y el hockey (Ice Skating and Hockey)

1.	el charco	pond
2.	el disco	puck
3.	el hielo	ice
4.	el palo de hockey	hockey stick
5.	el patinador (la patinadora) de figura	figure skater
6.	el patinador (la patinadora) olímpico	Olympic skater
7.	el patinador (la patinadora) de velocidad	speed skater
8.	el patinadero	skating rink
9.	los patines de hielo	ice skates
10.	el portero (la portera)	goalie

Ejercicios

A.   *Traduzca:*

1. The skater makes a figure 8.
2. The skater falls on the ice.
3. The speed skater wins the race.
4. She is an Olympic skater.
5. There is a skating rink inside the hotel.

B.   Las olimpíadas de invierno ponen **énfasis** especial   *(emphasis)*
en el patinaje sobre el hielo y otros deportes **invernales**.   *(winter)*
Kitzbuhel en Austria y Lake Placid en Nueva York son
las **mecas** de los deportistas. Abundan en América los   *(meccas)*
lugares para patinar sobre el hielo y para los partidos de
hockey. Muchos de estos programas se ven por televisión. ¿Cuál de estos deportes le interesa a Ud.? ¿Es
veterano o sólo **principiante**? Discuta este tema.   *(beginner)*

El esquí (Skiing)

1.	las botas de esquiar	ski boots
2.	el traje de esquiar	ski suit
3.	los esquíes	skis
4.	los palos de esquiar	ski poles
5.	la nieve	snow
6.	la montaña	mountain
7.	el telesilla	ski lift
8.	la colina de esquiar	ski slope
9.	la posada de esquiar	ski lodge
10.	el hogar	fireplace, hearth

Ejercicios

A. *Traduzca:*

1. The skiers put on their ski suits and ski boots.
2. Ski poles are necessary for skiing.
3. The snow on the mountain is a beautiful sight.
4. The skiers take the ski lift to the top of the ski slope.
5. The fireplace in the ski lodge is delightful after skiing.

B. La última olimpíada **tuvo lugar** en Sarajevo el año   *(took place)*
1984. El hermoso deporte de esquiar fue el tópico de conversación de mucha gente. ¿Qué alegría **deslizarse** por las   *(slide down/*
laderas del Monte Jahorina, o de las mountañas de Colo-   *sides)*
rado o de los Alpes! ¡**Ha probado** Ud. este deporte? ¿Qué   *(tried)*
suerte ha tenido? ¿Dónde fue? Hable sobre este asunto.

El boxeo y la lucha (Boxing and Wrestling)

1.	**el árbitro (la árbitra)**	*referee*
2.	**el asalto**	*round*
3.	**el boxeador (el pugilista, el luchador)**	*boxer (pugilist, fighter)*
4.	**el campeón**	*champion*
5.	**la campana, el timbre**	*bell*
6.	**el cuadrilátero**	*ring*
7.	**las cuerdas**	*ropes*
8.	**el golpe decisivo, el knockout**	*knockout*
9.	**el luchador**	*wrestler*
10.	**el puñetazo, el golpe**	*punch*

Ejercicios

A. *Traduzca:*

1. The boxer hits his opponent.
2. It's a hard punch.
3. The referee separates the boxers.
4. The fighter wins by a knockout.
5. The wrestler continues to fight after the bell.

B. Muhammad Ali ya es una **leyenda**, como lo fueron   *(legend)*
en su tiempo Joe Louis, Gene Tunney, Jack Dempsey y
otros muchos. **Y habrá** más leyendas y más campeones.   *(there will be)*
El boxeo, que es un deporte brutal, tiene, **sin embargo**,   *(nevertheless)*
sus entusiastas admiradores. También tiene sus

seguidores la lucha a pesar de las conocidas **bufonadas** *(antics)*
de los luchadores. ¿Qué opina Ud. del boxeo? ¿Recuerda
algunos **encuentros** famosos? ¿Por qué **entusiasma** a al- *(encounters/excite)*
gunos la lucha? Discuta los pros y los contras de estos
dos deportes.

Carreras y saltos (Track and Field)

1.	la carrera	*dash*
2.	la carrera a campo traviesa	*cross-country*
3.	el disco	*discus*
4.	la jabolina	*javelin*
5.	la pista de carreras	*track*
6.	el salto de altura (el salto de pértiga)	*high jump*
7.	el salto de longitud	*broad jump*
8.	el tiro de la pesa	*shotput*
9.	el tiro de pistola	*pistol shot*
10.	las vallas	*hurdles*

Ejercicios

A. *Traduzca:*

1. This athlete runs a 100-meter dash and cross-country.
2. I enjoy watching the javelin and discus.
3. What is next on the schedule? Broad jump or high jump?
4. Look *(tú)* at that runner go over the hurdle.
5. There goes the pistol shot. The race has started.

B. Desde los tiempos de Grecia y Roma los entusiastas
del deporte se han dedicado a multitud de actividades
para competir en **ligereza**, velocidad o **fortaleza del** *(swiftness/body*
cuerpo. Las universidades dedican mucho tiempo y di- *building)*
nero para **entrenar** a los atletas, y prepararlos para los *(to train)*
maratones ye las olimpíadas. ¿Cuál es el tiempo más *(marathons)*
breve en que se ha corrido una **milla?** Discuta este tema. *(mile)*

El camping (Camping)

1.	el bosque	*woods*
2.	el catre de tijera	*folding cot*
3.	el fogón	*campfire*
4.	los fósforos	*matches*
5.	la leña	*firewood*
6.	la linterna	*lantern*

7. la linterna de mano	*flashlight*
8. el mosquitero	*mosquito net*
9. el saco para dormir	*sleeping bag*
10. la tienda de campaña	*tent*

Ejercicios

A. *Traduzca:*

1. The boys go camping in the woods.
2. We will need matches and firewood in order to start a campfire.
3. Let's have the lantern and flashlight ready.
4. Shall I put the mosquito net over the cot or the sleeping bag?
5. The children sleep on the folding cots in the tent.

B. A los norteamericanos les gusta ir en sus autos y «trailers» a descubir **de nuevo** su país. Es un **placer** *(anew/pleasure)* sentir la **brisa** y escaparse de la ciudad y de la con- *(breeze)* taminación atmosférica. También es muy agradable pasar la noche al **aire libre**, levantarse con los primeros *(open air)* rayos del sol al amanecer, y preparar el desayuno en medio del **campo** o del bosque. **Exponga** sus ideas sobre *(meadow/expound)* estos aspectos de la vida.

Navegar en canoa (Canoeing)

1. la almohada, el cojín	*pillow*
2. la canoa de aluminio	*aluminum canoe*
3. la canoa de corteza de abedul	*birchbark canoe*
4. la canoa de lona	*canvas canoe*
5. la cascada	*waterfall*
6. las cataratas	*cataracts*
7. el chaleco flotante	*life jacket*
8. la mochila, la talega	*knapsack*
9. el remolino de agua	*whirlpool*
10. la paleta, el remo	*paddle, oar*

Ejercicios

A. *Traduzca:*

1. The girls put on their knapsacks and climb into their birchbark canoes.
2. When canoeing, (*tú*) be careful of cataracts, waterfalls, and whirlpools.
3. She puts her paddle into the water of the lake.
4. All canoeists must wear life jackets.
5. In case of accident, the cushions float and they will save your (*Ud.*) life.

B. Los indios americanos inventaron las canoas, sirviéndose de ellas para viajar, y para pescar en los lagos y los ríos. Hoy se usan las canoas como deporte, principalmente cuando hace mucho calor y no **llueve**. *(rain)*
¿Ha ido Ud. alguno vez en canoa? ¿Qué tiempo **hacía**? *(was)*
¿Con quién iba Ud.? ¿Por qué es **peligroso zozobrar**? *(dangerous/capsize)*
Discuta este tema.

Los deportes acuáticos (Water Sports)

1.	el esquiar por agua	*waterskiing*
2.	el nadar	*swimming*
3.	el nadador (la nadadora) submarino	*skin diver*
4.	el patín de mar	*surfboard*
5.	la piscina	*swimming pool*
6.	la regata	*boat racing (regatta)*
7.	el salto	*dive*
8.	el «surfing»	*surfing*
9.	el traje de baño, el bañador	*bathing suit*
10.	el trampolín	*diving board*

Ejercicios

A. *Traduzca:*

1. Young people enjoy surfing over the huge waves of the ocean.
2. Skin diving is an interesting sport.
3. I enjoy swimming in a pool.
4. It's a beautiful dive.
5. I can see the regatta on the river.

B. El deporte favorito del verano es la **natación** y *(swimming)* otros ejercicios relacionados con el agua. ¿A dónde va Ud. para nadar? ¿Qué deportes sobre el agua conoce Ud.? ¿Nada Ud. bien? ¿Cuándo aprendió? Desarrolle el tema.

La pesca (Fishing)

1.	el anzuelo	*fishhook*
2.	los aparejos de pescar	*fishing tackle*
3.	el bote de pescar, la barca de pesca	*fishing boat*
4.	la caña de pescar	*fishing rod*
5.	el carrete	*fishing reel*

6. **el cebo** (el gusano)   *bait (worm)*
7. **la cuerda de pescar**   *fishing line*
8. **el pescador** (la pescadora)   *fisherman (woman)*
9. **el plomo**   *sinker*
10. **la red de pescar**   *net*

Ejercicios

A. *Traduzca:*

1. We love to go fishing on a fishing boat.
2. I like my new fishing pole.
3. The sinker drops the fishing line to the bottom (*fondo*) of the ocean.
4. The fisherman puts bait on the hook.
5. Grab the fish with the net.

B. El pescar es más popular entre los hombres que
entre las mujeres. Sin embargo, se va extendiendo la
costumbre de matrimonios que van juntos de pesca. A
veces podemos ver en los ríos y arroyos a algunos pesca-
dores con enormes **polainas.** ¿Qué piensa Ud. de este   (*boots*)
deporte? ¿Es una pérdida de tiempo? ¿Ha pescado algu-
nos peces? ¿Qué hizo con ellos? ¿Le gusta limpiarlos?
Discuta este tema.

La caza (Hunting)

1. **la bala**   *bullet*
2. **el bosque**   *woods*
3. **el cazador** (la cazadora)   *hunter*
4. **la licencia de caza**   *hunting license*
5. **la munición**   *ammunition*
6. **el perro de caza**   *hunting dog*
7. **el rastro**   *track*
8. **la res**   *game*
9. **el rifle**   *rifle*
10. **el señuelo de caza**   *decoy*

Ejercicios

A. *Traduzca:*

1. It is necessary to purchase a hunting license in order to hunt.
2. He shoots his rifle with great care.
3. The hunter follows the deer into the woods.

4. The hunting dog follows the animal.
5. The hunter takes the bullet out of the game.

B. El deporte de la caza no **agrada** a los **amantes** de *(please/lovers)*
los animales. Sin embargo, opinan los **ecólogos** que es *(ecologists)*
necesario eliminar a muchos de los animales de la **selva**, *(forest)*
porque no hay comida suficiente para todos, a causa de
su excesiva proliferación. ¿Ha salido Ud. de caza alguna
vez? ¿Cuál es su caza predilecta? ¿En qué estados
abundan las **codornices** y los **conejos**? ¿Por qué es cruel *(quail/rabbit)*
el deporte de la caza? Discuta las preguntas formuladas.

Caminar y subir a las montañas (Hiking and Mountain Climbing)

1. **la altura** — *altitude, height*
2. **las botas** — *hiking shoes*
3. **el (la) caminante** — *hiker*
4. **el compás, la brújula** — *compass*
5. **la cuerda** — *rope*
6. **el mapa** — *map*
7. **la mochila** — *knapsack*
8. **la montaña** — *mountain*
9. **el pico** — *peak*
10. **la senda** — *trail*

Ejercicios

A. *Traduzca:*

1. It is a very high mountain.
2. The hiker uses her compass and her map.
3. My food is in the knapsack.
4. One needs a pick and a rope to climb this mountain.
5. The trail goes over the mountain peak.

B. El hombre **ha escalado** el monte Everest y otros *(has scaled)*
famosos picos del mundo. Los aficionados a las **alturas** *(heights)*
se contentan con subir a montañas menos altas, o seguir *(are satisfied)*
otros **senderos** pintorescos. ¿Cuál es la montaña más alta *(paths)*
que escaló Ud.? ¿Qué le parecen las **caminatas a pie**? *(hiking)*
¿Cuál es la distancia más larga que **ha recorrido**? Dis- *(have walked)*
cuta las ventajas de estos ejercicios al **aire libre** . *(open air)*

La carrera de caballos (Horse Racing)

1.	la apuesta	*bet*
2.	las apuestas desiguales, los puntos de ventaja	*odds*
3.	el caballo de carrera	*racehorse*
4.	el cercado	*paddock*
5.	el ganador (la ganadora), el premiado (la premiada)	*winner*
6.	el hipódromo	*racetrack*
7.	el jockey	*jockey*
8.	el programa	*racing form*
9.	la puerta de partida	*starting gate*
10.	el trotón	*trotter*

Ejercicios

A. *Traduzca:*

1. The winner is in the paddock.
2. I bet $2.00 on this race.
3. I prefer the trotters.
4. The jockey rides the racehorse proudly.
5. The racing form does not give the jockey's name.

B. Lo que era deporte de **reyes** se ha convertido en   *(kings)*
diversión de la clase media. A los aficionados a las carreras de caballos les son familiares los hipódromos de
Hialeah, Roosevelt, Churchill Downs, Kentucky Downs
y Saratoga Springs. ¿Qué hipódromo frecuenta Ud. más?
¿Cuáles han sido los jockeys más conocidos de estos últimos años? ¿Cómo reacciona la multitud ante las carreras? Exprese sus ideas sobre todo esto.

Los coches de carrera (Racing Cars)

1.	la bandera	*flag*
2.	el conductor (la conductora) de coches de carrera	*racing-car driver*
3.	el choque	*collision*
4.	el mecánico (la mecánica)	*mechanic*
5.	el motor	*engine*
6.	la parada	*pit stop*
7.	el recodo, la vuelta	*turn*

8.	la pista de carreras	speedway
9.	el reloj registrador	time clock
10.	la velocidad	speed

Ejercicios

A. *Traduzca:*

1. The flag goes down.
2. The racing cars speed over the speedway.
3. The mechanic repairs the racing car.
4. The driver takes a turn at high speed.
5. The two racing cars crash.

B. Los autos de carreras son bastante populares en este país. Son **bien conocidas** las que se celebran in Indianapolis y en Watkins Glen. Muchas familias tienen sus **propias** pistas en miniatura. ¿Tiene Ud. este tipo de pista? ¿Quién la usa? **¿Cómo es de grande?** Discuta el tema.

(well-known)

(own)
(how large is it?)

El casino (The Casino)

1.	el apostador (la apostadora)	gambler
2.	las apuestas (las apuestas desiguales)	bets (odds)
3.	el repartidor (la repartidora)	dealer
4.	los dados, el cubilete (el cuchumbo)	dice (dice box)
5.	el kino	keno
6.	las monedas (el cambista)	money (money changer)
7.	los naipes	playing cards
8.	ponerse las botas	hit the jackpot
9.	la ruleta	roulette
10.	tragamonedas, tragaperras	one-armed bandits, slot machines

Ejercicios

A. *Traduzca:*

1. The dealer starts the game, collects the money, and pays the winners.
2. I spend days and nights at the one-armed bandits.
3. All the young people find comfortable seats and play keno.
4. The gamblers spend all their money on the roulette wheels.
5. I lost all my money. Do you think the money changer will cash a check?

B. El **instinto** de jugar por dinero es muy fuerte **tanto** *(instinct)*
en los hombres **como en** las mujeres. Durante muchos *(as much .... as)*
años numerosas personas han ido a Las Vegas para
hacerse ricas, y han regresado completamente **arrui-** *(become)*
nadas. Y otro tanto se diga de los que visitan ahora a *(ruined)*
Atlantic City o viajan a Monte Carlo, lugares que atraen
a los **tahures** del mundo entero. El deseo de enri- *(professional gamblers)*
quecerse se ha **aumentado** con la autorización de lote- *(increased)*
rias en algunos estados. ¿Qué opina Ud. sobre las
apuestas? ¿Qué probabilidades hay de ganar? ¿Ha
ganado alguna vez, o ha perdido? Discuta este tema.

El juego de naipes (Playing Cards)

1.	**el as**	*the ace*
2.	**la baraja**	*the deck*
3.	**el bridge**	*bridge*
4.	**el comodín**	*joker*
5.	**la ficha**	*chip*
6.	**el póker**	*poker*
7.	**la reina**	*queen*
8.	**el rey**	*king*
9.	**la sota**	*jack*
10.	**la veintiuna**	*blackjack (21)*

Ejercicios

A.   *Traduzca:*

1.   The card player plays his ace.
2.   He shuffles (*baraja*) the cards.
3.   He bets (*apuesta*) three chips.
4.   I have a queen and a king.
5.   21—I win.

B.   El juego de naipes es un **pasatiempo** universal. Uno *(pastime)*
de los juegos **más extendidos** es el «bridge». Muchos *(played more often)*
hombres y mujeres juegan a él, en grandes y pequeñas
comunidades, en días **fijos**, y **hasta cuando** viajan en *(fixed/even when)*
tren. ¿Le gusta a Ud. jugar a los naipes? ¿Juega Ud. por
dinero? ¿Se necesita mucho dinero para ir a los casinos?
Hable sobre el juego de naipes.

El juego de damas y el ajedrez (Checkers and Chess)

1.	el alfil	bishop
2.	el caballo	knight
3.	la dama, la reina	queen
4.	la dama	king (checkers)
5.	el damero	checkerboard
6.	la ficha, la pieza	checker
7.	el paso, la jugada	move
8.	el peón	pawn
9.	el rey	king
10.	el roque, la torre	rook

Ejercicios

A. *Traduzca:*

1. He moves his checker.
2. It was a brilliant move.
3. The chess player lost his pawn and knight.
4. Each time I travel to Mexico I buy a checkerboard.
5. I can move in any direction with my king.

B. Los torneos de ajedrez entre los Estados Unidos y Rusia despiertan siempre **grandísimo** interés. ¿Juega *(the greatest)* Ud. al ajedrez? ¿Cuántas personas se necesitan para jugar? ¿Qué se necesita? Desarrolle el tópico, siguiendo las preguntas formuladas.

El picnic (Picnic)

1.	la bebida, el refresco	drink
2.	el bicho, el insecto	insect
3.	el bocadito (el bocadillo)	sandwich
4.	la cesta de comestibles	picnic basket
5.	los fiambres	cold cuts
6.	la frazada	blanket
7.	la heladera, la nevera portátil	cooler
8.	el plato de papel	paper plate
9.	el pollo frito	fried chicken
10.	la sombra	shade

Ejercicios

A.   *Traduzca:*

1.   Let's have our picnic in the shade.
2.   Are the drinks and the picnic basket on the blanket?
3.   Fried chicken is my favorite food.
4.   The cold cuts are in the cooler.
5.   There is an insect in my sandwich.

B.   ¡Qué experiencia tan **agradable** salir al campo en   *(enjoyable)*
un día **caluroso**, y **tender** una manta sobre el verde   *(hot / spread)*
césped, o descansar bajo la sombra de un árbol! ¿Hace
Ud. **jiras campestres?** ¿Qué **merienda** prefiere? Discuta   *(picnics / snack)*
este tópico.

Montar en bicicleta (Bicycle Riding)

1.	**el (la) biciclista**	*bicyclist, cyclist*
2.	**la cadena de la bicicleta**	*bicycle chain*
3.	**el freno de pedal, el freno de pie**	*brake*
4.	**la guía**	*handlebar*
5.	**la motocicleta**	*motorcycle*
6.	**la motoneta**	*motor scooter, motorbike (moped)*
7.	**el pedal**	*pedal*
8.	**la senda de bicicletas**	*bicycle path*
9.	**el tándem**	*tandem, bicycle built for two*
10.	**el triciclo**	*tricycle*

Ejercicios

A.   *Traduzca:*

1.   I enjoy bicycle riding very much.
2.   My girl friend and I often go bicycling together on a bicycle built for two.
3.   The pedal in reverse *(en reverso)* will give you the brake.
4.   When I am 18 years old Dad says I can buy a motorcycle.
5.   My baby brother loves his tricycle.

B.   Según los médicos, montar en bicicleta es excelente
para la salud. El movimiento de los pies sobre los
pedales es un buen ejercicio para mantener fuerte el
corazón. Al contrario, montar en una motocicleta es **pe-**
ligrosísimo y según las mismas autoridades médicas una   *(most dangerous)*
invitación al desastre. No hay duda que hay estudiantes
que no están de acuerdo con el **juicio** de los médicos.   *(judgment)*
¿Tiene Ud. una motocicleta o motoneta? ¿Quién repara

su bicicleta? ¿Ha montado Ud. un tándem alguna vez?
¿Dónde? ¿Con quién? ¿Fue divertido el deporte?

La fotografía (Photography)

1.	la ampliación	*enlargement*
2.	la bombilla de magnesio	*flashbulb*
3.	la diapositiva	*slide*
4.	la exposición	*exposure*
5.	la fotografía	*photograph*
6.	el fotómetro	*light meter*
7.	el lente	*lens*
8.	la máquina fotográfica	*camera*
9.	el negativo	*negative*
10.	la película	*film*

Ejercicios

A. *Traduzca:*

1. I use flashbulbs for night photography.
2. He checks the light with his light meter.
3. I love my new German camera.
4. A special lens is necessary for distance.
5. Is this film for slides or for photographs?

B. **Lo relacionado** con la fotografía ocupa una industria **valorada** en muchos millones. Es **espectáculo corriente** ver al turista, **correa** al hombro, de la que **cuelga** su cámara. Las fotos traen a la memoria momentos **felices** de la vida, y la imagen de nuestros **seres queridos**. ¿Qué fotos le gusta sacar? ¿Cuáles son sus mejores fotos? ¿Quién es el mejor fotógrafo de su familia? Discuta este tópico.

(All that is related/valued)
(common sight/ strap/hangs)
(happy)
(loved ones)

La jardinería (Gardening)

1.	el abono	*fertilizer*
2.	el árbol	*tree*
3.	el arbusto	*shrub*
4.	el bulbo	*bulb*
5.	el césped	*lawn*
6.	el estiércol	*manure*
7.	las herramientas del jardín	*garden tools*
8.	la maceta	*flowerpot*
9.	la tierra	*topsoil*
10.	la yerba (hierba) mala, la maleza	*weed(s)*

Ejercicios

A.   *Traduzca:*

1. The gardener puts topsoil on the lawn.
2. I plant shrubs in front of my new home.
3. Plant the seeds in a flowerpot.
4. Fertilizer will improve the growth of your shrubs, plants, and trees.
5. We buy new garden tools, seeds, and bulbs every year.

B.   Al terminar el invierno, que a veces es **sumamente** *(exceptionally)*
largo, vienen las primeras **señales** de la primavera. Viene *(signs)*
el **calor** del sol y **empiezan** a salir las primeras flores. La *(heat/begin)*
gente **se anima** para limpiar **alrededor de** las casas, y *(motivate themselves/*
plantar flores y legumbres. Con la primavera **renace** la *around/is reborn/*
vida y el entusiasmo para hacer cosas **mejores.** ¿Ha *better)*
plantado Ud. algo en su vida? ¿Qué fue? ¿Dónde? ¿Tuvo
Ud. éxito? ¿Qué prefiere plantar, legumbres o flores?
¿Por qué?

Sellos y monedas (Stamps and Coins)

1.	**el álbum**	*album*
2.	**el catálogo**	*catalogue*
3.	**el cuadrito sin usar**	*mint block*
4.	**la estampilla, el sello**	*stamp*
5.	**la fecha**	*date*
6.	**el (la) filatelista**	*philatelist*
7.	**la moneda**	*coin*
8.	**el sello del primer día**	*first day cover, first day stamp*
9.	**no usado**	*mint*
10.	**el valor**	*value*

Ejercicios

A.   *Traduzca:*

1. I save coins.
2. She saves stamps.
3. We put the coins and stamps in an album.
4. The philatelist looks for the stamp in the catalogue.
5. Do you save mint blocks or first day covers?

B. Uno de los **pasatiempos** más extendidos es el de coleccionar sellos nuevos o raros, y el de formar colecciones de monedas y **medallas** de valor. La **filatelia** y sobre todo la **numismática** requieren a veces conocimientos especiales. Las administraciones de Correos emiten **a menudo** nuevos sellos, no sólo para el consumo diario, sino para venderlos a los coleccionistas. En el caso de monedas y medallas, hechas de plata o de oro, su valor crece **a medida que** crece el valor de **dichos** metales. ¿Se dedica Ud. a coleccionar sellos? ¿De qué países? ¿Conoce a alguien que tenga una colección interesante? ¿Qué es un filatélico?

(pastimes)

(medals/stamp collecting/coin collecting)
(often)

(in proportion to/ said)

El circo y el parque de atracciones
(The Circus and the Amusement Park)

1.	el (la) acróbata, el jugador (la jugadora) (la prestidigitadora), de manos, el prestidigitador	acrobat, juggler, magician
2.	la casa de fieras, el espectáculo del circo	menagerie, sideshow
3.	el confite de algodón	cotton candy
4.	el desfile del circo	circus parade
5.	el entrenador (la entrenadora) de leones (tigres)	lion (tiger) tamer
6.	la gran rueda	Ferris wheel
7.	el juego de suerte	game of chance
8.	la montaña rusa	roller coaster
9.	el payaso	clown
10.	el tiovivo, los caballitos	merry-go-round, carousel

Ejercicios

A. *Traduzca:*

1. The clown is eating cotton candy.
2. I enjoy most watching the magician and the lion tamer.
3. I always feel sorry for the unfortunate people in the sideshow.
4. The very young children love to ride the Ferris wheel.
5. The games of chance take your money.

B.   A pesar de ser de origen europeo, el ver el desfile
de un circo con sus elefantes enormes, sus payasos, y su
música distintiva, forma gran parte de la escena ameri-
cana. Si hay un **terreno libre** en los alredededores de la   *(empty lot)*
ciudad, allí es donde se establece el circo o el mundo
mágico del carnaval. El Disneylandia de California y el
Disneymundo de la Florida han **cautivado** la imagina-   *(captured)*
ción de «niños de todas las edades». ¿Cuándo vio Ud. el
circo por primera vez? ¿Qué fue lo que más le impresio-
nó? ¿Qué le pareció el espectáculo? ¿Qué piensa de los
animales entrenados?

La fiesta de coctel (Cocktail Party)

1.	**el anfitrión (anfitriona)**	*host, (hostess)*
2.	**las bebidas**	*drinks*
3.	**el borracho (la borracha)**	*the drunk*
4.	**el cubito de hielo**	*ice cube*
5.	**el invitado (la invitada)**	*guest*
6.	**la música**	*music*
7.	**la ponchera**	*punch bowl*
8.	**los refrescos**	*soft drinks*
9.	**las tapas**	*appetizers*
10.	**el vaso**	*glass*

Ejercicios

A.   *Traduzca:*

1. The hostess is charming.
2. The drinks and the appetizers are excellent.
3. The music was sweet and low.
4. I prefer a soft drink from the punch bowl.
5. Put an ice cube in my drink.

B.   Una de las costumbres americanas más extendidas
y aceptadas es la hora del coctel para **amenizar** una   *(enliven)*
fiesta. Antes de la comida formal, en **casa ajena**, o en la   *(neighbor's house)*
propia, y hasta en la oficina, se levanta la **copa** del coctel *(goblet or glass)*
favorito, en un ambiente de alegría y locuacidad. Se
ofrecen, por lo común, con el coctel, sabrosas tapas y
otras cosas deliciosas para completar esta escena
típicamente americana. Discuta este tópico.

El «hazlotodo» (Handyman, Do-it-yourselfer)

1.	el trabajo, la tarea	*job*
2.	el cuarto, la habitación	*room*
3.	las herramientas	*tools*
4.	la escalera	*ladder*
5.	el taller del sótano	*cellar (basement) workshop*
6.	la regla, la cinta de medir	*ruler, tape measure*
7.	el engrapador	*stapler*
8.	la pizarra, los ladrillos, los bloques de cemento	*slate, bricks, cement blocks*
9.	los gabinetes	*cabinets*
10.	la carretilla	*wheelbarrow*

Ejercicios

A. *Traduzca:*

1. The handyman is going to do this job for me.
2. He brings his ladder and his tools into the room.
3. I have a workshop in the basement full of tools.
4. You *(tú)* need a ruler and a stapler to do this job.
5. We are building a patio. We'll need a wheelbarrow, slate, bricks, and cement.

B. Como la inflación sigue **en aumento**, y cuesta tanto *(on the rise)*
hacer los más pequeños arreglos, la gente ha empezado a
hacer cosas **por su cuenta**, para no pagar a profesionales. *(for themselves)*
¿ Quién es el **electricista** de su familia? ¿Y el carpintero? *(electrician)*
¿Quién **empapela las paredes?** Discuta este tópico. *(wallpapers the walls)*

La discoteca (The Discotheque)

1.	los bailarines	*dancers*
2.	los bailarines populares	*popular dancers*
3.	el conjunto musical	*musical group*
4.	el disco de éxito (de oro)	*hit record, (gold record)*
5.	el estéreo	*stereo*
6.	las luces psicodélicas	*psychodelic lights*
7.	la orquesta	*orchestra*
8.	el paso de baile	*dance step*
9.	la pista de baile	*dance floor*
10.	el tocadiscos	*record player*

Ejercicios

A. *Traduzca:*

1. The psychodelic lights shine on the dancers on the dance floor.
2. The record player plays their favorite tunes.
3. This musical group plays rock music.
4. The new dance steps are popular.
5. The stereo music is also enjoyed by those who do not dance the popular dances.

B. Centenares de grupos musicales ofrecen al público sus canciones para interpretar los bailes de modas populares. ¿Le gusta a Ud. bailar en la discoteca? ¿Por qué sí? ¿Por qué no? Nombre Ud. una discoteca en su ciudad. ¿Cuál es su baile favorito?

La corrida de toros (Bullfighting)

1.	**el banderillero, las banderillas**	*bullfighter that uses long darts, darts*
2.	**el desfile**	*parade of bullfighters*
3.	**la espada**	*sword*
4.	**la muleta**	*cape*
5.	**el matador, el torero**	*bullfighter who kills bull, bullfighter*
6.	**la oreja y el rabo**	*ear and tail—(awarded for bravery)*
7.	**el picador**	*bullfighter on horseback with sword*
8.	**la tauromaquia**	*art of bullfighting*
9.	**el toro**	*bull*
10.	**el traje de luces**	*bullfighter's suit*

Ejercicios

A. *Traduzca:*

1. What a beautiful sight—the parade of the bullfighters in their bullfighters' suits.
2. The dart thrower places the darts into the neck of the bull.
3. The picador wounds the bull.
4. The bullfighter works with his cape.
5. The bullfighter holds the sword.

B. Mucha gente no puede pensar en España sin pensar en las corridas de toros. La tauromaquia ha penetrado en el arte, en la literatura y hasta en el corazón de la mayoría de sus habitantes. El arte del toreo es uno de los **rasgos** más destacados de la tradición nacional española. Discuta este tema.   *(characteristics)*

PARTE 2
Gramática esencial

UNIT 1

Definite article

Nouns in Spanish are either masculine or feminine. The definite articles modifying them correspond both in gender and in number.

MASCULINE		FEMININE	
SINGULAR	PLURAL	SINGULAR	PLURAL
el número	**los números**	**la tienda**	**las tiendas**
the number	*the numbers*	*the store*	*the stores*
EXAMPLES		EXAMPLES	
el itinerario	**los itinerarios**	**la tarjeta**	**las tarjetas**
el folleto	**los folletos**	**la maleta**	**las maletas**
el pasaporte	**los pasaportes**	**la reservación**	**las reservaciones**

Indefinite article

Indefinite articles also agree with nouns in gender and in number.

MASCULINE		FEMININE	
SINGULAR	PLURAL	SINGULAR	PLURAL
un número	**unos números**	**una señorita**	**unas señoritas**
a number	*some numbers*	*a young lady*	*some young ladies*
EXAMPLES		EXAMPLES	
un viajero	**unos viajeros**	**una viajera**	**unas viajeras**
un billete	**unos billetes**	**una aduana**	**unas aduanas**
un viaje	**unos viajes**	**una guía**	**unas guías**

Uses of the definite article

The definite article in Spanish is used in many instances where English does not normally use it.

1. With abstract nouns:

La paciencia es una virtud.   *Patience is a virtue.*
El crimen es malo.   *Crime is evil.*

2. With nouns used in a general sense:

Los puertorriqueños son sentimentales.   *Puerto Ricans are sentimental.*
La carne es cara.   *Meat is expensive.*

3.   With species:

El **pescado** es barato.   *Fish is cheap.*
Las **plantas** son bonitas.   *Plants are pretty.*

4.   With languages:

El **inglés** es difícil.   *English is difficult.*
El **español** es popular.   *Spanish is popular.*

5.   With titles:

El **profesor García** es cubano.   *Professor Garcia is Cuban.*
El **general MacArthur** es un héroe.   *General MacArthur is a hero.*

In direct address, however, the article is not used.

Buenas días, **profesor Garcia.**   *"Good morning, Professor García."*

6.   With expressions of time:

Es **la una.**   *It's one o'clock.*
El **mediodía** es la hora de comer.   *Noon is the hour to eat.*

7.   With days of the week:

El **martes** es mi cumpleaños.   *Tuesday is my birthday.*
El **domingo** es el día de descanso.   *Sunday is the day of rest.*

8.   With academic subjects:

La **aritmética** es fácil.   *Arithmetic is easy.*
La **filosofía** es un estudio serio.   *Philosophy is a serious study.*

9.   With the names of some countries:

La **Argentina** es un país sudamericano.   *Argentina is a South American country.*
El **Canadá** es nuestro vecino.   *Canada is our neighbor.*

10.   With verbs used as nouns (verbal nouns):

El **viajar** es mi pasatiempo favorito.   *Travelling is my favorite pastime.*
El **nadar** es un deporte.   *Swimming is a sport.*

Ejercicios

A.   *Exprese en español:*

1.   You are a travel agent.
2.   He is a tourist.
3.   The car rental is cheap.
4.   The ticket is expensive.
5.   The suitcase is new.

6.   Are you a guide?
7.   They are travellers.
8.   The tickets are expensive.
9.   The suitcases are new.
10.   The trips are expensive.

B.   *Exprese los sujetos en español:*

1.   (*Tickets in first class*) no son económicos.
2.   (*Travel agents*) son ambiciosos.

3.   (*Suitcases*) son caros.
4.   (*The young woman*) es bonita.

5. (*The credit card*) es popular en
     España.
6. (*Sundays*) son los días de visita.
7. (*English*) y (*Spanish*) no son mis
     clases favoritas.

8. (*Numbers*) son fáciles.
9. (*Passports*) son importantes.
10. (*Travelling*) y (*swimming*) son dos
     pasatiempos buenos.

Conjugación del Verbo «llegar» (Conjugation of the verb «llegar»)

llegar   *to arrive*

Yo **llego** tarde.   I arrive late.
Tú **llegas** tarde.   You arrive late.
Él, Ella **llega** tarde.   He, She arrives late.
Usted **llega** tarde.   You arrive late.

Nosotros (–as) **llegamos** tarde.   We arrive late.
Vosotros (–as) **llegáis** tarde.   You arrive late.
Ellos, Ellas **llegan** tarde.   They arrive late.
Ustedes **llegan** tarde.   You arrive late.

Ejercicio

Use la forma apropiada del verbo **llegar:**

1. Yo _____ tarde a la agencia de viajes.
2. ¿Tú _____ a casa sin la tarjeta de crédito?
3. María _____ a la aduana.
4. El billete _____ a la casa.
5. Los folletos de viaje _____ de la agencia de viajes.

Estudio de palabras (Word study)

Many words with a *-tion* suffix in English have Spansih cognates that end in **-ción.** These nouns are feminine.

action	(la) **acción**	liberation	(la) **liberación**
ambition	(la) **ambición**	narration	(la) **narración**
consideration	(la) **consideración**	reception	(la) **recepción**
evaluation	(la) **evaluación**	satisfaction	(la) **satisfacción**
intuition	(la) **intuición**	transition	(la) **transición**

Ejercicio

Escriba las palabras siguientes en español:

1. the exclamation
2. the congregation
3. the conversation
4. the graduation
5. the imitation
6. the limitation

UNIT 2

Gender of nouns

1. Nouns ending in **-o** are generally masculine.

el piloto	*the pilot*	**el vuelo**	*the flight*
el asiento	*the seat*	**el aeropuerto**	*the airport*

2. Nouns denoting male beings are masculine.

el actor	*the actor*	**el florista**	*the florist*
el artista	*the artist*	**el gobernador**	*the governor*
el aviador	*the aviator*	**el maestro**	*the teacher*
el conductor	*the conductor*	**el paciente**	*the patient*
el estudiante	*the student*	**el presidente**	*the president*

3. Nouns ending in **-a** are generally feminine.

la maleta	*the suitcase*	**la viajera**	*the traveller*
la guía	*the guide; the guidebook*	**la agencia de viajes**	*the travel agency*

EXCEPTION: **el día** *the day*

4. Nouns denoting female beings are feminine.

la actriz	*the actress*	**la florista**	*the florist*
la artista	*the artist*	**la gobernadora**	*the governor*
la aviadora	*the aviator*	**la maestra**	*the teacher*
la conductora	*the conductor*	**la paciente**	*the patient*
la estudiante	*the student*	**la presidenta**	*the president*

EXCEPTIONS: **la persona** *the person*
                        la víctima *the victim*

5. Feminine nouns beginning with a stressed **a** use the singular article **el**. The plural article remains **las**.

el agua	*the water*	**las aguas**
el alma	*the soul*	**las almas**

6. Nouns of Greek origin ending in the suffixes **-ma, -pa,** and **-ta** are masculine.

el clima	*the climate*	**el planeta**	*the planet*
el drama	*the drama*	**el problema**	*the problem*
el enigma	*the enigma*	**el programa**	*the program*
el melodrama	*the melodrama*	**el tema**	*the theme*

7. Letters of the alphabet are feminine.

la a	*a*	**la zeta**	*z*
la b	*b*	**las aes**	*a's*
la che	*ch*	**las jotas**	*j's*

8. Abbreviations in Spanish keep their original gender.

el automóvil	*the automobile*	**el auto**
la fotografía	*the photograph*	**la foto**
la motocicleta	*the motorcycle*	**la moto**

9. The genders of all other nouns must be learned with the noun.

la mujer	*the woman*	**la reservación**	*the reservation*
el despegue	*the takeoff*	**la lección**	*the lesson*
la altitud	*the altitude*	**el calmante**	*the tranquilizer*

10. The days of the week, languages, rivers and oceans, points of the compass or directions, and musical notes are masculine in Spanish.

days:	**el lunes**	*Monday*	**el martes**	*Tuesday*
languages:	**el portugués**	*Portuguese*	**el castellano**	*Castilian*
rivers and oceans:	**el Atlántico, el Misisipí, el Río Grande**			
compass points:	**el norte, el sur, el este, el oeste**			
musical notes:	**el do, el re, el mi, el fa, el sol, el la, el si**			

11. The masculine article is used to form verbal nouns.

el comer	*eating*
el hablar	*talking, speaking*
el trabajar	*working*

El comer es necesario para vivir.	*Eating is necessary in order to live.*
El hablar es el trabajo del profesor.	*Speaking is the professor's work.*
El trabajar de dependiente no es interesante.	*Working as a salesman is not interesting.*

12. Nouns in the masculine plural may denote two or more people of different sex.

los abuelos	(**el abuelo y la abuela**)	*the grandparents*
los hermanos	(**el hermano y la hermana**)	*the brother and sister*
los hijos	(**el hijo y la hija**)	*the son and daughter*
los padres	(**el padre y la madre**)	*the parents*
los reyes	(**el rey y la reina**)	*the rulers*
los tíos	(**el tío y la tía**)	*the uncle and aunt*

Ejercicios

A. Diga en el plural:

1. el aeródromo
2. la azafata
3. el pasajero
4. la pasajera
5. el baño
6. la línea aérea
7. el piloto
8. el folleto
9. el viajero
10. la tarjeta
11. el rey
12. el agua

B. Diga en el singular:

1. los actores
2. unos dramas
3. los estudiantes
4. las maestras
5. los pilotos
6. los aviadores
7. los asientos
8. las ventanas
9. los vuelos
10. las puertas
11. las llegadas
12. las comidas

C. Complete las frases:

1. Mis (aunts and uncles) son los hermanos de mi padre.
2. (Name of river) separa a México de los Estados Unidos.
3. Usan muchos acondicionadores de aire en (the south) de España.
4. La madre de Rosa es (the president) del club.

D. Diga en español:

1. The Atlantic
2. eating
3. my parents
4. Portuguese
5. working
6. the patient (female)
7. Monday
8. your grand-parents
9. the west
10. the artist (male)

E. Exprese en español:

1. Mr. Luis García is the governor.
2. Swimming is a sport.
3. Travel is cheap.
4. Air travel is not expensive.
5. The teacher is an actress.
6. Flying is difficult.
7. Is flight insurance necessary?
8. My brother is buying an airplane.
9. The meal in flight is good.
10. The Mississippi is an important river.

Conjugación de los verbos «aprender» y «tener»

aprender

to learn

Yo **aprendo** la lección.
Tú **aprendes** la lección.
Él, Ella **aprende** la lección.
Usted **aprende** la lección.

I learn the lesson.
You learn the lesson.
He, She learns the lesson.
You learn the lesson.

Nosotros (–as) **aprendemos** la lección.
Vosotros (–as) **aprendéis** la lección.
Ellos, Ellas **aprenden** la lección.
Ustedes **aprenden** la lección.

We learn the lesson.
You learn the lesson.
They learn the lesson.
You learn the lesson.

Ejercicio

Use la forma apropiada del verbo **aprender**:

1. Pedro y Raúl _____ la lección.
2. Isabel y yo _____ los números.
3. La señorita _____ los verbos.

4. ¿ _____ Ud. el español?
5. ¿ _____ él la filosofia?

tener	*to have*
Yo **tengo** un problema.	I have a problem.
Tú **tienes** un problema.	You have a problem.
Él, Ella **tiene** un problema.	He, She has a problem.
Usted **tiene** un problema.	You have a problem.
Nosotros (–as) **tenemos** un problema.	We have a problem.
Vosotros (–as) **tenéis** un problema.	You have a problem.
Ellos, Ellas **tienen** un problema.	They have a problem.
Ustedes **tienen** un problema.	You have a problem.

Ejercicio

Use la forma apropiada del verbo **tener**:

1. El viajero no _____ alojamiento.
2. La agencia de viajes _____ muchos folletos de viajar.
3. Los turistas no _____ reservaciones.
4. Nosotros _____ una maleta grande.
5. Félix y yo _____ buenos asientos.

Estudio de palabras

Many words that end in *-sion* in English have Spanish cognates that are spelled the same or almost the same, with the addition of an accent on the **o**.

collision	(la) **colisión**	diversion	(la) **diversión**
confession	(la) **confesión**	emission	(la) **emisión**
confusion	(la) **confusión**	expression	(la) **expresión**
corrosion	(la) **corrosión**	incision	(la) **incisión**
depression	(la) **depresión**	occasion	(la) **ocasión**

Ejercicio

Exprese las palabras siguientes en español:

1. abrasion
2. accession
3. admission
4. explosion
5. fusion
6. inversion
7. mansion
8. mission
9. passion
10. precision
11. version
12. vision

UNIT 3
A. Plural of nouns

1. The plural of most nouns ending in an unaccented vowel is formed by adding -s.

el arte	*the art*	las artes
el horario	*the timetable*	los horarios
la carne	*the meat*	las carnes
el chocolate	*the chocolate*	los chocolates
la locomotora	*the locomotive*	las locomotoras
el metro	*the subway*	los metros

2. The plural of nouns ending in an accented vowel (except é) is formed by adding -es.

el capó	*the hood*	los capóes
el dominó	*the domino*	los dominóes
el hindú	*the Hindu*	los hindúes
el rubí	*the ruby*	los rubíes
el café	*the coffee*	los cafés

3. The plural of nouns that end in a consonant is formed by adding -es.

el automóvil	*the automobile*	los automóviles
el interés	*the interest*	los intereses
la lubricación	*the lubrication*	las lubricaciones
un millón	*a million*	unos millones
la mujer	*the woman*	las mujeres
el refrigerador	*the refrigerator*	los refrigeradores
el señor	*the gentleman*	los señores

4. The plural of nouns that end in -z is formed by changing the z to c and adding -es.

el lápiz	*the pencil*	los lápices
la luz	*the light*	las luces
el pez	*the fish*	los peces
la vez	*the time*	las veces
la voz	*the voice*	las voces

5. Nouns of more than one syllable that end in -s do not change in the plural.

el abrelatas	*the can opener*	los abrelatas
la crisis	*the crisis*	las crisis
el jueves	*Thursday*	los jueves
el lavaplatos	*the dishwasher*	los lavaplatos
el lunes	*Monday*	los lunes
el miércoles	*Wednesday*	los miércoles
el paréntesis	*the parenthesis*	los paréntesis
la sinopsis	*the synopsis*	las sinopsis

NOTE: el gas, los gases

6. Surnames in Spanish are invariable in the plural.

la familia Fernández	los Fernández	la familia Morales	los Morales
		la familia García	los García
la familia López	los López	la familia Ortiz	los Ortiz
la familia Martínez	los Martínez		

7. the plural of nouns that end in a diphthong with the final letter **y** is formed by adding **-es**.

el convoy	*the convoy*	los convoyes
el rey	*the king*	los reyes

Ejercicios

A. *Exprese en español*:

1. the rubies
2. the Fernández family
3. the Hindus
4. Mondays and
      Tuesdays
5. the synopsis of the
      verb
6. the aunt and uncle of
      the young lady
7. the seasons of the
      year
8. the customers
9. the conductors
10. the Villegas family
11. the luggage racks
12. the smoking cars

B. *Diga las oraciones siguientes en el plural*:

1. El señor portugués celebra la fiesta.
2. El mes del año es importante.
3. Él llega tarde alguna vez.
4. La mujer necesita un cinturón de
   seguridad.
5. El café y la carne están buenos.
6. El vagón de cola está en el túnel.

Conjugación de los verbos «escribir» y «hacer»

escribir   *to write*

Yo **escribo** una carta.   I write a letter.
Tú **escribes** una carta.   You write a letter.
Él, Ella **escribe** una carta.   He, She writes a letter.
Usted **escribe** una carta.   You write a letter.

Nosotros (–as) **escribimos** una carta.   We write a letter.
Vosotros (–as) **escribís** una carta   You write a letter.
Ellos, Ellas **escriben** una carta.   They write a letter.
Ustedes **escriben** una carta.   You write a letter.

Ejercicio

Use la forma apropiada del verbo **escribir**:

1. Ramón y Juana _____ una composición.
2. Vd. _____ muy bien.
3. Los jovenzuelos _____ en los libros.

4. ¿ _____ a su senador en Washington?
5. Vd. _____ a la familia Hernández.
6. _____ Vd. la oración.

hacer   *to do, make*

Yo **hago** el trabajo.   I do the work.
Tú **haces** el trabajo.   You do the work.
Él, Ella **hace** el trabajo.   He, She does the work.
Usted **hace** el trabajo.   You do the work.

Nosotros (–as) **hacemos** el trabajo.   We do the work.
Vosotros (–as) **hacéis** el trabajo.   You do the work.
Ellos, Ellas **hacen** el trabajo.   They do the work.
Ustedes **hacen** el trabajo.   You do the work.

Ejercicio

Use la forma apropiada del verbo **hacer**:

1. Juan _____ el trabajo.
2. El panadero _____ el pan.
3. María y Carmen _____ un viaje.

4. Las maestras _____ las lecciones.
5. El presidente _____ la decisión.
6. ¿ _____ bien tiempo?

Estudio de palabras

Many words that end in *-able* in English have cognates in Spanish also ending in **-able** and spelled the same or almost the same.

acceptable	**aceptable**	formidable	**formidable**
adaptable	**adaptable**	honorable	**honorable**
agreeable	**agradable**	inevitable	**inevitable**
comparable	**comparable**	interminable	**interminable**
educable	**educable**	probable	**probable**

Ejercicio

Use el adjetivo apropiado:

presentable	intolerable	penetrable	excusable	convertible
respetable	lamentable	venerable	revocable	definible

1. un señor _____
2. una idea _____
3. una caverna _____

4. una persona _____
5. un error _____
6. una situación _____

7. un manuscrito _____
8. un problema _____
9. un coche _____

Many English words ending in *-ible* have equivalents in Spanish also ending in **-ible** and spelled the same or almost the same.

accessible	**accesible**	divisible	**divisible**
admissible	**admisible**	flexible	**flexible**
combustible	**combustible**	possible	**posible**
comprehensible	**comprensible**	reducible	**reducible**
digestible	**digestible**	sensible	**sensible**

Ejercicio

Use el adjetivo apropiado:

imposible	incombustible	inflexible
inaccesible	indigestible	insensible
inadmisible	indivisible	irreducible

1. una fracción _____
2. un elemento _____
3. la evidencia _____

4. una comida _____
5. un individuo _____
6. una idea _____

7. un plan _____
8. un público _____
9. una nación _____

UNIT 4

Gender of adjectives

1. The adjective in Spanish changes gender to correspond to the noun it modifies. Adjectives that end in the vowel **-o** usually change the **-o** to **–a** to form the feminine.

La **Casa Blanca** está en **una avenida ancha** de Wáshington.
The White House is on a wide avenue of Washington.

Los domingos **nuestro tío favorito** va al cine **americano**.
On Sundays our favorite uncle goes to the American movies.

La **muchacha bonita** tiene un **pequeño perro negro**.
The pretty girl has a small black dog.

El **banquero rico** tiene **muchos bancos mexicanos**.
The rich banker has many Mexican banks.

2. Many adjectives ending in **-e, -l, -z,** and **-or** use the same form to modify masculine and feminine words.

El **café caliente** anima.
Hot coffee perks you up.

Esta **chaqueta** nueva es **ideal** para el invierno.
This new jacket is ideal for the winter.

El **león feroz** tiene hambre.
The ferocious lion is hungry.

Cuando paso por la **puerta exterior**, entro en un **patio interior**.
When I pass through the exterior door, I enter the interior patio.

3. Adjectives of nationality ending in consonants usually add the vowel **-a** to form the feminine.

un chico francés	*a French boy*
una chica francesa	*a French girl*
un señor irlandés	*an Irish man*
una señora irlandesa	*an Irish lady*
un muchacho español	*a Spanish boy*
una muchacha española	*a Spanish girl*
un libro alemán	*a German book*
una novela alemana	*a German novel*
un té japonés	*a Japanese tea*
una comida japonesa	*a Japanese meal*
un estudiante portugués	*a Portuguese student*
una maestra portuguesa	*a Portuguese teacher*

Ejercicios

A. *Diga en español:*

1. a rich girl
2. a French lady
3. hot coffee
4. the Irish woman
5. the Mexican airplane
6. a wide avenue of New York
7. Portuguese and German novels.
8. Irish coffee and Italian wine
9. the Japanese teacher *(feminine)* and the American student
10. a double decker bus
11. a front seat

B. *Responda en forma negativa según el modelo:*

MODELO: ¿Quiere Vd. tomar una gaseosa?
No, no quiero tomar una gaseosa.

1. ¿Quiere Vd. unos billetes?
2. ¿Quiere Vd. la comida en vuelo?
3. ¿Desea Vd. un asiento de atrás?
4. ¿Desea Vd. comprar los seguros de vuelo?

Plural of adjectives

1. The plural of adjectives ending in a vowel is formed by adding the consonant -s.

el libro interesante	*the interesting book*	**un perfume malo**	*a bad perfume*
los libros interesantes	*the interesting books*	**unos perfumes malos**	*some bad perfumes*

la estación nueva	*the new station*	**una chica buena**	*a good girl*
las estaciones nuevas	*the new stations*	**unas chicas buenas**	*some good girls*

2. The plural of adjectives ending in a consonant is formed by adding -es.

el automóvil azul	*the blue automobile*	**la caja gris**	*the gray box*
los automóviles azules	*the blue automobiles*	**las cajas grises**	*the gray boxes*

una clase formal	*a formal class*	**un tren local**	*a local train*
unas clases formales	*some formal classes*	**unos trenes locales**	*some local trains*

3. The plural of adjectives ending in -s is formed by adding -es. The plural of adjectives ending in -z is formed by changing the z to c and adding -es.

el dependiente cortés	*the courteous salesmen*	**el señor andaluz**	*the Andalusian man*
los dependientes corteses	*the courteous salesmen*	**los señores andaluces**	*the Andalusian men*

Ejercicio

Exprese en español:

1. many buses
2. the new students
3. some bad days
4. ten dollars
5. five blue trains
6. a good man
7. exact change
8. some Andalusian bus drivers

Conjugación del verbo «dar»

dar	*to give*
Yo **doy** una propina.	I give a tip.
Tú **das** una propina.	You give a tip.
Él, Ella **da** una propina.	He, She gives a tip.
Usted **da** una propina.	You give a tip.
Nosotros **damos** una propina.	We give a tip.
Vosotros **dais** una propina.	You give a tip.
Ellos, Ellas **dan** una propina.	They give a tip.
Ustedes **dan** una propina.	You give a tip.

Ejercicio

Use la forma apropiada del verbo **dar**:

1. Lolita y Pancho _____ una propina.
2. Yo _____ el dinero al dependiente.
3. El hombre _____ trabajo al estudiante.
4. Los tíos _____ unas galletas al chico.
5. ¿Tú _____ modelos de trenes a tu hijo?

Estudio de palabras

Some words ending in *-al* in English have exact cognates in Spanish.

accidental	**celestial**	**mental**	**rival**
animal	**eventual**	**mortal**	**sensual**
bestial	**jovial**	**plural**	**usual**

Ejercicio

Escriba oraciones en español con los cognados siguientes:

1. canal
2. capital
3. cerebral
4. dental
5. fatal
6. monumental
7. normal
8. principal
9. vital

UNIT 5

Position of adjectives

1. Qualifying adjectives concerned with properties of an object or person are generally placed after the noun.

El **padre generoso** compra un **automóvil nuevo** para su hija.
The generous father buys a new automobile for his daughter.

Jorge toca la **música moderna** en su **guitarra española**.
George plays modern music on his Spanish guitar.

2. Qualifying adjectives that express inherent or figurative characteristics of a noun are placed before the noun.

La **blanca nieve** es magnífica.	*The white snow is magnificent.*
El **célebre Bolívar** monta su caballo blanco.	*The celebrated Bolívar mounts his white horse.*
El **pobre panadero** tiene un problema.	*The poor (unfortunate) baker has a problem.*
BUT: **El panadero pobre** no tiene dinero.	*The (financially) poor baker has no money.*

3. Determinative adjectives that restrict the quantity of a noun precede the noun.

Cada mes yo voy al hospital.   *Each month I go to the hospital.*
El autor escribe **algunos textos y varias   *The author writes some texts and various
novelas.*   novels.*
Voy a comprar **dos seguros de vuelo.**   *I'm going to buy two flight insurance policies.*

Ejercicio

Complete las oraciones siguientes con palabras apropiadas:

1. La señorita _____ tiene un vaso de vino _____.
2. El agente de viajes nos vende _____ para ir a París y regresar a casa.
3. La mujer _____ deposita _____ en la cajita de vidrio del autobús _____.
4. El barbero _____ lava el pelo del turista _____.
5. _____ estudiante escribe una carta _____ a su novia.

Apocopation of adjectives

1. Some adjectives drop their final vowel when placed before a masculine singular noun.

Es un **flan bueno.**   *It's a good custard.*
Es un **buen flan.**
¿Es un **niño malo?**   *Is he a bad child?*
¿Es un **mal niño?**
Estamos en el **capítulo primero (tercero).**   *We are on chapter one (three).*
Estamos en el **primer (tercer) capítulo.**

2. **Ciento** drops the **-to** before nouns of both genders.

Hay **cien señoritas** aquí.   *There are one hundred young ladies here.*
Hay **cien automóviles** en la agencia.   *There are one hundred cars at the agency.*

3. **Santo** drops the **-to** before masculine names, except those beginning with **Do** or **To**.

Santa is invariable before feminine names.

San Fernando	*St. Ferdinand*	**Santo Tomás**	*St. Thomas*
San Juan	*St. John*	**Santa Bárbara**	*St. Barbara*
Santo Domingo	*St. Dominick*	**Santa Rosa de Lima**	*St. Rose of Lima*

4. When placed before nouns of either gender, **grande** drops the **-de** and takes on the meaning **great**. When used after the noun, **grande** means *large*.

El gran general es victorioso.   *The great general is victorious.*
El general grande es victorioso.   *The large general is victorious.*

5. **Alguno** and **ninguno** drop the **-o** before masculine singular nouns.

Él trabaja en **algún proyecto** interesante.

He is working on some interesting project.

Ningún hombre de aquí tiene dinero.
No man here has money.
Ninguna persona de aquí es rica.
No person here is rich.

6. **Cualquiera** drops the **-a** before nouns of both genders.

Cualquier libro es bueno.
Any book at all is good.
Compro **cualquier cosa** para su cumpleaños.
I am buying anything at all for her birthday.

Ejercicios

A. Repita las frases siguientes en el plural:

1. la muchacha pobre
2. ningún estudiante cortés
3. un mal niño
4. el primer corte de pelo
5. la gran fiesta
6. ninguna mujer

B. Repita las oraciones con los adjetivos delante de los nombres:

1. Es un profesor malo.
2. Voy a un hospital bueno.
3. Este hombre grande es generoso.
4. El *Camaro* es un automóvil bueno.
5. Estamos en la lección tercera del libro.
6. ¿Se emplea la frase «hombre ninguno»?

Conjugación del verbo «ir»

ir

to go

Yo **voy** al cine.
I go to the movies.
Tú **vas** al cine.
You go to the movies.
Él, Ella **va** al cine.
He, She goes to the movies.
Usted **va** al cine.
You go to the movies.

Nosotros (–as) **vamos** al cine.
We go to the movies.
Vosotros (–as) **vais** al cine.
You go to the movies.
Ellos, Ellas **van** al cine.
They go to the movies.
Ustedes **van** al cine.
You go to the movies.

Ejercicio

Exprese en el plural:

1. Yo voy al cine.
2. La madre va a la tienda.
3. El hermano de Conchita va al camarote.
4. El elefante va al río.
5. ¿Tú vas a la cubierta del barco?

Estudio de palabras

Many philosophical and literary words that end in -*ism* in English have Spanish cognates ending in **-ismo**.

Aristotelianism	**el aristotelismo**	naturalism	**el naturalismo**
asceticism	**el ascetismo**	neoclassicism	**el neoclasicismo**
Buddhism	**el budismo**	paganism	**el paganismo**
Catholicism	**el catolicismo**	Protestantism	**el protestantismo**
conceptism	**el conceptismo**	rationalism	**el racionalismo**
encyclopedism	**el enciclopedismo**	realism	**el realismo**
existentialism	**el existencialismo**	romanticism	**el romanticismo**
mysticism	**el misticismo**	spiritualism	**el espiritualismo**

Ejercicio

Complete en español:

1. el (*Americanism*) de Harry Truman
2. el (*communism*) de los rusos
3. el (*humanism*) de los autores renacentistas
4. el (*idealism*) de Don Quijote
5. El (*Marxism*) de Karl Marx
6. El (*materialism*) de Fidel Castro

UNIT 6

Augmentatives

Increased size or amount of what a noun or adjective expresses may be indicated by the addition of the suffixes **-ón** (**-ona**) or **-ote** (**-ota**) to the original form of the word if it ends in a consonant. If the word ends in a vowel, the vowel is dropped before adding the ending. The ending **-ote** may have a pejorative meaning at times.

grande	*large*	**grandote**	*very large*
guapo	*handsome*	**guapote**	*very handsome*
la silla	*the chair*	**el sillón**	*the large armchair*
la casa	*the house*	**el casón**	*the large house*

Mi primo tiene un perro **grandote**.	*My cousin has a large dog.*
El **hombrón** vive en este **casón**.	*The very big man lives in this large house.*
El **muchachón** tiene unas **manotas** peludas.	*The big boy has ugly, hairy hands.*

Diminutives

Smaller size or lesser amount of what a noun or adjective expresses may be indicated by the suffixes **-illo** (**-illa**), **-ito** (**-ita**), or **-cito** (**-cita**). The final vowel of the noun or adjective is dropped before the ending is added.

El **pequeñito** come en su silla alta.	*The little one is eating in his high chair.*
La **jovencita** da un beso al **niñito**.	*The young girl gives the little child a kiss.*
El **gatito** come con el **pajarito**.	*The little cat eats with the little bird.*
Fumo **cigarrillos**, no cigarros.	*I smoke cigarettes, not cigars.*

Pejoratives

Disdain or contempt for what an adjective or noun expresses may be indicated by the suffixes **-ucho** (**-ucha**), **-astro** (**-astra**), or **-aco** (**-aca**).

El hombre pobre vive en una **casucha** [casa].
The poor man lives in a shack.

Esa mujer **feúcha** [fea] nunca lava la cara del niño.
That ugly lady never washes the child's face.

El **poetastro** [poeta] escribe unos versos malos.
The poor (in ability) poet is writing some bad verses.

¡Mire el **pajarraco** [pájaro] grande!
Look at the big, ugly bird!

Ejercicios

A. *Exprese la forma peyorativa de:*

1. feo _____   un animal _____
2. médico _____   un _____ viejo
3. pájaro _____   un _____ enorme

Exprese el diminutivo de:

4. casa _____   una _____ blanca
5. pequeño _____   un bebé _____
6. chico _____   un _____ puertorriqueño

Exprese el aumentativo de:

7. large _____   un hombre _____
8. good _____   el suegro _____
9. handsome _____   el novio _____

B. Use la forma peyorativa:

1.   No es un pájaro. Es un _____.
2.   No es una casa. Es una _____.
3.   No es un poeta. Es un _____.

C. Use la forma diminutiva:

1.   (El bebé) come (el dulce).
2.   (El gato) es (un animal) bonito.
3.   (El muchacho) llega a (la casa).

D. Use la forma aumentativa:

1.   (Esa mujer) no es cortés.
2.   (El perro) no come bien cuando viaja en automóvil.
3.   (El hombre) tiene fotos de sus hijos.

Adverbs

Adverbs are formed in Spanish by adding the suffix **-mente** (corresponding to the English
-ly suffix) to the feminine singular form of the adjective.

alegre	*happy*	**alegremente**	*happily*
dulce	*sweet*	**dulcemente**	*sweetly*
fácil	*easy*	**fácilmente**	*easily*
hermosa	*beautiful*	**hermosamente**	*beautifully*
paciente	*patient*	**pacientemente**	*patiently*

La vieja trabaja **tristemente** en su oficina.
Puedo ver la luna **fácilmente** con ese
  telescopio.
El automóvil va **rápidamente** por la
  carretera.

The old woman works sadly in her office.
I can see the moon easily with that
  telescope.
The automobile goes rapidly along the
  highway.

Ejercicio

A. Diga en español:

1.   sadly
2.   jealously
3.   courteously
4.   ideally
5.   generously
6.   seriously
7.   easily
8.   pleasantly
9.   popularly

B. Exprese en español:

1. Give me the answer quickly and correctly. (—**mente** only appears on the last adverb)
2. The young man easily starts the car.
3. Seriously, don't smoke.
4. The father happily goes to the hospital to look at his first child.
5. Sadly the owners sell the store.

Conjugación del verbo «saber»

saber   *to know*

Yo **sé** la respuesta.   I know the answer.
Tú **sabes** la respuesta.   You know the answer.
Él, Ella **sabe** la respuesta.   He, She knows the answer.
Usted **sabe** la respuesta.   You know the answer.

Nosotros (–as) **sabemos** la respuesta.   We know the answer.
Vosotros (–as) **sabéis** la respuesta.   You know the answer.
Ellos, Ellas **saben** la respuesta.   They know the answer.
Ustedes **saben** la respuesta.   You know the answer.

Ejercicio

Use la forma apropiada del verbo con los sujetos entre paréntesis:

1. saber la respuesta (los estudiantes)
2. saber el nombre de la chica (el chico)
3. saber la fórmula (yo)
4. saber el trabajo (los hombres)
5. saber la solución (Raúl y yo)

Estudio de palabras

Many words ending in the suffix *-ude* in English have Spanish cognates which end in **-ud** and are spelled the same or almost the same.

aptitude	(**la**) **aptitud**	magnitude	(**la**) **magnitud**
attitude	(**la**) **actitud**	multitude	(**la**) **multitud**
gratitude	(**la**) **gratitud**	plenitude	(**la**) **plenitud**
latitude	(**la**) **latitud**	solicitude	(**la**) **solicitud**
longitude	(**la**) **longitud**	vicissitude	(**la**) **vicisitud**

Ejercicio

Complete las frases con las palabras del grupo mencionado arriba:

1. Una _____ deplorable.
2. La _____ de los profesores.
3. La _____ y _____ del Perú.
4. Una _____ de gente.
5. La _____ de la madre.
6. ¿Sabe Vd. _____ del problema?

UNIT 7

Comparison of adjectives

1. The positive degree of an adjective expresses a quality of the noun it modifies.

Una **gran** casa **blanca** está situada cerca de la playa.
A large white house is situated near the beach.

¿Venden este pan **delicioso** en la panadería **alemana**?
Do they sell this delicious bread in the German bakery?

Los hombres **buenos** van al cielo.
Good men go to heaven.

2. When comparing the quality of two nouns, the adjective is in the comparative degree. The comparative degree may express superiority using the construction **más** + adjective + **que** (*more . . .than*).

El perro es **más inteligente que** la vaca.   *The dog is more intelligent than the cow.*
Júpiter es **más grande que** Venus.   *Jupiter is larger than Venus.*

3. The comparative degree of an adjective may express inferiority using the construction **menos** + adjective + **que** (*less . . .than*).

La vaca es **menos inteligente que** el   *The cow is less intelligent than the dog.*
   perro.
La luna es **menos brillante que** el sol.   *The moon is less brilliant than the sun.*

4. The comparative degree of an adjective may express equality using the construction **tan** + adjective + **como** (*as . . .as*).

El caballo es **tan inteligente como** el   *The horse is as intelligent as the dog.*
   perro.
Esta cerveza es **tan sabrosa como** esa   *This beer is as tasty as that cider.*
   sidra.

5. In comparisons of superiority and inferiority, four Spanish adjectives have irregular forms.

grande	*large*	**más grande** or **mayor**	*larger, older*
pequeño	*small*	**más pequeño** or **menor**	*smaller, younger*
bueno	*good*	**mejor**	*better*
malo	*bad*	**peor**	*worse*

La leche es **mejor** que el vino.   *Milk is better than wine.*
Esta humedad es **peor** que el calor.   *This humidity is worse than the heat.*

Mayor and **menor** are preferred when speaking of the age of people.

Luis es **mayor** que Eduardo.	*Louis is older than Edward.*
Carmelita es **menor** que su hermana.	*Carmelita is younger than her sister.*
Somos **mayores** que Vds.	*We are older than you.*

Tanto . . .como

Tanto (**-a, -os, -as**) + noun + **como** (as much, as many . . .as) is used when comparing quantities. **Tanto** agrees with the noun it modifies.

Tengo **tanto dinero como** tú.	*I have as much money as you.*
Él come **tantas galletas como** tú.	*He eats as many cookies as you.*

Ejercicios

A. *Diga en español*:

1. smaller than	5. the taller boy	9. the more difficult problem
2. larger than	6. the shorter book	10. as tasty as
3. older	7. less pretty than	11. the less intelligent student
4. younger	8. as brilliant as	12. as much money as you

B. *Exprese en español*:

1. Anthony is richer than Charles.
2. Virginia is less rich than her sister.
3. Dorothy is as good as her brother.
4. The classroom is as large as your house.
5. Arithmetic is more difficult than Spanish.
6. I have as many cars as he.

Conjugación del verbo «conocer»[1]

conocer	*to know, to be acquainted with*
Yo **conozco** a María.	I know Mary.
Tú **conoces** a María.	You know Mary.
Él, Ella **conoce** a María.	He, She knows Mary.
Usted **conoce** a María.	You know Mary.
Nosotros (–as) **conocemos** a María.	We know Mary.
Vosotros (–as) **conocéis** a María.	You know Mary.
Ellos, Ellas **conocen** a María.	They know Mary.
Ustedes **conocen** a María.	You know Mary.

---

1. **conocer** + **a** + person.

Ejercicio

Complete las oraciones siguientes:

1. Yo _____ a José.
2. Los Pérez no _____ a los García.
3. El agente no _____ al dueño.
4. El piloto y yo _____ a nuestros viajeros.

5. ¿_____ Vd. al señor Gómez?
6. ¿_____ Dolores a su vecino?

Estudio de palabras

Many words ending in *-ty* in English have Spanish cognates ending in **-tad** or **-dad**.

ability	**(la) habilidad**	liberty	**(la) libertad**
difficulty	**(la) dificultad**	maternity	**(la) maternidad**
faculty	**(la) facultad**	mentality	**(la) mentalidad**
futility	**(la) futilidad**	nationality	**(la) nacionalidad**
humanity	**(la) humanidad**	possibility	**(la) posibilidad**

Ejercicio

Escriba las palabras siguientes en español. Use el vocabulario al final del libro para verificarlas:

1. (*clear*) claro; (*clarity*) _____
2. (*curious*) curioso; (*curiosity*) _____
3. (*intense*) intenso; (*intensity*) _____
4. (*probable*)probable; (*probability*)_____
5. (*real*) real; (*reality*) _____

6. (*sane*) sano; (*sanity*) _____
7. (*tranquil*)tranquilo;(*tranquility*)_____
8. (*vane*) vano; (*vanity*) _____
9. (*virgin*) virgen; (*virginity*) _____
10. (*virtuous*) virtuoso; (*virtuosity*) _____

Many English words ending in *-ty* have Spanish cognates ending in **-ez** or **-eza**.

acidity	**(la) acidez**	lividity	**(la) lividez**
certainty	**(la) certeza**	nudity	**(la) desnudez**
entirety	**(la) entereza**	rigidity	**(la) rigidez**
ferocity	**(la) fiereza**	stupidity	**(la) estupidez**
gentility	**(la) gentileza**	validity	**(la) validez**

Ejercicio

Use las palabras siguientes en oraciones españolas:

1. escasez
2. frigidez

3. nobleza
4. pobreza

5. pureza
6. rareza

Unit 8

Superlative degrees of comparison

1. When comparing the qualities of three or more nouns, the adjective is in the superlative degree. The following construction is used:

definite article + **más** or **menos** + adjective + **de**

Cándida es **la muchacha más alta de** la clase.
Candida is the tallest girl in the class.

Consuelo es **la muchacha más pequeña de** la clase.
Consuelo is the shortest girl in the class.

Australia es **el menos grande (el menor) de** los continentes.
Australia is the smallest of the continents.

2. When describing a very high or low degree of the quality of a noun, the adjective is in the absolute superlative degree. It is formed by dropping the final vowel from the adjective, if there is one, and adding the suffix **-ísimo** (**-a, -os, -as**). A substitute form is **muy** (*very* or *most*) + the adjective.

El vino de su padre es **clarísimo**.	*His father's wine is very clear.*
Lucía es **hermosísima**.	*Lucy is very beautiful.*
Estas manzanas son **deliciosísimas**.	*These apples are very delicious.*
Es un problema **dificilísimo**.	*It is a very difficult problem.*
Es un problema muy **difícil**	*It is a very difficult problem.*

Comparison of adverbs

1. The comparative degree of adverbs is formed in the same way as that of adjectives. The superlative of adverbs differs from that of adjectives in that no article is used.

Por favor, hable Vd. **más despacio.**	*Please speak more slowly.*
Viven **más cerca que** Juan.	*They live closer than John.*
Esta ciudad está **más cerca**.	*This city is nearer.*
El tren no puede ir **más rápidamente**.	*The train can't go more rapidly (any faster).*
El tiempo pasa **más rápidamente**.	*Time passes more rapidly.*

2. Four adverbs have irregular forms.

bien	*well*	**mejor**	*better, best*
mal	*bad*	**peor**	*worse, worst*
mucho	*much*	**más**	*more, most*
poco	*little*	**menos**	*less, least*

Rosa baila **mejor que** Susana.	*Rose dances better than Susan.*

3. **Tan . . .como** may also be used with adverbs to form comparisons of equality.

Llega **tan pronto como** tú.	*He arrives as quickly as you.*
Vemos **tan bien como** ellas.	*We see as well as they.*

Ejercicios

Exprese en español:

1. the best stock
2. the most beautiful girl
3. the tallest of the boys
4. the very high prices
5. the most generous client
6. the youngest of the children
7. the oldest son
8. the most rapid car

9. very difficult
10. as slowly as possible
11. The brightest planet is Venus.
12. Henry is the tallest boy in the class.
13. The best pie is apple pie.
14. It is very good tea.
15. It is the worst book.
16. the least of my problems

Conjugación del verbo «decir»

decir

to say, tell

Yo **digo** la verdad.
Tú **dices** la verdad.
Él, Ella **dice** la verdad.
Ud. **dice** la verdad.

I tell the truth.
You tell the truth.
He, She tells the truth.
You tell the truth.

Nosotros (–as) **decimos** la verdad.
Vosotros (–as) **decís** la verdad.
Ellos, Ellas **dicen** la verdad.
Uds. **dicen** la verdad.

We tell the truth.
You tell the truth.
They tell the truth.
You tell the truth.

Ejercicio

Exprese las oraciones en la forma plural:

1. Yo digo la verdad.
2. Ella dice «muchas gracias».
3. Tú dices poco.

4. ¿Dice Vd. «adiós» a sus amigos?
5. ¿Dice él «dispénseme»?
6. Eso digo yo.

Estudio de palabras

Many English words ending in -*ic* have Spanish cognates ending in **-ico**.

artistic	**artístico**	graphic	**gráfico**
characteristic	**característico**	linguistic	**lingüístico**
comic	**cómico**	magnetic	**magnético**
cosmic	**cósmico**	photographic	**fotográfico**
enigmatic	**enigmático**	platonic	**platónico**
genetic	**genético**	sadistic	**sadístico**

Ejercicio

Exprese las palabras siguientes en inglés:

1. diabético
3. fantástico
5. intrínseco
7. romántico
2. eléctrico
4. genérico
6. profético
8. supersónico

UNIT 9

Uses of «ser»

1. **Ser** is used before predicate adjectives, that is, adjectives which describe the subject's essential and characteristic qualities of age, character appearance, and financial status.

Es viejo.	*He is old.*	(age)
Son buenos.	*They are good.*	(character)
Soy delgado.	*I am skinny.*	(appearance)
Somos ricos.	*We are rich.*	(financial status)

2. **Ser** is used to express nationality, religion, shape, size, color, and number.

Soy mexicano.	*I am Mexican.*	(nationality)
Es judío.	*He is Jewish.*	(religion)
Es redondo.	*It is round.*	(shape)
Son grandes.	*They are large.*	(size)
Es rojo.	*It is red.*	(color)
Son muchos.	*They are many.*	(number)

3. **Ser** is used in impersonal expressions.

Es necesario.	*It is necessary.*	**Es una lástima.**	*It's a pity.*
Es verdad.	*It is true.*	**Es posible.**	*It is possible.*

Telling time

1. **Ser** is used with **la** or **las** and the cardinal numbers to express the time of day. The gender of the article is determined by the word **hora** (hour), which is understood.

Es la una.	*It is 1:00.*	**Son las cinco.**	*It is 5:00*
Son las dos.	*It is 2:00.*	**Son las siete.**	*It is 7:00*

Es is used to express time between 12:30 and 1:30 and **son** is used when giving other times.

2. Time past the hour and extending to the half hour is introduced by **y**.

Es la una **y diez.**	*It is 1:10.*
Son las dos **y dos.**	*It is 2:02.*
Son las cuatro **y veinticinco.**	*It is 4:25.*

3. Time past the half hour is expressed by the number of the next hour minus (**menos**) the amount of time that must yet elapse before that hour. Often **faltar** with the number of minutes plus **para** is used as a substitute for the **menos** construction.

Son las seis **menos diez**.	*It is 5:50.*	Es la una **menos veinte,**	*It is 12:40.*
Faltan diez minutos para	*It is 5:50.*	**Faltan veinte minutos para**	*It is 12:40.*
las seis		**la una**	

4. Fifteen minutes before or after the hour may be expressed by **cuarto** (*quarter*).

Es la una **menos cuarto**.	*It is 12:45.*
Son las ocho **y cuarto**.	*It is 8:15.*

5. Half past the hour is expressed by **media** (*half*).

Son las nueve **y media**.	*It is 9:30.*
Son las tres **y media**.	*It is 3:30.*

6. *In* or *at* in phrases such as *in the morning* or *at night* is expressed by **de**.

Son las cinco **de la mañana**.	*It is 5:00 in the morning.*
Son las cinco **de la tarde**.	*It is 5:00 in the afternoon.*
Son las once **de la noche**.	*It is 11:00 at night.*

7. Expressions and words relating to time

¿Qué hora es?	*What time is it?*	**las tres y pico**	*a little after 3:00*
Es la medianoche.	*It's midnight.*	**a las ocho de la**	*at 8:00 P.M.*
Es el mediodía.	*It's noon.*	**noche**	
las seis en punto	*6:00 sharp*		

Hay

There is and *there are* are idiomatic forms in Spanish and are both expressed by the verb **hay**.

Hay un hombre en la casa.	*There is a man in the house.*
Hay dos hombres en la casa.	*There are two men in the house.*
¿Hay hombres en la casa?	*Are there men in the house?*

Ejercicios

A. *Exprese en español*:

1. We are skinny.
2. They are Mexicans.
3. She is old.
4. It is red and round.
5. It is true and necessary.
6. There is an order of meat in the truck.
7. There are lamb chops in the kitchen.
8. *You (fam., sing.)* are old.
9. You *(form., pl.)* are good girls.

10. You (*form.*, *sing.*) are a good boy.
11. There is a man in the store. He is a rich man.
12. The Italian and Spanish students are good.
13. The Mexican is old and rich.
14. There is a woman in the butcher shop that is skinny.
15. Is it true that he wears a toupee?
16. David is Jewish and Pilar is Catholic.

B. Diga en español:

1. 5:15
2. 1:30
3. 4:40
4. 2:40
5. 10:10
6. 8:50
7. 6:30
8. 1:45
9. 9:02 P.M.
10. 3:25 A.M.

C. ¿Qué hora es?

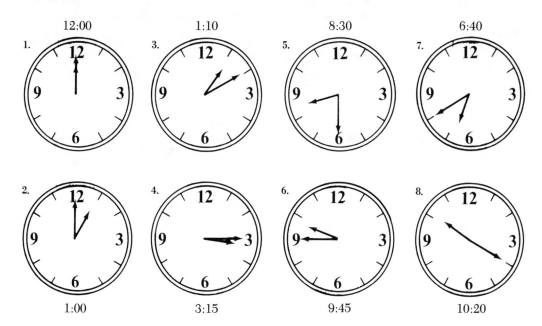

| 12:00 | 1:10 | 8:30 | 6:40 |
| 1:00 | 3:15 | 9:45 | 10:20 |

Conjugación del verbo «querer»

querer   *to want, wish, love*

Yo **quiero** a una muchacha.   I love a girl.
Tú **quieres** a una muchacha.   You love a girl.
El, Ella **quiere** a una muchacha.   He, She loves a girl.
Usted **quiere** a una muchacha.   You love a girl.
Nosotros (–as) **queremos** a una muchacha. We love a girl.
Vosotros (–as) **queréis** a una muchacha.   You love a girl.
Ellos, Ellas **quieren** a una muchacha.   They love a girl.
Ustedes **quieren** a una muchacha.   You love a girl.

Ejercicio

Forme una oración con la persona indicada como sujeto:

1. querer a una muchacha (Yo)
2. querer pan tostado (Mi familia)
3. querer aprender español (Mis compañeras de clase)
4. querer pagar la cuenta (El agente y yo)
5. querer la verdad (Los profesores)

Estudio de palabras

Many words ending in -*ist* in English have Spanish cognates ending in -**ista**. Such words may be used with both the masculine and feminine articles to refer to masculine and feminine persons.

activist	**activista**	masochist	**masoquista**
artist	**artista**	pacifist	**pacifista**
classicist	**clasicista**	pianist	**pianista**
communist	**comunista**	protagonist	**protagonista**
dentist	**dentista**	socialist	**socialista**
falangist	**falangista**	traditionalist	**tradicionalista**
florist	**florista**	violinist	**violinista**

Ejercicio

Escriba las palabras siguientes en español:

1. chauvinist
2. federalist
3. guitarist
4. humanist
5. novelist
6. surrealist

UNIT 10

«estar»

The irregular verb **estar** (*to be*) is used in the following situations.

1. To express the temporary or permanent location of the subject.

Los estudiantes **están en el gimnasio**.	*the students are in the gymnasium.*
Sevilla **está en España**.	*Seville is in Spain.*
La batería no **está en la cámara**.	*The battery is not in the camera.*

2. To express a state or condition of the subject that is temporary, transitory, or accidental.

El agua **está sucia**.	*The water is dirty.*	La puerta **está cerrada**.	*The door is closed.*
Estoy triste hoy.	*I am sad today.*		
Su esposa **está de pie** ahora.	*His wife is standing now.*		

3. To express the taste, appearance, or state of health of the subject.

La sopa **está buena** hoy.	*The soup is good today.*
Está elegante con su traje de etiqueta.	*He is very elegant in his tuxedo.*
Roberto **está enfermo**.	*Robert is sick.*
La fruta **está verde**.	*The fruit is green.*
Sus abuelos **están cansados**.	*His grandparents are tired.*

4. With a present participle to form the progressive tenses. The progressive tenses express the development or continuity of an action or describe an act in progress at a given moment. The present participle of regular verbs is formed in Spanish by adding **-ando** to the stem of **-ar** verbs, and **-iendo** to the stem of **-er** and **-ir** verbs, and always ends in **-o**.

tomar:	**tomando**	*taking*
comer:	**comiendo**	*eating*
escribir:	**escribiendo**	*writing*

Está lloviendo hoy.
It is raining today.

El profesor **está enseñando** el verbo **estar**.
The professor is teaching the verb **estar**.

Estamos comiendo (una) paella.
We are eating paella.

El Presidente de los Estados Unidos **está hablando** ahora por televisión.
The President of the United States is speaking now on television.

Los chicos **están patinando**.
The children are skating.

Ser, estar, venir (*to come*), **ir**, and **tener** are not used in the progressive tense construction.

Comparison of «**ser**» and «**estar**»

Ser plus an adjective indicates a permanent quality of the subject, whereas **estar** plus an adjective indicates a temporary condition.

ser	estar
El muchacho **es ciego**.	La muchacha **está ciega de cólera**.
The boy is blind.	*The girl is blind with rage.*
Mi padre **es sordo**.	La maestra **está sorda hoy**.
My father is deaf.	*The teacher is deaf today.*
La jovencita **es bonita**.	La jovencita **está bonita con su nuevo vestido**.
The young girl is pretty.	*The young girl is pretty in her new dress.*

El tabernero **es atento**.   El tabernero **está atento a mis palabras**.
The bartender is attentive.   *The bartender is attentive to my words.*

Rockefeller **es rico**.   Los accionistas **están ricos hoy**.
Rockefeller is rich.   *The stockholders are rich today.*

La sopa **es buena para la salud**. La sopa de este restaurante **está buena estos días**.
Soup is good for the health.   *The soup in this restaurant is good these days.*

El asesino **es malo**.   El niño **está malo esta mañana**.
The assassin is bad.   *The boy is sick this morning.*

Ese hombre **es muy aburrido**.   **Está aburrido** el viejo.
That man is very boring.   *The old man is bored.*

Ejercicios

A. Diga en español:

1. It is raining.
2. They are eating fruit.
3. I am speaking Spanish.
4. The meat is good today.
5. He is teaching English.
6. He is blind for a moment.
7. My father is deaf.
8. The bartender is rich.

9. Rome is in Italy.
10. The lens is dirty.
11. Madrid is not in Mexico.
12. The store is closed.
13. The students are sad.
14. She is sick.
15. His wife is beautiful.
16. Sergio is Cuban.

B. Exprese en español:

1. The children are eating paella in a Spanish restaurant.
2. The professor is eating with his pupils.
3. The young lady is writing a book.
4. Is the barber in the barber shop?
5. We are talking on the telephone.
6. The old man is bored, but he is not sad.
7. Paul is a Cuban, but he is not in Cuba now.
8. Where are his parents? My parents are in Guantánamo.
9. She is a very beautiful girl, but she is not beautiful in the photograph.
10. The bartender is blind with rage.

Conjugación del verbo «poner»

poner   *to place, put*

Yo **pongo** un sello.   I place a stamp.
Tú **pones** un sello.   You place a stamp.

Él, Ella **pone** un sello.	He, She places a stamp.
Usted **pone** un sello.	You place a stamp.
Nosotros (–as) **ponemos** un sello.	We place a stamp.
Vosotros (–as) **ponéis** un sello.	You place a stamp.
Ellos, Ellas **ponen** un sello.	They place a stamp.
Ustedes **ponen** un sello.	You place a stamp.

Ejercicio

Convierta las oraciones siguientes en interrogativas:

1. Yo pongo un sello.
2. Vicente y Gloria ponen el vaso sobre la mesa.
3. El mecánico pone agua en el radiador.
4. Beatriz y yo ponemos dinero en el banco.
5. Vosotros ponéis las cámaras en venta.
6. Tú pones el cheque en el sobre.

Estudio de palabras

The sound designated by the English letters *ph* is designated by *f* in Spanish.

Alphonse	**Alfonso**	pharynx	**(la) faringe**
elephant	**(el) elefante**	phase	**(la) fase**
geography	**geografía**	Philadelphia	**Filadelfia**
graphic	**gráfico**	philanthropic	**filantrópico**
pamphlet	**panfleto**	Philippine	**filipino**
phantom	**(el) fantasma**	photographer	**(el) fotógrafo**

Ejercicio

Dé el equivalente en inglés de las siguientes palabras españolas:

1. alfabeto
2. farmacia
3. Felipe
4. fenómeno
5. filología
6. fonógrafo
7. fosfato
8. fotografía
9. frase
10. física
11. teléfono
12. filosofía

UNIT 11

Spanish negative structure

1. Negative words

nada	*nothing*
nadie	*no one, nobody, not anybody, not anyone*
ninguno (-a, -os, -as)	*no one, none, not one, not any, not anyone*
ningún (before m. sing. noun)	
nunca	*never, not ever*

ni	*nor, neither (either)*
ni . . .ni	*neither . . .nor*
tampoco	*neither, not either*
ni . . .tampoco	*nor . . .either*
jamás	*never* (in negative sentences), *ever* (in affirmative sentences)

2.   **No** is placed before the verb to make a sentence negative.

Alicia **no está** presente hoy.	*Alice is not present today.*
No es cubana. Es puertorriqueña.	*She is not Cuban. She is Puerto Rican.*
No hablan español en Haití.	*They do not speak Spanish in Haiti.*

3.   Negative words may be placed before the verb.

Nadie está en casa.	*Nobody is at home.*
Nunca va al cine.	*He never goes to the movies.*
Nunca invita a nadie.	*He never invites anybody.*
Ni Elena ni Josefina quiere ir.	*Neither Helen nor Josephine wishes to go.*

4.   Negative words may also follow the verb, in which case **no** is placed before the verb.
     Unlike English, Spanish commonly uses this double negative construction.

No está nadie en casa.	*Nobody is in the house.*
No va nunca al cine.	*He never goes to the movies.*
El paciente **no come nada**.	*The patient doesn't eat anything.*

Affirmative indefinites

alguien	*somebody, someone, anybody, anyone* (opposite of **nadie**)
algo	*something, anything, somewhat* (opposite of **nada**)
alguno	*some, any, someone, anyone* (opposite of **ninguno**)
o. . .o. . .	*either . . .or . . .* (opposite of **ni . . .ni . . .**)
también	*also, too* (opposite of **tampoco**)

Alguien está llamando la ambulancia.	*Somebody is calling the ambulance.*
Está comprando **algo** para su novia.	*He is buying something for his girlfriend.*
O Jaime **o** Antonio va a pagar la cuenta.	*Either James or Anthony is going to pay the bill.*

Ejercicios

A. Diga en español:

1.   He is not talking.
2.   Nobody is crying.
3.   Florence never eats.
4.   Nobody is here.
5.   Nothing is new today.

6.   There is somebody in the store.
7.   Never ignore anybody.
8.   Neither Carmen nor Charles has an idea.

9.   I do not want anything.
10.   . . .nor Christina either.

B. *Exprese en español*:

1. Either Mother or Dad is going to fly to Peru.
2. My neighbor never does anything for anybody.
3. I never eat anything in the morning.
4. Somebody is calling my parents.
5. None of the men wants to watch the baby.

Conjugación del verbo «mostrar»

mostrar	to show
Yo **muestro** una película.	I show a movie.
Tú **muestras** una película.	You show a movie.
Él, Ella **muestra** una película.	He, She shows a movie.
Usted **muestra** una película.	You show a movie.
Nosotros (–as) **mostramos** una película.	We show a movie.
Vosotros (–as) **mostráis** una película.	You show a movie.
Ellos, Ellas **muestran** una película.	They show a movie.
Ustedes **muestran** una película	You show a movie.

Ejercicio

Complete con una frase adversativa, utilizando el mismo verbo de la oración:

1. Yo muestro una película, pero Joaquín no . . .
2. Tú muestras las fotografías, pero los otros fotógrafos no . . .
3. El chófer muestra su licencia, pero el oficial y yo no . . .
4. Los dependientes muestran sellos, pero los clientes no . . .
5. La abuela muestra métodos de cocinar pollo, pero el abuelo no . . .

Estudio de palabras

Many words ending in *-e* in English have cognates in Spanish ending in **-o** or **-a**.

active	**activo**	mine	**(la) mina**
concise	**conciso**	plate	**(el) plato**
crude	**crudo**	positive	**positivo**
curve	**(la) curva**	precise	**preciso**
defense	**(la) defensa**	relative	**relativo**
false	**falso**	rose	**(la) rosa**
fame	**(la) fama**	serene	**sereno**
fortune	**(la) fortuna**	severe	**severo**

Ejercicio

Dé el equivalente en inglés de las siguientes frases españolas:

1. una fortuna adversa
2. una capa azul
3. una captura heroica
4. un grado de centígrado
5. una figura hermosa
6. una pipa vieja
7. una ruptura de relaciones
8. un vaso precioso
9. un vestíbulo pequeño
10. un voto importante
11. un plan definitivo
12. una oración ofensiva

UNIT 12

Possession

Possession is expressed in Spanish with **de** plus the possessor. This construction corresponds to the English *'s* and *s'*.

el libro de Susana	*Susan's book*	**los juguetes de los niños**	*the children's toys*
el hotel de ella	*her hotel*	**el automóvil de Carlos**	*Charles' automobile*
la barbería de él	*his barber shop*		

Contractions

1. The preposition **de** and the masculine article **el** form the contraction **del. De la, de los,** and **de las** are not contracted.

los juguetes **del** nene	*the baby's toys*	el precio **de las** fragancias	*the price of the perfumes*
las fotos **de los** niños	*the photographs of the children*	la riqueza **de la** nación	*the nation's wealth*

2. The preposition **a** and the masculine article **el** form the contraction **al. A la, a los,** and **a las** are not contracted.

Los primos van **al** cine.	*The cousins go to the movies.*
Los turistas van **a la** aduana.	*The tourists go to the custom house.*
Mamá va **a las** tiendas.	*Mama goes to the stores.*
Los hombres van **a los** casinos.	*The men go to the casinos.*

Direct objects and the personal «a»

1. The direct object of a verb is the person or thing that receives the action of the verb.

    Compro **una flor.**   *I'm buying a flower.*

2. When the direct object is a person, it is preceded by the preposition **a**, which is called the personal "**a**" in this usage.

Busco **al niño**.	*I am looking for the boy.*
¿Conoce Ud. **a ese señor**?	*Do you know that man?*
No escuchas **a nadie**.	*You don't listen to anybody.*
Ella quiere **a otro** y no **a él**.	*She loves somebody else and not him.*

3. The personal "a" is also used when an intelligent or domesticated animal is the direct object of a verb.

Veo **al perro** todos los días.	*I see the dog every day.*
Miro **al gatito** con su plato de leche.	*I am looking at the kitten with its plate of milk.*

4. The personal "a" is used when the name of a geographical location is the direct object of the verb.

Conozco muy bien **a Madrid**.	*I know Madrid very well.*
Visito **al Canadá** cada verano.	*I visit Canada each summer.*

5. The personal "a" is not used after **tener** (*to have*)

Tengo una vaca que da buena leche.	*I have a cow that gives good milk.*
Alicia **tiene tres hermanos**.	*Alice has three brothers.*
Tienen un hijo y quieren más.	*They have one child and they want more.*

Ejercicios

A. *Diga en español*:

1. Do you know the boy?
2. He looks for the kitten.
3. Dolores loves Nicholas.
4. The Mexican boy has a donkey.
5. He sees the cow.
6. The doctor visits the woman in the hospital.
7. Rose has three sons.
8. She teaches Spanish students.
9. He doesn't love anybody.
10. Joe is listening to the boys.
11. the customer's check
12. Susan's wig
13. the country's lakes
14. the barber's scissors
15. Richard's money
16. I have a dog.
17. Feed the dog.

B. *Exprese en español*:

1. Chile's capital is Santiago de Chile.
2. Puerto Rico's and Haiti's beaches are very good.
3. Panama's steamships are numerous.
4. England's salesmen are courteous.
5. Canada's motels are very expensive.

Conjugación del verbo «oír»

oír	*to hear, listen*
Yo **oigo** la música.	I hear the music.
Tú **oyes** la música.	You hear the music.

Él, Ella **oye** la música.   He, She hears the music.
Usted **oye** la música.   You hear the music.

Nosotros (–as) **oímos** la música.   We hear the music.
Vosotros (–as) **oís** la música.   You hear the music.
Ellos, Ellas **oyen** la música.   They hear the music.
Ustedes **oyen** la música.   You hear the music.

Ejercicio

Cambie el sujeto y el verbo al singular o al plural según la oración:

1. Yo oigo la música.
2. Tú oyes el disco.
3. Nosotros oímos al ministro.
4. Ellas oyen los gritos de los niños.
5. Vd. oye la explosión de la dinamita.

Estudio de palabras

Many English words ending in the suffix *-ure* have Spanish cognates ending in **-ura**.

adventure	**(la) aventura**	nature	**(la) natura**
caricature	**(la) caricatura**	posture	**(la) postura**
censure	**(la) censura**	sculpture	**(la) escultura**
culture	**(la) cultura**	stature	**(la) estatura**
manicure	**(la) manicura**	structure	**(la) estructura**
miniature	**(la) miniatura**	temperature	**(la) temperatura**

Ejercicio

Complete las frases con las palabras siguientes:

la aventura   la dentadura   la temperatura
la agricultura   la escultura   la tortura
la captura   la Sagrada Escritura
la caricatura   la legislatura

1. _____ de México   5. _____ de Tarzán   9. el texto de _____
2. _____ de la Inquisición   6. _____ de los trópicos   10. _____ del Ratón Miguelito
3. _____ del paciente   7. _____ del criminal
4. _____ de Nueva York   8. _____ de Venus de Milo

UNIT 13

Demonstrative adjectives

MASCULINE SINGULAR	FEMININE SINGULAR	
este	esta	*this*
ese	esa	*that* (near speaker)
aquel	aquella	*that* (far away)

MASCULINE PLURAL	FEMININE PLURAL	
estos	estas	*these*
esos	esas	*those* (near speaker)
aquellos	aquellas	*those* (far away)

Spanish expresses the English demonstrative *that* (*pl. those*) with two forms. The **ese** form refers to an entity near, connected with, or possessed by the person addressed. The **aquel** form refers to an entity far away or unrelated to both the speaker and the person addressed. Demonstrative adjectives agree in gender and number with the nouns they modify and are usually repeated before each noun.

Este muchacho y esa (aquella) muchacha son polacos.
This boy and that girl are Polish.

Esta botella de cerveza, **esta lata** de guisantes y **esta sopa** son mías.
This bottle of beer, this can of peas, and this soup are mine.

Déme **esa carta**.
Give me that letter.

Aquel árbol es un olmo.
That tree out yonder is an elm.

Aquellas montañas y aquellas nubes son hermosas.
Those mountains and those clouds are beautiful.

Demonstrative pronouns

MASCULINE SINGULAR	FEMININE SINGULAR	
éste	ésta	*this, this one*
ése	ésa	*that, that one* (near)
aquél	aquélla	*that, that one* (far away)

MASCULINE PLURAL	FEMININE PLURAL	
éstos	éstas	*these*
ésos	ésas	*those* (near)
aquéllos	aquéllas	*those* (far away)

Examples

esa bebida y **ésta**	*that drink and this one*
aquella cerveza y **ésa**	*that beer (far away) and that one*
ese mostrador y **éste**	*that counter and this one*
aquel cuadro y **ése**	*that picture (far away) and that one*
ese atleta y **aquél**	*that athlete and that one (far away)*
estos documentos y **ésos**	*these documents and those*
esas manzanas y **aquéllas**	*those apples and those (far away)*
este libro y **ése**	*this book and that one*

Creo que **ésta** es su hermana y **ésa** es su prima.
I believe that this one is his sister and that one is his cousin.

Quédate con **ésa**.
Keep that one.

1. Demonstrative pronouns consist of the demonstrative adjective forms plus a written accent on the stressed vowels. The relationship of distance expressed by demonstrative pronouns is the same as that expressed by demonstrative adjectives. The pronouns agree in gender and number with the nouns they replace.

2. **Éste** may express the English *the latter*, while **aquél** may express *the former*. Unlike English, which places *the former* before *the latter*, Spanish places **éste** before **aquél**.

Teresa y Salvador son amigos; **éste** es italiano y **aquélla** es irlandesa.
Theresa and Salvatore are friends; the former is Irish and the latter is Italian.

Neuter demonstratives

Esto, eso, and **aquello** are the neuter demonstrative pronouns. They bear no written accent because there are no neuter adjectives from which to distinguish them. Neuter pronouns are always singular and refer to a vague, intangible, indefinite entity, or to a previously expressed idea. They are often used in interrogative statements when gender is unknown or unidentified.

¿Qué es **esto**?	*What is this?*	**Eso** no me gusta.	*I don't like that.*
No quiero hacer **esto**.	*I do not want to do this.*	**Aquello** está confuso.	*That is confusing.*

Here and there

aquí, acá	*here*
ahí	*there* (near person addressed)
allí, allá	*there* (far away)

Acá and allá are less definite than aquí and allí and are used with verbs of motion.

¡**Ven acá**!   *Come here!*

Va allá todos los días.   *He goes there every day.*

Ejercicios

A. *Diga en español*:

1. this son
2. that family (*near*)
3. that hotel (*far*)
4. that cloud (*far*)
5. this dentist
6. these telephones
7. those nurses (*near*)
8. those football players (*far*)
9. these girls and those boys
10. these boats and those airplanes
11. this stretcher and that one (*near*)
12. that spark plug and that one (*far*)
13. these X-rays and those
14. this dog and those (*far*)
15. those houses and this one
16. that hospital and this one
17. I want this one or that one.
18. Those (far away) are very large.
19. What is that?
20. This is the price of the permanent.

B. *Exprese en español*:

1. This car and this bus are for the children.
2. These problems are difficult for those new students.
3. This automobile near me needs tires and that convertible in the distance needs gasoline.
4. Give me that money now and I will go buy those inexpensive airplane tickets.
5. This bus driver drives this bus like a madman.
6. These stewardesses and those in the airport are from Iberian Airlines.
7. This is Mr. Sanchez's daughter and that (one) is his son.
8. John and Henry are professional men; the former is a professor and the latter is a doctor.
9. This is horrible but that is magnificent.
10. There are tourists in this store, in that one and in the one next to the beauty parlor.

Conjugación del verbo «poder»

poder   *to be able*

Yo **puedo** caminar.   I can walk.

Tú **puedes** caminar.   You can walk.

Él, Ella **puede** caminar.   He, She can walk.

Usted **puede** caminar.   You can walk.

Nosotros (–as) **podemos** caminar.   We can walk.

Vosotros (–as) **podéis** caminar.   You can walk.

Ellos, Ellas **pueden** caminar.   They can walk.

Ustedes **pueden** caminar.   You can walk.

Ejercicio

Responda a las preguntas:

1. ¿Quiénes no pueden ir a la universidad?
2. ¿Por qué no puede caminar el paciente?
3. ¿Qué carne no pueden vender en esta ciudad?
4. ¿Qué legumbre puede Ud. comprar por poco dinero?
5. ¿Quiénes pueden rezar en el templo?

Estudio de palabras

Many English words ending in -*ence* have Spanish cognates ending in **-encia**.

coexistence	**(la) coexistencia**	existence	**(la) existencia**
competence	**(la) competencia**	influence	**(la) influencia**
condolence	**(la) condolencia**	innocence	**(la) inocencia**
convalescence	**(la) convalecencia**	insistence	**(la) insistencia**
difference	**(la) diferencia**	persistence	**(la) persistencia**
essence	**(la) esencia**	reference	**(la) referencia**

Ejercicio

Exprese en español:

1. la (*convenience*) de vivir en la ciudad
2. la (*inference*) del insulto
3. la (*intelligence*) del perro
4. la (*malevolence*) del criminal
5. la (*negligence*) del chofer

6. la (*presence*) del actor
7. la (*prudence*) de la madre
8. la (*violence*) del incidente
9. la (*correspondence*) de los amigos
10. la (*residence*) de los estudiantes

UNIT 14

Possessive adjectives (unstressed forms)

SINGULAR POSSESSOR

mi libro	*my book*
mi poesía	*my poem*
tu vestido	*your dress*
tu sábana	*your sheet*
su hijo	*his, her, your son*
su hija	*his, her, your daughter*

mis libros	*my books*
mis poesías	*my poems*
tus vestidos	*your dresses*
tus sábanas	*your sheets*
sus hijos	*his, her, your sons*
sus hijas	*his, her, your daughters*

PLURAL POSSESSOR

nuestro carro	*our car*
nuestra casa	*our house*
vuestro balcón	*your balcony*
vuestra toalla	*your towel*
su banco	*their, your bank*
su tienda	*their, your store*
nuestros carros	*our cars*
nuestras casas	*our houses*
vuestros balcones	*your balconies*
vuestras toallas	*your towels*
sus bancos	*their, your banks*
sus tiendas	*their, your stores*

In Spanish, unlike English, the possessive adjective agrees in gender and number with the thing possessed, not with the possessor. The unstressed possessive adjective is usually repeated before each noun it modifies.

Mi hijo y **su esposo** están en la casa.	**Mi hijo** y **mi esposo** están en la casa.
My son and your husband are in the house.	*My son and husband are in the house.*

Possessive adjectives (stressed forms)

SINGULAR POSSESSOR

el libro **mío**	*my books*
la poesía **mía**	*my poem*
el vestido **tuyo**	*your dress*
la sábana **tuya**	*your sheet*
el hijo **suyo**	*his, her, your son*
la hija **suya**	*his, her, your daughter*
los libros **míos**	*my books*
las poesías **mías**	*my poems*
los vestidos **tuyos**	*your dresses*
las sábanas **tuyas**	*your sheets*
los hijos **suyos**	*his, her, your sons*
las hijas **suyas**	*his, her, your daughters*

PLURAL POSSESSOR

el carro **nuestro**	*our car*
la casa **nuestra**	*our house*
el balcón **vuestro**	*your balcony*
la toalla **vuestra**	*your towel*
el banco **suyo**	*their, your bank*
la tienda **suya**	*their, your store*
los carros **nuestros**	*our cars*
las casas **nuestras**	*our houses*
los balcones **vuestros**	*your balconies*
las toallas **vuestras**	*your towels*
los bancos **suyos**	*their, your banks*
las tiendas **suyas**	*their, your stores*

The stressed form of the possessive adjective always follows the noun it modifies and agrees with it in gender and number. The stressed form is used in exclamations, in direct address, and to emphasize the possessor.

¡Dios **mío**!	*My God!*
Ven acá, hija **mía**.	*Come here, my daughter.*
Es el dinero **mío**, no el **tuyo**.	*It's my money, not yours.*

Ejercicios

A. *Diga en español:*

1. my tennis racquet
2. your golf clubs
3. his football
4. our team
5. your basketball court
6. your rifle
7. their playing cards
8. her baseball and bat
9. their boats
10. his racing car
11. her tennis ball
12. my pistol

B. *Exprese en español:*

1. My tennis racquet is a Spalding but her tennis racquet is a Wilson.
2. Their permanent waves are cheap, but our permanents are expensive.
3. His house and his garage are dirty.
4. My hair and your hair are blond.
5. The cleaner is pressing our sheets and your towels.

Conjugación del verbo «venir»

venir	*To come*
Yo **vengo** a las ocho.	I come at eight o'clock.
Tú **vienes** a las ocho.	You come at eight o'clock.
Él, Ella **viene** a las ocho.	He, She comes at eight o'clock.
Usted **viene** a las ocho.	You come at eight o'clock.

Nosotros (-as) **venimos** a las ocho.	We come at eight o'clock.
Vosotros (-as) **venís** a las ocho.	You come at eight o'clock.
Ellos, Ellas **vienen** a las ocho.	They come at eight o'clock.
Ustedes **vienen** a las ocho.	You come at eight o'clock.

Ejercicio

Sustituya los sujetos entre paréntesis:

1. Yo vengo a las ocho. (el chófer, el aeromozo)
2. Tú vienes a la playa. (los niños, su estudiante)
3. Andrés viene al hotel. (el turista, los médicos)
4. Nosotros venimos a la iglesia. (el sacerdote, las monjas)
5. Ellos vienen a comer temprano. (yo, tu madre y yo)

Estudio de palabras

Many English words ending in *-ant* have Spanish cognates ending in **-ante.**

abundant	**abundante**	militant	**militante**
brilliant	**brillante**	pedant	**(el, la) pedante**
constant	**constante**	radiant	**radiante**
dominant	**dominante**	redundant	**redundante**
exorbitant	**exorbitante**	resonant	**resonante**
exuberant	**exuberante**	stimulant	**(el) estimulante**
ignorant	**ignorante**	triumphant	**triunfante**

Ejercicio

Complete la frase con una de las palabras siguientes:

elegante	inmigrante	mutante	radiante
extravagante	importante	predominante	vigilante

1. una novia _____   3. un precio _____   5. una madre _____
2. una decisión _____   4. una planta _____   6. un hijo _____

UNIT 15

Possessive pronouns

SINGULAR POSSESSOR

el mío	**la mía**	*mine*
los míos	**las mías**	
el tuyo	**la tuya**	*yours*
los tuyos	**las tuyas**	

PLURAL POSSESSOR

el nuestro	**la nuestra**	*ours*
los nuestros	**las nuestras**	
el vuestro	**la vuestra**	*yours*
los vuestros	**las vuestras**	

| el suyo | la suya | his, hers, yours | el suyo | la suya | theirs, yours |
| los suyos | las suyas | | los suyos | las suyas | |

1. The possessive pronoun is composed of the definite article plus the possessive adjective. It agrees in gender and number with the object possessed.

Yo llevo mi gato y Jorge lleva **el suyo**.   *I take my cat and George takes his.*
Él va con su amigo y yo voy con **el mío**.   *He goes with his friend and I go with mine.*
Escriba bien **los suyos**.   *Write yours well.*

2. The article is omitted after the verb **ser**.

Es mío.   *It's mine.*
Son suyos.   *They are yours.*
¿Es tuya o mía la bebida?   *Is the drink yours or mine?*

"Lo" + *Possessive pronoun*

Lo used with the masculine singular possessive pronouns indicates possession of an indefinite or abstract idea or quality.

Lo mío es suyo.   *What's mine is yours.*
Déme **lo mío** con **lo suyo**.   *Give me mine with yours.*
Lo tuyo vale mucho y **lo nuestro** también.   *Yours is worth a lot and ours is also.*

Clarification of "el suyo"

The definite article, agreeing with the thing possessed, + **de** + a prepositional pronoun (**él, ella, ellos, ellas, Vd., Vds.**) or name is often used in place of the **el suyo** constructions in order to clarify the identity of the possessor.

La señorita García es mi maestra y **la de ellos**.
Miss García is my teacher and theirs.

Mis amigos y **los de él** son boticarios.
My friends and his are druggists.

Mi carro y **el de Carmen** están en el parque de estacionamiento.
My car and Carmen's are in the parking lot.

Ejercicios

A. *Diga en español:*

1. your class and mine
2. It's yours (*indef. fam.*).
3. his boy and mine
4. my children and yours (*fam.*)
5. his money and hers
6. our medicine and theirs

7. their book and his
8. her stationery and ours
9. my cigarettes and yours (*form.*)
10. our pipes or his
11. her stateroom and his
12. your train ticket and ours (*fam.*)

B. *Exprese en español*:

1. James says that his is the best automobile on the street.
2. Here is my glass and this one is yours.
3. Here is my money. Where is yours?
4. My son David is a pharmacist, but yours is a doctor.
5. Our drink is Pepsi Cola, but theirs is wine.
6. That's his surfboard. Where is ours?

Conjugación del verbo «ver»

ver
Yo **veo** el espectáculo.
Tú ves el espectáculo.
Él, Ella **ve** el espectáculo.
Usted **ve** el espectáculo.

Nosotros (–as) **vemos** el espectáculo.
Vosotros (–as) **veis** el espectáculo.
Ellos, Ellas **ven** el espectáculo.
Ustedes **ven** el espectáculo.

to see
I see the show.
You see the show.
He, She sees the show.
You see the show.

We see the show.
You see the show.
They see the show.
You see the show.

Ejercicio

Cambie la oración al singular o al plural, según el caso:

1. El niño ve el espectáculo.
2. El doctor ve al paciente.
3. Yo veo la película.
4. Los maestros ven a los estudiantes.
5. El tintorero ve la mancha.
6. Tú ves al infeliz.

Estudio de pàlabras

Some English words that end in the suffix *-ment* have Spanish cognates with the suffix *-miento*.

compartment	**el compartimiento**	disarmament	**el desarmamiento**
confinement	**el confinamiento**	discernment	**el discernimiento**
contentment	**el contentamiento**	enlistment	**el alistamiento**

Ejercicio

Escriba oraciones con las palabras arriba mencionadas.

UNIT 16

Direct object pronouns

	SINGULAR		PLURAL
me	*me*	**nos**	*us*
te	*you* (fam.)	**os**	*you* (fam.)
le	*him, you* (form.)	**los**	*them, you* (form.)
lo	*him, you* (form.), *it*	**las**	*them, you* (form.)
la	*her, you* (form.), *it*		

1. In Spain, **le** is preferred for the direct object when it represents a male person, and **lo** is preferred for a thing of masculine gender. In Spanish America, **lo** usually refers both to a male person and a thing of masculine gender.

2. The direct object pronoun precedes the conjugated verb and the negative command, but it follows **no**.

Lo quiere.   *She loves him.*
No lo deje Vd.   *Don't leave it.*

3. The direct object pronoun is attached to the affirmative command and may be attached to the present participle. It may also be attached to the infinitive when it is the object of the infinitive.

    In the first two cases, a written accent is placed on the syllable of the verb which was stressed before the addition of the pronoun.

Cómalas después.   *Eat them later.*
Está **diciéndome** una mentira.   *He is telling me a lie.*
Quiero **cantarla**.   *I want to sing it.*

    When the pronoun is the object of the conjugated verb and not the infinitive, it precedes the conjugated verb.

La veo venir.   *I see her coming*

4. When an infinitive or present participle is preceded by a conjugated verb, the pronoun may either be attached to the infinitive or present participle, as described above, or may precede the conjugated verb.

Tu madre **desea verte**.
Tu madre **te desea ver**.   *Your mother wants to see you.*

Están **vendiéndolos** ahora.
Los están vendiendo ahora.   *They are selling them now.*

Ejercicios

A. Diga en español:

1. Write the exercise. Write it.
2. Don't read the novel. Don't read it.
3. He is giving money. He is giving it.
4. Leave it.
5. I have the books. I have them.
6. We visit Henry. We visit him.
7. I want to see Rose. I want to see her.
8. They invite our family. They invite us.
9. Nobody knows me.
10. She loves you (*fam.*).

B. Exprese en español:

1. Florence has some stamps for Tom and he is going to use them.
2. To see you and to dine with you is a pleasure.
3. The students are waiting for him at school. Is he visiting you now?
4. Xavier says to her, "No, I don't love you."
5. I like it better when she irons it for me.

Conjugación del verbo «pensar»

pensar	to think
Yo **pienso** un rato.	I think a while.
Tú **piensas** un rato.	You think a while.
Él, Ella **piensa** un rato.	He, She thinks a while.
Usted **piensa** un rato.	You think a while.
Nosotros (–as) **pensamos** un rato.	We think a while.
Vosotros (–as) **pensáis** un rato.	You think a while.
Ellos, Ellas **piensan** un rato.	They think a while.
Ustedes **piensan** un rato.	You think a while.

Ejercicio

Forme oraciones con los sujetos indicados:

1. pensar un rato (yo, ella)
2. pensar en lo mío (mi madre, los corredores)
3. pensar en la fiesta (Graciela y yo, los niños)
4. pensar bien de él (el banquero, tú y mamá)
5. pensar en las épocas difíciles (los inmigrantes, el poeta)

Estudio de palabras

Many English words ending in -ine have Spanish cognates ending in -ino or -ina.

aquamarine	**el aguamarina** (*f.*)	discipline	**la disciplina**
Argentine	**la Argentina**	doctrine	**la doctrina**
benzedrine	**la bencedrina**	gasoline	**la gasolina**
benzine	**la bencina**	marine	**marino**
brilliantine	**la brillantina**	medicine	**la medicina**
caffeine	**la cafeína**	mine	**la mina**
Caroline	**Carolina**	quinine	**la quinina**
concubine	**la concubina**	sardine	**la sardina**

Ejercicio

Complete la frase con una palabra apropiada del grupo siguiente:

benedictino   salino
calamina   sanguino
fino   Sistina

1. la loción de _____   4. la solución _____
2. el misionero _____   5. los polvos _____
3. el cadáver _____   6. la capilla _____

UNIT 17

Indirect object pronouns

SINGULAR		PLURAL	
me	*to, for me*	**nos**	*to, for us*
te	*to, for you* (fam.)	**os**	*to, for you* (fam.)
le	*to, for him*	**les**	*to, for them* (masc. & fem.)
	to, for her		*to, for you* (form.)
	to, for you (form.)		
	to, for it		

1. The position of an indirect object pronoun in a sentence is identical to that of the direct object pronoun. When both the direct and indirect object pronouns are used in the same expression, the indirect precedes the direct.

Ana **me lo** da.	*Anna gives it to me.*
Ellos **nos lo** venden.	*They sell it to us.*
No **me la** manden Vds.	*Don't send it to me.*
No **me los** compren.	*Don't buy them for me.*
Él quiere prestár**noslo**.	*He wishes to lend it to us.*

Ella ofrece cantár**mela**.	*She offers to sing it to me.*
El carnicero está cortándo**nosla**.	*The butcher is cutting it for us.*
Léa**melo**.	*Read it to me.*
Quíte**noslo**.	*Take it from us.*

2. If both the direct and indirect object pronouns appear in the same expression in the third person (singular or plural), the indirect object **le** or **les** changes to **se**. This change is made for the sake of harmonious sound.

Se las lleva a Vd.	*He takes them to you.*
No **se los** preste a él.	*Don't lend them to him.*
Ella quiere escribír**selo** a ella.	*She wishes to write it to her.*
Ella **se lo** quiere escribir.	*She wishes to write it to her.*
Díga**selo** a ellos.	*Tell it to them.*
Están lavándo**selos**.	*They are washing them for her.*
Se los están lavando.	*They are washing them for her.*

3. The indirect object pronoun **se** means *to him, to her, to you* (sing, or pl.), *to them,* and *to it.* In order to make clear the meaning of **se**, a redundant prepositional form of the pronoun is used. The expression **se lo da** has many possible meanings without clarification. The addition of the subject pronoun reduces them to six meanings: **Ella se lo da.** Clarification of the pronoun allows one possible interpretation:

Ella se lo da a él.	*She gives it to him.*
Se lo da **a él**.	*He, She gives it to him.*
Se lo da **a ella**.	*He, She gives it to her.*
Se lo da **a Vd**.	*He, She gives it to you* (sing.).
Se lo da **a ellos**.	*He, She gives it to them.*
Se lo da **a ellas**.	*He, She gives it to them.*
Se lo da **a Vds**.	*He, She gives it to you* (pl.).
Se lo da **a él**.	*You give it to him.*
Se lo da **a ella**.	*You give it to her.*
Se lo da **a ellos**.	*You give it to them.*
Se lo da **a ellas**.	*You give it to them.*

Ejercicio

A. Exprese en español:

1. Give it to her.
2. Don't give it to him.
3. I am singing it for him.
4. He wants to lend it to me.
5. She is taking them to you.

6. They are selling it to us.
7. Wash it for him.
8. Don't open them for us.
9. They give it to them (*masc.*).
10. They give it to them (*fem.*).

11. Santa Claus has a present and he is going to give it to you.

12. He takes it to her and she says "Thank you" to him.

13. The lady wants to buy it from him.

14. First he buys it for her and then she gives it to you.

15. Buy it for him. Don't buy it for us.

Conjugación del verbo «volver»

volver

Yo **vuelvo** mañana.
Tú **vuelves** mañana.
Él, Ella **vuelve** mañana.
Usted **vuelve** mañana.

Nosotros (–as) **volvemos** mañana.
Vosotros (–as) **volvéis** mañana.
Ellos, Ellas **vuelven** mañana.
Ustedes **vuelven** mañana.

to return

I return tomorrow.
You return tomorrow.
He, She returns tomorrow.
You return tomorrow.

We return tomorrow.
You return tomorrow.
They return tomorrow.
You return tomorrow.

Ejercicio

Complete la oración utilizando la forma apropiada del verbo **volver**:

1. El florista _____ en una hora.
2. Los bomberos _____ inmediatamente.
3. Pancho y yo _____ mañana.
4. ¿Cuándo _____ ella?
5. Tú y Luisa _____ del mercado.
6. Nosotras _____ pronto.

Estudio de palabras

Many English adjectives ending in *-ive* have Spanish cognates ending in *-ivo*.

active	**activo**	festive	**festivo**
alternative	**alternativo**	inclusive	**inclusivo**
collective	**colectivo**	primitive	**primitivo**
conclusive	**conclusivo**	sensitive	**sensitivo**
constructive	**constructivo**	superlative	**superlativo**
exclusive	**exclusivo**	tentative	**tentativo**

Ejercicio

Complete la frase con la palabra apropiada del grupo siguiente:

explosivo	extensivo	pasivo	posesivo
expresivo	intensivo	positivo	productivo

1. una situación _____
2. el adjetivo _____
3. el grado _____
4. una hacienda _____
5. unas vacaciones _____
6. una palabra _____

UNIT 18

Reflexive pronouns

SINGULAR		PLURAL	
me	*myself*	nos	*ourselves*
te	*yourself* (fam.)	os	*yourselves* (fam.)
se	*himself, herself,*	se	*themselves, yourselves* (form.)
	yourself (form.), *itself*		

1. A reflexive pronoun is an object pronoun which refers to the subject of the verb. In a reflexive construction, the subject performs the action of the verb to itself. Many verbs in Spanish are generally used with reflexive pronouns.

Me lavo la cara.	*I wash my face.*
Se sienta.	*He sits down.*

2. Reflexive pronouns precede all other object pronouns and, like object pronouns, are attached to infinitives, present participles, and affirmative commands.

Ella **se lava** la cara.	*She washes her face.*
Ella **se la lava.**	*She washes it.*
Se me acerca.	*He approaches me.*
Quiere **bañarse** en el río.	*He wants to bathe in the river.*
Estamos **limpiándonos** el polvo.	*We are cleaning off the dust from us.*
Levántese Vd.	*Get up.*
No se levante Vd.	*Don't get up.*

3. When the reflexive pronoun is used with some verbs, a change in meaning occurs.

hacer	*to make, to do*
hacerse	*to become*

Hago mucho trabajo.	*I do a lot of work.*
Quiere **hacerse** abogado.	*He wants to become a lawyer.*

poner	*to place*
ponerse	*to become*

Pongo el centavo en la máquina.	*I put the penny in the machine.*
Se pone triste.	*He becomes sad.*

hallar	*to find*
hallarse	*to find oneself*

Hallo tranquilidad en el bosque.	*I find tranquility in the woods.*
Me hallo contento con mis ganancias.	*I find myself happy with my earnings.*

4. Some non-reflexive intransitive verbs use the reflexive pronoun to indicate emphasis or a special interest on the part of the subject in the action or state of the verb.

Yo **me voy** al campo.   *I am going to the country.*
Quédese Vd. aquí.   *Stay here.*
Nos marchamos después del almuerzo.   *We are leaving after lunch.*

5. Reciprocal action between two or more subjects is indicated with reflexive pronouns.

Él y ella se saludan amablemente.   *He and she greet each other amiably.*
Tú y yo nos queremos como buenos amigos.   *You and I love each other as good friends.*

6. In reflexive constructions, the possessive adjective is replaced by the definite article.

Él se lava **los pies**.   *He washes his feet.*
Ella se lava **el pelo**.   *She washes her hair.*

Ejercicio

Exprese en español:

1. I comb my hair.
2. You wash your face.
3. He gets up.
4. We go away.
5. John and Mary love each other.
6. Albert washes his face, eats his breakfast, and goes to work each day at eight o'clock.
7. The old man becomes nervous, combs his hair, and gets up from the chair.
8. The girls look at themselves in the mirror and put on their lipstick and powder.
9. Father bathes each morning at seven thirty and shaves his beard.
10. She becomes very sad and approaches me with her problems.

Conjugación del verbo «sentarse»

sentarse   *to sit down*

Yo **me siento** en el sofá.   I sit down on the sofa.
Tú **te sientas** en el sofá.   You sit down on the sofa.
Él, Ella **se sienta** en el sofá.   He, She sits down on the sofa.
Usted **se sienta** en el sofá.   You sit down on the sofa.

Nosotros (–as) **nos sentamos** en el sofá.   We sit down on the sofa.
Vosotros (–as) **os sentáis** en el sofá.   You sit down on the sofa.
Ellos, Ellas **se sientan** en el sofá.   They sit down on the sofa.
Ustedes **se sientan** en el sofá.   You sit down on the sofa.

Ejercicio

Complete las oraciones con la forma apropiada del verbo **sentarse:**

1. Mi padre _____ en el sofá.
2. Los niños _____ en el tren.
3. Pepe y yo _____ las sillas de cubierta.

4. ¿Dónde quieres _____ ?
5. Su abuela _____ en el autobús.
6. _____ en el avión.

Estudio de palabras

Athens	**Atenas**	theme	**(el) tema**
Catherine	**Catalina**	Theodore	**Teodoro**
mathematics	**(las) matemáticas**	theorem	**(el) teorema**
method	**(el) método**	therapeutic	**terapéutico**
myth	**(el) mito**	thermal	**termal**
north	**(el) norte**	thermometer	**(el) termómetro**
rhythm	**(el) ritmo**	thrombosis	**(la) trombosis**
theatre	**(el) teatro**	throne	**(el) trono**

Ejercicio

¿Cuál es el cognado inglés de las palabras siguientes?

1. Itaca	5. termodinámico	9. termos
2. metano	6. teológico	10. Tesauro
3. teocéntrico	7. teólogo	11. tesis
4. teocracia	8. termoeléctrico	12. tórax

UNIT 19

Prepositional pronouns

SINGULAR		PLURAL	
para **mí**	*for me*	para **nosotros (–as)**	*for us*
para **tí**	*for you*	para **vosotros (–as)**	*for you*
para **él**	*for him, for it* (masc.)	para **ellos**	*for them*
para **ella**	*for her, for it* (fem.)	para **ellas**	*for them*
para **Vd.**	*for you*	para **Vds.**	*for you*
para **ello**	*for it* (neuter)		

1. The prepositional pronoun is used as the object of a preposition. It may also be used in a redundant construction to emphasize or clarify the meaning of a direct or indirect object pronoun.

Papá está comprando una radio **para nosotros**.	*Papa is buying a radio for us.*
El cartero trae unas cartas **para ella**.	*The mailman brings some letters for her.*
Hablo **de ellos** ahora.	*I am speaking of them now.*
Alguien **le** llama a **él**.	*Somebody is calling him.*
Te quiere a **tí**.	*He loves you.*

2. The preposition **entre** is an exception and uses a subject pronoun as its object.

Entre tú y yo no hay problemas.   *Between you and me there are no*
                                                  problems.

Ella va **conmigo** al muelle.   *She goes with me to the pier.*
No hay problemas **contigo**.   *There aren't any problems with you.*

Reflexive prepositional pronouns

SINGULAR		PLURAL	
para **mí**	*for myself*	para **nosotros** (–as)	*for ourselves*
para **ti**	*for yourself*	para **vosotros** (–as)	*for yourselves*
para **sí**	*for himself*	para **sí**	*for themselves*
	for herself		*for yourselves*
	for yourself		
	for itself		

1. The reflexive prepositional pronouns have the same forms as the prepositional pronouns
    with the exception of the third person singular and plural.
    Habla **para sí**.   *He is talking to himself.*
    Ellos hacen esto **para sí**.   *They do this for themselves.*

2. The reflexive prepositional pronoun **sí** combines with the preposition **con** to form **consigo**.

Ella tiene el dinero **consigo**.   *She has the money with her.*

3. **Mismo** (–a, –os, –as) may be used with the reflexive prepositional pronouns for emphasis.
    It agrees in gender and number with the pronoun.

Tú lo haces **para ti mismo**.   *You do it for yourself.*
Ellos trabajan **para sí mismos**.   *They work for themselves.*

Table of personal pronouns

SUBJECT SINGULAR	DIRECT OBJECT	INDIRECT OBJECT	REFLEXIVE	PREPOSITIONAL	REFLEXIVE PREPOSITIONAL
yo	me	me	me	mí	mí
tú	te	te	te	ti	ti
él	(le) lo	le	se	él	sí
ella	la	le	se	ella	sí
usted	(le) lo, la	le	se	usted	sí
ello	lo	le	se	ello	sí

PLURAL

nosotros (–as)	nos	nos	nos	nosotros (–as)	nosotros (–as)
vosotros (–as)	os	os	os	vosotros (–as)	vosotros (–as)
ellos	los	les	se	ellos	sí
ellas	las	les	se	ellas	sí
ustedes	los, las	les	se	ustedes	sí

Ejercicios

A. Diga en español:

1. for herself
2. for themselves
3. for ourselves
4. for yourself (*fam.*)
5. for yourself (*form.*)

6. I do it for myself.
7. He speaks to himself
8. Work for yourselves.
9. That beautiful girl believes in herself.
10. They think only of themselves.

B. Exprese en español:

1. I have a letter for her.
2. The money is for you (*fam.*).
3. My brother lives near me.
4. The child sits down with us.
5. Do you know her?
6. Don't eat the potatoes with it.
7. Paul receives a present from them.

8. These pills are for me but those near you (*fam.*) are for us.
9. He loves her but he never sends her money.
10. Helen and Virginia are with me in the bookstore. Is the baby with you?
11. He speaks to her but she never answers him.

Conjugación del verbo «dormir»

dormir

Yo **duermo** la siesta.
Tú **duermes** la siesta.
Él, Ella **duerme** la siesta.
Usted **duerme** la siesta.

Nosotros (–as) **dormimos** la siesta.
Vosotros (–as) **dormís** la siesta.
Ellos, Ellas **duermen** la siesta.
Ustedes **duermen** la siesta.

to sleep

I sleep the siesta. (I take a nap.)
You sleep the siesta.
He, She sleeps the siesta.
You sleep the siesta.

We sleep the siesta.
You sleep the siesta.
They sleep the siesta.
You sleep the siesta.

Ejercicio

Use la forma apropiada del verbo **dormir:**

1. Pancho _____ la siesta cerca de un cacto.
2. Los pilotos nunca _____ en los aviones.

3. No me gusta _____ en ese motel.
4. El soldado y yo _____ todo el domingo.
5. No puedo _____; tengo que ir a la catedral.

Estudio de palabras

Many English words beginning with *s* have Spanish cognates beginning with **es**.

scandalous	**escandaloso**	squadron	**(el) escuadrón**
scenery	**(el) escenario**	stable	**(el) establo**
skeleton	**(el) esqueleto**	stomach	**(el) estómago**
Spanish	**español**	strait	**(el) estrecho**
spectator	**(el) espectador**	strict	**estricto**
spinach	**(las) espinacas**	student	**(el, la) estudiante**
spiritual	**espiritual**	stupid	**estúpido**
spy	**(el, la) espía**	style	**(el) estilo**

Ejercicio

Exprese en inglés:

1. la *escuela* elemental
2. un *estudiante* brillante
3. la *estación* de ómnibus
4. el *estado* artificial
5. un *estudio* independiente
6. el *estadio* olímpico
7. el *espacio* sin límites
8. la *esfera* celeste

UNIT 20

«*Para*»

The preposition **para** is used in the following situations to express:

1. Destination.

Trae unos juguetes **para los muchachos**.
Los Morales salen **para México** en avión.
La carta es **para mí**.

He brings some toys for the children.
The Morales leave for Mexico by plane.
The letter is for me.

2. Purpose or use.

Estas químicas son **para un experimento**.
Usan cemento **para construir la casa**.
Voy a la farmacia **para comprar
    calmantes**.

These chemicals are for an experiment.
They use cement to construct the house.
*I am going to the drug store to buy
    tranquilizers.*

3.   Comparisons or contrasts.

Su padrino no está mal **para su edad**.	*His godfather is not bad for his age.*
Para uno tan rico, vive en una casa muy pobre.	*For one so rich, he lives in a very poor house.*
Para ser español, hablas bien el inglés.	*For a Spaniard, you speak English well.*

4.   A definite point in future time.

El postre es **para mañana**.	*The dessert is for tomorrow.*
Va a terminar el proyecto **para el sábado**.	*He is going to finish the project for Saturday.*
Déjelo **para el invierno próximo**.	*Leave it for next winter.*

5.   After **estar** to state something about to happen.

Los jóvenes **están para casarse**.	*The young people are about to get married.*
Está para nevar.	*It is about to snow.*

«Por»

The preposition **por** is used to express:

1.   Exchange, price, terms, unit of measure, rate, or multiplication.

Compre Vd. este cuadro **por cien dólares**.	*Buy this picture for a hundred dollars.*
Deseo cambiar esta falda **por ésa**.	*I want to exchange this skirt for that one.*
Tres **por tres** son nueve.	*Three times three are nine.*

2.   Duration of time.

Estudio **por dos horas** cada noche.	*I study for two hours each night.*
Está sufriendo **por muchos años**.	*He has been suffering for many years.*
Podemos descansar **por un rato**.	*We can rest for a while.*

3.   The cause, motive, or reason for an action.

La castigan **por desobediente**.	*They punish her for being disobedient.*
No trabaja en esa fábrica **por razones conocidas**.	*He doesn't work in that factory for known reasons.*
No puedo pagar la renta **por falta de pesos**.	*I can't pay the rent for lack of pesos (money).*

4.   The means, manner, or instrument by which something is done.

Mandan los papeles **por correo**.	*They send the papers by mail.*
Por ese camino Vd. llega a la pirámide.	*By that road you arrive at the pyramid.*

5.   Indefinite or vague location.

Los ratones corren **por el sótano**.	*The rats run through the cellar.*
Por aquí no hay nadie.	*There is nobody around here.*

Buscan **por todas partes** al perro perdido.   *They are looking everywhere for the lost dog.*

El tren pasa **por el túnel**.   *The train passes through the tunnel.*

6.   On account of, for the sale of, in behalf of.

Muere **por su familia**.   *He dies for his family.*
Voy al fin del mundo **por Carmen**.   *I am going to the ends of the earth for Carmen.*

Ejercicios

A.   *Diga en español:*

1.   This engagement ring is for you.
2.   He is young for his age.
3.   The work is for tomorrow.
4.   Leave it for next week.
5.   Two times two are four.

6.   They work in order to live.
7.   I can buy the painting for $150.
8.   Send the book by mail.
9.   He is about to arrive.
10. We return by five o'clock.

B.   *Exprese en español:*

1.   In order to build a new house, we are going to ask for a mortgage.
2.   The bowling tournament is for tomorrow, but for now you may practice on this bowling alley.
3.   She is youthful for her age, but he is about to die.
4.   I am doing this for you, not for him.
5.   For someone so young, he is very intelligent.

Conjugación del verbo «*morir*»

morir   *to die*

Yo **muero** mil veces.   I die a thousand times.
Tú **mueres** mil veces.   You die a thousand times.
Él, Ella **muere** mil veces.   He, She dies a thousand times.
Usted **muere** mil veces.   You die a thousand times.

Nosotros (–as) **morimos** mil veces.   We die a thousand times.
Vosotros (–as) **morís** mil veces.   You die a thousand times.
Ellos, Ellas **mueren** mil veces.   They die a thousand times.
Ustedes **mueren** mil veces.   You die a thousand times.

Ejercicio

Complete las oraciones empleando el verbo **morir**.

1.   Los soldados . . .
2.   El paciente . . .
3.   Las víctimas del fuego . . .

4.   El asesino . . .
5.   Yo . . .
6.   Los criminales . . .

Estudio de palabras

The letter *y* in many English words is often the equivalent of **i** in Spanish cognates.

anonymous	**anónimo**	myth	**(el) mito**
crystal	**(el) cristal**	mythology	**(la) mitología**
cylinder	**(el) cilindro**	nylon	**(el) nilón**
encyclopedia	**(la) enciclopedia**	oxygen	**(el) oxígeno**
motorcycle	**(la) motocicleta**	rhyme	**(la) rima**
my	**mi**	syllable	**(la) sílaba**
myriad	**(la) miríada**	Tony	**Toni**
mystic	**(el) místico**	xylophone	**(el) xilófono**

Ejercicio

Complete las oraciones:

1. _____ es mi compañero de cuarto.
2. Me falta _____.
3. Santa Teresa es _____.
4. Mi hijo tiene un piano y mi hija tiene un _____.

5. Mi coche tiene ocho _____.
6. La palabra tiene tres _____.

UNIT 21

Relative pronouns

The commonly used Spanish relative pronouns are listed below. The relative pronoun may not be omitted in Spanish as it often is in English.

que	(invariable) *who, whom, which, that*
quien(es)	*who, whom, he who*
el (la) que	*that which, who, the one who*
los (las) que	*those which, who, those who*
lo que	(neuter) *which, what*
el (la) cual	*which, who*
los (las) cuales	*which, who*
lo cual	(neuter) *which, that, what*

1. The invariable **que** is the most common of the relative pronouns. It may be used as the subject or object and may refer to persons or things. After a preposition **que** refers only to things.

Te presento a Magdalena, Gloria e Isabel, **que** son mis primas.
I present to you Magdalen, Gloria, and Isabel, who are my cousins.

Saludos a tus vecinos **que** viven en la esquina.
Greetings to your neighbors that live on the corner.

La casa en **que** vives es cómoda.
The house in which you live is comfortable.

2.   **Quienes** always refers to persons even after prepositions. As the object of a verb it is used with the personal "**a.**"

Mis alumnos, **quienes** son muy perezosos, van a sufrir un examen hoy.
My pupils, who are very lazy, are going to take an examination today.

Quien no se aventura, no pasa el mar.
He who doesn't adventure doesn't cross the sea. (Nothing ventured, nothing gained.)

No sé **a quién** vamos a visitar.
I don't know whom we are going to visit.

3.   The definite articles are used with the relative **que** to avoid repetition of nouns.

Estos zapatos **y los que** están en la caja me quedan bien.
These shoes and those that are in the box fit me.

Voy a comprar las manzanas rojas y también **las que** todavía están verdes.
I am going to buy the red apples and also those that are still green.

The definite articles are also used with **que** to distingusih the gender and number of the antecedent, thus avoiding ambiguity in sentences that have two possible antecedents.

Va al baile con la hermana del francés, **la que** le interesa mucho.
He is going to the dance with the Frenchman's sister, who interests him a great deal.

El amigo de Patricia, **el que** está en Europa, regresa mañana.
Patricia's friend, who is in Europe, will return tomorrow.

El que may be used instead of **quien** to begin a sentence.

El que no se aventura, no pasa el mar.
He who doesn't adventure, doesn't cross the sea. (Nothing ventured, nothing gained.)

4.   The definite articles are also used with **cual(es)** to refer to persons or things in order to avoid ambiguity in sentences that have two possible antecedents. These forms are not used to begin a Spanish sentence.

El hijo de Emilia, **el cual** trabaja en la casa de bomberos, está casado con mi hija.
Emily's son, who works in the firehouse, is married to my daughter.

5.   **Lo que** and **lo cual** are the neuter relative pronouns. They refer to a statement or previously mentioned idea.

El aumento de salario es **lo que** (**lo cual**) me interesa.
The increase in salary is what interests me.

The relative possessive adjective «cuyo»

Cuyo (–a, –os, —as) is the relative possessive adjective and agrees in gender and number with the thing possessed (usually the noun that immediately follows). **Cuyo** corresponds to the English *whose, of whom, of which.*

Esa chica, **cuyo** hermano es **mi amigo**, es muy linda.
That girl, whose brother is my friend, is very pretty.

Daniel, **cuya** madre es mi abuela, está en el hospital.
Daniel, whose mother is my grandmother, is in the hospital.

Esos helados en el mostrador, **cuyos** sabores son deliciosos, son muy caros.
Those ice creams on the counter, whose flavors are delicious, are very expensive.

Ejercicios

A. *Diga en español:*

1. The baker who works at night . . .
2. He who seeks . . .
3. To whom you write . . .
4. Frank, whose house is wooden . . .
5. The 747, the plane that you prefer . . .
6. The girl to whom you are speaking . . .
7. The doctor who is here . . .
8. Bernard's sister, who works there . . .

B. *Exprese en español:*

1. The teacher who comes from Argentina speaks English very well.
2. Those students who study a great deal are going to receive an A.
3. The father-in-law to whom you are writing is a very nice man.
4. Anthony, whose mother is in Italy, is going to visit Rome next year.
5. The sofa, which is more comfortable than the chair, is very inexpensive.

Conjugación del verbo «traer»

traer   *to carry, bring*

Yo **traigo** la leña.   I carry the wood.
Tú **traes** la leña.   You carry the wood.
Él, Ella **trae** la leña.   He, She carries the wood.
Usted **trae** la leña.   You carry the wood.

Nosotros (–as) **traemos** la leña.   We carry the wood.
Vosotros (–as) **traéis** la leña.   You carry the wood.
Ellos, Ellas **traen** la leña.   They carry the wood.
Ustedes **traen** la leña.   You carry the wood.

Ejercicio

Complete las oraciones:

1. El pastelero nos _____ los pasteles.
2. ¡_____ los libros a clase!
3. Mis padres _____ la comida a casa.

4. El boticario me _____ el yodo.
5. El bombero y yo _____ el perro herido al dueño.

Estudio de palabras

Many English words with the prefix *dis* have Spanish cognates with the prefix **des**.

disappearance	**(la) desaparición**	disloyalty	**(la) deslealtad**
discovery	**(el) descubrimiento**	disobedience	**(la) desobediencia**
disdain	**(el) desdén**	disorder	**(el) desorden**
disillusionment	**(la) desilusión**	disproportion	**(la) desproporción**
disinterest	**(el) desinterés**	dishonor	**(la) deshonra**

Ejercicio

Use los adjetivos siguientes en oraciones españolas:

1. desagradable (*disagreeable*)
2. desanimado (*discouraged*)
3. descorazonado (*disheartened*)
4. descortés (*discourteous*)

5. desinteresado (*disinterested*)
6. desorganizado (*disorganized*)
7. desposeído (*dispossessed*)
8. desventajoso (*disadvantageous*)

UNIT 22

Interrogative pronouns

1. The forms of the interrogative pronouns are the same as those of the relative pronouns, with the addition of an accent mark and without the definite articles before **que** and **cual**.

¿Qué . . . ?	¿**Qué** compras en la tienda?	*What are you buying in the store?*
¿Cuál . . . ?	¿**Cuál** de los perros es tuyo?	*Which of the dogs is yours?*
¿Cuáles . . . ?	¿**Cuáles** paquetes son tuyos?	*Which packages are yours?*
¿Quién . . . ?	¿**Quién** se atreve a comer ese plato?	*Who dares to eat that dish?*
¿Quiénes . . . ?	¿**Quiénes** son esos muchachos?	*Who are those boys?*
¿Cuánto (–a, –os, –as) . . . ?	¿**Cuántos** van a la playa?	*How many are going to the beach?*

2. Question marks are not used in indirect questions, but the accent is still required on the interrogative pronoun.

Dígame **qué** va a comprar en la tienda.

Tell me what you are going to buy in the store.

Exclamatory pronouns

Exclamatory pronouns employ the same forms as the interrogative pronouns. Exclamation points precede and follow the sentence instead of question marks to indicate surprise, doubt, or some other strong emotion.

1. ¡**Qué** . . .!

What a . . . .! How . . .!

¡**Qué** hombre tan guapo!
¡**Qué** mujer más linda!
¡**Qué** vista!
¡**Qué** bueno!
¡**Qué** bien!

What a handsome man!
What a beautiful woman!
What a view!
How good!
How well!

When **qué** is used with a noun modified by an adjective, **tan** or **más** is usually included in the expression.

2. ¡**Cuánto** (–a, –os, –as) . . .!

How much . . .! How many . . .!

¡**Cuánta** gente!
¡**Cuántos** vienen!
¡**Cuánto** tengo!

How many people!
How many are coming!
How much I have!

Interjections

1. Interjections commonly used in conversation

¡**Abajo**!	*Down with . . .!*	¡**Diantre**!	*The deuce!*
¡**Adelante**!	*Straight ahead!*	¡**Diga**!	*Tell me!*
¡**Alerta**!	*Keep alert!*	¡**Ea**!	*Come!*
¡**Alto**!	*Halt!*	¡**Eh**!	*Hey!*
¡**Anda**!	*Go on!*	¡**Fuego**!	*Fire!*
¡**Ay**!	*Ouch!*	¡**Fuera**!	*Out!*
¡**Bobo**!	*Fool!*	¡**Hola**!	*Hello!*
¡**Caballero**!	*Sir!*	¡**Hombre**!	*Man!*
¡**Caramba**!	*Heck!*	¡**Huy**!	*Phew!*
¡**Cáspita**!	*Can you imagine!*	¡**Ja, ja**!	*Ha, ha!*
¡**Claro**!	*Of course!*	¡**Mire** (–a)!	*Look!*
¡**Cuidado**!	*Be careful!*	¡**Muera** . . .!	*Death to . . .!*
¡**Chas**!	*Oops!, Boom!*	¡**Oiga**! (¡**Oye**!)	*Listen!*
¡**Chist**!	*Sh-sh!, Be quiet!*	¡**Ojo**!	*Attention!*

¡Olé!	*Bravo!, Encore!*	¡Upa!	*Upsy daisy! (to lift)*
¡Quita!	*Stop!*	¡Vamos!	*Come on!*
¡Señor!	*My dear fellow!*	¡Vaya!	*Of course!, indeed!*
¡Silencio!	*Silence!*	¡Viva . . .!	*Long live . . . !*
¡Socorro!	*Help!*	¡Ya!	*I see!, Indeed!*

2.   Interjections used with animals

¡arre!	*giddap!*	¡mis, mis!	*puss, puss!*
¡bee!, bah!	*bah! (lamb or goat)*	¡mu-u!	*moo!*
¡firme!	*steady!*	¡quiquiriqui!	*cock-a-doodle-do!*
¡guau, guau!	*bow wow!*	¡so!	*whoa!*
¡miau!	*meow!*	¡zape!	*scat!*

3.   Divine interjections

Divine interjections are commonly used in Spanish with no blasphemous intent. A literal translation does not convey a precise meaning of these words.

¡Ave María!	¡Jesús!	¡Cielos!
¡Ave María Purísima!	¡Virgen santísima!	¡Válgame Dios!
¡Cristo!	¡Dios!	¡Jesucristo!

4.   Any combination of words in Spanish that expresses exhortation, surprise, disgust, fear, joy, sorrow, desire, anger, or other intense personal emotion that is spontaneously expressed is considered an exclamatory construction.

¡Salta de ahí ahora mismo!	*Get out of there right now!*
¡Pobre hombre!	*Poor man!*
¡Castañas!, ¡Maní!	*Chestnuts!, Peanuts!*
¡Piña deliciosa! ¡A la buena piña!	*Delicious pineapple! Come get your pineapple!*
¡Me alegra verte!	*I'm happy to see you!*

Ejercicios

A.   *Diga en español:*

1.   What is this?
2.   Whom do you pay?
3.   Who are the tourists?
4.   How many persons are here?
5.   How sweet it is!

6.   Silence, please!
7.   Be careful, fool!
8.   Help!
9.   Gosh! What a stupid man!
10.   Long live the Queen!

B.   *Exprese en español*:

1.   Which of the two students is your girl friend? That one. Man! What a doll!
2.   How many of that group are going to college?
3.   I don't know how many are going to the butcher shop.
4.   Children! Stop! Don't go near the fire!
5.   Heavens! Another D in Spanish. The deuce with it!
6.   Ouch! These desks are not comfortable. I should say not!

Conjugación del verbo «salir»

salir   *to leave*

Yo **salgo** a las ocho.   I leave at eight o'clock.
Tú **sales** a las ocho.   You leave at eight o'clock.
Él, Ella **sale** a las ocho.   He, She leaves at eight o'clock.
Usted **sale** a las ocho.   You leave at eight o'clock.

Nosotros **salimos** a las ocho.   We leave at eight o'clock.
Vosotros **salís** a las ocho.   You leave at eight o'clock.
Ellos, Ellas **salen** a las ocho.   They leave at eight o'clock.
Ustedes **salen** a las ocho.   You leave at eight o'clock.

Ejercicio

Forme oraciones con los sujetos indicados y la forma apropiada del verbo **salir**:

1.   salir ahora (Juan y yo, el relojero)
2.   salir temprano (nosotros, los mecánicos)
3.   salir a las cinco (Vd., el empleado)
4.   salir con tu padre (tú, yo)
5.   salir antes de comer (ellos, los bomberos)
6.   salir del país (los pobres, ella)

Estudio de Palabras

Many English words with a double consonant have Spanish cognates with a single consonant.

appetite	(el) apetito	massage	(el) masaje
battery	(la) batería	necessary	necesario
centennial	(el) centenario	occupation	(la) ocupación
commission	(la) comisión	offensive	(la) ofensiva
different	diferente	passive	pasivo
fission	(la) fisión	possible	posible
grippe	(la) gripe	rebellion	(la) rebelión
Hellenic	helénico	symmetry	(la) simetría
lottery	(la) lotería	tennis	(el) tenis

Ejercicio

Complete las frases con las palabras siguientes:

la acomodación	inteligente	
la asociación	el misionero	(*missionary*)
la atención	la oferta	(*offer*)
la batalla	(*battle*)	el pudín	(*pudding*)
la hamaca	(*hammock*)	la sílaba	

1. _____ de los estudiantes
2. _____ de Waterloo
3. la religiosidad del _____
4. _____ del marinero
5. _____en el hotel

6. las ideas de las personas _____
7. el sabor del _____
8. la pronunciación de _____
9. _____ del cliente

UNIT 23

Infinitives

1. Infinitives may be used as subjects or objects and may directly follow conjugated verbs when there is no change in subject.

Vivir bien es agradable.
Quiero **regresar** a casa.
Los turistas deciden **ir** a Roma.
¡Esto sí que es **vivir**!

To live well is pleasant.
I want to return home.
The tourists decide to go to Rome.
This is really living!

2. The infinitive is employed as the object of prepositions.

Necesitamos comer para **vivir**.
One must eat in order to live.

Después de **satisfacer** las deudas, nunca jamás voy a **trabajar**.
After I satisfy my debts, I am never going to work again.

3. **Al** plus an infinitive expresses the English *on, when, upon* plus a verb.

Al entrar, se sienta a la mesa.
On entering he sits at the table.

Al terminar el curso, vas a recibir un automóvil.
When you finish the course you are going to receive an automobile.

4. In Spanish, the infinitive preceded by the definite article **el** is used as a verbal noun. The present participle is used as a verbal noun in English.

El nadar es mi deporte favorito.
Swimming is my favorite sport.

5. The infinitive preceded by **a** is often used as a command.

¡**A trabajar**, compadre!   *Get to work, friend!*
¡**A nadar**!   *Let's go swimming!*

Infinitives used with prepositions

The prepositions most often used with infinitives are **con, a, de**, and **en**.

1. **Con** is commonly used with the following verbs:

bastar con	*to be enough*	**contentarse con**	*to be content with*
contar con	*to count on*	**soñar con**	*to dream of*
casarse con	*to marry*	**tropezar con**	*to stumble on, run into*
comprometerse con	*to become engaged to*		

Basta con eso.   *Enough of that.*
Yo **cuento con** tu amistad.   *I'm counting on your friendship.*

2. **A** is commonly used with the following verbs:

acertar a	*to happen to*	**incitar a**	*to incite*
acostumbrarse a	*to accustom oneself to*	**invitar a**	*to invite*
aprender a	*to learn to*	**ir a**	*to go to*
apresurarse a	*to be in a hurry to*	**llegar a**	*to arrive at*
asistir a	*to attend*	**negarse a**	*to refuse*
asomarse a	*to lean out of*	**obligarse a**	*to oblige oneself to*
atreverse a	*to dare to*	**oponerse a**	*to oppose*
ayudar a	*to help*	**parecerse a**	*to resemble*
comenzar a	*to begin*	**persuadir a**	*to persuade*
decidirse a	*to decide on*	**prestarse a**	*to lend oneself*
disponerse a	*to be disposed to*	**renunciar a**	*to renounce*
empezar a	*to begin to*	**resignarse a**	*to resign oneself to*
enseñar a	*to teach to*		

Se atreve a subir esa montaña.   *He dares to climb that mountain.*
Ella **renuncia a** las tentaciones del diablo.   *She renounces the temptations of the devil.*

3. **De** is commonly used with the following verbs:

acabar de + inf.	*to have just* + inf.	**cansarse de**	*to be tired of*
acordarse de	*to remember*	**carecer de**	*to lack*
alegrarse de	*to be happy*	**cesar de**	*to cease*
alejarse de	*to move away from*	**despedirse de**	*to take leave of*
arrepentirse de	*to repent*	**disfrutar de**	*to enjoy*
asombrarse de	*to be surprised*	**enamorarse de**	*to fall in love with*
burlarse de	*to make fun of*	**encargarse de**	*to take charge of*

enterarse de	*to find out about*	gozar de	*to enjoy*
equivocarse de	*to be mistaken (wrong) in*	olvidarse de	*to forget*
		quejarse de	*to complain*
extrañarse de	*to be surprised at*	tratar de	*to try to*

El presidente **se burla del** incidente.
El paciente **trata de** caminar.

The president makes fun of the incident.
The patient tries to walk

4.   **En** is commonly used with the following verbs.:

acordar en	*to reach an accord about*	insistir en	*to insist on*
		molestarse en	*to be bothered with*
confiar en	*to confide in*	ocuparse en	*to busy oneself in*
consentir en	*to consent to*	pensar en	*to think of*
convenir en	*to agree to*	persistir en	*to persist in*
empeñarse en	*to persist in*	quedarse en	*to remain in*
entrar en	*to enter into*	tardar en	*to be late in*
fijarse en	*to pay attention to*	vacilar en	*to vacilate in*

Insiste Benjamín **en** pagar la cuenta.
Nunca **confía** Alicia **en** su madre.

Benjamín insists on paying the bill.
Alice never confides in her mother.

Ejercicios

A.   *Diga en español*:

1.   to eat well
2.   I like to eat spinach.
3.   He wants to see you.
4.   We decide to go.
5.   on entering the building
6.   after starting the work
7.   when I decided to invite you
8.   Getting married is a good idea.
9.   My grandfather likes to tell stories.
10.   Enjoy life!

B.   *Exprese en español*:

1.   Enough of that language.
2.   I want to marry María.
3.   I'm surprised at him.
4.   He is opposed to that question.
5.   We bump into the teacher every day.
6.   I have just done my work.
7.   You are wrong in that idea.
8.   Pay attention to the lesson, and don't make fun of him.
9.   She resembles her daughter.
10.   He insists on reading that romantic novel about the old lady who marries her gardener.
11.   We repent being wrong in our actions.
12.   You are late in arriving and you remain in the office for only half a day.
13.   She persists in calling me.
14.   I'm not in love with her.

Conjugación del verbo «caber»

caber	to fit
Yo **quepo** en el ascensor.	I fit in the elevator.
Tú **cabes** en el ascensor.	You fit in the elevator.
Él, Ella **cabe** en el ascensor.	He, She fits in the elevator.
Usted **cabe** en el ascensor.	You fit in the elevator.
Nosotros (–as) **cabemos** en el ascensor.	We fit in the elevator.
Vosotros (–as) **cabéis** en el ascensor.	You fit in the elevator.
Ellos, Ellas **caben** en el ascensor.	They fit in the elevator.
Ustedes **caben** en el ascensor.	You fit in the elevator

Ejercicio

Exprese en español:

1. I fit in the elevator.
2. The pie fits in the box.
3. The fat lady does not fit in that seat.
4. We cannot fit in that bus.
5. George and I fit well in the small car.
6. They fit in the back seat.

Estudio de palabras

The *o, oo* or *ou* in many English words are often the equivalents of **u** or **ue** in Spanish cognates.

accord	(el) acuerdo	discourse	(el) discurso
account	(la) cuenta	force	(la) fuerza
announcer	(el) anunciador	knot	(el) nudo
censorship	(la) censura	post	(el) puesto
cross	(la) cruz	secondary school	(la) escuela secundaria
custom	(la) costumbre	South America	Suramérica
discount	(el) descuento		(Sudamérica)
discovery	(el) descubrimiento		

Ejercicio

Use las frases en una oración y tradúzcalas al inglés:

1. la blusa de seda
2. una idea común
3. el descubridor hispánico
4. la fuente
5. el mes de octubre
6. la cubierta de nieve
7. uno por uno
8. el champú
9. el curso de español
10. la escuela sudamericana

UNIT 24

Present participle

1. The present participle is formed by adding **–ando** to the stem of first conjugation (**–ar**) verbs and **–iendo** to the stem of second (**–er**) and third conjugation (**–ir**) verbs. It is an invariable construction and always ends in **–o**.

tomar: tomando *taking*   **comer: comiendo** *eating*   **vivir: viviendo** *living*

2. Some verbs have irregular present participles.

caer:	**cayendo**	*falling*		**leer:**	**leyendo**	*reading*
creer:	**creyendo**	*believing*		**poder:**	**pudiendo**	*being able to*
decir:	**diciendo**	*telling*		**venir:**	**viniendo**	*coming*
ir:	**yendo**	*going*				

3. The Spanish present participle expresses means, manner, cause, or condition and maintains an adverbial posture or function.

Quitándose el abrigo, empieza a dictar inmediatamente a su estenógrafo.
Taking his coat, he immediately begins to dictate to his stenographer.

Escuchando bien, vas a entender.
By listening closely, you will understand.

4. The present participle is used in the progressive tenses.

Estoy escribiendo una carta.
I am writing a letter.

Los alumnos **están leyendo** una novela de Cervantes.
The students are reading a novel of Cervantes.

5. The verbs **seguir** and **continuar** are used with the present participle and not with the infinitive, as in English.

Emilio **sigue viviendo** en el barrio.
Emil continues to live in the ghetto.

Continúan manejando el coche por las tierras de Andalucía.
They continue to drive the car through the lands of Andalusia.

Coordinating conjunctions

The principal coordinating conjunctions are **y** (*and*); **e** (*and*); **pero** (*but*); **sino** (*but*); **o** (*or*); and **u** (*or*).

1. The conjunction **y** becomes **e** before words that begin with an **i** or **hi**.

Padre e hijo están en la cárcel.
Father and son are in jail.

Necesito una **aguja e hilo** para coser la camisa.
I need a needle and thread to sew the shirt.

2. **Sino** means *but, but on the contrary,* or simply *on the contrary.* It is used to contrast or contradict a preceding negative statement.

El edificio no es de piedra **sino** de ladrillo.
The building is not (made) of stone but of brick.

No es Douglas **sino** Eduardo quien está en la piscina.
It isn't Douglas but Edward who is in the swimming pool.

3. O becomes **u** before words that begin with **o** or **ho**.

¿Es hombre **joven u hombre** viejo?
Is he a young man or an old man?

¿Hay **siete u ocho** congresistas allí?
Are there seven or eight congressmen there?

Ejercicios

A. *Diga en español:*

1. We are learning Spanish.
2. They are eating.
3. The boys are drinking beer.
4. Dancing is popular.
5. washing the dishes
6. taking off her dress
7. telling the truth
8. coming and going
9. thinking of you (*fam.*)
10. cooking the bacon
11. yesterday or today
12. summer or autumn
13. father and son
14. bread and butter
15. schools and churches
16. not yellow but blue
17. not this but that
18. Anna and Ines
19. Joseph or Olga
20. overcoats and raincoats

B. *Exprese en español:*

1. Henrietta is not going to stay in Madrid or Olmedo.
2. Is it a girl or a boy? It's not a girl but a boy.
3. Patricia doesn't want to go to Madrid but to London and Athens.
4. She doesn't want to go by sea but by air.
5. Robert's watch is not gold but silver, and his sweater is not green but red.
6. The tourists are sitting in the cafe, eating paella, and drinking wine.
7. The students are studying, reading, writing, and counting numbers.
8. By believing in himself and enjoying life, my father still lives at ninety years of age.

Conjugación del verbo «oler»

oler   *to smell*

Yo **huelo** las flores.   I smell the flowers.
Tú **hueles** las flores.   You smell the flowers.
Él, Ella **huele** las flores.   He, She smells the flowers.
Usted **huele** las flores.   You smell the flowers.

Nosotros (–as) **olemos** las flores.   We smell the flowers.
Vosotros (–as) **oléis** las flores.   You smell the flowers.
Ellos, Ellas **huelen** las flores.   They smell the flowers.
Ustedes **huelen** las flores.   You smell the flowers.

Ejercicio

Complete las oraciones:

1. Yo _____ la rosa.
2. Margarita y yo _____ el perfume.
3. Tú _____ la comida.
4. Los soldados _____ el polvo del cañón.
5. El florista _____ los claveles.

Estudio de palabras

Many English words that end in *-or* have Spanish cognates that also end in **-or**.

ambassador	(**el**) **embajador**	inventor	(**el**) **inventor**
candor	(**el**) **candor**	investigator	(**el**) **investigador**
conductor	(**el**) **conductor**	liberator	(**el**) **libertador**
dictator	(**el**) **dictador**	major	(**el**) **mayor**
exterior	(**el**) **exterior**	minor	(**el**) **menor**
governor	(**el**) **gobernador**	perpetrator	(**el**) **perpetrador**
interior	(**el**) **interior**	senator	(**el**) **senador**

Ejercicio

Complete las frases con las palabras siguientes:

el actor   el mentor   el terror
el color   el sector   el vector
el horror   el tenor   Víctor

1. _____ de mi tesis
2. _____ de la ópera
3. _____ noroeste
4. _____ del suicidio
5. la esposa de _____
6. _____ de la guerra
7. _____ de Hollywood
8. _____ del problema
9. _____ del crimen

UNIT 25

Imperfect tense

hablar	aprender	escribir
hablaba	aprendía	escribía
hablabas	aprendías	escribías
hablaba	aprendía	escribía
hablábamos	aprendíamos	escribíamos
hablabais	aprendíais	escribíais
hablaban	aprendían	escribían

1. The imperfect tense is formed by dropping the infinitive ending and adding **-aba, -abas, -aba, -ábamos, -abais, -aban** for **-ar** verbs, and **-ía, -ías, -ía, -íamos, -íais, -ían** for **-er** or **-ir** verbs. The imperfect expresses the English *was* or *were* plus a present participle, or *used to* plus an infinitive.

Los cadetes **aprendían** a volar aviones en la Fuerza Aérea.
The cadets were learning to fly airplanes in the Air Force.

En el verano los amantes **escribían** palabras románticas en la arena.
In the summer the lovers used to write romantic words in the sand.

2. The imperfect tense is used to express a state or condition in the past, or an action that was continuous, habitual, or recurrent in the past.

Había mucha gente en la fiesta.
There were many people at the party.

Los agricultores siempre **cultivaban** los campos en la primavera.
The farmers always cultivated the lands in the spring.

Leonardo y su hermano Raúl **tomaban** helado todas las noches mientras **miraban** la televisión.
Leonard and his brother Raúl used to eat ice cream every night while they watched television.

3. The imperfect tense is used to describe persons or things in the past.

Raimundo **era** inteligente e industrioso.   *Raymond was intelligent and industrious.*
El trabajo no **estaba** terminado todavía.   *The work was not completed yet.*

4. The verbs **ir**, **ser**, and **ver** have irregular forms in the imperfect tense.

ir	*to go:*	iba, ibas, iba, íbamos, ibais, iban
ser	*to be:*	era, eras, era éramos, erais, eran
ver	*to see:*	veía, veías, veía, veíamos, veíais, veían

Esos jóvenes **iban** a misa todos los domingos cuando eran pequeños.
Those young people used to go to mass every Sunday when they were small.

Veíamos a Laurencio a menudo en sus paseos diarios por el Malecón.
We used to see Lawrence often on his daily walks along the Malecón.

The imperfect of **hay** is **había** (*there was, there were*).

Había nubes en el cielo.   *There were clouds in the sky.*

5.   The imperfect of **estar** plus a present participle form the past progressive tense.

Ella **estaba cortándose** las uñas de los pies en el cuarto de baño.
She was cutting her toenails in the bathroom.

Los huelguistas **estaban gritando** obscenidades.
The strikers were shouting obscenities.

Ejercicios

A.   *Exprese en español:*

1.   They were learning to read and write.
2.   We were eating and drinking.
3.   The students used to arrive late for class.
4.   I was walking and singing.
5.   The spinach was cooked in a cream sauce.
6.   They were drinking the soda with a straw.
7.   He used to work in a dress factory.
8.   The workers cultivated the ground every spring.
9.   The soldier was looking at the airplane in the sky.
10. The butcher was cutting the meat and selling it to his customers.

B.   *Dé el equivalente en español:*

1.   The children got up at eight o'clock every morning and ate their breakfast.
2.   Victor was singing in the bathroom and Katherine was singing in the bedroom.
3.   I was reading a novel and my cousin was baking a cake.
4.   The husband and wife were living happily in Mexico.
5.   My girlfriend always used to wear a red skirt and a black sweater.
6.   Their son and daughter were in the cafe drinking lemonade.
7.   The President used to speak to the people on radio and television.
8.   My grandson visited us every Christmas and decorated the house with lights and flowers.
9.   Many widows used to help us in the hospital, working as receptionists and stenographers.
10. Her brother-in-law swam in the family pool every Sunday.
11. When I was married, I used to go to the movies every week and it was very expensive.
12. In church the American ladies wore hats but Spanish women went without them.
13. The grandmother was talking to her granddaughter, telling her that she was interested in her new boyfriend.
14. I used to see my nurse in the cafeteria every afternoon. Was she beautiful!
15. Christina and Jim walked along the beach and looked for shells in the white sand.

Conjugación del verbo «valer»

valer	to be worth
Yo **valgo** una fortuna.	I am worth a fortune.
Tú **vales** una fortuna.	You are worth a fortune.
Él, Ella **vale** una fortuna.	He, She is worth a fortune.
Usted **vale** una fortuna.	You are worth a fortune.
Nosotros (–as) **valemos** una fortuna.	We are worth a fortune.
Vosotros (–as) **valéis** una fortuna.	You are worth a fortune.
Ellos, Ellas **valen** una fortuna.	They are worth a fortune.
Ustedes **valen** una fortuna.	You are worth a fortune.

Ejercicio

Dé un sujeto apropiado:

1. _____ valen veinticinco centavos.
2. _____ valen cinco dólares.
3. _____ valen cien dólares.
4. _____ valen un peso.
5. _____ vale un beso.
6. _____ vale la consideración.

Estudio de palabras

Many English words that end in *-ar* have Spanish cognates that also end in **–ar**.

altar	(el) altar	lunar	lunar
angular	angular	popular	popular
bar	(el) bar	radar	(el) radar
circular	circular	scholar	(el) escolar
czar	(el) zar	semicircular	semicircular
familiar	familiar	solar	solar
Gibraltar	Gibraltar	triangular	triangular
quadrangular	cuadrangular	vehicular	vehicular

Ejercicio

Complete las frases utilizando las palabras siguientes:

solar	molar	Oscar	regular
dólar	ocular	polar	secular

1. El señor estudia el sistema _____ .
2. Juan tiene dos mil _____ en el banco.
3. Le duele un _____.
4. Es el nervio _____ que causa la enfermedad de los ojos.
5. _____ es mi colega.
6. Los soldados están en una expedición _____.
7. La maestra _____ está ausente.
8. Es un padre _____ de la iglesia de Miraflores.

UNIT 26

Preterit tense

hablar	**aprender**	**escribir**
hablé	aprendí	escribí
hablaste	aprendiste	escribiste
habló	aprendió	escribió
hablamos	aprendimos	escribimos
hablasteis	aprendisteis	escribisteis
hablaron	aprendieron	escribieron

1. The preterit tense endings are added to the stem of the infinitive. Notice that the endings for **–er** and **–ir** verbs are the same. The Spanish preterit corresponds to the English simple past: *did* plus the verb.
2. The preterit is used to express (1) an action that is definitely past or completed, with no emphasis on the duration of the action: (2) a series of actions complete in themselves or viewed as a whole. The preterit is the only simple past tense that expresses a complete action.

Anoche **hablé** con mi compañero de cuarto.
Last night I spoke (did speak) to my roommate.

Mi hermano **aprendió** el español en diez lecciones.
My brother learned (did learn) Spanish in ten lessons.

La víctima del accidente **escribió** una carta a la compañía de seguros.
The victim of the accident wrote a letter to the insurance company.

Contestaste bien cuando te lo **preguntaron**.
You answered well when they asked you (about it).

Ejercicio

Exprese en español:

1. Mother prepared supper.
2. I did work in a tobacco shop last year.
3. Yesterday Henry walked for two hours.
4. My godfather bought the newspaper.
5. That boy loved football.
6. We drove the car to Acapulco.
7. The captain stayed at the dinner for ten minutes.
8. The old lady ate the paella.
9. The boys did drink rum all night long.
10. Did they study for the test?
11. He altered the suit, sewed the jacket, and shortened the slacks.

12. He paid for the trousers, the tie, and the pajamas, but the owner of the store did not send the clothes to his home.
13. I loved you when we got married but I hate you now.
14. My grandmother knitted me a pair of gloves, a sweater, and a scarf, but I didn't like any of them because they were woolen.

Conjugación del verbo «traducir»

traducir

Yo **traduzco** la oración.
Tú **traduces** la oración.
Él, Ella **traduce** la oración.
Usted **traduce** la oración.

Nosotros (–as) **traducimos** la oración.
Vosotros (–as) **traducís** la oración.
Ellos, Ellas **traducen** la oración.
Ustedes **traducen** la oración.

to translate

I translate the sentence.
You translate the sentence.
He, She translates the sentence.
You translate the sentence.

We translate the sentence.
You translate the sentence.
They translate the sentence.
You translate the sentence.

Ejercicio

1. El profesor _____ el poema.
2. ¿ _____ tú la lección de español?
3. Miguel y yo _____ el capítulo.
4. Los estudiantes _____ el menú al español.

5. Yo siempre _____ bien.
6. Ellos y yo _____ el ensayo.

Estudio de palabras

Many English words that end in -*ous* have Spanish cognates that end in -**oso**.

amorous	**amoroso**	malicious	**malicioso**
anxious	**ansioso**	marvelous	**maravilloso**
curious	**curioso**	mountainous	**montañoso**
delicious	**delicioso**	mysterious	**misterioso**
fabulous	**fabuloso**	nervous	**nervioso**
famous	**famoso**	numerous	**numeroso**
furious	**furioso**	precious	**precioso**
generous	**generoso**	vigorous	**vigoroso**
glorious	**glorioso**	virtuous	**virtuoso**

Ejercicio

Complete las frases:

1. un experimento _____
2. un incidente _____
3. un cuento _____
4. un caballero _____

5. un león _____
6. una mujer _____
7. una joya _____
8. un presidente _____

9. una comida _____
10. una tierra _____
11. un héroe _____
12. una novela _____

UNIT 27

Irregular preterit forms

1. Irregular verbs in the preterit

dar	ser, ir	traer
di	fui	traje
diste	fuiste	trajiste
dio	fue	trajo
dimos	fuimos	trajimos
disteis	fuisteis	trajisteis
dieron	fueron	trajeron

Although **dar** is an **-ar** verb, it uses the **-er** and **-ir** endings in the preterit. **Ser** and **ir** have the same forms in the preterit. The meaning can be distinguished by the context.

El estudiante **fue** a la clase   *The student went to class.*
El estudiante **fue** brillante ayer.   *The student was brilliant yesterday.*

Note that the i of the ending is dropped in the third person plural of **traer**.

2. Irregular verbs in the preterit with an **i** stem

decir	hacer	querer	venir
dije	hice	quise	vine
dijiste	hiciste	quisiste	viniste
dijo	hizo	quiso	vino
dijimos	hicimos	quisimos	vinimos
dijisteis	hicisteis	quisisteis	vinisteis
dijeron	hicieron	quisieron	vinieron

The stress falls on the stem in the first and third persons singular of i-stem preterits. There are no written accents as in the regular preterit endings. Note that the i of the ending is dropped in the third person plural of **decir**. The third person singular of **hacer** is spelled with a **z**.

3. Irregular verbs in the preterit with a **u** stem

estar	poder	poner	saber	tener
estuve	pude	puse	supe	tuve
estuviste	pudiste	pusiste	supiste	tuviste
estuvo	pudo	puso	supo	tuvo
estuvimos	pudimos	pusimos	supimos	tuvimos
estuvisteis	pudisteis	pusisteis	supisteis	tuvisteis
estuvieron	pudieron	pusieron	supieron	tuvieron

The endings of **u**-stem preterits are the same as those of i-stem preterits.

4.   Verbs with spelling changes in the preterit

buscar	comenzar	empezar	llegar
bus**qué**	comen**cé**	empe**cé**	lle**gué**
buscaste	comenzaste	empezaste	llegaste
buscó	comenzó	empezó	llegó
buscamos	comenzamos	empezamos	llegamos
buscasteis	comenzasteis	empezasteis	llegasteis
buscaron	comenzaron	empezaron	llegaron

Before the ending -**é** of the first person singular of the preterit:
verbs ending in -**car** change the **c** to **qu**;
verbs ending in -**gar** change the **g** to **gu**;
verbs ending in -**zar** change the **z** to **c**.

Ejercicio

Complete en español:

1.   Yo (*told*) el cuento del carnicero.
2.   Mi hermano (*did*) todo el trabajo en la fábrica.
3.   Los invitados (*came*) temprano a mi fiesta de cumpleaños.
4.   Tú (*had*) mucho dinero esta mañana.
5.   Nosotros (*brought*) una botella de vino.
6.   Yo lo (*looked for*) ayer en la casa de correos.
7.   Alfonso y Carmen (*went*) al cine.
8.   Vd. (*were*) estudiante el año pasado.
9.   Yo (*began*) el experimento.
10. Ellos (*were*) en la Corte a las dos.

Conjugación del verbo «dirigir»

dirigir   *to direct*

Yo **dirijo** la comedia.   I direct the play.
Tú **diriges** la comedia.   You direct the play.
Él, Ella **dirige** la comedia.   He, She directs the play.
Usted **dirige** la comedia.   You direct the play.

Nosotros (–as) **dirigimos** la comedia.   We direct the play.
Vosotros (–as) **dirigís** la comedia.   You direct the play.
Ellos, Ellas **dirigen** la comedia.   They direct the play.
Ustedes **dirigen** la comedia.   You direct the play.

Ejercicio

Complete las oraciones con la forma apropiada del verbo **dirigir**:

1. Yo _____ el drama.
2. Miguel, el policía, _____ a la gente a la estación de servicio.
3. Los senadores _____ la palabra al Congreso.
4. Tú _____ demasiado la atención a los animales.
5. El artista _____ su energía a la pintura.

Estudio de palabras

English words ending in *-ary* generally have Spanish cognates ending **-ario**.

adversary	**(el) adversario**	monetary	**monetario**
anniversary	**(el) aniversario**	notary	**(el) notario**
arbitrary	**arbitrario**	salary	**(el) salario**
contrary	**contrario**	secondary	**secundario**
corollary	**(el) corolario**	secretary	**(el) secretario**
coronary	**coronario**	sedentary	**sedentario**
dictionary	**(el) diccionario**	tributary	**(el) tributario**

Ejercicio

Complete las frases con las palabras siguientes:

el comentario   el diario
imaginario   el ovario
parlamentario   planetario
sanguinario   sanitario
temporario   primario

1. _____ de César
2. _____ de la planta
3. un cuento _____
4. _____ de la chica
5. el procedimiento ___
6. una misión _____
7. una escena _____
8. una enfermedad ___
9. una botella _____
10. una razón _____

Many English words ending in *-ory* have Spanish cognates ending in **-orio**.

condemnatory	**condenatorio**	purgatory	**(el) purgatorio**
conservatory	**(el) conservatorio**	reformatory	**(el) reformatorio**
depilatory	**(el) depilatorio**	sensory	**sensorio**
laboratory	**(el) laboratorio**	suppository	**(el) supositorio**
obligatory	**obligatorio**	territory	**(el) territorio**
preparatory	**preparatorio**	transitory	**transitorio**

Ejercicio

Complete la oración con una de las palabras arriba mencionadas:

1. Tiene plantas en su _____.
2. _____ de lenguas
3. _____ de los indios
4. Hoy no es _____ entrar en el servicio militar.

5. El chico malo está en _____.
6. _____ del paciente.

UNIT 28

Past participles

1. The regular past participle of a verb is formed by adding **-ado** to the stem of **-ar** verbs, and **-ido** to the stem of **-er** and **-ir** verbs.

tomar	tomado	*taken*
comer	comido	*eaten*
vivir	vivido	*lived*

2. The most common irregular past participles are:

abrir	abierto	*opened*
cubrir	cubierto	*covered*
decir	dicho	*said*
descubrir	descubierto	*discovered*
escribir	escrito	*written*
freír	frito	*fried*
hacer	hecho	*made, done*
imprimir	impreso	*printed*
morir	muerto	*died*
poner	puesto	*placed*
prender	preso	*seized*
romper	roto	*broken*
satisfacer	satisfecho	*satisfied*
ver	visto	*seen*
volver	vuelto	*returned*

3. When the stem of a verb ends in a strong vowel (**a**, **e**, **o**) the **i** of the past participle ending has a written accent to prevent the two vowels from forming a diphtong.

caer	caído	*fallen*
leer	leído	*read*
oír	oído	*heard*
traer	traído	*brought*

4. The past participle may be used as an adjective, in which case it agrees in gender and number with the noun it modifies.

La paella está **comida** y los invitados están **satisfechos**.
The paella is eaten and the guests are satisfied.

La patata está **asada.**
The potato is baked.

Los huevos y el tocino están **fritos.**
The eggs and bacon are fried.

Los niños se encuentran **cansados.**
The children find themselves tired.

5. Many past participles are equivalents of English present participles.

Papá está **acostado**.   *Papa is lying down.*
Las zarzuelas a veces son **pesadas**.   *The zarzuelas at times are boring.*

6. Past participles may have a noun value.

Los fracasados se matriculan en la escuela de verano.
The failures matriculate in summer school.

Regresan **los heridos** de la guerra.
The wounded return from the war.

7. **Lo** with the past participle has a noun value.

Lo divertido del incidente es que lo encontraron dormido.
The funny thing about the incident is that they found him asleep.

Jorge gasta todo **lo ganado** y siempre es pobre.
George spends all he earns and is always poor.

Ejercicio

Exprese en español:

1. The pharmacy is open.
2. His favorite song is played often.
3. The clients are very satisfied.
4. Books printed in the U.S. are more expensive.
5. Fried potatoes are very popular.
6. The electric shavers are covered with dust.
7. Be careful of the broken glass.
8. The written word is law.
9. Her engagement ring was made in Spain.
10. The interested people will not be absent.
11. This woolen blanket made in Mexico was given to me by my dead wife.
12. Do you like fried pork chops? No, I prefer roasted meat.

13. The tired children are lying down.
14. The signed contracts will give your employees work for a whole year.
15. I am interested in what is done and not what is said.

Conjugación del verbo «caer»

caer   *to fall*

Yo **caigo** en una trampa.   I fall into a trap.
Tú **caes** en una trampa.   You fall into a trap.
Él, Ella **cae** en una trampa.   He, She falls into a trap.
Usted **cae** en una trampa.   You fall into a trap.

Nosotros (–as) **caemos** en una trampa.   We fall into a trap.
Vosotros (–as) **caéis** en una trampa.   You fall into a trap.
Ellos, Ellas **caen** en una trampa.   They fall into a trap.
Ustedes **caen** en una trampa.   You fall into a trap.

Ejercicio

Dé la forma apropiada del verbo **caer:**

1. Teodoro _____ en el jardín.
2. ¿Dónde _____ el criminal?
3. Nosotros _____ en esta batalla.
4. Tú siempre _____ en casa.
5. Yo _____ en sus manos.
6. Los chicos _____ del árbol.

Estudio de palabras

Many verbs ending in *-ate* in English have Spanish cognates that are **-ar** verbs.

accelerate	**acelerar**	evaporate	**evaporar**
accentuate	**acentuar**	facilitate	**facilitar**
accumulate	**acumular**	imitate	**imitar**
agitate	**agitar**	meditate	**meditar**
associate	**asociar**	negotiate	**negociar**
celebrate	**celebrar**	relate	**relatar**
conjugate	**conjugar**	terminate	**terminar**
delegate	**delegar**	vacilate	**vacilar**

Ejercicio

Use las palabras siguientes en oraciones españolas:

1. **abrogar** (*abrogate*)
2. **aliviar** (*alleviate*)
3. **calcular** (*calculate*)
4. **estimar** (*estimate*)
5. **interrogar** (*interrogate*)
6. **navegar** (*navigate*)
7. **separar** (*separate*)
8. **tolerar** (*tolerate*)

UNIT 29

Passive voice

In the active voice, the subject performs the action denoted by the verb.

Los muchachos comen las manzanas.   *The boys eat the apples*

In the passive voice, the subject is acted upon by a person or thing, called the agent. The passive voice in Spanish is formed by **ser** plus a past participle, which agrees in number and gender with the subject.

Las manzanas **son comidas por** los   *The apples are eaten by the boys.*
   muchachos.
El edificio **fue construido por** los   *The building was constructed by the*
   carpinteros.   *carpenters.*

Substitutes for the passive voice

1.   If the subject of a passive construction is not a person and an agent is not expressed, the reflexive **se** may be used with a verb in the third person as a substitute for the true passive.

Se cierra la puerta.   *The door is closed.*
Se habla español aquí.   *Spanish is spoken here.*
Se comen uvas.   *Grapes are eaten.*
Se celebran las fiestas.   *The holidays are celebrated.*

2.   The third person plural of the verb may be used as a substitute for the true passive.

Dicen muchas cosas interesantes.
Many interesting things are said. (They say . . .)

Preparan un buen desayuno y almuerzo.
A good breakfast and lunch are prepared. (They prepare . . .)

Montan los caballos.
The horses are mounted. (They mount . . .)

Cantan unas canciones.
Some songs are sung. (They sing . . .)

Resultant condition

Estar with a past participle is used to express a condition resulting from an action and is not to be confused with any passive constructions.

La puerta **está cerrada**.   *The door is closed.*
La carta **está escrita**.   *The letter is written.*
Las ventanas **están abiertas**.   *The windows are open.*

Ejercicios

A. Diga en español:

1. The music is heard.
2. Soldiers are wounded.
3. Gasoline was not sold today.
4. English is spoken here.
5. Money is needed.
6. The doctors are consulted.
7. The books are opened.
8. The contracts are signed.

B. Exprese en español:

1. The novel was read diligently by all the students.
2. Swimming is prohibited here, and there is also a sign that says, "No Trespassing."
3. French is spoken in Haiti and Quebec, and Spanish is spoken in Texas and Arizona.
4. The store was opened at ten o'clock this morning, but the customers were not given enough time to purchase the ties on sale.
5. The criminal was arrested by the policeman and was put in jail.

Conjugación del verbo «huir»

huir

Yo **huyo** de la autoridad.
Tú **huyes** de la autoridad.
Él, Ella **huye** de la autoridad.
Usted **huye** de la autoridad.

Nosotros (–as) **huimos** de la autoridad.
Vosotros (–as) **huís** de la autoridad.
Ellos, Ellas **huyen** de la autoridad.
Ustedes **huyen** de la autoridad.

to flee

I flee from the authorities.
You flee from the authorities.
He, She flees from the authorities.
You flee from the authorities.

We flee from the authorities.
You flee from the authorities.
They flee from the authorities.
You flee from the authorities.

Ejercicio

Complete con la forma apropiada del verbo **huir**:

1. El criminal _____ de la ley.
2. Los niños _____ del incendio.
3. Nosotros _____ del ejército.
4. Tú _____ de tus padres.
5. Yo _____ del enemigo.

Estudio de palabras

Many English words ending in -y have Spanish cognates ending in -ía.

agony	(la) **agonía**	biography	(la) **biografía**
artillery	(la) **artillería**	chronology	(la) **cronología**
astrology	(la) **astrología**	company	(la) **compañía**
autobiography	(la) **autobiografía**	courtesy	(la) **cortesía**
battery	(la) **batería**	infantry	(la) **infantería**

| photography | (la) **fotografía** | refinery | (la) **refinería** |
| pornography | (la) **pornografía** | seismology | (la) **sismología** |

Ejercicio

Exprese en español:

1. anatomy
2. astronomy
3. biology
4. geometry

5. cosmology
6. geography
7. ontology
8. ornithology

9. paleontology
10. parisitology
11. philosophy
12. psychology

UNIT 30

Review of verbs with spelling changes

Many verbs in Spanish have certain regular changes in spelling in order to preserve their characteristic sounds.

1. Verbs ending in **–car** and **–gar** change the **c** and **g** to **qu** and **gu** respectively before **e** in the first person singular of the preterit and in the command.

buscar   *to look for*

bus**qué**, buscaste, buscó, buscamos, buscasteis, buscaron
bus**que**, bus**quen**

Yo **busqué** los tomates maduros.   *I looked for ripe tomatoes.*

llegar   to arrive

lle**gué**, llegaste, llegó, llegamos, llegasteis, llegaron
lle**gue**, lle**guen**

Llegué a tiempo.   *I arrived on time.*

2. Verbs ending in **-guar** change the **gu** to **gü** before **e** in the first person singular of the preterit and the command.

averiguar   *to ascertain*

averi**güé,** averiguaste, averiguó, averiguamos, averiguasteis, averiguaron
averi**güe**, averi**güen**.

Averigüé los hechos.   *I ascertained the facts.*

3. Verbs ending in **-guir** drop the **u** before **a** and **o** in the first person of the present indicative and the command.

seguir   *to follow*

sigo, sigues, sigue, seguimos, seguís, **siguen**
siga, sigan

Yo **sigo** al líder.   *I follow the leader.*

4. Verbs ending in **-ger** and **-gir** change the **g** to **j** before **a** and **o** in the first person singular of the present indicative and the command.

escoger   *to choose*

escojo, escoges, escoge, escogemos, escogéis, escogen
escoja, escojan

Escoja la forma apropiada del verbo.   *Choose the appropriate form of the verb.*

5. ' Verbs ending in **-cer** and **-cir** preceded by a consonant change the **c** to **z** before **a** and **o** in the first person of the present indicative and the command.

convencer   *to convince*

convenzo, convences, convence, convencemos, convencéis, convencen
convenza, convenzan.

Yo **convenzo** al profesor.   *I convince the professor.*

6. Verbs ending in **-cer** and **-cir** preceded by a vowel insert **z** before the **c** in the first person of the present indicative and the command.

conocer   *to know*

conozco, conoces, conoce, conocemos, conocéis, conocen
conozca, conozcan

Conozco a Pablo.   *I know Paul.*

7. Verbs ending in **-zar** change the **z** to **c** before **e** in the first person singular of the preterit and the command.

empezar   *to begin*

empecé, empezaste, empezó, empezamos, empezasteis, empezaron
empiece, empiecen

Empecé la lección   *I began the lesson.*

8. Verbs ending in **-iar** and **-uar** (except **-guar**) have a written accent on the **i** and **u** respectively throughout the singular and in the third person plural of the present indicative and in the command.

enviar   *to send*

envío, envías, envía, enviamos, enviáis, envían
envíe, envíen

Envío un telegrama.   *I send a telegram.*

continuar   *to continue*

continúo, continúas, continúa, continuamos, continuáis, continúan
continúe, continúen

Continúa su viaje.   *He continues his trip.*

9. Verbs whose stem ends in a vowel (**-aer, -eer, -uir**) change the **i** of endings beginning
    with **ie** or **io** to **y**. The stressed **i** is not changed to **y**.

caer   *to fall*

caí, caíste, ca**yó**, caímos, caísteis, ca**yeron**
ca**yendo**.

Vds. **cayeron** en la trampa.   *You fell into the trap.*

creer   *to believe*

creí, creíste, cre**yó**, creímos, creísteis, cre**yeron**
cre**yendo**

No **creyeron** la verdad.   *They didn't believe the truth.*

concluir   *to conclude*

concluyo, concluyes, concluye, concluimos, concluís, concluyen
concluí, concluíste, concluyó, concluimos, concluisteis, concluyeron
concluyendo

Concluyó la tarea.   *He concluded the homework.*

10. Verbs ending in **-eír**.

reír to laugh

río, ríes, ríe, reímos, reís, ríen
reí, reíste, rió, reímos, reísteis, rieron
riendo
Siempre **río** cuando veo a Cantinflas.   *I always laugh when I see Cantinflas.*
Siempre **me río** de él.   *I always laugh at him.*

Ejercicios

A.   *Diga en español:*

1. I looked for the money.
2. I arrived late.
3. I ascertained the truth.
4. I began to work.
5. He believed the rabbi.

6. They laugh at him.
7. They concluded the assignment.
8. She sends a letter.
9. You continue your studies.
10. I convince the butcher.

B.   Exprese en español:

1.   I know the man who was a witness in the case.
2.   I follow you but you do not follow me.
3.   I am going to convince the government officials of it. They fell into a trap.
4.   Anita laughed when Gloria completed the sweater that she began to knit a year ago.
5.   They are sending a telegram to the President of the United States in order to convince him to sign the law giving more money to postal workers.

Conjugación del verbo «recordar»

recordar	*to remember*
Yo **recuerdo** el chiste.	I remember the joke.
Tú **recuerdas** el chiste.	You remember the joke.
Él, Ella **recuerda** el chiste.	He, She remembers the joke.
Usted **recuerda** el chiste.	You remember the joke.
Nosotros (–as) **recordamos** el chiste.	We remember the joke.
Vosotros (–as) **recordáis** el chiste.	You remember the joke.
Ellos, Ellas **recuerdan** el chiste.	They remember the joke.
Ustedes **recuerdan** el chiste.	You remember the joke.

Ejercicio

Dé la forma apropiada del verbo **recordar**:

1.   recordar los guantes (Doris y Graciela, yo)
2.   recordar el nombre del cartero (el chico, tú)
3.   recordar el error (los alumnos, vosotros)
4.   recordar el viaje (el turista, los chóferes)
5.   recordar (tú y yo, los abuelos)

Estudio de palabras

Many English words that end in *-ium* have Spanish cognates that end in **-io**.

aquarium	**(el) acuario**	gymnasium	**(el) gimnasio**
auditorium	**(el) auditorio**	honorarium	**(el) honorario**
colloquium	**(el) coloquio**	medium	**(el) medio**
compendium	**(el) compendio**	paramecium	**(el) paramecio**
equilibrium	**(el) equilibrio**	sanatorium	**(el) sanatorio**

Ejercicio

Dé el cognado español de las palabras siguientes:

1.   barium
2.   calcium
3.   helium
4.   magnesium
5.   radium
6.   sodium

UNIT 31

Radical changing verbs

Radical-changing verbs have irregularities in the radical (stem) vowel. These radical changes fall into the following three classes.

CLASS 1. Verbs of the first and second conjugations with the radical vowel **e** or **o**

The stressed **e** changes to **ie** and the stressed **o** changes to **ue** throughout the singular and in the third person plural of the present indicative and in the command.

perder *to lose*		**morder** *to bite*	
pierdo	perdemos	muerdo	mordemos
pierdes	perdéis	muerdes	mordéis
pierde	pierden	muerde	muerden
pierda, pierdan		muerda, muerdan	

CLASS 2. Verbs of the third conjugation with the radical vowel **e** or **o**

The stressed **e** changes to **ie** and the stressed **o** changes to **ue** throughout the singular and in the third person plural of the present indicative and in the command. The **e** changes to **i** and the **o** changes to **u** in the third person singular and plural of the preterit and in the present participle.

PRESENT

mentir *to lie*		**dormir** *to sleep*	
miento	mentimos	duermo	dormimos
mientes	mentís	duermes	dormís
miente	mienten	duerme	duermen

PRETERIT

mentí	mentimos	dormí	dormimos
mentiste	mentisteis	dormiste	dormisteis
mintió	mintieron	durmió	durmieron
mienta, mientan		duerma, duerman	
mintiendo		durmiendo	

CLASS 3. Verbs of the third conjugation with the radical vowel **e**

The stressed **e** changes to **i** throughout the singular and in the third person plural of the present indicative and in the command. The **e** also changes to **i** in the third person singular and plural of the preterit and in the present participle.

vestir   *to dress*

PRESENT		PRETERIT	
visto	vestimos	vestí	vestimos
vistes	vestís	vestiste	vestisteis
viste	visten	vistió	vistieron

vista, vistan
vistiendo

1.   Common verbs of the first class like **perder**

acertar	*to figure out*	empezar	*to begin*
apretar	*to squeeze*	encender	*to ignite*
ascender	*to ascend*	entender	*to understand*
atravesar	*to cross*	gobernar	*to govern*
calentar	*to warm*	manifestar	*to manifest*
cerrar	*to close*	negar	*to deny*
comenzar	*to begin*	pensar	*to think*
concertar	*to arrange*	quebrar	*to break*
confesar	*to confess*	regar	*to irrigate*
defender	*to defend*	sembrar	*to seed*
descender	*to descend*	sentarse	*to sit*
despertar	*to awaken*	temblar	*to tremble*
desterrar	*to exile*	tender	*to spread out*

2.   Common verbs of the first class like **morder**

acordar	*to agree upon*	moler	*to grind*
almorzar	*to lunch*	mostrar	*to show*
apostar	*to bet*	mover	*to move*
avergonzar	*to shame*	probar	*to prove*
colgar	*to hang*	recordar	*to remember*
consolar	*to console*	rogar	*to pray*
contar	*to count*	soltar	*to free*
costar	*to cost*	soñar	*to dream*
forzar	*to force*	volver	*to return*

3.   Common verbs of the second class like **mentir**

advertir	*to warn*	hervir	*to boil*
arrepentirse	*to repent*	invertir	*to invert*
conferir	*to confer*	preferir	*to prefer*
convertir	*to convert*	referir	*to refer*
divertirse	*to amuse oneself*	sentir	*to feel*
herir	*to wound*	sugerir	*to suggest*

4.   Common verbs of the second class like **dormir**

morir	*to die*

5. Common verbs of the third category like **vestir**

competir	*to compete*	**medir**	*to measure*
concebir	*to conceive*	**pedir**	*to ask for*
despedir	*to take leave of*	**repetir**	*to repeat*
elegir	*to elect*	**seguir**	*to follow*
impedir	*to obstruct*	**servir**	*to serve*

Ejercicios

A.   Diga en español:

1. He loses the ticket.
2. The dog bites the girl.
3. You lie.
4. I sleep every afternoon.
5. I dress for the dance.

6.   You amuse the family.
7.   He heats the apartment.
8.   She counts the money.
9   He prefers the opera.
10.   I ask for a glass of water.

B.   Exprese en español:

1.   He asks for the engagement ring and she begins to cry.
2.   Is he now confessing that he bets on the horses and lies to his wife?
3.   He returns to the farm, sows his seed, and irrigates the fields.
4.   The soldiers defend the city and they do not move from their positions.
5.   First the child frees the horses and then he ignites the barn.
6.   The king governs well and manifests to the people that he is dreaming of peace.
7.   While I measure the carpet she serves the children their lunch.
8.   I remember the day when children used to go to school in fine clothes. Is it true today they sit on the floor? I'm beginning to show my age.
9.   The eggs cost $1.00 a dozen and I bet he breaks them all.
10.   I descend into the mine while he ascends in an elevator.

Conjugación del verbo «contar»

contar	*to count*
Yo **cuento** los días.	I count the days.
Tú **cuentas** los días.	You count the days.
Él, Ella **cuenta** los días.	He, She counts the days.
Usted **cuenta** los días.	You count the days.
Nosotros (–as) **contamos** los días.	We count the days.
Vosotros (–as) **contáis** los días.	You count the days.
Ellos, Ellas **cuentan** los días.	They count the days.
Ustedes **cuentan** los días.	You count the days.

Ejercicio

Use la forma apropiada del verbo **contar:**

1. contar los días (Alfredo y Jaime, yo)
2. contar el dinero (el campesino, tú)
3. contar las tarjetas de Navidad (mamá y papá, mi primo)
4. contar las palabras (el maestro, los autores)
5. contar los números (los niños, mi nieto)
6. contar las hojas de papel (yo, Ana)

Estudio de palabras

Many English words containing a *k* have Spanish cognates with a **k**, **c**, or **qu**.

bank	**(el) banco**	Korea	**Corea**
dike	**(el) dique**	New Yorker	**(el) neoyorkino, neoyorquino**
disk	**(el) disco**	park	**(el) parque**
Key West	**Cayo Hueso**	pick	**(el) pico**
khaki	**(el) caqui**	poker	**(el) pócar**
kiosk	**(el) kiosko, quiosco**	rock	**(la) roca**

Ejercicio

Complete las oraciones utilizando las palabras siguientes:

el canguro	*(kangaroo)*	Dinamarca	*(Denmark)*
Catalina	*(Katherine)*	el duque	*(duke)*
el cheque	*(check)*	el paquete	*(package)*
la cucaracha	*(cockroach)*	la quilla	*(keel)*

1. _____ de Australia
2. el rey de _____
3. _____ del banco
4. _____ del bote
5. _____ de Braganza
6. _____ del apartamento
7. _____ del correo
8. _____ de Inglaterra

UNIT 32

Future tense

hablar**é**	apender**é**	escribir**é**
hablar**ás**	aprender**ás**	escribir**ás**
hablar**á**	aprender**á**	escribir**á**
hablar**emos**	aprender**emos**	escribir**emos**
hablar**éis**	aprender**éis**	escribir**éis**
hablar**án**	aprender**án**	escribir**án**

1. The endings for the future tense are added to the infinitive and are the same for **–ar,**
    –er, and **–ir** verbs. The future tense in Spanish corresponds to the English.

Enriqueta **hablará** con la policía sobre el delito.
Henrietta will speak to the police concerning the crime.

Los inmigrantes cubanos **aprenderán** fácilmente el inglés.
The Cuban immigrants will learn English easily.

Te **escribiré** un poema de amor.
I shall write a love poem for you.

Mañana **me levantaré** muy tarde.
Tomorrow I shall get up very late.

2. The future tense in Spanish may be used to express probability or conjecture in present
    time.

El boxeador puertorriqueño probablemente **ganará** el campeonato.
The Puerto Rican boxer is probably going to win the championship.

Ahora el difunto **estará** en el cielo.
Now the deceased is probably in heaven.

Lloverá en unos minutos.
It will probably rain in a few minutes.

3. The following verbs have irregular stems in the future tense.

caber	*to fit*	**cabré**
decir	*to say, tell*	**diré**
haber	*to have*	**habré**
hacer	*to do, make*	**haré**
poder	*to be able, can*	**podré**
poner	*to put, place*	**pondré**
querer	*to wish, love, want*	**querré**
saber	*to know*	**sabré**
salir	*to go out*	**saldré**
tener	*to have*	**tendré**
valer	*to be worth*	**valdré**
venir	*to come*	**vendré**

Ejercicios

A. *Dé el equivalente en español:*

1. The doctor will operate tomorrow.
2. Victoria will marry Edward next Sunday.
3. Shall I be able to eat sweets after leaving the hospital?
4. Next month my family and I will go to Italy.
5. Will you go out with me tonight?

6. The Puerto Rican students will probably sing in the chorus.
7. The teachers will play baseball with the students.
8. Will you accompany me to the opera?
9. John is probably working many more hours for Christmas.
10. The Americans are probably going to Europe.

B. *Exprese en español:*

1. I wonder what time it is. It's probably a quarter after four.
2. Although it rained yesterday, tomorrow will probably be fine weather. Whatever will be, will be.
3. In six hours the PAN AM 707 will arrive in Paris and we shall be able to take our luggage to the hotel.
4. Where is my driver's license? It is probably in the glove compartment of the car.
5. The children will probably learn to read and write better and quicker than their parents.

Conjugación del verbo «reírse»

reírse

Yo **me río** a carcajadas.
Tú **te ríes** a carcajadas.
Él, Ella **se ríe** a carcajadas.
Usted **se ríe** a carcajadas.

Nosotros (–as) **nos reímos** a carcajadas.
Vosotros (–as) **os reís** a carcajadas.
Ellos, Ellas **se ríen** a carcajadas.
Ustedes **se ríen** a carcajadas.

to laugh

I laugh heartily.
You laugh heartily.
He, She laughs heartily.
You laugh heartily.

We laugh heartily.
You laugh heartily.
They laugh heartily.
You laugh heartily.

Ejercicio

Use la forma apropiada del verbo **reírse**:

1. Yo _____ a carcajadas.
2. Mi pobre padre nunca _____.
3. El cartero y yo _____ del incidente.
4. Los peatones _____ de la policía.
5. Los niños _____ de los animales en el circo.
6. Ellos _____ de Santa Claus.

Estudio de palabras

Many English words that end in the suffix -*ment* have Spanish cognates with the suffix **–mento.**

cement	(el) **cemento**	experiment	(el) **experimento**
complement	(el) **complemento**	firmament	(el) **firmamento**
condiment	(el) **condimento**	fragment	(el) **fragmento**
department	(el) **departamento**	increment	(el) **incremento**
element	(el) **elemento**	ligament	(el) **ligamento**

| moment | **(el) momento** | temperament | **(el) temperamento** |
| monument | **(el) monumento** | torment | **(el) tormento** |

Ejercicio

Complete las frases utilizando las palabras siguientes:

(el) apartamento	**(el) instrumento**
(el) argumento	**(el) lamento**
(el) armamento	**(el) parlamento**
(el) campamento	**(el) sacramento**
(el) filamento	**(el) sedimento**

1. _____ de la comedia
2. _____ del soltero
3. _____ de la viuda
4. _____ del músico

5. _____ del edificio
6. _____ del soldado
7. _____ de Inglaterra
8. _____ de la bombilla

9. _____ del presidente
10. _____ del matrimonio

UNIT 33

Conditional tense (also referred to as the Conditional mood)

hablaría	aprendería	escribiría
hablarías	aprenderías	escribirías
hablaría	aprendería	escribiría
hablaríamos	aprenderíamos	escribiríamos
hablaríais	aprenderíais	escribiríais
hablarían	aprenderían	escribirían

1. The endings of the conditional are added to the infinitive and are the same for **-ar**, **-er**, and **-ir** verbs. The conditional in Spanish corresponds to the English *would* or *should* plus a verb.

Yo iría, pero tengo demasiado trabajo.
I would go, but I have too much work.

El cartero me aseguró que **encontraría** la carta perdida.
The postman assured me that he would find the lost letter.

2. The conditional may be used to express probability or conjecture in the past.

La víctima del accidente **estaría** en ruta al hospital.
The accident victim was probably on route to the hospital.

Serían las dos de la mañana cuando mi vecino regresó borracho de la fiesta.
It was probably two o'clock in the morning when my neighbor returned drunk from the party.

3. The following verbs have irregular stems in the conditional tense.

caber	**cabría**	querer	**querría**
decir	**diría**	saber	**sabría**
haber	**habría**	salir	**saldría**
hacer	**haría**	tener	**tendría**
poder	**podría**	valer	**valdría**
poner	**pondría**	venir	**vendría**

4. The stems of the future and the conditional tenses are the same for both regular and irregular verbs.

5. *Should* meaning *ought to* (an obligation) is expressed by the present tense of **deber**.

Debo asistir a clase todos los días.   *I ought to go to class every day.*
Los niños **deben** respetar a sus padres.   *Children should respect their parents.*

Ejercicios

A. *Dé el equivalente en español*:

1. You should take your vitamins.
2. That girl should receive the highest grades.
3. I would get up at six A.M., but I'm tired.
4. Would you write to her?
5. I would not go alone.
6. It would be difficult to give you more money.
7. At what time would the plane arrive?
8. Would you eat spaghetti without Italian cheese?
9. Vendors of drugs should be in jail.
10. You should marry.

B. *Exprese en español*:

1. Would you listen to the music of the Bee Gees or would you prefer Barry Manilow?
2. The men would not dance or drink beer in this cabaret.
3. Would you believe that terrible thing happened to that lovely girl?
4. Some said that we would live like kings in other countries.
5. Students should listen to their parents but they should also express their ideas.

Conjugación del verbo «encontrarse»

encontrarse   *to meet*

Yo **me encuentro** con un amigo.   I meet with a friend.
Tú **te encuentras** con un amigo.   You meet with a friend.
Él, Ella **se encuentra** con un amigo.   He, She meets with a friend.
Usted **se encuentra** con un amigo.   You meet with a friend.

Nosotros (–as) **nos encontramos** con un amigo.	We meet with a friend.
Vostros (-as) **os encontráis** con un amigo.	You meet with a friend.
Ellos, Ellas **se encuentran** con un amigo.	They meet with a friend.
Ustedes **se encuentran** con un amigo	You meet with a friend.

Ejercicio

Use la forma apropiada del verbo **encontrarse**:

1. _____ con una amiga. (yo, Juanita)
2. _____ con los soldados enemigos. (los generales, tú)
3. _____ con el profesor. (el alumno, nosotros)
4. _____ con el líder. (los jóvenes, vosotras)
5. _____ con la policía. (el chófer, la joven)

Estudio de palabras

Many English words ending in *-ent* or *-ant* have Spanish cognates ending in **-ente** or **-iente**.

ardent	**ardiente**	Orient	**(el) Oriente**
client	**(el, la) cliente**	patent	**patente**
current	**corriente**	patient	**(el, la) paciente**
dependent	**(el, la) dependiente**	persistent	**persistente**
descendent	**(el, la) descendiente**	president	**(el, la) presidente**
different	**diferente**	prudent	**prudente**
excellent	**excelente**	servant	**(el, la) sirviente**
indifferent	**indiferente**	valiant	**valiente**

Ejercicio

Use la palabra apropiada del grupo arriba mencionado:

1. Los _____ están en el hospital.
2. El_____ de los Estados Unidos gana mucho.
3. _____ sirvió la comida.
4. _____. habló con el cliente.
5. El señor será _____ .
6. Hoy brilla un sol _____ .

UNIT 34

Present perfect

hablar	comer	escribir
he hablado	**he comido**	**he escrito**
has hablado	**has comido**	**has escrito**
ha hablado	**ha comido**	**ha escrito**

hemos hablado	hemos comido	hemos escrito
habéis hablado	habéis comido	habéis escrito
han hablado	han comido	han escrito

The present perfect tense is formed with the present tense of **haber** and a past participle. It expresses a past or completed action in the recent past. The English equivalent is **have** plus a past participle.

He comido el emparedado.
I have eaten the sandwich.

El padre **ha visto** al recién nacido.
The father has seen the newborn baby.

Los turistas **han volado** al Canadá para visitar la Exposición.
The tourists have flown to Canada to visit the Exposition.

Pluperfect

había hablado	había comido	había escrito
habías hablado	habías comido	habías escrito
había hablado	había comido	había escrito
habíamos hablado	habíamos comido	habíamos escrito
habíais hablado	habíais comido	habíais escrito
habían hablado	habían comido	habían escrito

The pluperfect tense is formed with the imperfect tense of **haber** and a past participle. It expresses an action that was completed before another action took place in the past. It is therefore dependent upon another action or circumstance. The English equivalent is *had* plus a past participle.

Ya **habías cenado** cuando yo te llamé por teléfono.
You had already eaten supper when I called you on the phone.

El estudiante **había llegado** mucho antes que yo.
The student had arrived long before I (did).

Ejercicios

A. *Dé el equivalente en español:*

1. John has eaten the orange.
2. We have repaired the shoes.
3. The astronaut has reached the moon.
4. The farmers have sown the fields.
5. I have drunk my milk.
6. I had washed the clothes.
7. The witness had given his testimony.
8. The policemen and the firemen had arrived at the fire.

9.   The jeweler and the silversmith had purchased all the diamonds.
10. Elmer and I had lost our sneakers in the woods.

B.   *Exprese en español*:

1.   I had brushed my shoes before breakfast.
2.   We have sent a telegram to our son and he has already answered.
3.   The guests had eaten all the dessert and had drunk all the wine.
4.   He had broken the glass and had cut his hand.
5.   He has been in Spain and has enjoyed the night clubs in Malaga and Madrid.

Conjugación del verbo «coger»

coger   *to take, grab*

Yo **cojo** el martillo.   I grab the hammer.
Tú **coges** el martillo.   You grab the hammer.
Él, Ella **coge** el martillo.   He, She grabs the hammer.
Usted **coge** el martillo.   You grab the hammer.

Nosotros (–as) **cogemos** el martillo.   We grab the hammer.
Vosotros (–as) **cogéis** el martillo.   You grab the hammer.
Ellos, Ellas **cogen** el martillo.   They grab the hammer.
Ustedes **cogen** el martillo.   You grab the hammer.

Ejercicio

Complete la oración con un sujeto y un objecto apropiado:

1. _____ cojo _____ .   4. _____ cogemos _____ .
2. _____ cogen _____ .   5. _____ coge _____ .
3. _____ coges _____ .   6. _____ cogéis _____ .

Estudio de palabras

DERIVATIVES AND COMPOUND WORDS

banco	*bank*	**banquero**	*banker*	**banquete**	*banquet*
boleto	*ticket*	**boletería**	*ticket office*	**boletín**	*bulletin*
calzar	*to shoe*	**calzado**	*shoe*	**calcetín**	*sock*
calle	*street*	**callejón**	*alley*	**callejuela**	*narrow street*
campo	*field*	**campesino**	*peasant*	**camposanto**	*cemetery*
carne	*meat*	**carnal**	*carnal*	**carnicero**	*butcher*
carro	*car*	**carreta**	*wagon*	**carretera**	*highway*
carta	*letter*	**cartero**	*letter carrier*	**cartón**	*cardboard*
flor	*flower*	**florero**	*vase*	**floreciente**	*flowering*
llano	*plain*	**llanero**	*plainsman*	**llanura**	*plains*
mar	*sea*	**marino**	*marine*	**mareo**	*seasickness*

materia	matter	material	material	materialismo	materialism
peso	weight	pesado	heavy	pesadumbre	sadness
sal	salt	salero	salt shaker	salado	salty
silla	chair	sillón	armchair	sillería	pews
sombra	shade	sombrero	hat	sombrío	somber
toro	bull	toreador	bullfighter	torero	bullfighter

Ejercicio

Dé las palabras de las cuales son derivadas las siguientes:

1. el blanqueador
2. la enfermedad
3. la perrera
4. la planchadora
5. nombrar
6. la lavandera
7. el perchero
8. el jardinero
9. dependiente
10. trabajar
11. el panadero
12. el carnicero

Many Spanish nouns are related directly to verbs.

el abrazo	embrace	abrazar	el peso	weight	pesar
el beso	kiss	besar	la planta	plant	plantar
el canto	song	cantar	el rey	king	reinar
la cocina	kitchen	cocinar	el saludo	greeting	saludar
la cruz	cross	cruzar	el toro	bull	torear
el número	number	numerar	la visita	visit	visitar
el ojo	eye	ojear	el vuelo	flight	volar

Ejercicios

A. *Dé un verbo relacionado con los nombres siguientes. Consulte el vocabulario si es necesario:*

1. los ahorros (*savings*)
2. el ataque (*attack*)
3. el cantante (*singer*)
4. el camino (*walk*)
5. la celebración (*celebration*)
6. la construcción (*construction*)
7. el dependiente (*salesman*)
8. el grito (*shout*)
9. el peine (*comb*)
10. la lluvia (*rain*)

B. *Dé un nombre relacionado con los verbos siguientes:*

1. alimentar (*to eat*)
2. bailar (*to dance*)
3. mostrar (*to show*)
4. dibujar (*to draw*)
5. invitar (*to invite*)
6. fabricar (*to manufacture*)
7. nombrar (*to name*)
8. quejarse (*to complain*)
9. trabajar (*to work*)
10. reaccionar (*to react*)

COMPOUND WORDS: NOUN AND ADJECTIVE COMBINATIONS

agrio	(*sour*)	+ dulce	(*sweet*)	= agridulce	(*bittersweet*)
agua	(*water*)	+ ardiente	(*fiery*)	= aguardiente	(*brandy*)

alta	(loud)	+ voz	(voice)	= altavoz	(loud speaker)
barba	(beard)	+ negro	(black)	= barbinegro	(black-bearded)
gentil	(genteel)	+ hombre	(man)	= gentilhombre	(gentleman)
hispano	(Spanish)	+ americano	(American)	= hispanoamericano	(Spanish American)
mano	(hand)	+ obra	(work)	= maniobra	(hand work)
ojo	(eye)	+ negro	(black)	= ojinegro	(black-eyed)

COMPOUND WORDS: VERBS AND NOUNS

abrir	(to open)	+ latas	(cans)	= abrelatas	(can opener)
cortar	(to cut)	+ plumas	(pens)	= cortaplumas	(penknife)
cubrir	(to cover)	+ cama	(bed)	= cubrecama	(bedspread)
espantar	(to scare)	+ pájaros	(birds)	= espantapájaros	(scarecrow)
pasar	(to pass)	+ puerto	(port)	= pasaporte	(passport)
quitar	(to remove)	+ manchas	(stains)	= quitamanchas	(stain remover)
rascar	(to scratch)	+ cielos	(skies)	= rascacielos	(skyscraper)

Ejercicio

¿Cuál es el nombre compuesto de las palabras siguientes? Consulte el vocabulario si es necesario:

1. sacar, corchos — corkscrew
2. salvar, vidas — life preserver
3. tocar, discos — phonograph
4. pelo, rubio — blond-haired
5. radio, oyente — radio listener

UNIT 35

Future perfect

hablar	comer	escribir
habré hablado	habré comido	habré escrito
habrás hablado	habrás comido	habrás escrito
habrá hablado	habrá comido	habrá escrito
habremos hablado	habremos comido	habremos escrito
habréis hablado	habréis comido	habréis escrito
habrán hablado	habrán comido	habrán escrito

1. The future perfect tense is formed with the future tense of **haber** and a past participle. It expresses a future action that is certain to take place. The English equivalent is *will have* plus a past participle.

Yo **habré terminado** el trabajo antes de su regreso.
I shall have finished the work before his return.

La fiesta **habrá empezado** antes de la fecha oficial.
The fiesta will have begun before the official date.

Ellas **habrán comido** para las siete.
They will have eaten by seven o'clock.

2.   The future perfect may be used to express probability in present time.

El jardinero (probablemente) **habrá cortado** el césped.
The gardener probably has cut the lawn.

¿**Habrá llegado** el estéreo?
I wonder if the stereo has arrived.

Conditional perfect

hablar	comer	escribir
habría hablado	habría comido	habría escrito
habrías hablado	habrías comido	habrías escrito
habría hablado	habría comido	habría escrito
habríamos hablado	habríamos comido	habríamos escrito
habríais hablado	habríais comido	habríais escrito
habrían hablado	habrían comido	habrían escrito

1.   The conditional perfect expresses an action that was possible or incomplete. The English equivalent is *would have* plus a past participle.

Mi hijo **habría venido** a visitarme.
My son would have come to visit me.

Le dijeron que Carmelita **habría ido** al cine.
They told him that Carmelita would have gone to the movies.

Se habrían hecho ricos con las acciones de Anaconda.
They would have become rich with the Anaconda stock.

2.   The conditional perfect may be used to express probability in the past.

¿Lo **habría visto**?

I wondered if she had seen it.

¡**Se habrían burlado** de él, sus compañeros de clase!
His classmates had probably (must have) made fun of him!

Idiomatic uses of «tener» and «haber»

1.   **tener que**   *to have to*

Tengo que pagar la cuenta.   *I have to pay the bill. (I must pay the bill.)*

2. **haber de**   *to be supposed to, must*
The obligation expressed is less than that expressed by **tener que**.

He de ir a la escuela.	*I must go to school.*
Los hombres **han de pagar**.	*The men are supposed to pay.*

3. **hay**   *there is, there are*
    había   *there was, there were*

Hay seis soldados en esa tienda.	*There are six soldiers in that store.*
Había siete gusanos en la lata.	*There were seven worms in the can.*

4. **hay que**   *it is necessary, one must*

Hay que decir la verdad.	*It is necessary to tell the truth.*

Ejercicio

Exprese en español:

1.   He would have gone to South America.
2.   They will have taken the child to the doctor.
3.   I wonder if daddy has come home.
4.   My daughter would have come to the hospital.
5.   He had probably arrived early.
6.   I must go to the dentist.
7.   You are supposed to take your medicine.
8.   One must rest at times.
9.   There were five skiers on the mountain.
10. There is a fly in my soup.
11. I wondered if she had seen it. But she would have told me.
12. My classmates had probably gone to the beach.
13. One must take the good with the bad.
14. She would have known the truth earlier.
15. Winter will have arrived before his birthday.

Conjugación del verbo «jugar»

jugar	*to play*
Yo **juego** a la pelota.	I play ball.
Tú **juegas** a la pelota.	You play ball.
Él, Ella **juega** a la pelota.	He, She plays ball.
Usted **juega** a la pelota.	You play ball.
Nosotros (–as) **jugamos** a la pelota.	We play ball.
Vosotros (–as) **jugáis** a la pelota.	You play ball.
Ellos, Ellas **juegan** a la pelota.	They play ball.
Ustedes **juegan** a la pelota.	You play ball.

Ejercicio

Emplee las frases siguientes en oraciones:

1. jugar al béisbol	4. jugar al balompié
2. jugar al tenis	5. jugar a los naipes (*cards*)
3. jugar al ajedrez	6. jugar con los niños

Estudio de palabras

Many English words which refer to occupations and professions and end in **-er** and **-or** have Spanish cognates ending in **-dor**.

aviator	**(el) aviador**	investigator	**(el) investigador**
boxer	**(el) boxeador**	legislator	**(el) legislador**
collaborator	**(el) colaborador**	operator	**(el) operador**
emperor	**(el) emperador**	orator	**(el) orador**
exterminator	**(el) exterminador**	senator	**(el) senador**

Ejercicio

Busque las palabras siguientes en el vocabulario y combínelas con el adjetivo **español**:

MODELO: solicitor
          el solicitador español

1. conqueror	3. discoverer	5. governor
2. curator	4. explorer	6. spectator

APÉNDICE

Subjunctive and Command Forms

SUBJUNCTIVE MOOD

1. The verb tenses presented thus far are part of the indicative mood. They express what is known or certain. The subjunctive mood in Spanish likewise includes several tenses, but it expresses uncertainty or doubt. The subjunctive is generally used in a dependent clause in the following construction.

main verb (indicative)	+	**que**	+	dependent verb (subjunctive)
I prefer		*that*		*you come.*

The subjunctive verb in the dependent clause is not to be treated as an isolated fact or idea, but in terms of its dependent relationship to the main clause of the sentence. The subjunctive mood is rapidly disappearing in English, but it still has a foothold in Spanish.

2. To form the present subjunctive, **-ar** verbs change the distinctive vowel of the present indicative endings from **a** to **e**, and **-er** and **-ir** verbs change the characteristic vowels from **e** and **i** to **a**. These endings are added to the stem of the first person singular of the present indicative.

hablo **hable**   hago **haga**   salgo **salga**

hablar   **comer**   **escribir**

hable	hablemos	coma	comamos	escriba	escribamos
hables	habléis	comas	comáis	escribas	escribáis
hable	hablen	coma	coman	escriba	escriban

The present subjunctive expresses an action that can occur now or in the future. It is dependent on a verb in the present or future tense or a command in the main clause.

3. There are six verbs in Spanish that have irregular forms in the present subjunctive.

dar	dé,	des,	dé,	demos,	deis,	den
estar	esté,	estés,	esté,	estemos,	estéis,	estén
haber	haya,	hayas,	haya,	hayamos,	hayáis,	hayan
ir	vaya,	vayas,	vaya,	vayamos,	vayáis,	vayan
saber	sepa,	sepas,	sepa,	sepamos,	sepáis,	sepan
ser	sea,	seas,	sea,	seamos,	seáis,	sean

4. Radical-changing verbs have the same vowel changes in the present subjunctive as in the present indicative. In addition, Class II and Class III verbs have another change: **e** becomes **i** and **o** becomes **u** in first and second person plural forms.

Class I: **pensar piense, pienses, piense, pensemos, penséis, piensen**
          volver vuelva, vuelvas, vuelva, volvamos, volváis, vuelvan
Class II: **sentir sienta, sientas, sienta, sintamos, sintáis, sientan**
          dormir duerma, duermas, duerma, durmamos, durmáis, duerman
Class III: **pedir pida, pidas, pida, pidamos, pidáis, pidan**

Ejercicios

A. *Dé la forma apropiada del presente de subjuntivo de los verbos siguientes:*

1. que él cante   (escribir, ir, venir)
2. que yo hable   (buscar, llegar, empezar)[1]
3. que nosotros vivamos   (poder, dejar, comer)
4. que tú estés   (ser, saber, beber)
5. que ellos preparen   (dar, conocer, saludar)

B. *Diga en español:*

1. _____ that we may sleep
2. _____ that Ernest may think
3. _____ that it may go
4. _____ that Philip may have
5. _____ that Helen and Anita may know
6. _____ that Eleanor and I may kiss
7. _____ that you enjoy yourselves (*fam.*)
8. _____ that Rudolph and Eugene may buy
9. _____ that the general returns
10. _____ that we lose

IMPERFECT SUBJUNCTIVE

The imperfect subjunctive is formed by dropping the **-ron** ending of the third person plural of the preterit and adding either the **-ra** or **-se** endings.

hablar		**comer**		**escribir**	
hablara	hablase	comiera	comiese	escribiera	escribiese
hablaras	hablases	comieras	comieses	escribieras	escribieses
hablara	hablase	comiera	comiese	escribiera	escribiese
habláramos	hablásemos	comiéramos	comiésemos	escribiéramos	escribiésemos
hablarais	hablaseis	comierais	comieseis	escribierais	escribieseis
hablaran	hablasen	comieran	comiesen	escribieran	escribiesen

1. Spelling changes that occurred in the first person singular of the preterit also take place in all forms of the present subjunctive.

PRESENT PERFECT SUBJUNCTIVE

The present perfect subjunctive is formed with the present subjunctive of the auxiliary verb **haber** (haya) plus the past participle.

hablar	comer	escribir
haya hablado	haya comido	haya escrito
hayas hablado	hayas comido	hayas escrito
haya hablado	haya comido	haya escrito
hayamos hablado	hayamos comido	hayamos escrito
hayáis hablado	hayáis comido	hayáis escrito
hayan hablado	hayan comido	hayan escrito

PLUPERFECT SUBJUNCTIVE

The pluperfect subjunctive is formed with the imperfect subjunctive of the verb **haber** (**hubiera or hubiese**) plus the past participle.

hablar

hubiera hablado	hubiese hablado
hubieras hablado	hubieses hablado
hubiera hablado	hubiese hablado
hubiéramos hablado	hubiésemos hablado
hubierais hablado	hubieseis hablado
hubieran hablado	hubiesen hablado

comer

hubiera comido	hubiese comido
hubieras comido	hubieses comido
hubiera comido	hubiese comido
hubiéramos comido	hubiésemos comido
hubierais comido	hubieseis comido
hubieran comido	hubiesen comido

escribir

hubiera escrito	hubiese escrito
hubieras escrito	hubieses escrito
hubiera escrito	hubiese escrito
hubiéramos escrito	hubiésemos escrito
hubierais escrito	hubieseis escrito
hubieran escrito	hubiesen escrito

Ejercicio

Cambie los infinitivos al imperfecto, al perfecto y al pluscuamperfecto del modo subjunctivo (imperfect, present perfect, and pluperfect subjunctive):

1. que (necesitar)
2. que (ocurrir)
3. que (creer) eso
4. que Vd. (dormir) en toda la noche
5. que (estar) en el Perú
6. que (volver) a casa
7. que (tomar) esas píldoras
8. que lo (preferir)
9. que (cumplir) con tus obligaciones
10. que (decir) tal cosa

SUBJUNCTIVE IN NOUN CLAUSES

1. A noun clause is a dependent clause that functions as a noun and may be used as the object of the verb in the main clause. In Spanish the verb in a noun clause is in the subjunctive mood when (1) the main verb (or expression) denotes or implies the subject's volition, emotion, or doubt; and (2) the subject of the noun clause is different from the subject of the main clause. The noun clause is introduced by the relative **que**.

2. If the main verb expresses or implies a wish, the verb in the dependent clause is in the subjunctive.

Quiero que Vd. **regrese** a casa temprano.
I want you to return home early.(. . .that you return . . .)

Su madre **había deseado que** Cristina **se casara** el año próximo.
Her mother had wanted Christina to get married next year. (. . . that Christina marry . . .)

No **desean que** sus hijos **vayan** a esa fábrica a trabajar.
They don't want their children to go to work in that factory. (. . . that their children go . . .)

Preferí que me **pagaran** en dólares americanos.
I preferred to have them pay me in American dollars. (. . . that they pay me . . .)

But: Yo **quiero regresar.**
       I want to return.

       Su madre **había deseado casarse.**
       Her mother had wanted to get married.

3. If the main verb expresses an order, permission, advice, prohibition, supplication or necessity, the dependent verb in the noun clause is in the subjunctive.

Dígale que no tome whisky con las píldoras.
Tell him not to take whiskey with the pills.

El comandante **mandó que** las tropas **avanzaran.**
The commander ordered the troops to advance.

Permito que vayas esta vez.
I permit you to go this time.

Le aconsejé que tomara la ruta más directa.
I advised him to take the most direct route.

La ley **impide que cobren** más del nueve por ciento de interés.
The law prevents them from charging more than nine percent interest.

Le suplico que mande esta carta por correo aéreo.
I implore you to send this letter air mail.

El cliente **necesita que** la corbata **sea** roja.
The customer needs the tie to be red.

Le ruego que ponga su firma al dorso de la solicitud.
I beg you to put your signature on the reverse side of the application.

El maestro **prohibió que** los estudiantes **saliesen** del aula de clase.
The teacher prohibited the students from leaving the classroom.

El jefe **había pedido que no insistiéramos** en días de vacaciones.
The boss had asked us not to insist on vacation days.

4. If the main verb expresses doubt, uncertainty, disbelief, or denial, the verb in the
    dependent clause is in the subjunctive mood. **No dudar** is considered a verb of certainty
    and does not govern the subjunctive. **No creer** and **¿cree?** take the subjunctive if the
    speaker feels an element of doubt; when there is certainty, however, these expressions
    call for the indicative mood.

    Yo **dudo que vengan, pero él no duda que vienen**.
    I doubt that they will come, but he doesn't doubt that they will come.

    No creí que papá **recibiese** su cheque del Seguro Social a tiempo.
    I didn't believe that Papa would receive his Social Security check on time.

    No estoy seguro que mi sobrino **diga** la verdad.
    I am not sure my nephew is telling the truth.

    ¿Quiénes **dudan que** este carro **cueste** tres mil pesos?
    Who doubts that this car costs three thousand dollars?

    El Ministro **no cree que haya** peligro de guerra.
    The Minister does not believe that there is danger of war.

    ¿Cree que lo haga?
    Do you believe he will do it?

5. If the main verb is one of emotion (joy, surprise, fear, anger, sorrow, and so on), the
    dependent verb is in the subjunctive mood.

Me alegro de que haya tenido suerte en la lotería nacional.
I am happy that you had luck in the national lottery.

Siento que no puedas venir a nuestra fiesta.
I am sorry that you are not able to come to our party.

El médico **teme que muera** el viejo.
The doctor is afraid that the old man will die.

Tuve miedo que los astronautas no aterrizasen sobre la luna.
I feared that the astronauts would not land on the moon.

SUBJUNCTIVE AFTER IMPERSONAL EXPRESSIONS

Impersonal expressions and impersonal verbs which express an attitude of uncertainty as to the outcome of the dependent clause call for the subjunctive in the dependent clause. Dependent verbs following **es cierto, es claro**, and **es verdad** express a positive attitude of certainty and are in the indicative mood.

Es cierto que un general **va** a aparecer en el bar.
It is certain that a general will appear in the bar.

No es cierto que un general **vaya** a aparecer.
It is not certain that a general will appear.

Es dudoso que salga bien en sus estudios.
It is doubtful he will do well in his studies.

Será extraño que no vendan colchones en esa tienda.
It will be unusual for them not to sell mattresses in that store.

Fue lástima que los obreros **no encontrasen** empleo.
It was a pity that the workers didn't find jobs.

Sería necesario que los pobres **continuaran** viviendo en tales condiciones deplorables.
It would be necessary that the poor continue to live in such deplorable conditions.

Es imposible que paguemos el alquiler este mes.
It is impossible for us to pay the rent this month.

Es posible que los precios **se rebajen.**
It is possible for the prices to go down.

Es probable que los deportistas mexicanos **obtengan** la victoria; **basta que mantengamos** el
    segundo lugar.
*It's probable that the Mexican athletes will win; it will be enough for us to maintain second
    place.*

SUBJUNCTIVE IN EXCLAMATIONS

When the main clause contains a vehement expression or exclamation of desire, the dependent verb is in the subjunctive.

¡Ojalá que él **haya salido** de Cuba!
I hope that he got out of Cuba!

¡Ojalá que mi esposa **estuviera** aquí ahora!
Would that my wife were here now! (I wish my wife were here now.)

¡Ojalá que lleva!
Oh, that it may rain! (I hope it rains.)

¡Ojalá que lloviese!
Oh, that it might rain! (I wish it would rain.)

INFINITIVE TO REPLACE SUBJUNCTIVE

In Spanish the infinitive may be used in place of a noun clause with a subjunctive when the subject of the dependent verb is a pronoun which may be regarded as the indirect object of the main verb. This possibility generally occurs with the verbs **mandar, dejar, impedir, permitir**, and **prohibir**.

El jefe **nos mandó hacer** este trabajo.
     or
El jefe **nos mandó que hiciésemos** este trabajo.
The boss ordered us to do this job.

Mi madre **no me deja que beba**.
Mi madre **no me deja beber**.
My mother doesn't allow me to drink.

El choque **nos impide pasar**.
El choque **nos impide que pasemos**.
The accident prevents us from passing.

Ejercicio

Exprese en español:

1. Everybody doubts she did it.
2. We advise you to pay.
3. It was certain that Lupe entered the store.
4. Oh, if it would only snow!
5. I hope she will get out of the hospital today.
6. Do you believe that Fred is fifty years old?
7. I want to go to the movies.

8. It is necessary to arrive at the party early.
9. The captain ordered the soldiers to put their rifles in the barracks.
10. He is so happy that he can walk again.
11. Tell him to bring the corporal here and order the rest of the men to clean the mess hall.
12. I shall be very sad if she returns the engagement ring to her boyfriend. He wants so much to marry her.
13. Don't you believe the truth when you hear it or is it necessary for me to give you a written document?
14. Will you want them to sleep in your home, or shall I advise them to make a reservation at a motel?
15. It is not enough for him to finish college; I also want him to be a doctor.

SUBJUNCTIVE IN ADJECTIVE CLAUSES

An adjective clause is a dependent clause which is used as an adjective and which may modify a noun or pronoun antecedent in the main clause. When the antecedent is negative, indefinite, uncertain, or not definitely known to exist, the subjunctive is used in the dependent clause. If the antecedent is definite, the dependent verb is in the indicative mood. These clauses are introduced by **que**.

Busco **un guía que hable** bien el inglés.
I am looking for a guide who speaks English well.

¿Hay alguien que sepa bailar el tango?
Is there anybody who knows how to dance the tango?

No conozco a **nadie que haya visto** el monstruo.
I don't know anyone who has seen the monster.

Haré **lo que Vd. quiera.**
I'll do whatever you wish.

But:

Busco al **guía que habla** inglés.
I am looking for the guide who speaks English.

Conozco a la **chica que entiende** ruso.
I know the girl who understands Russian.

SUBJUNCTIVE IN ADVERBIAL CLAUSES

1. An adverbial clause is a dependent clause used as an adverb. It is introduced by a conjunction or an adverb and may modify a verb in the main clause. The subjunctive is used in adverbial clauses only when referring to something yet to be accomplished or realized in a future or indefinite time. If the statement expresses a material fact, the verb

is in the indicative. The most frequently used conjunctions and adverbs that may introduce a clause with a subjunctive are:

antes (de) que	*before*	**hasta que**	*until*
así que	*as soon as*	**luego que**	*as soon as*
aunque	*although*	**mientras que**	*while*
cuando	*when*	**siempre que**	*as long as*
después (de) que	*after*	**tan pronto como**	*as soon as*
en cuanto	*as soon as*		

Te avisaré **cuando llegue** el tren.
I shall let you know when the train arrives.

Déme la llave **tan pronto como me acerque** a la puerta.
Give me the key as soon as I approach the door.

Lograremos conseguir el dinero **siempre que sigamos** las instrucciones del jefe.
We shall succeed in getting the money as long as we follow the instructions of the boss.

2. The subjunctive is also used in adverbial clauses of purpose, result, supposition, provision, negation, exception, concession, and condition. The following common conjunctions govern the subjunctive:

en caso de que	*in case*	**para que**	*in order that*
a fin de que	*in order that*	**de manera que**	*so that*
a menos que	*unless*	**de modo que**	*so that*
a no ser que	*unless*	**con tal que**	*provided that*
a pesar de que	*in spite of the fact that*	**sólo que**	*except that*
dado que	*provided that*	**sin que**	*without*

Te llevaré al gimnasio **a fin de que puedas** jugar al baloncesto.
I'll take you to the gymnasium so that you can play basketball.

Dado que estés aquí durante las vacaciones, te atenderé bien.
As long as you will be here during the vacation period, I shall take good care of you.

Los herederos fueron invitados a la oficina del abogado **para que se firmasen** los papeles oficiales del testamento.
The heirs were invited to the lawyer's office so that the official papers of the will might be signed.

THE SUBJUNCTIVE IN **IF-CLAUSES**

1. In adverbial sentences of condition that express uncertainty, doubt, or a statement that is contrary to fact or impossible to realize, the verb in the *if*-clause (dependent clause) is in the imperfect or pluperfect subjunctive, while the main verb (result clause) is in the conditional or conditional perfect.

Si él **hubiera estado** en casa, no **habría sucedido** el robo.
If he had been at home, the robbery would not have taken place.

Si **tuviese** dinero suficiente, **compraría** una piscina.
If I had enough money, I would buy a swimming pool.

Si **hubiésemos visitado** a México, **habríamos necesitado** una vacunación.
If we had visited Mexico, we would have needed a vaccination.

2.   When **si** is the equivalent of *whether* or expresses a possibility that can be realized, the verb is in the indicative mood, not the subjunctive.

No sabía **si Alberto iría** al teatro.
I didn't know whether Albert would go to the theatre.

Era difícil averiguar **si Roberto estaría** en Londres el año próximo.
It was difficult to ascertain whether Robert would be in London next year.

Todavía no sé **si voy**.
I still don't know if I'm going.

SEQUENCE OF TENSES

The following sequence of tenses is applicable only to those sentences that need the subjunctive mood. If the verb in the main clause is in the present, future, or present perfect, or is a command, the verb in the dependent clause is in the present subjunctive or present perfect subjunctive. If the verb in the main clause is in the imperfect, preterit, pluperfect, or conditional, the verb in the dependent clause is in the imperfect subjunctive. If the action in the dependent clause happened before a past action in the main clause, the pluperfect subjunctive is used in the dependent clause.

VERB IN MAIN CLAUSE	TENSES OF SUBJUNCTIVE IN DEPENDENT CLAUSE	
	Incomplete Action	Completed Action
1. Present 2. Future 3. Present perfect 4. Commands	Present	Present perfect
5. Imperfect 6. Preterit 7. Pluperfect 8. Conditional	Imperfect	Pluperfect

EJEMPLOS

1. Manda que venga.
2. Mandará que venga.
3. Ha mandado que venga.
4. ¡Mande Vd. que venga!
5. Mandaba que viniera.

6. Mandó que viniera.
7. Había mandado que viniera.
8. Mandaría que viniera.
9. Vino antes de que lo hubiera mandado.

Ejercicio

Exprese en español:

1. . . . in case we fly to Europe.
2. . . . whether Nicholas would stay home.
3. . . . if I were God.
4. . . . so that the birds do not fly.
5. . . . in spite of the fact that the girl has money.
6. . . . when she receives the gift.
7. . . . as soon as I see him.
8. . . . provided that the money is paid.
9. I am looking for a man with red trousers.
10. I am looking for the man with red trousers.
11. I don't know anybody who has ever seen a unicorn.
12. If I were President of the United States, I would work with the most intelligent men in the country.
13. The doctor suggests I go to the hospital so that I may get an X-ray of my broken bone.
14. As soon as you are twenty-one years of age, I shall give you the house and you can pay the mortgage.
15. The judge would give me a job in the court provided that I did what he wants.

COMMANDS

1. Affirmative familiar

canta (tú)   **bebe (tú)**   **escribe (tú)**
cantad (vosotros)   **bebed (vosotros)**   **escribid (vosotros)**

The singular of the familiar command is the same as the third person singular of the present indicative. The plural is formed by dropping the **r** of the infinitive and adding **d**.

2. Negative familiar

no cantes (tú)   **no bebas (tú)**   **no escribas (tú)**
no cantéis (vosotros) **no bebáis (vosotros)** **no escribáis (vosotros)**

All negative commands have the same form as the corresponding person in the present subjunctive.

3. The polite commands (singular and plural) have the same form as the present subjunctive.

(no) cante Vd.   **(no) beba Vd.**   **(no) escriba Vd.**
(no) salga Vd.   **(no) haga Vd.**   **(no) ponga Vd.**

4. Object pronouns are attached to all affirmative commands. If necessary, a written accent is added to preserve the original stress of the word.

Déselo Vd. al capitán.   *Give it to the captain.*

The final **d** of familiar plural commands is dropped before the reflexive pronoun **os** is added. **Irse** is an exception.

levantaos   **acostaos**   **idos**

5. In negative commands, the object pronouns precede the verb.

No se lo des a la secretaria.   *Don't give it to the secretary.*

6. The first person plural of the present subjunctive is used for the first person plural command.

Lavemos los platos.   *Let us wash the dishes.*

7. **Vamos a** plus the infinitive may be substituted for the first person plural command if the action is to be performed in the near future.

Vamos a ponernos las gafas para verlo.   *Let us put on our glasses to see it.*

8. *Let* may also be expressed as a command in the third person singular and plural with **que** plus the corresponding subjunctive forms of the verb.

Que lo haga Enrique.   *Let Henry do it.*

9. Irregular Familiar Commands

decir:	di	decid	salir:	sal	salid
hacer:	haz	haced	ser:	sé	sed
ir:	ve	id	tener:	ten	tened
irse:	vete	idos	venir:	ven	venid
poner:	pon	poned			

Ejercicios

A. *Diga en español*:

1. Tommy, go to the store.
2. Drink your milk, kitty.
3. Put your hands on the table.
4. Speak to me.
5. Go away.
6. Let's go swimming.
7. Have another beer.
8. Make your bed.
9. Kiss me.
10. Be careful.

B.   *Exprese en español:*

1.   "Eat , drink, and be merry" is a popular refrain.
2.   Go in peace and remember your neighbors.
3.   Go to the courtroom and tell the judge the truth.
4.   Rest, stay in bed, drink orange juice, and take one aspirin every four hours.
5.   Wash your face, comb your hair, and don't forget to clean out the bathtub before you leave the bathroom.

Vocabularios

The Spanish-English vocabulary includes words needed to complete the *Cuestionario, Vamos a hablar* sections, and other exercises, as well as unglossed words from the *Diálogo* and *Dichos y refranes*. The vocabulary does not include those words that are part of the special vocabulary of the individual units (*Expresiones apropiadas* and *Expresiones útiles*). Such word categories may be located through the Index. Close cognates are not included. The English-Spanish vocabulary includes words needed to complete the *Vocabulario en acción* sections.

ABREVIATURAS

adj.	adjective	*interj.*	interjection	*p.p.*	past participle
com.	command	*m.*	masculine	*pl.*	plural
f.	feminine				

Español-Inglés

a to, at, for, on, upon, in, into, by, from
abajo below
abogado (a) *m., f.* lawyer
abrigo *m.* overcoat, clothing
abril *m.* April
abrir to open
abuela *f.* grandmother
abuelo *m.* grandfather
abundancia *f.* abundance
abundar to abound
aburrir to bore, to get bored
acabar de to have just
acción *f.* share of stock, action
accionista *m. & f.* stockholder, shareholder
aceite *m.* oil; **aceite de oliva** *m.* olive oil
acera *f.* sidewalk
acompañar to accompany
acontecimiento *m.* event

acordar to resolve
acostarse to go to bed
acostumbrado accustomed to
actitud *f.* attitude
actualmente at present
acudir to respond
acuerdo: de acuerdo in agreement
adecuado appropriate
adelgazar to make thin
además de besides
¡adiós! good-bye!
adivinar to guess
¿adónde? where?
aeropuerto *m.* airport
afeitada *f.* shave
aficionado (a) *m., f.* fan
agencia *f.* agency
agradable pleasant, agreeable
agradecer to thank
agua *f.* (*article* el) water

aguja *f.* needle
ahora now
ahorrar to save
ahorros *m. pl.* savings
ajedrez *m.* chess
al = a + el
alabanza *f.* compliment
alegrarse to be happy
alegre happy
alegría *f.* happiness
alemán German
alfiler *m.* straight pin
alfombra *f.* rug
algo something
algodón *m.* cotton
alguien somebody
alguno some, any
alimento *m.* food
aliviar to alleviate
almacén *m.* warehouse, store, department store

almeja *f.* clam
almuerzo *m.* lunch
alojamiento *m.* lodging
alrededor around
alto high, tall
altoparlante *m.* loudspeaker
alumno *m.* pupil, student
allí there
amable nice
amanecer *m.* dawn
amar to love
amarillo yellow
ambos both
ambulante roving
amigo (a) *m., f.* friend
amor *m.* love
ampliación *f.* enlargement
anaranjado orange
andar to go
angelito *m.* little angel
anillo de compromiso *m.*
  engagement ring
aniversario *m.* anniversary
ansiar to covet, to yearn
anterior before
antes de before
antiguo old
anunciador (a) *m., f.*
  announcer
anunciar to announce
anuncio *m.* commerical,
  announcement
año *m.* year
aparecer to appear
apenas hardly
aplicar to apply
apodo *m.* nickname
apreciar to appreciate
aprender to learn
apretar to squeeze
apropiado appropriate, correct
aquí here
árbol *m.* tree
arena *f.* sand
arreglar to adjust, to fix, to
  arrange
arriba above, upward, upstairs
arroz con pollo *m.* chicken
  with rice
arruga *f.* wrinkle
artesano(a) *m., f.* artisan
asesion *m.* assassin
asistir to attend, to assist
aspiradora *f.* vacuum cleaner

astilla *f.* splinter
asunto *m.* matter
atacar to attack
atleta *m. & f.* athlete
atravesar to cross
atribuir to attribute
atún *m.* tuna
aumentar to increase
aún still, yet
aunque although
ausentar to drive away
ausente absent
autobús *m.* bus
autor(a) *m., f.* author
autoridad *f.* authority
aventura *f.* adventure
aventurar to venture
avión *m.* airplane
avisar to advise, to inform, to
  warn
¡ay! alas!, ouch!; ¡ay de mí! my
  goodness!
ayer yesterday
ayuda *f.* help
ayudar to help
azúcar *f.* sugar
azucarero *m.* sugar bowl
azul blue

bailar to dance
baile *m.* dance
bajada *f.* fall
bajar to go down
bajo below
balompié *m.* football
banco *m.* bank
banquero(a) *m., f.* banker
banquete *m.* banquet
baño *m.* bath, bathroom
baratillo bargain goods
barato cheap, inexpensive
barba *f.* beard, whiskers, chin
barbacoa *f.* barbecue
barbaridad outrage; **¡qué**
  barbaridad! how awful!
barbería *f.* barbershop
barbero(a) *m., f.* barber
barniz *m.* varnish
barquillero *m.* waffle iron
barredera *f.* street sweeper
barriga *f.* belly
barrio *m.* ghetto,
  neighborhood
basta enough

bastante enough
basura *f.* garbage
batalla *f.* battle
bate *m.* bat
batear to bat
bebé *m.* baby
beber to drink
bebida *f.* drink
bebito *m.* little baby
béisbol *m.* baseball
bendito blessed
besar to kiss
beso *m.* kiss
biblioteca *f.* library
bicicleta *f.* bicycle
bien well, all right
bienvenido welcome
billete de ida y vuelta *m.*
  round-trip ticket
bizcocho *m.* biscuit, cookie,
  cake
blanco white
blanqueador *m.* bleach
blusa *f.* blouse
boca *f.* mouth
  boca de agua *f.* hydrant
bocado *m.* bite, mouthful
bocina *f.* horn
boda *f.* wedding
bolsillo *m.* pocket
bombero(a) *m., f.* firefighter
bombilla *f.* bulb
bonita pretty
bono *m.* bond
bordo: a bordo de on board
borracho *m.* drunkard
bosque *m.* forest
bote *m.* boat
botella *f.* bottle
botón *m.* button
breve brief
bruja *f.* witch
bueno good
buscar to look for
butaca *f.* armchair

caballero *m.* gentleman
caballo *m.* horse
cabellera *f.* head of hair
cabello *m.* hair
cabeza *f.* head
cacto *m.* cactus
cada each
caer to fall

café *m.* coffee
caja *f.:* **caja de seguridad** safe-deposit box; **caja registradora** cash register; **caja de primer auxilio** first-aid kit
cajero(a) *m., f.* teller, cashier
calamidad *f.* calamity
calvicie *f.* baldness
calvo bald
calzado *m.* shoes, footwear
callarse to be quiet
calle *f.* street
cama *f.* bed
cambiar to change
caminar to walk
camión *m.* truck; **camión basurero** garbage truck
camioneta *f.* station wagon
camisa *f.* shirt
campana *f.* bell
campeonato *m.* championship
campo *m.* countryside, field
cana *f.* gray hair
cansado tired
cantar to sing
cantidad *f.* quantity
cañón *m.* cannon
capa *f.* cape, cloak
capaz capable of
capilla *f.* chapel
capítulo *m.* chapter
capó *m.* hood of car
cara *f.* face
carabela *f.* caravel
¡caramba! gracious!, darn!
carcajada *f.* burst of laughter
cárcel *f.* jail
caricatura *f.* caricature, cartoon
caridad *f.* charity
cariño *m.* affection; dear, honey, love
carne *f.* meat
caro expensive
carpintería *f.* carpentry
carrera *f.* race, run
carretera *f.* highway
carrito *m.* wagon; **carrito de compras** shopping cart
carro *m.* car, cart
carta *f.* letter; **carta de navegar** chart
cartel *m.* poster

casa *f.* home, house; **casa de seguros** insurance company
casarse to marry
casi almost
catedral *f.* cathedral
causa: **a causa de** because of
causar to cause
caza *f.* hunting
cazador *m.* hunter
cebolla *f.* onion
celebrar to celebrate
celibato *m.* bachelorhood
celoso jealous
cena *f.* supper
cenar to dine, to eat supper
ceniza *f.* ash
centavo *m.* cent
centro *m.* center, marketplace, shopping center
cepillo *m.* brush
cerca (de) near
cerdo *m.* pig
cerebro *m.* brain
certificado registered *m.* certificate
cerveza *f.* beer
cerrar to close, to lock
cielo *m.* heaven, sky
cien hundred
científico scientific
cierto certain
cigarrillo *m.* cigarette
cinco five
cincuenta fifty
cine *m.* movie, movies
circo *m.* circus
ciruela *f.* plum
cirujano(a) *m., f.* surgeon
cirugía *f.* surgery
citación *f.* date, appointment
ciudad *f.* city
claro que sí (no) indeed (not)
clase *f.* kind, species
clavel *m.* carnation
clavo *m.* nail
cliente *m. & f.* customer, client
clima *m.* climate
cobrar to change
cocina *f.* kitchen, cooking
coctel *m.* cocktail
cocinar to cook
cocinero(a) *m., f.* cook, chef
coche *m.* car

colega *m. & f.* colleague
colgar to hang
comedia *f.* play
comentario *m.* commentary
comer to eat
comercio *m.* business
comestibles *m. pl.* provisions, food
comida *f.* meal
como as, how; ¿cómo? how?
cómodo comfortable
compañero(a) *m., f.* companion; **compañero de cuarto** roommate
compañía *f.* company
complejo *m.* complex
complicado complicated
compra *f.* purchase
comprar to buy
comprensión *f.* comprehension
computador *m.* computer
común common
con with
concejo *m.* council
condenar to condemn
conducir to drive
confianza *f.* confidence
conmigo with me
conocer to know, to be acquainted with
conseguir to get, to achieve
consejero(a) *m., f.* adviser
conservar to conserve
consigo with him (her, you)
construir to construct
consulta *f.* consultation
consumador(a) *m., f.* consumer
consumir to consume
contar to tell
contenir to contain
contento content, happy
contestar to answer
contigo with you
contra against
contrario *m.* opposite
convencer to convince
convenir to suit
corazón *m.* heart
coro *m.* chorus
correr to run
corrida *f.* bullfight, race
corte *f.* court; **corte de pelo** *m.* haircut

cortés polite, courteous
corto short
cosa f. thing
coser to sew
costar to cost
costumbre f. custom
crecer to grow
creer to believe
crema f. cream
cremera f. creamer
crimen m. crime
crónica f. chronicle,
newspaper
crucero m. cruise, crossing
cruzar to cross
cual as, such as, which, who;
¿cuál? which?, what?, which
one?
cualquier(a) any
cuando when, although, since;
¿cuándo? when
¿cuánto? how much?
cuarenta forty
cuarto m. room, fourth,
quarter past (of)
cuatro four
cubierta f. deck, over
cubo de basura m. garbage
can
cuchillería f. cutlery
cuchillo m. knife
cuello m. collar, neck
cuenta f. bill
cuero m. leather
cuerpo m. body
cuidado m. care, attention
cuidar to take charge of
culpa f. blame
culpable m. culprit
cumpleaños m. birthday
cuna f. cradle
curar to cure
curso m. course
cutis m. skin
cuyo(a) whose, of whom
chaleco salvavidas m. life
jacket
champú m. shampoo
chapa de circulación f. license
plate
charla f. chat
charlar to chat
cheque m. check
chica f. girl

chico m. boy, lad, youngster
chimenea f. fireplace, chimney
chino Chinese
chiquito very small
chiste m. joke
chófer m. chauffeur, driver
choque m. crash
chuleta f. chop

dañar to harm
daño m. harm, hurt, damage
dar to give
de of, from, about
debajo below
deber ought to, must; deber
de faltar must be missing
decidir to decide
decir to say, to tell
dedo m. finger, toe
dejar to leave
delgado thin
delicioso delicious
demasiado too much
demorar to delay, to linger
depender to depend
dependiente(a) m., f. salesman
(woman)
deporte m. sport
deportista m., f. participant in
sports
deportivo sport
derecha f. right
derecho m. right
desaparecido disappeared
desayuno m. breakfast
descansar to rest
desconocido m. stranger
describir to describe
descripción f. description
desde since
desear to desire, to wish
desempeñar to act
deseo m. desire
desierto m. desert
después after
destinado destined
desventaja f. disadvantage
desventajoso disadventageous
detalle m. detail
detrás (de) behind
día m. day
diablo m. devil
diario daily
dibujo m. drawing, illustration

dicho m. saying
diente m. tooth
difícil difficult
dificultad f. difficulty
diga com. state, tell, say
dinamita f. dynamite
dinero m. money
Dios m. God
dirección f. direction
dirigir to direct
disco m. record
disculpar to forgive, to excuse,
to pardon
discutir to discuss
diseñador(a) m., f. designer
disfrutar to make the most of
distinguir to distinguish
distinto distinct
distribuidor(a) m., f.
distributor
doce twelve
docena f. dozen
dólar m. dollar
doler to hurt
doliente aching, suffering,
sorrowful
dolor m. pain
donde where; ¿dónde? where?
dormir to sleep
dormitorio m. bedroom,
dormitory
dos two
droga f. drug
ducha f. shower
dueño(a) m., f. owner
dulce sweet
durante during

e and
echar to throw
edad f. age
edificio m. building
educado educated
educador(a) m., f. educator
efecto eléctrico m. electrical
appliance
ejemplar m. copy
ejemplo m. example; por
ejemplo for example
ejercicio m. exercise
ejército m. army
eléctrico electric
elefante m. elephant
elogio m. compliment

embajador(a) *m., f.*
  ambassador
empanada *f.* meat pie
empezar to begin
empleado(a) *m., f.* employee
emplear to use
en in, into, on, at
encaje *m.* lace
encantar to love
encargarse de to take charge
  of
encontrar to meet, to find, to
  be faced with
endorsar (endosar) to endorse
enemigo *m.* enemy
energía *f.* energy
enfermedad *f.* sickness,
  malady
enfermero(a) *m., f.* nurse
enfermo sick
enfrentar to confront
engañar to deceive
enlazar to tie, to connect
enriqueser to enrich
ensalada *f.* salad
enseñar to teach
entender to understand
entero entire, whole
entonces then, so
entrada *f.* ticket, entrance
entrar to enter
entre between, among
entregar to deliver
entretenimiento *m.*
  entertainment
enumerar to enumerate
envejecerse to become old
enviar to send
envidia *f.* envy
época *f.* epoch, age, time
equipaje *m.* luggage
equipo *m.* team
equivocado wrong, in error
escala *f.* stopover
escaparate *m.* shop window
escasez *f.* scarcity
escaso limited
escena *f.* scene
escoger to choose
esconder to hide
escribir to write
escritorio *m.* desk
escuela *f.* school
escultura *f.* sculpture

esmoquin *m.* tuxedo
eso that
espacio *m.* space; **espacio en
  blanco** blank
España *f.* Spain
especialidad *f.* specialty
especializarse to specialize
espectáculo *m.* show
espejo *m.* mirror
esperar to wait for, to hope
espina *f.* thorn
espíritu *m.* spirit
esposa *f.* wife
esposo *m.* husband; *pl.*
  husband and wife *f. pl.*
  handcuffs
esquiar to ski
estación *f.* station, season
estacionar to park
estado *m.* state
Estados Unidos (de América)
  m. pl. United States (of
  America)
estadounidense American
estante *m.* shelf
estar to be
estatua *f.* statue
este this
esterilizar to sterilize
estilo *m.* style
estipulación *f.* stipulation
esto this
estómago *m.* stomach
estudiante *m., f.* student
estudios *m. pl.* studies
excursión *f.* excursion, trip,
  cruise
explicar to explain
exportador exporting
extranjero foreign; *m.* foreign
  land
extrañar to be surprised at
extraño strange, foreign

fábrica *f.* factory
fabricar to make
fábula *f.* fable, fairy tale
fácil easy
falta: por falta de for lack of
faltar to be lacking
familia *f.* family
farmacéutico(a) *m., f.*
  pharmacist, druggist

farmacia *f.* pharmacy,
  drugstore
favor: por favor please
fecha *f.* date
felicitar to congratulate
fenómeno *m.* phenomenon
feo ugly
feria *f.* fair
ferrovia: linea ferrovia
  railroad line
festejar to entertain
ficción *f.* fiction
ficha *f.* checker
fiebre *f.* fever
fiesta *f.* party
figura *f.* figure
fijar to fix, to set
filosofía *f.* philosophy
filtro *m.* filter
fin: a fin de in order to
final: al final in the end
financiero financial
firma *f.* signature
firmar to sign
física *f.* physics
flecha *f.* arrow
florería *f.* flower shop
florista *m. & f.* florist
fonógrafo *m.* phonograph
fortuna *f.* fortune
fósforo *m.* match
foto (fotografía) *f.* photo
  (photograph)
fracción *f.* fraction
francés(-esa) *m. & f.* French
  person
frase *f.* phrase, sentence
frente: en frente de in front
  of
fresa *f.* strawberry
fresco fresh
frío *m.* cold
frito fried
frontera *f.* border, frontier
fuego *m.* fire
fuente *f.* fountain
fuerte strong
fumar to smoke
función *f.* performance
funcionar to function

gabinete de medicina *m.*
  medicine cabinet
gafas *f. pl.* eyeglasses

galopear to gallop

galletica *f.* little biscuit, cookie

gallina *f.* chicken

gallo *m.* rooster

ganancia *f.* gain, advantage

ganar to earn, to gain; **ganar la vida** to earn one's living

ganga *f.* bargain

garantía *f.* guarantee

garganta *f.* throat

gastar to spend, to waste

gato *m.* cat

gaveta *f.* drawer

generalmente generally

genérico generic

generoso generous

gente *f.* people

gobierno *m.* government

goma *f.* tire

gordo fat

gozar to enjoy

gracias *f. pl.* thanks, thank you

grado *m.* degree

gran (grande) large

gratis free

gritar to shout

guante *m.* glove

guardar to keep, to preserve, to protect

guerra *f.* war

guiar to guide

guisante *m.* pea

guitarra *f.* guitar

guitarrista *m. & f.* guitarist

gustar to like

haba *f.* lima bean

habitación *f.* room

habitante *m. & f.* inhabitant

hábito *m.* habit, clothes

hablar to speak

hacer to make, to do; **hacer falta** to need, to lack; **hacer juego** to match; **hacer lucir** to make shine; **hacer un juicio** to make a judgment

hacienda *f.* country estate

hallar to find

hambre *f.* hunger

hasta: hasta luego see you later; **hasta que** until

hay there is, there are; **hay que** it is necessary; **¿qué hay de nuevo?** what's new?

helado *m.* ice cream

herida *f.* wound

hermana *f.* sister

hermano *m.* brother

hermoso handsome, beautiful

héroe *m.* hero

hígado *m.* liver

hija *f.* daughter

hijito *m.* little son

hijo *m.* son; *pl.* children

hilo *m.* thread

himno *m.* hymn

hispánico Hispanic

historia *f.* story, history

hogar *m.* home, hearth

hola hello

hombre *m.* man; **hombre de negocios** businessman

hora *f.* hour

horizonte *m.* horizon

horno *m.* oven

hoy today; **hoy día** today, nowadays

huele it smells

huelga *f.* strike

huevo *m.* egg

huir to flee

humo *m.* smoke

humor *m.* humor

identificar to identify

iglesia *f.* church

igual equal

ilustre illustrious

imaginar to imagine

importado imported

incendio *m.* fire

increíble incredible

indio *m.* Indian

individuo *m.* individual

inferencia *f.* inference

inmediatamente immediately

inmediato immediate

inmigrante *m.* immigrant

inscribir to report, to sign up

insuperable unsurpassable

interés *m.* interest

invernadero *m.* greenhouse

invierno *m.* winter

invitado(a) *m., f.* guest

ir to go; **ir de compras** to go shopping; **ir de pesca** to go fishing

isla *f.* island

jabón *m.* soap

jamás never

jamón *m.* ham

Japón *m.* Japan

jardín *m.* garden

jardinería *f.* gardening

jefe(a) *m., f.* chief

joven young

joya *f.* jewel

jubilado retired

juez *m.* (**la señora juez**) judge

jugar to play

juguete *m.* toy

juntarse to join together

junto a next to

juventud *f.* youth

ladrar to break

ladrón *m.* thief

lago *m.* lake

lámpara *f.* lamp

lana *f.* wool

langosta *f.* lobster

largo long, abundant

lástima: qué lástima what a pity

lavado *m.* laundry

lavar to wash

lección *f.* lesson

leche *f.* milk

lechería *f.* dairy

lechuga *f.* lettuce

leer to read

legislatura *f.* legislature

legumbre *f.* vegetable

lengua *f.* language, tongue

lente *m.* lens; *pl.* eyeglasses

leña *f.* wood, firewood

león *m.* lion

levantarse to get up

ley *f.* law

leyenda *f.* legend

libra *f.* pound

librarse to free oneself

libre free

libro *m.* book; **libro de referencia** reference book

líder *m.* leader

lima *f.* lime

limpiar to clean
lindo pretty
lírico lyrical
listo ready, alert
litro *m.* liter
llama *f.* llama (Andean animal)
llamar to call
llamarse to be called
llegada *f.* arrival
llegar to arrive (at), to reach
llenar to fill
lleno full
llevar to carry, to wear
llorar to cry
llover to rain
lluvia *f.* rainfall
loco crazy
lograr to succeed in, to obtain
lugar *m.* place
lujo *m.* luxury
luna de miel *f.* honeymoon
lunes *m.* Monday

madera *f.* wood
maderería *f.* lumberyard
madre *f.* mother
maestro(a) *m., f.* teacher
maleta *f.* suitcase
maletero *m.* trunk of car
mal(o) bad, evil
mandar to send, to order
mandato *m.* commandment
manejar to drive
manera *f.* manner
mano *f.* hand
manta *f.* blanket
mantel *m.* tablecloth
manzana *f.* apple
mañana *f.* morning, tomorrow
maquillaje *m.* makeup
máquina *f.* machine
mar *m.* sea
maravilloso marvellous
marca *f.* brand, trade name
margarita *f.* daisy
marido *m.* husband
marina *f.* navy
marinero *m.* sailor
más more
masaje *m.* massage
matar to kill
matrimonio *m.* marriage, matrimony, married couple

mayor greater, older
mayoría *f.* majority
mecánico(a) *m., f.* mechanic
medianoche *f.* midnight
medicina *f.* medicine
médico(a) *m., f.* doctor
medida *f.* size
medio half; **en medio de** in the midst of
mejor better
mencionar to mention
menos less; **al menos** at least
mensaje *m.* message
mentira *f.* lie
mercado *m.* market, business world
mes *m.* month
mesa *f.* table
meter to bring in
método *m* method
mi my
miedo *m.* fear
miembro *m.* member
mientras while
mil thousand
militar military
milla *f.* mile
mío mine, of mine
mirar to look at
mismo *m.* same, own, very
moda *f.* style
mole de hielo *f.* iceberg
molestar to bother, to molest
momentico *m.* wee moment
mona *f.* monkey
moneda *f.* currency
monja *f.* nun
monje *m.* monk
montaña *f.* mountain
monte *m.* mount, mountain
montura *f.* saddle
morder to bite
moreno(a) *m. & f.* brunette
morir to die
mosca *f.* fly
mostrador *m.* counter, showcase
mostrar to show
motocicleta *f.* motorcycle
mover to move
muchacha *f.* girl
muchacho *m.* boy
mucho much
mueble *m.* piece of furniture

muerte *f.* death
muerto dead
mujer *f.* woman, lady, wife
mundo *m.* world; **todo el mundo** everybody
museo *m.* museum
muy very

nación *f.* nation
nada nothing, anything, not at all
nadar to swim
naranja *f.* orange
narrar to tell
nata *f.* cream
naufragio *m.* shipwreck
Navidad *f.* Christmas
necesitar to need
necio *m.* fool
negocios *m. pl.* business
nervio *m.* nerve
ni . . .ni . . . neither . . .nor
nieve *f.* snow
ningún (ninguno) no, none, nobody
niña *f.* little girl, child
niño *m.* little boy, child; *pl.* children, little boys
nobleza *f.* nobility
noche *f.* night
nombrar to name
nombre *m.* name, noun
noroeste *m.* northwest
norteamericano *m.* North American, American
nota *f.* grade (school); note (music)
novia *f.* financée, girl friend
novio *m.* fiancé, boyfriend
nuestro our
nuevo new; **de nuevo** again, anew
número *m.* number
numeroso numerous
nunca never, ever

o or
obediente obedient
objeto *m.* object
obra *f.* work
obsequiar to give, to present
obtener to obtain
ocurrir to occur
oficina *f.* office

oficio m. trade
ofrecer to offer
oído m. hearing
oír to hear, to listen
ojo m. eye
oler to smell
olimpíadas f. pl. olympics
olor m. smell, odor
olvidar to forget
olla f. pot
ómnibus m. bus
once eleven
opinar to opine, to think
oración f. sentence, prayer
orden f. order
oreja f. ear
órgano m. organ
oro m. gold
otro other, another; otra vez
again
oveja f. lamb
oyente m. listener

paciente m. & f. patient
padre m. father, priest; pl.
parents, father and mother
pagar to pay
página f. page
pago m. pay
país m. country
paisaje m. landscape
pájaro m. bird
palabra f. word
paleta f. paddle
palmada m. slap
pan m. bread; pan de centeno
rye bread; pan tostado toast
panadería m. bakery
panadero(a) m., f. baker
panecillo m. roll
papel m. paper, role
par m. pair
para to, for, toward, in order
to; para que in order that
parabrisas m. windshield
parada f. bus stop
parar to stop
parecer to seem
pared f. wall
parque m. park; parque
zoológico zoo
parráfo m. paragraph
partidario partisan
partido m. game, contest

pasa f. raisin
pasajero(a) m., f. passenger
pasar to pass, to spend, to
happen
pasatiempo m. pastime
Pascua Florida f. Easter
Sunday
paso m. step
pastel m. pie, cake
patinar to skate
patrulla f. patrol
payaso m. clown
paz f. peace
peatón m. pedestrian
pedido m. request
pedir to ask for
pegado stuck
peinarse to comb
película f. film, movie
peligro m. danger
peligroso dangerous
pelo m. hair
peluca f. wig
peluquero(a) m., f. hairdresser
pensamiento m. thought
pensar to think
peor worse
pequeño small
perchero m. clothes rack
perder to lose
pérdida f. loss
perezoso lazy
periódico m. newspaper
permiso m. permit, permission
pero but
perrera f. doghouse, kennel
perro m. dog; perro caliente
hot dog
personalidad f. personality
pesar: a pesar de in spite of
pesar to weigh
pescadería f. fish store
pescado m. fish
pescar to fish
peso m. weight
pez m. fish
pie m. foot; a pie on foot; al
pie de la letra to the letter
piedra f. stone
piel f. skin
pierna f. leg
pintar to paint; pintar al óleo
to paint with oil

pintor m. painter
pintura f. paint
piña f. pineapple
pipa f. pipe
pirámide f. pyramid
piso m. floor
placer m. pleasure
planchadora f. press
planchar to iron
planeta m. planet
planta f. plant
plata f. silver, money
platillo m. saucer
plato m. plate, dish
playa f. beach
pleito m. dispute, quarrel,
lawsuit
población f. population
pobre poor
pobreza f. poverty
poco little, few
poder to be able
poesía f. poetry
poeta (poetisa) m., f. poet
policía m. & f. policeman,
policewoman
político(a) m. & f. politician
polvo m. powder
poner to put, to place; poner
fin to put an end
por by, through, over, in, for,
for the sake of, on account
of, in exchange for, in place
of
¿por qué? why?
porque because
portaguantes m. glove
compartment
portarse to behave
portilla f. porthole
postre m. dessert
precaución f. precaution
precio m. price
precioso precious
predilecto favorite
preferir to prefer
pregunta f. question
preguntar to ask
premio m. prize
prenda f. personal effect
preocuparse to worry
preparar to prepare
preparativo m. preparations

presentar to present;
  presentarse to present
  oneself
préstamo *m.* loan
prestar to lend
prevenido forewarned
primavera *f.* spring
primera clase *f.* first class
primer(o) *m.* first
probar to try on
procedimiento *m.* proceeding
profético prophetic
prohibido prohibited
prohibir to prohibit
propiedad *f.* property
propina *f.* tip
propio own
proponer to propose
proteger to protect
provecho *m.* advantage,
  benefit, profit
próximo next
prueba *f.* test, trial
psicólogo(a) *m., f.* psychologist
psiquiatra *m. & f.* psychiatrist
pueblo *m.* town
puente *m.* bridge
puerco *m.* pork, pig
puerta *f.* door
puertorriqueño Puerto Rican
pues then, well, anyhow
pulga *f.* flea
pulmón *m.* lung
pulsera *f.* bracelet
punto *m.* point
pureza *f.* purity
purga *f.* purge

que that, which, who, whom,
  ¿qué? what?, which?, how?,
  what a?; **¿qué hay de
  nuevo?** what's new?; **¿qué
  tal?** hello, how is
  everything?
quedar to remain, to fit;
  quedar bien to fit well
quedarse to remain
quehacer *m.* chore, odd job
queja *f.* complaint
quejarse to complain
quemar to burn
querer to want, to wish;
  querer decir to mean
querido *m.* dear, dearie

quien who, whom; **¿quién?**
  who?, whom?
quitarse to take off
quizás perhaps

rábano *m.* radish
ranchero(a) *m., f.* rancher
raqueta *f.* racket
rareza *f.* rarity
rascar to scratch
rato *m.* while
rayo ultravioleta *m.* ultraviolet
  ray
razón *f.* reason; **con razón** no
  wonder, of course; **tener
  razón** to be right
reaccionar to react
realidad *f.* reality
recibir to receive
recién recently
reclamar to claim
recluta *m.* recruit
recoger to gather, to pick up
recordar to remember
recorrer to pass through
recto straight
rechazar to reject
rechinar to grind, to grate
red *f.* net
refrán *m.* proverb, saying
regalar to give
regalo *m.* gift
regatear to bargain
reglamento *m.* regulations
regresar to return
reina *f.* queen
rejuvenecerse to become
  rejuvenated
relacionado related
relatar to tell
relato *m.* story
reloj *m.* watch
relucir to glitter, to shine
relleno *m.* stuffing, padding
remediar to relieve
remo *m.* oar
remolacha *f.* beet
remover to remove, to stir
reparación *f.* repair
repetir to repeat
representante *m. & f.*
  representative
requerir to require
requisito *m.* requisite

resolver to solve
respirar to breathe
responder to answer, to
  respond
respuesta *f.* response, answer
resultado *m.* result
reunir to collect
revisar to review
revista *f.* magazine, review
rey *m.* king
rezar to pray
rico rich
ridículo ridiculous
riesgo *m.* danger, risk
río *m.* river
robar to rob
robo *m.* robbery
rodar to roll, to rotate, to
  move
rojo red
romper to break
roncar to snore
ropa *f.* clothes
rosa *f.* rose
rosado pink
roto broken
ruido *m.* noise
ruina *f.* ruin
ruptura *f.* rupture
ruso Russian

saber to know
sabor *m.* taste
sacar to take, to take out, to
  take off
sacerdote *m.* priest
saco *m.* sack, bag
sala de recreo *f.* den,
  recreation room
salario *m.* salary
salir to leave, to turn out
salón de belleza *m.* beauty
  parlor
saltar to jump
salud *f.* health
saludable healthy
saludo *m.* greeting
salvado saved
salvamento *m.* rescue
salvar to save
san (santo) *m.* saint
sangre *f.* blood
sargento *m.* sergeant
secar to dry

seda *f.* silk
seguida: en seguida at once, right away, immediately
seguir to follow
según according to, as per, depending on circumstances
segundo second
seguridad *f.* security, collateral
seguro certain, sure
seis six
sello *m.* stamp
semana *f.* week
senador(a) *m., f.* senator
sentarse to sit down
sentir to feel, to feel sorry
señal *f.* signal
señal de carretera *f.* road sign
señor *m.* gentleman
señora *f.* lady
señorita *f.* miss
separar to separate
ser to be
serio serious
servicio militar *m.* military service
servilleta *f.* napkin
servir to serve, to help
sesenta sixty
setenta seventy
severo severe
si if, whether
sí yes
siempre always
siete seven
siglo *m.* century
siguiente following, next
silla de cubierta *f.* deck chair
sillón *m.* armchair
símbolo *m.* symbol
simpático nice, likable
sin without
sino but, except
sobrar to exceed, to excel
sobre on, on top of, about, concerning
socorro *m.* help
solamente only
soldado *m.* soldier
solito alone
solo alone, only
soltero *m.* bachelor
sombra *f.* shade
son *m.* sound
soneto *m.* sonnet

sonriente smiling
soñar to dream
sopa *f.* soup
sorbete *m.* sherbet
su your, his, her, its, their
subir to rise
suceder to happen
sucio dirty
suegra *f.* mother-in-law
suegro *m.* father-in-law; *pl.* mother-and father-in-law
suelo *m.* floor
suerte *f.* luck
sufrir to suffer
sugerir to suggest
Suiza *f.* Switzerland
sujeto *m.* subject
suma *f.* sum
supermercado *m.* supermarket
suyo his, hers, yours, theirs

tabaco *m.* cigar, tobacco
tabernero(a) *m., f.* tavern keeper, bartender
tal: tal vez perhaps
  ¿qué tal? how are you?
talla *f.* size
también also, too
tampoco neither, not either
tan so; **tan solo** only
tanque *m.* tank
tanto so much
tardar to be long, to be late
tarde late
tarde *f.* afternoon
tarjeta *f.* card
taxista *m. & f.* taxi driver
taza *f.* cup
teatro *m.* theater
techo *m.* ceiling
tela *m.* fabric
teléfono *m.* telephone
tema *m.* theme, subject
templo *m.* temple
temprano early
tendero(a) *m., f.* shopkeeper, storekeeper
tenedor *m.* fork
tener to have; **tener lugar** to take place; **tener prisa** to be in a hurry; **tener razón** to be right; **tener que** to have to, must
tercero third

terminar to end, to terminate
tesis *f.* thesis
testigo *m. & f.* witness
ti you
tía *f.* aunt
tiempo *m.* time
tienda *f.* store, tent
tijeras *f. pl.* scissors
tinte *m.* tint
tiñer to tint
tío *m.* uncle; *pl.* aunt and uncle
típico typical
tipo *m.* type
tirar to pull
tocar to play
todavía still, yet
todos all
tonto stupid, foolish, fool
toro *m.* bull
tortura *f.* torture
tostadora *f.* toaster
trabajar to work
trabajo *m.* work
traducir to translate
traducción *f.* translation
traer to bring
traje *m.* suit; **traje de baño** bathing suit; swimsuit
trampolín *m.* diving board
tranquilidad *f.* tranquillity
tranquilizar to tranquilize
transparencia *f.* slide
tratar to treat, to try to
tres three
tripulación *f.* crew
triste sad
trópico *m.* tropics
tu your
tulipán *m.* tulip
túnel *m.* tunnel
turista *m. & f.* tourist

u or
últimamente lately
último last, latest
universidad *f.* university
universitario university
universo *m.* universe
uno: uno por uno one by one; *pl.* some
uña *f.* fingernail
usar to use
utilizar to use, to utilize

vaca *f.* cow
vacaciones *f. pl.* vacation
vacío empty
vajilla *f.* tableware
valer to be worth
valor *m.* value
valla *f.* hurdle
vanidoso vain
vapor *m.* ship
vaso *m.* glass
vecindario *m.* neighborhood
vecino(a) *m., f.* neighbor
vejez *f.* old age
velita *f.* candle
velozmente swiftly
vencer to conquer
vendedor(a) *m., f.* seller,
  peddler
vender to sell
venir to come
venta *f.* sale; en venta on sale

ventaja *f.* advantage
ventajoso advantageous
ventana *f.* window
ver to see; a ver let's see
verano *m.* summer
verdad *f.* truth
verde green
verificar to verify, to check
vestido *m.* suit, dress
vestir to dress
vez *f.* time; en vez de instead
  of; otra vez again; a veces
  at times
viajar to travel
viaje *m.* trip, voyage
viajero(a) *m., f.* traveler
vida *f.* life
viejo old
viento *m.* wind
viernes Friday

vino *m.* wine
visita *f.* visit
visitar to visit
viuda *f.* widow
vivir to live
volar to fly
volver to return
voto *m.* vote, vow
voz *f.* voice
vuelo *m.* flight

y and
ya already, now, finally, at
  once
yerno *m.* son-in-law
yo I

zanahoria *f.* carrot
zapatero(a) *m., f.* cobbler
zapato *m.* shoe

Inglés-Español

absent ausente
accident accidente *m.*
accuracy exactitud *f.*,
  precisión *f.*
actress actriz *f.*
admission admisión *f.*, entrada
  f.
adventurous aventuroso
advise aconsejar
after después
afternoon tarde *f.*, good
  afternoon buenas tardes
again otraz vez
age edad *f.*
ago hace; a year ago hace un
  año
air conditioner aire
  acondicionado *m.*
airplane avión *m.*, aeroplano
  m.
all todo
also también
alter alterar
always siempre

amuse (oneself) divertir(se)
animal animal *m.*
another otro
answer respuesta *f.*
anybody alguien
apple manzana *f.*, apple pie
  pastel de manzana *m.*
approach acercarse
arithmetic aritmética *f.*
arrive llegar
artist artista *m. & f.*
as tan, tanto; as many as tan
  (tanto, tantas) . . .como; as
  soon as tan pronto como
ascertain averiguar
ask preguntar; to ask for pedir
aspirin aspirina *f.*
assignment tarea *f.*
astronaut astronauta *m. & f.*
astronomy astronomía *f.*
athlete atleta *m. & f.*
Atlantic Atlántico *m.*
attend asistir

aunt tía *f.*; aunt and uncle
  tíos *m. pl.*
avenue avenida *f.*

bacon tocino *m.*
bake cocer al horno
baker panadero(a) *m., f.*
bankbook libreta de banco *f.*
bat bate *m.*; batear
bathroom baño *m.*, cuatro de
  baño *m.*
bathtub bañera *f.*, bañadera *f.*
be ser, estar
beach playa *f.*
bean frijol *m.*
beard barba *f.*
beautiful hermoso
bed cama *f.*
bedroom alcoba *f.*, dormitorio
  m.
beer cerveza *f.*
before antes de
best el (la) mejor
bet apuesta *f.*; apostar

big grande
billion billón *m.*
biology biología *f.*
bite morder
black negro
blanket manta *f.*, frazada *f.*
blender licuadora *f.*
blessed bendecido, bendito
blind ciego
blonde rubio
blue azul
bone hueso *m.*
book libro *m.*
boss jefe(a) *m.*, *f.*
box caja *f.*
boy chico *m.*, niño *m.*,
    muchacho *m.*
boyfriend novio *m.*
bread pan *m.*
breakfast desayuno *m.*
bridge puente *m.*
brilliant brillante
bring traer
broken roto
brother hermano *m.*
brother-in-law cuñado *m.*
brown castaño, pardo
build construir
building edificio *m.*
bump chocar
bus ómnibus *m.*, autobús *m.*
butcher carnicero(a) *m.*, *f.*
butter mantequilla *f.*
buy comprar

café café *m.*
cafeteria cafetería *f.*
call llamar
can poder
candle vela *f.*, candela *f.*
canoe canoa *f.;* pasear en
    canoa
capital capital *f.*
captain capitán *m.*
car carro *m.*, coche *m.*, auto
    m., automóvil *m.*
careful cuidado; **to be careful**
    tener cuidado
carefully con cuidado
carnation clavel m.
case: in case (of) en case de
    (que)
catch coger
center centro *m.*

certain cierto
chair silla *f.*
chauvinist chauvinista *m. & f.*
cheap barato
check cheque *m.;* chequear
cheese queso *m.*
cherry cereza *f.*
child hijo *m.*, niño *m.*
children hijos *m.*
Chinese chino
Christmas Navidad *f.*
church iglesia *f.*
city ciudad *f.*
class classe *f.*
classroom sala de clase *f.*
clean limpiar
client cliente *m. & f.*
climb subir
close cerrar
closed cerrado
cloud nube *f.*
club club *m.*
coffee café *m.*
college universidad *f.*
colored de color, en colores
comb peinarse
come venir
comfortable cómodo
competition competición *f.*
complete completo
**concern: to whom it may
    concern** a quien
    corresponda
conclude concluir
congregation congregación *f.*
continue continuar
contract contrato *m.*
convenience conveniencia *f.*
conversation conversación *f.*
convince convencer
cookie pastelito *m.*, galletica
    f., galleta *f.*
cordially yours cordialmente
correctly correctamente
correspondence
    correspondencia *m.*
count contar
country país *m.*, campo *m.*
courteous cortés
courteously cortésmente
cousin primo *m.* prima *f.*
crash choque *m.;* chocar
cow vaca *f.*
cream crema *f.*, nata *f.*

credit card tarjeta de crédito
    f.
criminal criminal *m. & f.*
cry llorar
Cuban cubano *m.*, cubana *f.*
cultivate cultivar
curiosity curiosidad *f.*
customer cliente *m. & f.*
cut cortar

dad, daddy papá, papacito
dance baile *m.;* **to dance**
    bailar
dancing el bailar *m.*, bailando
day día *m.*
dead muerto
deaf sordo
Dear Madam Estimada señora
Dear Sir Muy señor mío
decide decidir
delightful deleitoso
dentist dentista *m. & f.*
desk escritorio *m.*
dessert postre *m.*
diamond diamante *m.*
difficult difícil
diligent diligente
diligently diligentemente
dine cenar, comer
dinner cena *f.*
direction dirección *f.*
dirty sucio
dishwasher lavaplatos *m.*
distance distancia *f.*
doctor médico(a) *m.*, *f.*
document documento *m.*
dog perro *m.*
dollar dólar *m.*
donkey asno *m.*, **burro** *m.*,
    burrico *m.*
doubt dudar
dream sueño *m.*
dress vestirse
drink beber
drive manejar
drug droga *f.*
during durante
dust polva *m.*

each cada
early temprano
easily fácilmente
eat comer
eating el comer *m.*, comiendo

either ...or o ...o
electric: electric blanket
frazada eléctrica f.; electric
shaver afeitadora eléctrica f.
employee empleado(a) m., f.
engagement ring anillo de
compromiso m.
England Inglaterra f.
English inglés
enjoy disfrutar, gozar
enter entrar
enough basta, suficiente
Europe Europa f.
every cada
everybody todo el mundo
exercise ejercicio m.
examination examen m.
excessively excesivamente
expensive caro
expert experto
express expresar

fabric tela f.
face cara f.
factory fábrica f., factoría f.
faint marearse
fall caerse
family familia f.
fast rápido
fat gordo
father padre m.
father-in-law suegro m.
favorite favorito, predilecto
few poco(s)
fifth quinto
fifty cincuenta
fight lucha f., luchar
film película f.
finish terminar, acabar
first primer(o)
fish pescado m., pez m. (alive)
fit caber
float flotar
flower flor f.; flower shop
florería f.
follow seguir
food alimento m.
football balompié m.
forget olvidar
fourth cuarto
French francés
Friday viernes m.
fried frito

friend amigo(a) m., f.
fruit fruta f.

garden jardín m.
gasoline gasolina f.
generous generoso
generously generosamente
geography geografía f.
German alemán
get obtener, conseguir
get up levantarse
gift regalo m.
girl niña f., muchacha f.
girl friend novia f.
give dar
given dado
glass vidrio m.
glove guante m.
glue cola f.; pegar
go ir; go away irse; go down
bajar; to go to bed acostarse
golden de oro, dorado
good bueno; good afternoon
buenas tardes; good
morning buenos días
governor gobernador(a) m., f.
graceful gracioso
graduation gradución f.
granddaughter nieta f.
grandfather abuelo m.
grandmother abuela f.
grandparents abuelos m. pl.
grandson nieto m.
gravity gravedad f.
green verde
ground tierra f.
group grupo m.
guide guía m. & f.
gymnasium gimnasio m.

Haita Haití m.
half medio
handsome guapo
hanging plants plantas
colgantes f.
happily alegremente
happy alegre, contento
hard duro
hardware store ferretería f.
hat sombrero m.
hate odiar
have tener, haber; to have to
tener que
heard oído, escuchado

heart corazón m.
heat calentar
heaven cielo m.
help socorro m; ayudar
her su, sus
here aquí
high alto
his su, sus
hit dar; dar contra
home casa f.
horrible horrible
hose medias f. pl.
hospital hospital m.
hot caliente
hour hora f.
house casa f.
hundred cien
husband esposo m.

I am in receipt of Obra en mi
poder
ice cream helado m., ice
cream parlor heladería f.
idea idea f.
idealism idealismo m.
ideally idealmente
if si
imitation imitación f.
important importante
improve mejorar
inside dentro (de)
in order to para, por
intelligence inteligencia f.
intelligent inteligente
interested interesado
interesting interesante
introduce presentar
Irish irlandés m.
iron plancha f.
Italian italiano
Italy Italia f.

jacket chaqueta f.
jai alai jai-alai m.
jail cárcel f.
Japanese japonés
jealously celosamente
job trabajo m., puesto m.,
oficio m.
judge juez m.
jump saltar

kill matar
kitchen cocina f.

kitten gatito *m.*
knit tejer
know saber, conocer

lady señora *f.*, dama *f.*
lake lago *m.*
lamb chop chuleta de cordero *f.*
language lengua *f.*, idioma *m.*
large grande
late tarde; **to be late** tardar en
laugh reírse
law ley *f.*
learn aprender
least: at least al menos
leave dejar
lemonade limonada *f.*
lend prestar
lens lente *m.*
lentil lenteja *f.*
less menos
lesson lección *f.*
license plate placa de matrícula *f.*
lie mentir
life vida *f.*
light luz *f.*
like gustar
limitation limitación *f.*
lipstick lápiz labial *m.*
listen escuchar
little pequeño
live vivir
loan préstamo *m.*
look: to look at mirar; **to look for** buscar
long live viva
lose perder
lot: a lot (of) mucho(s)
louder en voz más alta
love amar

madam señora *f.*
made hecho
magnificent magnífico
mail correo *m.*
make hacer; **to make fun of** burlarse de
mama mamá *f.*
man hombre *m.; old man* viejo *m.*
mansion mansión *f.*
many muchos; **as many as** tan (tantos, tantas) ... como

march marzo *m.*
materialism materialismo *m.*
meat carne *f.*
mechanic mecánico(a) *m.*, *f.*
mention mencionar
merging traffic confluencia *f.*
mess hall salón comedor *m.*
Mexican mejicano, mexicano
Mexico México *m.*
million millón *m.*
mine mío
minus menos
mirror espejo *m.*
Miss señorita *f.*
miss faltar; echar de menos
mission misión *f.*
mom, mommy mamá *f.*, mamacita *f.*
moment momento *m.*
Monday lunes *m.*
money dinero *m.*
month mes *m.*
more más
morning mañana *f.; good morning* buenos dís *m. pl.*
mortgage hipoteca *f.*
motel motel *m.*
mother madre *f.*
mountain montaña *f.*
move mover
movies cine *m.*
Mr. señor *m.*
Mrs. señora *f.*
music música *f.*
must tener que
my mi, mis
myself me

name nombre *m.; be named* llamarse
narrow angosto, estrecho
necessary necesario
need necesitar
needed necesitado, se necesita
negligence negligencia *f.*
neighbor vecino(a) *m.*, *f.*
nervous nervioso
next siguiente
new nuevo
newspaper periódico *m.*
New York Nueva York
next próximo; **next to** junto a
nice simpático, amable
night noche *f.*

no no
nobody nadie
nobody ninguno
not no
novel novela *f.*
novelist novelista *m. & f.*
now ahora
number número *m.*
nurse enfermero(a) *m.*, *f.*

ocean océano *m.*
often a veces, a menudo
oil aceite *m.*
old viejo, de edad; **old man** viejo *m.*
once una vez
onion cebolla *f.*
opal ópalo *m.*
open abierto; **to open** abrir
opera ópera *f.*
operate operar
oppose oponer
orange naranja *f.; orange juice* jugo (zumo) de naranja *m.*
order: in order to para
ouch ay
our nuestro(s)
over sobre
overcoat abrigo *m.*, sobretodo *m.*
owner dueño(a) *m.*, *f.*

paella paella *f.*
painting cuadro *m.*
pajamas pijama *m.*
papa papá *m.*
parents padres *m. pl.*
party fiesta *f.*, reunión *f.*
passenger pasajero(a) *m.*, *f.*
patient paciente *m. & f.*
pay pagar; **to pay attention** prestar atención
payment pago *m.*
peace paz *f.*
people gente *f.*
person persona *f.*
pharmacy farmacia *f.*
philosophy filosofía *f.*
pie pastel *m.*
planet planeta *m.*
play jugar
pleasantly agradablemente

please por favor, hágame el
  favor de
pleasure gusto *m.*, placer *m.*
plus y
pool piscina *f.*
poor pobre
popular popular
popularly popularmente
pork chop chuleta de puerco
  f.
Portuguese portugués *m.*
postal postal
postman (woman) cartero(a)
  m., f.
potato patata *f.*, papa *f.*
powder polvo *m.*
precision precisión *f.*
prefer preferir
presence presencia *f.*
present regalo *m.*
press planchar
pretty bonito
printed impreso
probability probabilidad *f.*
probably probablemente
problem problema *m.*
professional profesional
professor profesor(a) *m., f.*
prohibited prohibido, se
  prohibe
proud orgulloso
provided that con tal que
prudence prudencia *f.*
psychology psicología *f.*
Puerto Rican puertorriqueño
pupil alumno(a) *m., f.*
purchase compras *f.;* comprar
**purpose: my purpose in
  writing is** es mi propósito al
  escribir
put poner

Quebec Quebec
question pregunta *f.*
quickly rápidamente

rabbi rabino *m.*
radio radio *m. & f.*
rain llover
raincoat impermeable *m.*
rapid rápido
reach alcanzar
reality realidad *f.*
ready listo

reason razón *f.*
receptionist recepcionista *m.*
  & f.
red rojo
refrain dicho *m.*
refrigerator nevera *f.*
**regret: we regret to inform
  you** mucho nos duele
remain quedar
repair reparar, remontar
  (zapatos)
repeat repetir
repent arrepentirse
reply: in reply en contestación
resemble asemejarse, parecerse
  a
reservation reservación *f.*
residence residencia *f.*
rest: to rest descansar; **the rest
  (of)** los demás
restaurant restaurante *m.*
return vuelta *f.;* **to return**
  volver, regresar
rich rico
ride montar
right turn virar a la derecha
river río *m.*
rocking chair mecedora *f.*
rose rosa *f.*
round redondo
ruby rubí *m.*
run correr

sad triste
sadly tristemente
said dicho
sail navegar
sailor marinero *m.*
sale: on sale en venta
salesman dependiente *m.*
  vendedor *m.*
saleswoman dependienta *f.*,
  vendedora *f.*
Santa Claus Santa Claus, San
  Nicolás
Saturday sábado *m.*
sauce salsa *f.*
save guardar
say decir; **say it** dígalo
scarf bufanda *f.*
school crossing zona escolar *f.*
scissors tijeras *f.*
seasick mareado
second segundo

see ver
seek buscar
sell vender
separate separar
September septiembre *m.*
seriously seriamente, en serio
serve servir
service: at your service a sus
  órdenes
sew coser
sewing machine máquina de
  coser *f.*
ship barco *m.*
short corto
shorten acortar
shrimp camarón *m.*
shuffle barajar
sick enfermo
sign signo *m.*, señal *f.*, letrero
  m.; **to sign** firmar
signed firmado
silence silencio *m.*
silversmith platero *m.*
sing cantar
sir señor *m.*
sis hermanita *f.*
sister hermana *f.*
sit sentar
skate patinar
skier esquiador(a) *m., f.*
skinny delgado
skirt falda *f.*
slacks pantalones *m. pl.*
sleep dormir
sleeve manga *f.*
slow lento, despacio
small pequeño
smoke fumar
sneaker zapato de tenis *m.*
snow nevar
so that de manera que, de
  modo que
soda gaseosa *f.*, soda *f.*
sodium sodio *m.*
sofa sofá *m.*
sold vendido, se vende
soldier soldado *m.*
some unos, algunos
somebody alguien
son hijo *m.*
soon: as soon as tan pronto
  como
sow sembrar
space espacio *m.*

Spanish español
spark plug bujía *f.*
special especial
speed velocidad *f.*
spinach espinacas *f. pl.*
spite: in spite of a pesar de
  que
spoken hablado, se habla
sport deporte *m.*
spring primavera *f.*
stadium estadio *m.*
start empezar, comenzar
state estado *m.*
stay quedar
steak biftec *m.*, bistec *m.*
still todavía
stock acción *f.*
stop parada *f.;* alto
store tienda *f.*
story cuento *m.*
straw pajita *f.*
street calle *f.*
strict estricto
strong fuerte
student estudiante *m. & f.*
study estudio *m.*
suggest sugerir
Sunday domingo *m.*
supper cena *f.*
surgeon cirujano(a) *m., f.*
surprise sorprender
sweat sudar
sweater suéter *m.*
sweet dulce; **sweets** dulces *m.*
  pl.
swim nadar
swimming el nadar

table mesa *f.*
tablecloth mantel *m.*
tailor sastre(a) *m., f.*
take tomar
talk hablar
tall alto
tasty sabroso
tea té *m.*
teach enseñar
teacher maestro(a) *m., f.*
  profesor(a) *m., f.*
telegram telegrama *m.*
television set televisor *m.*
ten diez
test examen *m.*, prueba *f.*
Texas Tejas

than que
that ese, esa, aquel(la); **so that**
  de manera que, de modo
  que
their su, sus
these estos, estas
think pensar
third tercero
this este, esta
those esos, esas, aquellas
thousand mil
three tres
throw tirar
Thursday jueves *m.*
ticket boleto *m.*, billete *m.*
tie corbata *f.*
time tiempo *m.;* **at times**
  a veces
times *(multiplication sign)* por
tire goma *f.*, llanta *f.*
tired cansado
today hoy
tomorrow mañana
tonight esta noche
top of mountain cumbre *f.*
toupee tupé *m.*
tourist turista *m. & f.*
toward hacia
tranquility tranquilidad *f.*
traveler viajero(a) *m., f.*
trip viaje *m.*
Tuesday martes *m.*
twenty veinte
twice dos veces
two dos

ugly feo
uncle tío *m.*
under bajo
understand entender
United States Estados Unidos
  m. pl.
until hasta
up arriba
upon sobre
us nos
use usar

vacuum cleaner aspiradora *f.*
vanity vanidad *f.*
vegetable legumbre *f.*
version versión *f.*
vice-president
  vicepresidente(a) *m., f.*

violence violencia *f.*
virtuosity virtuosidad *f.*
visit visitar
vitamin vitamina *f.*
voice voz *f.*

waiter camarero *m.*
waitress camarera *f.*
wall pared *f.*
want querer
warmth calor *m.*
wash lavarse
washing machine lavadora *f.*
watch reloj *m.;* mirar
water agua *f.* (*article* el)
wave ola *f.*
wear llevar
Wednesday miércoles *m.*
week semana *f.*
west oeste *m.*
what: what a! ¡qué!; **what's
  new?** ¿qué hay de nuevo?
wheel alignment ajuste de las
  ruedas *m.*
when cuando
where donde
whether si
white blanco
whole todo
**whom: to whom it may
  concern** a quien
  corresponda
wide ancho
widow viuda *f.*
wife esposa *f.*
wig peluca *f.*
win ganar
wine vino *m.*
witness testigo *m.*
woman señorita *f.*, mujer *f.*
wood leña *f.*
woolen de lana
word palabra *f.*
work trabajo *m.*
worker obrero *m.*
working el trabajar,
  trabajando
world mundo *m.*
worst el peor
wounded herido
written escrito
wrong: to be wrong
  equivocarse

X ray rayo X *m.*, radiografía *f.*

year año *m.*
yell gritar
yellow amarillo
yes sí
yesterday ayer

yet todavía
yield ceda el paso
you usted, ustedes, tú, vosotros
young joven *m. & f.;* **young people** jóvenes *m. & f.*

your su, sus; tu, tus
yours truly de Ud. atto. s.s.

zero cero *m.*

ÍNDICE